STRATEGIC
DATABASE
TECHNOLOGY:
MANAGEMENT FOR THE YEAR
2000

STRATEGIC
DATABASE
TECHNOLOGY:
MANAGEMENT FOR THE YEAR
2000

Alan R. Simon

Morgan Kaufmann Publishers, Inc.
San Francisco, California

Information Technology

Executive Editor: Bruce M. Spatz
Production Manager: Yonie Overton
Assistant Editor: Douglas Sery
Production Editor: Elisabeth Beller
Copyeditor: Gary Morris
Composition and Design: Rebecca Evans & Associates
Proofreader: Ken DellaPenta
Indexer: Ted Laux
Printer: Courier Corporation

Morgan Kaufmann Publishers, Inc.
Editorial and Sales Office
340 Pine Street, Sixth Floor
San Francisco, CA 94104-3205
USA
Telephone 415/392-2665
Facsimile 415/982-2665
Internet mkp@mkp.com

Library of Congress Cataloging-in-Publication Data is available for this book.

ISBN 1-55860-264-x

Contents

Preface   xvii
A Road Map of This Book   xxi
Acknowledgments   xxv

PART I Background and Introduction

1 Setting the Stage   3

1.1   Introduction   3

1.2   Terminology   4

1.3   Major Information Systems Trends   6
   1.3.1 Distribution and Decentralization   6
   1.3.2 Heterogeneity   7
   1.3.3 Standards   8
   1.3.4 Real-World Modeling   9

1.4   How IM Relates to Other IS Disciplines   9

1.5   Days of Future . . . in the Past   10
   1.5.1 The Early Days: Pre-DBMS   11
   1.5.2 Hierarchical and Network Databases   13
   1.5.3 The Relational Model   15
   1.5.4 Distribution and Extended Database Models   18
   1.5.5 Object-Oriented Databases   18
   1.5.6 Hypertext and Hypermedia   20
   1.5.7 Database Languages   21

1.6   Into the 1990s   22
   1.6.1 Third-Generation Data Base System Manifesto   22
   1.6.2 The Object-Oriented Database System Manifesto   25
   1.6.3 The National Science Foundation Workshop   25

1.7   A Perspective on Future Directions   28

1.8   Conclusion   30

Outlook   30
Additional Reading   31
Endnotes   31

PART II Distributed Databases and Information Management

2 Principles of Distributed Information Management 37

2.1 Introduction 37

2.2 Definition and Characteristics of Distributed Database Systems 39

2.3 Distributed Information Management: The Ultimate Scenario 43

2.4 Distributed Database Models 45
  2.4.1 Homogeneous versus Heterogeneous Systems 46
  2.4.2 Top-Down versus Bottom-Up Distributed Databases 47

2.5 Conclusion 53

Outlook 53
Additional Reading 54
Endnotes 54

3 Client/Server Databases and Middleware 55

3.1 Introduction 55

3.2 Client/Server Guidelines and Evaluation Criteria 60

3.3 Client/Server Information Management Standards 61
  3.3.1 SQL Access Group and DRDA 61
  3.3.2 SAG CLI-Based Standards 63

3.4 Middleware 65

3.5 Database Interoperability 66

3.6 Conclusion 67

Outlook 68
Additional Reading 68
Endnotes 68

4 Data Warehouses 71

4.1 Introduction 71

4.2 Principles of the Data Warehouse 72

4.3 Multiple Media 77

4.4 Data Summarization 78

4.5 Distributed Data Warehouses 79

4.6 Rewriting History 82

4.7   Data Warehouses and Other Information Management Technology   83
　　4.7.1   Client/Server Databases and Applications   83
　　4.7.2   Active Databases   85
　　4.7.3   Hypertext   86
　　4.7.4   Temporal Databases   86
4.8   Digital Libraries and Information Highways   87
4.9   Conclusion   87
　　Outlook   87
　　Additional Reading   88
　　Endnotes   88

5   Partitioning and Replication: The Next Generation   89

5.1   Introduction   89
5.2   MPP and Parallel Database System Concepts   90
5.3   Partitioning Models for Parallel Database Systems   94
5.4   Parallel Relational Operators and Index Structures   97
5.5   The Future Direction of Parallel Database Systems   98
5.6   Revisiting Replication   99
5.7   Conclusion   101
　　Outlook   102
　　Additional Reading   102
　　Endnotes   102

6   Heterogeneous Federated Databases and Multidatabase Systems   105

6.1   Introduction   105
6.2   Distributed Database Systems Revisited: A Taxonomy   106
6.3   A Conceptual Architecture of a Multidatabase System   111
6.4   Database Services   113
6.5   Conflict Resolution   115
6.6   Mediators   117
6.7   Cross-Database Integrity   118
6.8   The Role of Standards in Heterogeneous Information Management   119
6.9   Problems and Issues with Multidatabase Environments   120
6.10   Conclusion   120
　　Outlook   121
　　Additional Reading   121
　　Endnotes   122

7 Conclusions: Future Directions of
Distributed Information Management **123**

7.1 Introduction 123
7.2 Where Are We Today? 124
  7.2.1 Multiple Models of Information Distribution 125
  7.2.2 Parallel Database Machines 132
7.3 Problem Areas in Distributed Information Management 133
  7.3.1 Semantic Inconsistency 133
  7.3.2 Browsing 134
  7.3.3 Security 134
  7.3.4 Site Scale-Up 134
  7.3.5 Transaction Processing 135
  7.3.6 Distributed Design 135
  7.3.7 Distributed Query Processing 135
7.4 Promising Areas in Distributed Information Management 136
7.5 Conclusion 137
  Outlook 137
  Additional Reading 138
  Endnotes 138

PART III Object-Oriented Databases

8 Principles of Object-Oriented Databases **141**

8.1 Introduction 141
8.2 Rationale and Characteristics of Object-Oriented Databases 142
8.3 Concepts of Object-Oriented Databases 148
  8.3.1 Object Identity 149
  8.3.2 Attributes 149
  8.3.3 Methods 149
  8.3.4 Classes 150
  8.3.5 Class Hierarchies and Inheritance 150
8.4 Persistence 150
8.5 Development Methodology and Programming Languages 152
8.6 Conclusion 154
  Outlook 154
  Additional Reading 155
  Endnotes 155

9 Hybrid and Extended Relational Forms
of Object Management   **157**

9.1 Introduction   157
9.2 Hybrid Versus Extended Relational Approaches   159
   9.2.1 Uses and Trends of the Hybrid and Extended Relational
         Approaches   162
9.3 Extended Relational Languages   164
9.4 Object-Oriented Languages and SQL   165
9.5 Conclusion   166
   Outlook   167
   Additional Reading   167
   Endnotes   168

10 Object-Oriented Engines and Models   **169**

10.1 Introduction   169
10.2 The Object-Oriented Database System Manifesto   170
10.3 The ODMG Standardization Effort   174
10.4 ODMG Contents   175
10.5 ODMG Languages   177
10.6 Conclusion   178
   Outlook   179
   Additional Reading   179
   Endnotes   180

11 Other Issues in Object-Oriented Information Management   **183**

11.1 Introduction   183
11.2 Transaction Processing for Object-Oriented Environments   184
11.3 Distributed Object Management and Object Request Brokers   188
11.4 Security in OODBMS Environments   191
11.5 A Final Look at Object-Oriented Information Management   192
11.6 Conclusion   193
   Outlook   193
   Additional Reading   194
   Endnotes   194

PART IV Database and Information Management Languages

12 SQL Futures 197

12.1 Introduction   197

12.2 SQL History   198

12.3 The SQL-92 Standard   203
    12.3.1 Leveling   203
    12.3.2 Implementation Issues   204
    12.3.3 SQL-92 Language Features   205

12.4 The SQL3 Standard   212
    12.4.1 SQL3 Advanced Relational-Like Database Concepts   213
    12.4.2 MOOSE   216
    12.4.3 Issues   217
    12.4.4 Related Standards Efforts   218

12.5 Conclusion   219

    Outlook   220
    Additional Reading   220
    Endnotes   220

13 ODMG Languages for Object-Oriented Databases 223

13.1 Introduction   223

13.2 Review of ODMG Principles   224

13.3 Object Definition Language (ODL)   225

13.4 Object Query Language (OQL)   229

13.5 ODMG and C++   231
    13.5.1 C++ and ODL   231
    13.5.2 C++ and OQL   232
    13.5.3 C++ and OML   232

13.6 Smalltalk and ODMG   234

13.7 Conclusion   234

    Outlook   235
    Additional Reading   235
    Endnotes   235

14 Xbase and Other Desktop Databases 237

14.1 Introduction   237

14.2 Desktop Databases and Xbase: A Brief History   238

14.2.1 dBASE and Related Products 238
14.2.2 Other PC Databases 240

14.3 Xbase and ANSI X3J19 242
14.3.1 Standardization Efforts 244
14.3.2 Xbase Standardization Concerns 245

14.4 Graphical User Interfaces (GUIs) to PC Databases 246

14.5 Object Orientation 248

14.6 PC Databases and Architectures 250
14.6.1 The .DBF File Format 250
14.6.2 IBM Desktop Databases: Future Directions 251
14.6.3 Representative PC Database Architectures 252

14.7 Conclusion 252

Outlook 253
Additional Reading 254
Endnotes 254

PART V Future Database and Information Management Models

15 **Time Is on Your Side: Temporal Databases** **257**

15.1 Introduction 257

15.2 Principles of Temporal Databases 262

15.3 Models of Temporal Databases 264

15.4 Temporal Extensions to Database Languages 268
15.4.1 TempSQL 268
15.4.2 TSQL 269
15.4.3 HSQL 270
15.4.4 Other SQL Extensions 271
15.4.5 Standardized Temporal SQL 272

15.5 Metadata and Temporal Databases 272

15.6 Object-Oriented Temporal Databases 274

15.7 Indexes for Temporal Database Support 275

15.8 Conclusion 276

Outlook 276
Additional Reading 277
Endnotes 277

16 Database Intelligence: The Active Database Approach   **279**

16.1 Introduction 279

16.2 Principles of Active Database Systems 280
    16.2.1 Constraints and Assertions 283
    16.2.2 Stored Procedures 285
    16.2.3 Triggers 285

16.3 Extensions to the Active Database Model 286

16.4 Transaction Models and Active Databases 287

16.5 Limitations of Active Database Models 288

16.6 Production Rules and Database Environments 289

16.7 Artificial Intelligence and Database Technology 289

16.8 Conclusion 290

Outlook 291
Additional Reading 291
Endnotes 291

17 Space, Shapes, and Words: Spatial Databases, Multimedia and Image Information Management, and Text Management Systems   **293**

17.1 Introduction 294

17.2 Principles of Spatial Data 295
    17.2.1 Navigational Systems: A Case of Spatial Data Management 296

17.3 Image Information Systems 302

17.4 Multimedia Information Systems 304
    17.4.1 Architecture 305
    17.4.2 Standards 307
    17.4.3 Application Development Methodology 307

17.5 Text Retrieval and Document Management Systems 307
    17.5.1 Document Check-in 310
    17.5.2 Index Structure 310
    17.5.3 Index Loading 311
    17.5.4 Component Document Management 311
    17.5.5 Future Directions and Issues 312

17.6 Conclusion 314

Outlook 314
Additional Reading 315
Endnotes 315

18 Hypertext and Hypermedia 317

18.1 Introduction 317
18.2 Definitions of Hypertext and Hypermedia 318
18.3 Architecture of Hypermedia Systems 320
18.4 Hypermedia and Information Management 322
18.5 Future Directions in Hypermedia 324
18.6 Conclusion 325
    Outlook 326
    Additional Reading 326
    Endnotes 326

PART VI Supporting Functions

19 Repositories and Metadata Management 329

19.1 Introduction 329
19.2 Principles of Repositories 330
19.3 Repository Standards 334
19.4 Distributed Repository Capabilities 336
19.5 Granularity Issues 340
19.6 Repository Tools 342
19.7 Conclusion 343
    Outlook 344
    Additional Reading 344
    Endnotes 344

20 Transaction Processing 347

20.1 Introduction 347
20.2 Background in Transaction Processing Fundamentals 348
20.3 Transaction Principles and Models 351
    20.3.1 Flat Transactions 351
    20.3.2 Savepoints 352
    20.3.3 Chained Transactions 354
    20.3.4 Nested Transactions 354

20.4 Encina and DCE   357

20.5 X/Open DTP   360

20.6 Transaction Processing System Classification   361

20.7 Transaction Languages   362

20.8 Third-Generation TP Monitors Revisited   363

20.9 Conclusion   364

Outlook   365
Additional Reading   365
Endnotes   365

21 Database Security 369

21.1 Introduction   369

21.2 A Basic Database Security Model   373
    21.2.1 Authorization   373
    21.2.2 Authentication   373

21.3 Multilevel Secure Databases   375

21.4 Polyinstantiation   379

21.5 Covert Channels   383

21.6 Secure Distributed Database Environments   385

21.7 Languages for Secure Databases   389

21.8 Secure OODBMSs   391

21.9 Conclusion   392

Outlook   394
Additional Reading   394
Endnotes   395

PART VII The Finishing Touches

22 Other Database and Information Management Topics 399

22.1 Introduction   399

22.2 Databases and Information Management for Mobile Computing
Environments   400

22.3 Benchmarking   404

22.4 Data Compression   405

22.5 Main Memory Databases   407

22.6 Tertiary Storage   409

22.7 Design Models and CASE Tools   411

22.8 Network Operating System Databases   411

22.9 Conclusion   412

Outlook   412
Additional Reading   413
Endnotes   413

23 **Managerial and Business Issues**   **417**

23.1 Introduction   417

23.2 Interrelationships of Information Management Disciplines   418

23.3 Utilize Technology Specific to Your Environment   420

23.4 Assessing Next-Generation Vendor Products and
Research Advances   421

23.5 Getting from Here to There: Transitioning to New Information Management
Technology   422
23.5.1 Same-Product Transitioning   423
23.5.2 Same Model, Different Product   424
23.5.3 Intermodel Transition   425

23.6 Conclusion   426
23.6.1 Joy's Law   426
23.6.2 RAID   427
23.6.3 Future Challenges   427

Outlook   428
Endnotes   428

Index   **429**

PREFACE

Welcome to the future.

This book is intended to provide a single, consolidated source for management, MIS decision-makers, and technology planners. Effective use of database resources is essential for any company to remain competitive for the long term (or, if you prefer, for the next millennium). This book will help you make the best choices for your corporate applications and systems. The old adage that those who don't study and learn from history are doomed to repeat it pertains to technology as well; today's legacy systems were state-of-the-art ten or twenty years ago. Understanding the motivations and fundamental concepts behind the technologies in this book will help you avoid many of the problems inherent in the legacy systems of today. For those planners and decision-makers developing information systems to carry organizations into the next millennium, knowing the potential of alternatives within the basic technology is just as important as knowing available products and pricing.

The future is by definition uncertain. No one can predict with 100% accuracy the products available at given points between now and the year 2000. We can't know the features available to developers or even what the dominant technologies will be. We've all seen announcements for remarkable products that appear years late or never show up at all. Uncertainty is further fostered by merger activity among vendors and the creation of new companies. Products that your company has relied upon for years will be retired, and new ones will appear on the scene (bringing risks as well as benefits). The good news is that you can minimize the uncertainty by having good control over available information. You can't know the future, but you'll be in a better position to evaluate and choose from available technologies if you know where the technologies are likely to come from, the factors that influence their development, and their potential capabilities and limitations.

Uncertainty about the future can also be mitigated by closely studying the state-of-the-art of a given technology and the directions being pursued by the best commercial and academic researchers, and, of course, the results of those research and development efforts. Unfortunately, the sheer volume of information on technology would intimidate even the most avid reader.

Synthesizing and distilling this wealth is the goal of this book. The chapters that follow reflect the thinking of the best minds in the database and information management business. They also summarize the myriad opinions and information provided by limited distribution technical reports, journals, and trade periodicals.

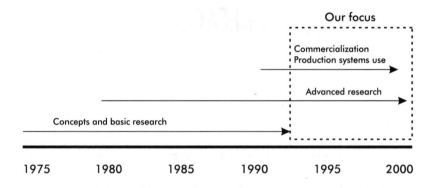

To find out as much as possible about the future directions of, say, transaction processing or object-oriented databases, who better to go to than the leaders in those fields? But for most of us, this isn't even a possibility. A unique aspect of this book are the personal interviews with technical authorities that form the basis of the chapter content in each area. As with any of the technical books I've written, my research efforts have also included exhaustive searches of journals, magazines, and other periodicals, as well as interviews with product representatives and technical staff members at major vendors. To further ensure the long-term value of the presentations you'll read, the manuscript was carefully reviewed by technical experts and MIS professionals. The comments and suggestions provided by these distinguished technologists helped shape the final draft as well as validate the premises and conclusions drawn. I can't help but feel that this is a collaborative effort with the best of the database community.

What You'll Find Inside

The idea for this book was originally conceived in 1990, when I was a distributed database product manager at Digital Equipment. Part of my job was to track advances and emerging technologies in all corners of the database world, and the idea dawned on me that a single volume discussing the many different areas of database technology would be a valuable resource for information systems strategic planners, decision makers, and technologists.

My original intention was to write individual chapters about significant areas such as distributed databases, object-oriented databases, languages, transaction processing, security, and the other topics included in this volume. As the research progressed, though, I found that the complexity of the material on distributed information management, object-oriented technology, and languages, combined with the goal of producing a comprehensible overview, required that multiple chapters be devoted to each information management subject for adequate discussion. For example, the area of distributed information management covers a wide range of topics from client/server databases to the class of information commonly called "truly distributed database systems." To relate a great deal of material without resorting to a single, overwhelmingly large chapter, each aspect of these primary areas is given a separate chapter, with a summary chapter at the end of the part.

Each of these parts is actually a collection of chapters about related technologies. The three major database languages are discussed in individual chapters; each object-oriented database approach is discussed separately along with an introductory chapter to object-oriented database technology; and distributed information management contains multiple subjects: client/server databases, data warehousing, classical distributed database technology, and new approaches to database replication. Other subjects, such as temporal (time-oriented) databases, intelligent databases, and transaction processing, are covered in separate chapters at a depth appropriate to the general nature of this book.

Finally, I reserved one chapter for mobile database technology, main memory databases, tertiary databases, and benchmarking. This chapter contains topics (with the exception of benchmarking) that represent the newly-emerging fringes of information management just now being investigated in the research community, areas with many unanswered questions regarding their underlying technologies. For example, the discussion of mobile (nomadic) databases, just now hitting its stride in the research community, includes a list of the areas for which a great deal of additional research must be conducted. Similarly, how fruitful will main-memory databases be for information systems in the year 2000? Opinions vary, but a discussion may help you decide for yourself. Many unanswered questions also remain with respect to transaction management and distributed query processing, among others. The brevity of coverage is not a reflection of potential importance but of how little we know at present (and as with all topics in the book, ample references are included to direct the reader to sources of additional information). The preview of these topics included here will help you understand their importance to your organization in the upcoming years.

Each chapter also provides background and historical information on the ground from which the state-of-the-art technology grew and suggestions as to where it is headed over the next five years. For example, research and development in object-oriented databases (specifically, the two major branches of the discipline, extended relational models and "pure" object-oriented databases, as discussed in Chapters 9 and 10) were initially guided by two landmark documents, "Third-Generation Data Base System Manifesto" and "Object-Oriented Database System Manifesto." Though by some measures these documents might be considered dated or of limited relevance to the vendor or research communities, note that initial research and development was influenced by these documents and resulted in the products and standards we have today such as the Object Database Management Group [ODMG]-93 standard ODMG-93 rel 1.2. Such vendor consortia will, in turn, influence research and development over the next five years. Knowing foundational concepts will cushion you from the many incremental shifts in products and technologies expected in the years ahead.

The road map that follows indicates the subjects covered in this book as well as where discussion can be found. I've also included special sections within chapters, wherever appropriate. Anyone wanting a quick glimpse of the topic at hand before studying the chapter in detail should start with these. They are shaded for easy visibilty. A Note to the CIO, Executive Summary, and What This Technology Can Do for You, should help even the most harried MIS professionals get an immediate sense of whether or not a topic is relevant to their needs.

I hope this book provides you with the resources to feel more confident in making the best decisions for the future. The risk associated with uncertainty can be dramatically reduced by thoroughly investigating the past, the present, and *likely* directions for future technologies. The rapid pace of technological change requires a forward-looking orientation even if it must be somewhat speculative. New technologies will emerge, others will fade into the information management background, their promise never fully realized, and still others will seem temporary or fleeting, only to be revived as tremendously important solutions for many organizations. Data warehousing and replication, each considered a temporary approach until "real" distributed databases with superior performance arrived, are prime examples of reborn information management technologies.

As important as any of the specific technical discussions in this book, though, are the pointers to the work of leading database and information management authorities who lent their support to this work. The interconnected world in which we all live and work, with electronic mail and other rapid communications technologies, enables unprecedented access to the knowledge of others. The large number of online databases now available gives the reader the power to browse the universe of computer-related periodicals and conduct keyword searches for recent articles and papers about object-oriented databases, complex transaction models, or any other area of interest. Perhaps the most valuable contribution of this book is its role in giving you a starting point to pursue the future for yourself.

A Road Map of This Book

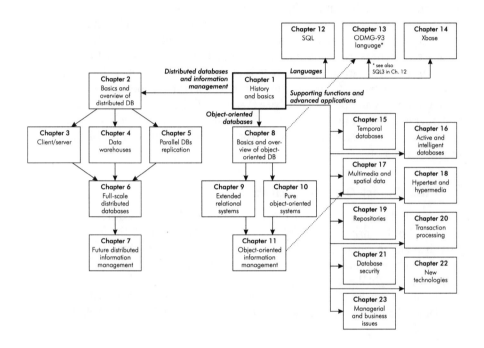

This book is divided into seven parts, as follows:

Part I: Background and Introduction

A single chapter, "Setting the Stage," provides the background for our discussions in the rest of the book. That background—the historical development and evolution of database and information management technology—focuses on the state of information management technology in the 1990s and current major trends such as distributed databases and object-oriented DBMSs.

For many readers, a good deal of this chapter will cover familiar territory, though some of the discussion at the end of the chapter with respect to future-oriented thinking will be new to most.

Part II: Distributed Databases and Information Management

The six chapters in this part focus on different areas of distributed database management. (A slight caveat is that our subject matter in Chapter 4—data warehouses—need not imply distribution of data assets, though the future direction of data warehousing is certainly toward distributed architectures.)

Following an introductory chapter in which the principles of distributed databases, such as partitioning, replication, top-down versus bottom-up creation, and so on, are discussed, we look at areas of distribution with varying levels of complexity—from directions in client/server technology, through data warehouses and parallel database systems, all the way to multidatabase and federated distributed database environments. The last chapter in this part, Chapter 7, will consider discussions from previous chapters together and provide a wrap-up.

Part III: Object-Oriented Databases

This part deals with all aspects of object-oriented databases. Our discussion in Chapter 8 of the principles of OODBs and OODBMSs leads to the following two chapters on different directions in the OODB world. Chapter 9 discusses OODB technology built from a relational foundation, while Chapter 10 deals with what might be termed "pure" OODBMSs (that is, those without a relational history). Finally, Chapter 11 considers other topics related to OODBs.

Other chapters in this book will also cover aspects of OODBs and OODBMSs, specifically

- a discussion in Chapter 12 of the object-oriented extensions to SQL in the SQL3 standard
- the ODMG languages, which are discussed in Chapter 13
- "extensions" to a basic object-oriented model to handle multimedia, spatial, and image data, which are discussed in Chapter 17

Part IV: Database and Information Management Languages

The three chapters in this part deal with different aspects of database language standards. Chapter 12 discusses the SQL world, from the recently released SQL-92 standard to the work currently underway in SQL3. Chapter 13 covers the efforts of OODBMS vendors to develop language standards under the ODMG umbrella. Chapter 14 discusses standardization efforts in the PC database world for the Xbase language.

Any database environment includes one or more languages through which database operations are invoked, so readings in this part of the book are strongly recommended to suggest directions in which the language(s) most applicable to your organization's information management environment are headed.

Additionally, Chapter 14 discusses the directions of desktop (that is, PC and workstation) databases as well as the Xbase language. Since nearly every organization either has or will have some level of desktop involvement in their database and information management picture, this material is also recommended.

Part V: Future Database and Information Management Models

Most of the discussion in this part of the book falls under what might be termed "extensible information management," that is, the foundations of relational and object-oriented technology discussed in the earlier chapters also serve as the basis for new database models in specialized application areas. For example, Chapter 15 discusses temporal databases in which historical and time-sensitive information is captured within the context of the database structures themselves, rather than by user-created tables or objects that must be populated and manipulated by applications. Temporal databases are not applicable to all types of application environments, but if your organizational information needs fit this description, a perusal of the principles of and directions in temporal database models will be most valuable.

Similarly, the discussion in Chapter 16 of active databases focuses on extensions to basic models that go beyond the traditionally passive nature of information management. Many of the technologies and models discussed elsewhere in the book (data warehouses, for example) can benefit from active databases, so corollary study might be in order.

The other chapters in this part of the book that deal with different data forms (spatial, image, textual, and other aspects of multimedia) may, as with the discussion of temporal databases, be more applicable to some organizations than others. These chapters are valuable because they provide information about areas other than "managing flat data."

Part VI: Supporting Functions

None of the areas discussed thus far stand alone. Specifically, there are three topical areas common to basic relational databases, extended relational DBMSs, object-oriented databases, and other technologies. These are

- metadata management
- transaction processing
- security

The three chapters in this part deal with these subjects and are recommended reading for all.

Part VII: The Finishing Touches

The last two chapters in the book deal with a conglomeration of subjects. Chapter 22 discusses a number of topics such as mobile computing databases, benchmarking, and memory and tertiary storage databases. Chapter 23 covers managerial issues, from methodologies for incorporating emerging information management technology into your organization, to a discussion of how to evaluate vendor and research community products and systems.

Many of you will be "database aficionados" and likely to want to read all the chapters in this book. Others may wish to focus on one area, such as future directions in object-oriented information management, so only certain chapters will be of interest to you. You can use this road map to guide you to the portions of the book that are of most interest. Keep in mind, though, that as your organization's information management needs, or your job description, change over time, topics that were of little interest to you at one time could suddenly become very important. Therefore, this volume may serve as a "living reference" because of its future-oriented approach.

Finally, it's important to note that many diverse subjects are covered in this book and that much detailed information is available from other sources. At the end of each chapter you will find suggested readings for additional information on the subject matter of that chapter as well as endnotes that may also provide sources for further information.

Acknowledgments

I'd like to acknowledge many people for their roles in making this book a reality.

First, and definitely foremost, is Bruce Spatz, Executive Editor at Morgan Kaufmann Publishers. Not only did Bruce show his faith in this project, bringing the book to life five years after I had first envisioned it, but he was instrumental in a number of ways throughout the writing process. His comments on the early draft chapters helped steer me in the right direction with respect to the organization of the material as well as a great deal of the content. Without Bruce's editorial skills, which provided an organized framework for the numerous subjects I cover throughout the book, the writing process would have been extremely difficult.

Throughout the period in which I worked on the manuscript, Bruce put me in touch with many of those acknowledged below, all of whom sent me copies of papers they had written or spent time with me discussing their thoughts about the future of their respective areas of expertise in the database and information world.

Bruce and Doug Sery—also of Morgan Kaufmann—made their considerable internal library of trade magazines, journals, and conference proceedings available to me for my research. Without Bruce and the staff at Morgan Kaufmann, the research for this book, considerable and time-consuming as it was, would have been much more difficult.

I'd also like to thank my once and future coauthor of SQL-related books, Jim Melton, not only for taking the time to discuss SQL and other language futures with me, but for lending his expertise in the database arena as well.

Jim Gray was also instrumental in steering this book in the right direction. He commented on early versions of the table of contents, gave me a number of additional topics to consider for inclusion, and spent a long evening on the phone with me discussing the book project and helping provide the finishing touches to the material.

Many other people contributed their time to help me with reference material, manuscript review and commentary, and personal observations. I am grateful to the following: Marco Emrich of Cincom Systems, Mary E.S. Loomis of Hewlett-Packard, Toby Teorey of the University of Michigan, Ahmed Elmagarmid of Purdue University, John Hawkins of *Data Based Advisor,* Sushil Jajodia of George Mason University, Rafael Alonso of Matsushita Labs, Andrea Skarra of AT&T, Jennifer Widom of IBM, Rick Cattell of SunSoft, Jacob Stein of Sybase, Joe Celko, independent consultant, Tom Kregel, independent consultant, and Frank Manola of GTE Labs.

PART I

Background and Introduction

CHAPTER

1

Setting the Stage

A Note to the CIO

If your career in information systems started in an area other than information management (general software development, marketing, or product management, for instance), this chapter will give you enough background on database and information management to put our discussion in the rest of the book in context. Specifically, this chapter will have a flavor of future-oriented thinking, focusing on past milestones in information management and how they were influenced by significant events that drove researchers in certain directions.

1.1 Introduction

In this book, we'll discuss what directions the many aspects of database and information management are taking. To put our discussion in the proper context, we must first set the stage with respect to the historical background of the information management discipline. In this first chapter, we'll take a look at some basic terminology that will guide our discussion throughout the book and we'll discuss some of the major trends that affect computer and information systems. Finally, we'll take a journey through the history of databases and information management, from early file management systems to the state of the art today.

Executive Summary

The roots of database and information management go back to the days of tape-based file systems. In the late 1960s and early 1970s, various research models and implementations of database management systems brought control and consistency to an information management world rife with redundant, often out-of-synch data.

Today's information world is somewhat of a paradox. Though the dominant database paradigm is the relational model, the majority of corporate and government data are stored in the file systems and older, mostly hierarchical, databases referred to as the legacy systems of these organizations. Tremendous effort is underway in most organizations to migrate from legacy systems to more modern systems based on

1.2 Terminology

To best understand the material in this book, we need to discuss two terms: database management and information management.

Database management is a formal discipline in the computer world, complete with various data models (hierarchical, network, relational, or object-oriented) under which user data and their definitions (metadata) reside *and are controlled via formal policies*. These policies deal with the concurrency, integrity, and other aspects of the data and metadata, ensuring that haphazard access to and modification of the data does not occur.

Information management, in contrast, is a much looser, more all-encompassing model. Database management falls under the information management umbrella, and so do many other models for providing access to data that do *not* exhibit the requisite behaviors of a database or its database management system-based management (Figure 1-1). Examples of this type of information management include

- *Hypertext*, in which links are traversed in a random manner by a user to access many different types of data. To date, hypertext has fallen outside the realm of database management, though it's certainly a valuable model of managing information for certain classes of applications. (We'll discuss hypertext further in Chapter 18.)
- *File systems* (so-called flat files), which still store a significant percentage of organizational data even today. Though operating systems provide access controls, directory structures, and other services for file systems, they do not exhibit the characteristics that would classify them as databases.

client/server computing, standards-based interfaces, and other emerging technologies.

Information management, like other computer and communication fields, is undergoing dramatic change in a number of areas: storage and access models, the scale of systems being built, and underlying technologies.

Finally, quirks of fate often play a role in the evolution of any technology, and database and information management are no exception. Decisions made by dominant vendors (e.g., IBM in the 1970s) have influenced the directions taken to date, and no doubt similar vendor choices will play a role in how information management technology evolves toward the year 2000.

To classify the storage and management of data as a database, certain conditions must be satisfied:[1]

- The data must have a known format; that is, the format of the data must be well defined to the computer system, not just to application programs that use it. This format is defined by the *metadata*, or data about data.

- The data should be stored, retrieved, and modified only by a special type of computer program, called a *database management system*, or DBMS.

- The data should be under *transaction control*, that is, subject to a formal set of rules and guidelines to ensure that integrity is maintained during and after operations on data. Transaction control is especially important when multiple users and applications are simultaneously accessing the data.

Databases are managed by database management systems (DBMSs). While this statement appears to do little more than state the obvious, it is important to recognize that policies and controls such as concurrency and data integrity are ideally established and managed *not* by applications software but by a subsystem of the overall systems software environment (the whole package containing the operating systems, communications software, device drivers, and so on). The software subsystem with that particular responsibility is the DBMS.

We will distinguish between database management and general information management when appropriate, because throughout this book we'll discuss many topics that fall under one or the other of these classifications.

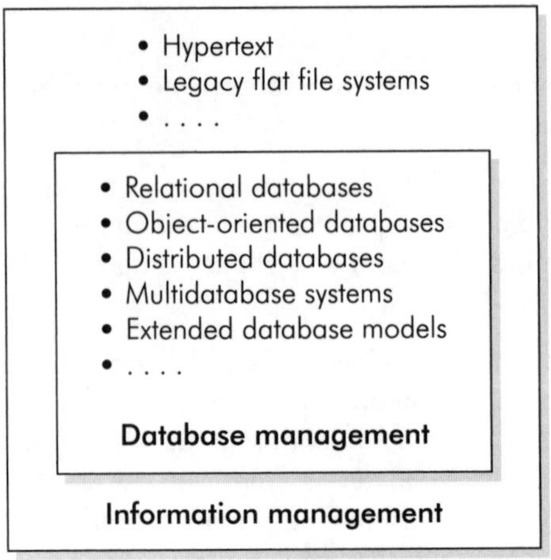

Figure 1-1 The Relationship of Database Management and Information Management

Much of our discussion, but not all of it, will focus on database-related areas. Other topics, although equally important to the management of information as a corporate or organizational asset, may fall outside the realm of database management.

1.3 Major Information Systems Trends

Many of the future directions in database and information management are heavily influenced by general information systems trends. In this section, we'll discuss four major trends, briefly focusing on those aspects specific to information management. The four trends are

1) Distribution and decentralization of information management resources

2) Heterogeneity of information systems components

3) Growth of standards

4) Inclusion of real-world modeling in information systems

Let's take a look at each of these.

1.3.1 Distribution and Decentralization

Nearly everyone in the computer field, as well as much of the general populace, is familiar with the trend toward distribution and decentralization of computing resources. Downsizing computer hardware (to borrow a term usually applied to personnel) has brought about small-scale yet very powerful processors and computer systems as viable alternatives to mainframe systems. These computer systems, from desktop personal computers and workstations to mid-range systems, are commonly tied together through communications capabilities (e.g., local area networks, or LANs) to provide a collective computing power on a par with or exceeding that of centralized, mainframe systems of the recent past.

Accompanying the distribution of computing resources is a much greater decentralization of control than was customary in centralized environments in which the data center typically had strong control over mainframe resources. And, this is still true for mainframe components in most large organizations. However, desktop PCs and workstations, along with department-level, mid-range systems, have provided a greater degree of resource control to individual users.

One positive aspect of decentralization is the faster turnaround for many areas of corporate computing: application installation and development, peripheral attachment, system expansion, and the like. On the negative side, however, the proliferation of personally owned applications (e.g., personal copies of spreadsheet and PC-based database software) has led to a loss of control over the data. Individual users have much faster access to data they "own" than they had to centrally managed resources, and they can easily and rapidly create new data as needed. However, the collective whole of organizational data tends to have a high instance of integrity problems, due to lack of synchronization of updates, for example, and there is a general confusion in the category of "who owns what, and where is it."

Distribution and decentralization apply directly to database and information management. While most organizations still have mainframe-based corporate information systems with centralized information management, we have seen an explosion since the mid-1980s in department-owned systems for specific point applications and desktop PCs with personal applications, including database management systems. In fact, database management, word processing, spreadsheet management, and graphics represent the so-called Big 4 of PC horizontal applications. Lesser satellites include mailing lists, personnel databases, client and customer rosters—the list of personalized applications (and personalized data) goes on and on. In most organizations, attempts by the data center to impose mainframe-like controls on PC usage, and specifically data management, have met with a tremendous degree of resistance. Distribution and decentralization have brought unprecedented control of information to the "corporate masses" and they will not give up that control.

1.3.2 Heterogeneity

The days of single-vendor environments are rapidly dwindling away. Even the "standard" corporate data center model—one based on some type of IBM mainframe and one or more operating systems—is gaining a heterogeneous

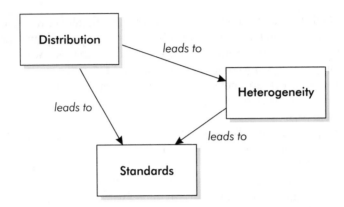

Figure 1-2 Relationship of Distribution, Heterogeneity, and Standards

flavor as hardware and software from other vendors find their way into those environments. More significant than just the presence of these newcomer systems is their *demand* for connectivity and interoperability, despite the brand differences.

The model of heterogeneity applies to information management as well. Legacy systems—typically, hierarchical databases or flat file systems that contain and manage long-standing corporate data—must share information with relational databases residing on the same mainframe systems, as well as with departmental and PC-based databases. All of this sharing must occur regardless of product brands and, increasingly, the interoperability spans multiple information models (e.g., combining relational and object-oriented data).

1.3.3 Standards

Much of the interoperability for heterogeneous environments described in the previous section is based on standards. Standards pervade every area of computing, from communications (e.g., the Open Systems Interconnection [OSI] Reference Model) to database management (e.g., SQL, which we'll discuss in Chapter 12).

Despite some contrary opinions regarding their role in information systems, standards are here to stay, primarily due to user demand. By themselves, standards have little value. In the context of the two major trends we've discussed so far (distribution and heterogeneity) standards become *very* important (Figure 1-2). Users want the freedom to switch hardware and/or software in their systems without being forced to start over from scratch with all of the interfaces incumbent in their environments. For example, switching from one DBMS product to another ideally should be accomplished without having to rewrite applications code or the code of other services in the environment, such as communications or user interfaces.

1.3.4 Real-World Modeling

Throughout the history of business computer systems, there has been some degree of disconnection between the information systems themselves and the real-world constructs they were developed to support. Examples of this disconnection include

- Applications sets that required multiple iterations of data input and paper-intensive information sharing among users from different business areas.

- The software and systems development process itself, with development methodologies and models that have required an awkward and error-prone mapping between the conceptual phase of development and the implementation of the applications and systems.

The 1980s brought about a closer coupling of information systems paradigms and the systems that they represent and support. Some examples of bringing real-world models to the computer systems world include

- *Graphical user interfaces* (GUIs), which brought a more natural look and feel to applications.

- *Object-oriented models*, the principles of which have been applied to programming and data management and (through capabilities such as inheritance and methods discussed in Part III on objected-oriented databases) brought a closer relationship between the conception and implementation stages of the development process.

- *Work flow management*, in which work flows among users and interrelationships among applications can be defined and managed. Work flow–based systems enable the flow of control and data among applications and users to more closely model the "natural way of doing business" than do paper-intensive means that require a high degree of human intervention.

1.4 How IM Relates to Other IS Disciplines

Obviously, the discipline of information management does not stand alone in the world of computer systems. The most powerful, robust databases and information management systems have little value without corollary capabilities, such as presenting information to users or enabling communications among distributed systems.

The open systems "movement," with its many standards efforts, has cemented a classification of different *service areas* in the information systems world, all of which serve distinct needs. *Reference models* encompass these various service areas and provide frameworks that relate information management to other disciplines. An example of such a reference model is the Open Systems Environment Application Portability Profile (OSE/1 APP), which is sponsored and specified by the National Institute of Standards and Technology (NIST), providing recommendations (not mandates) of standards for services in the following areas:[2]

- Operating systems
- User interface
- Programming
- Data management
- Data interchange
- Graphics
- Network

In short, the many areas of database and information management are interdependent with these other service areas. Distributed databases require network services; data sublanguages require programming services; and so on.

1.5 Days of Future . . . in the Past

The study of history in any discipline, including information management, is important for many reasons. For our purposes, the primary reason is that much of that history remains with us to this day. Most large corporations retain the bulk of their data in hierarchical databases or flat file systems. This tells us two significant things:

1) For most organizations, implementation of upcoming database technology, such as temporal or spatial databases, will require some degree of transition of data assets from antiquated forms of information management to futuristic models.

2) Whether or not transition efforts are put in place, *interoperability* must typically occur, meaning that historical information models will continue to play a role in the organizational information systems of the future. For example, implementation of a heterogeneous, distributed database environment (models and scenarios of which are discussed in Chapter 2) often requires incorporation not only of newly developed database segments built on state-of-the-art technology but legacy systems perhaps based on file systems or hierarchical databases.

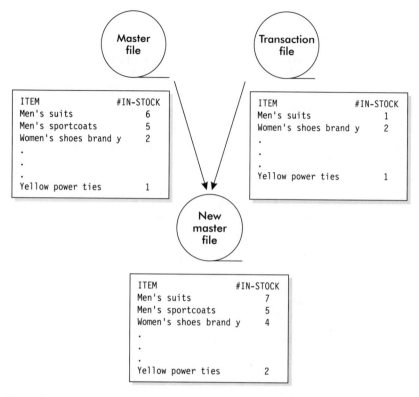

Figure 1-3 Tape-Based Master/Transaction File Interaction

With this in mind, let's take a brief tour through the history of information management, with an eye toward major events that have influenced directions in the past.

1.5.1 The Early Days: Pre-DBMS

The early days of business information systems were dominated by a file-oriented processing model. Initially, the primary storage mechanism was magnetic tape (with a healthy supplemental dose of punched cards and punched tape in some environments), the serial nature of which necessitated a standard processing model built around master and transaction files (Figure 1-3). For example, a clothing store system might have a magnetic tape with data organized in alphabetical order by merchandise type; that tape or a series of tapes would represent the master inventory file. A transaction file organized in the same manner would then be processed against the master file periodically, with program logic (typically written in COBOL) updating inventory counts according to the applicable business rules.

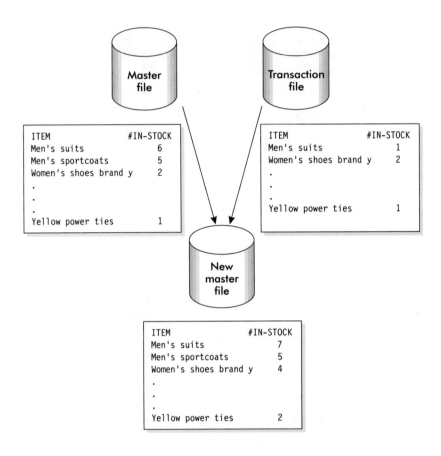

Figure 1-4 Disk-Based Master/Transaction File Interaction

Once directly accessible storage media such as disk drives arrived, new models for business information processing became available. Initially, disk drives were used as surrogate storage devices in place of tape-based files (Figure 1-4); the same master-transaction processing could take place with disk-based files. As new applications were developed and older ones transitioned to the cutting edge, replacement interaction models such as that shown in Figure 1-5 became common. Transactions could be applied directly against master files without the need for serial processing and the creation of a new generation of the master files.

A number of problems were evident in file-based application environments. Chief among these problems was the repetition of data in different files, with frequent inconsistencies. For example, a clothing store customer checkout application might permit changes of address to be processed against its customer log file, but those changes might not be reflected in the customer master file used by the promotional mailing application. Similarly, the sales

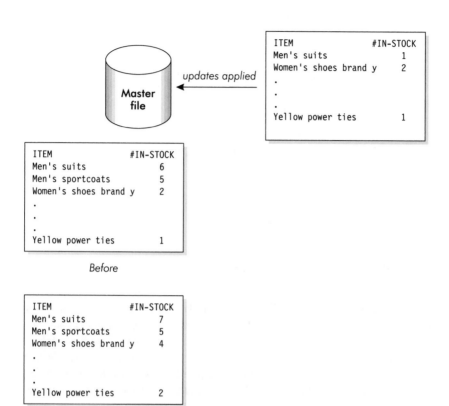

Figure 1-5 Transactions Applied Directly Against Disk-Based Master Files

log and clothing inventory files might have inconsistencies in inventory counts against one another. Additionally, the models used by most operating systems for access to and locking of data files made simultaneous application use tricky at best and, in many cases, almost impossible. These very problems gave rise to the early generations of database management systems.

1.5.2 Hierarchical and Network Databases

Though many different architectures competed for predominance in the early days of the "data base" or the "data bank" (a term we don't hear much anymore), the *hierarchical* database model rose to prominence, led by IBM's Information Management System (IMS) and its database language Data Language/I (DL/I). IMS and DL/I were commercially introduced in 1968 through a joint venture of IBM and North American Aviation (now Rockwell International Corporation).[3] Due to IBM's dominance of the mainframe computer market, many applications typically featured COBOL and DL/I databases.[4] This dominance made IMS the de facto standard among databases.

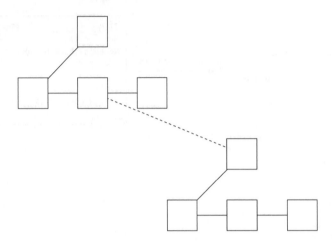

Figure 1-6 Tree-Structured Hierarchical Databases

The hierarchical model in general, and DL/I databases specifically, were implemented via tree structures, with root *segments* having physical pointers to other segments (Figure 1-6). One of the disadvantages of such a database model is that the real world can't easily fit in tree structures with a single root segment. Hierarchical databases provided pointers among different database trees, but the processing of the data through such linkages could sometimes be awkward.

The important advantage of these early databases, however, was the reduction in duplicate data. They also freed the data management discipline from the even more constraining flat file systems. Interobject associations among logically related data elements, instantiated through physical pointers, could be modeled and implemented with much greater ease than the earlier file processing systems.

Further, the principles of database management discussed in section 1.2 (e.g., having a known format of data under DBMS control) were beginning to assert themselves in business processing environments.

Around the same time, a competitive database model was taking form, one which would also find itself instantiated through commercial products. The network database model, first implemented in General Electric's Integrated Data Store (IDS) DBMS, was enthusiastically promoted by Charles Bachman.[5]

Unlike the case with the hierarchical model, however, the standards community turned its attention to formalizing the network model. The Conference on Data Systems Languages (CODASYL) formed a Data Base Task Group (DBTG) which published a report in 1969 that was updated in 1971.[6]

One of the major contributions of the DBTG model was the introduction of the *data definition language* (DDL) and *data manipulation language* (DML), formal languages to define and manipulate, respectively, database

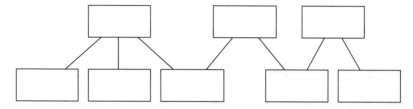

Figure 1-7 Structure of a Network Database

contents. DL/I databases did not feature a DDL, relying instead on assembly language macros to define database contents.[7] This demarcation among different language types within database management systems has grown over the years to include transaction management languages, schema manipulation languages, and other language groupings.

Figure 1-7 shows the structure of network databases. In contrast to hierarchical databases, a root record is not necessary in a network database, since *sets* can be created between record types without the artificial constraints of a hierarchy. As with hierarchical databases, though, associations are managed through physical pointers. It was during the 1970s that database research became dominated by a revolutionary database model not dependent on physically implemented pointers: the relational database model.

1.5.3 The Relational Model[8]

In June 1970, *Communications of the ACM* published a paper by Dr. E. F. Codd, then of the IBM Research Laboratory (IBM Corporation) in San Jose, California. This paper, entitled "A Relational Model of Data for Large Shared Data Banks"[9] was the first hint that many people had of the new relational model for databases.

As defined by Dr. Codd in his landmark paper, the relational model of data provides a number of important characteristics that make database management and use relatively easy, error-resistant, and predictable. The most important characteristics of the relational model are

- It describes data with its "natural" structure, without adding any additional structure for machine representation or implementation purposes.

- It provides a mathematical basis for the treatment of derivability, redundancy, and consistency of relations.

- It provides independence of the data from the physical representation of the data, of the relationships between the data, and of implementation considerations related to efficiency and like concerns.

The mathematical foundations of the relational model provide an interesting and important characteristic: closure. The basic element in the relational model is the relation. For most people, the usual visualization of a relation is a "table." A table, as it is known to us in other contexts, has rows and columns. The columns of a relation correspond to the "data items" for each of the "records" that are represented by the rows of the relation. The primary distinction between a relation and a table (the latter as implemented in most relational DBMS products) is that a relation cannot have duplicate tuples (i.e., records in a file), while a table is permitted to contain duplicate rows.

All relational operations on relations produce relations. This closure makes it feasible to prove the correctness of many manipulation operations. The various operators that have been defined on relations have precise mathematical characteristics. For example, some are commutative, some are distributive, and some are associative. These characteristics offer practical applications; for instance, they might be used by optimizers in production-quality products to determine faster and more effective methods of data manipulation.

Dr. Codd, having developed the model, became one of the chief proponents of relational databases, and IBM began several research and prototype products aimed at producing relational DBMSs. This work continued for most of the 1970s. In the early 1980s, a flurry of commercial relational DBMS products—from IBM, Oracle Corporation, Relational Technology, Inc. (RTI, later known as Ingres Corp. and still later as ASK/Ingres), and others—legitimized the relational database model as one around which real-life applications could be developed.

The inherent simplicity in the relational model was, however, accompanied by a corresponding increase in the complexity required of a supporting DBMS product. Whereas application developers writing hierarchical or network database applications had control over how linkages were defined and traversed, much of this processing was pushed into the DBMS itself in relational products. Therefore, query optimization became a major factor (and, initially, a performance inhibitor) in relational DBMS products.

Arguably, the dominance of the relational model and its corresponding products was assisted by the accelerating trend throughout the 1980s of smaller-scale computer hardware. On one front, the minicomputer market boomed, led primarily by Digital Equipment Corporation and accompanied by other vendors, such as Data General. While Digital Equipment did indeed have a CODASYL DBMS product (VAX/DBMS for VAX/VMS systems, and earlier products for the DEC-10 computer family), they and others encouraged the third-party DBMS vendors such as Oracle and RTI to develop relational DBMS products for their platforms. As these mid-range systems surged in popularity throughout the early and mid-1980s, so too did relational DBMS products and the applications built on top of those products.

An even more important second front, however, was the proliferation of personal computers. As PCs became legitimized in corporate environments, the Big 4 personal productivity software suite emerged: word processing, spreadsheet analysis, graphics, and database management. (These four were later joined by desktop publishing as the horizontal applications common to most organizations.) In response to the increasing PC presence, some vendors took the approach of downsizing the network DBMS model to the desktop environment; while the products were powerful, the inherent complications of the network model proved too cumbersome for the average PC software developer. Other vendors, particularly Ashton-Tate, concentrated on creating PC database products based upon the relational model. With the success of Ashton-Tate's dBASE family (initially dBASE II, and later dBASE III, dBASE III+, and dBASE IV, all owned by Borland now) and other relational DBMS products, the relational model easily became the major force in desktop database management.

As small businesses acquired PCs, they purchased commercial products or hired consultants to build relational-based applications for everything from mailing lists to accounting systems. The ease with which relational tables could be defined and the accompanying power of sophisticated languages (very similiar to fourth-generation languages, or 4GLs), such as dBASE and forms managers, provided PC users with a tremendous amount of power without the accompanying overhead (in computer resources and personnel) required in earlier database environments.

This one–two punch from the minicomputers and from the desktop brought such dominance to the relational database model and relational DBMS products that the 1980s ended and the present decade began with little argument as to the winner in the database wars. (Although, as we will discuss later in this chapter, the relational model is currently under siege from the object-oriented model for dominance of this decade's information management.) This doesn't mean, however, that all aspects of applied relational databases are perfect; nor are relational databases the ultimate solution to database management. One of the major advantages of relational databases— the ease with which database tables and columns can be defined—can lead to haphazard, hopelessly redundant data definitions for applications, particularly in PC environments. Such problems typically arise when the definition is done by "amateurs," that is, end users or others unfamiliar with database design concepts as opposed to database-trained computer professionals.

Early on, the discipline of *conceptual database design* (also known as *data modeling*) was typically absent from the design process as people put a table with columns here and put another table with other columns there, without regard for relational principles such as *normalization* (a formal set of rules that governs which columns should be in which tables, based on functional dependencies among those columns).[10] While shortcomings due to user and developer unfamiliarity can hardly be blamed on the relational database model itself, the result for some organizations has been a form of chaos with respect to relationally managed data. Attempts to introduce database interoperability and integration under the catch-all umbrella of "distributed databases" have sometimes led to mixed results that can be directly attributed to poor conceptual design.

1.5.4 Distribution and Extended Database Models

Because of the trend towards distribution of computing resources discussed earlier, it became apparent that relational DBMS products required some degree of distribution, both of the applications' data and of the products themselves. The 1980s saw a great deal of research in the relational model come to fruition based on work begun in the preceding decade, and the 1980s devoted much of its research to the area of distributed databases and distributed DBMSs.

Another major research direction of the 1980s was in the area of extensions to the relational database model. In 1979, Dr. Codd published a paper entitled "Extending the Database Relational Model to Capture More Meaning,"[11] partially in response to the *semantic modeling* movement in which researchers explored ways to capture more meaning within native database structures than is typically possible through basic relations.[12] Extended relational database models became a growth industry in database research.

In Part II of this book, we'll discuss distributed database management in detail, beginning in Chapter 2 with its underlying principles. In later chapters, we will move on to discuss temporal databases, hybrid relational/object-oriented database models, and other models based on extended relational capabilities.

1.5.5 Object-Oriented Databases

Earlier, we mentioned some shortcomings of the relational database model. One problem is straightforward enough: the relational model is simply difficult to use for some types of applications. Even though most relational DBMS vendors take liberties with the "pure" relational model, relational databases are still built around tables made up of rows and columns.

Chief among the application types for which it is difficult to build relational applications are computer-aided design (CAD) and computer-aided software engineering (CASE). Developers of commercial products in such areas that have an underlying relational DBMS as the storage manager must go through data contortions to make their models fit into the table and column structure. In areas such as CAD, CASE, and others, conventional wisdom says that a new database model—the object-oriented model—is the appropriate platform on which these applications and systems should be built.

However, as we'll see in our discussion of future directions of object-oriented information management, there is major dissension as to the "correct" direction this discipline should take. Some propose object-oriented databases as an entirely new discipline, without the baggage of relational DBMS roots. A contrary opinion holds that object-oriented database capabilities should be added as extensions to relational products and architectures in much the same way that other extensions (e.g., temporal, spatial, and semantic) have been explored. We'll discuss these contrasting points of view in detail in Part III, which is devoted to object-oriented databases, but we'll take a brief look at some of the driving forces behind the two camps in section 1.6.

An object-oriented database (OODB) is, as the name states, built around objects. (You might view the relational model as the "table-oriented" database model, since conforming databases are built around tables and, as we mentioned earlier, a relation is the formal name for a table.)

Because OODBs and OODBMSs are relatively new compared with the relational database and other information management ancestors, they have a number of problems, including in particular a lack of agreement about basic precepts and terminology. It is nearly impossible to get full agreement on the precise definition of the term "object," as well as on many other terms that deal with OODBs, which accounts for a good deal of the confusion and disagreement in the OODB world about base technology and product directions. Additionally, database practitioners, both from within the OODB field and from the more general information management field, disagree vehemently as to what the major contributions to databases actually are.

As an example, some claim that the unification of programming language and database facilities is the greatest advantage of OODBMS systems over relational and navigational (hierarchical, network) systems, yet the PC database (particularly Xbase systems, as we'll discuss in Chapter 14) has had this close coupling paradigm since the early 1980s. Others note that the unification of programming language and database sublanguage systems in OODB systems is not particularly desirable anyway, citing the trend toward compartmentalization of information systems along different service lines (information management, user interface, programming language, operating system services, graphics, and so on); these practitioners claim that the OODBMS coupling with programming languages like C++ and Smalltalk is leaning in the wrong direction, away from compartmentalization.

Other practitioners claim that inheritance through a robust, abstract data typing system (described below) is the greatest advantage of OODBMSs compared to older alternatives, while still others argue that other aspects are the greatest contribution. It's important not to get caught up in the rhetoric of OODBs and OODBMSs when evaluating current technology and future directions; each attribute of this technical area is important in its own right but needs to be evaluated in view of the needs of an individual organization.

OODBs feature objects (that's fairly obvious from the name), from which other objects can be defined, using a concept known as *inheritance*, in which some or all *attributes* (or properties) of the defining object are inherited by some other object, others are added, and some might be deleted.

For example, we might have some object called a STORE in our OODB. A STORE has some attributes true of all stores, such as STORE_ID, STORE_NAME, and ADDRESS. Some stores are MUSIC_STORES, and we wish to retain information about such attributes as CD_REVENUE and CASSETTE_REVENUE. Still other stores are VIDEO_STORES, for which we manage information about VHS_REVENUE and VHS_UNITS_RENTED. By defining a simple OODB structure, as shown in Figure 1-8, we can represent such information through the inheritance of these properties.

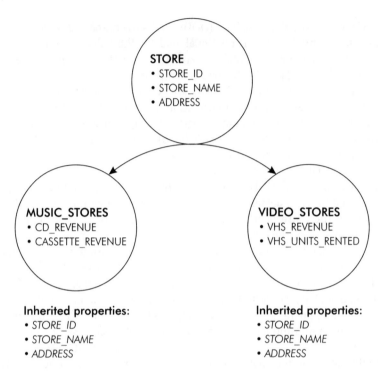

Figure 1-8 Sample Object-Oriented Database Portion

1.5.6 Hypertext and Hypermedia

In 1984, Apple Computer, Inc. introduced the Macintosh personal computer, a system which brought such features as graphical user interfaces (GUIs), windows, pull-down menus, and dialog boxes—all of which are now common-place—into the mainstream of computing. These areas had been introduced some years before and had even been used by Apple in their predecessor to the Macintosh, the Lisa. One could argue that Apple did indeed "bring computing to the masses" with their revolutionary system.

Another commercial introduction by Apple several years later initially drew raves, yet curiously faded somewhat from the spotlight. This area is known as *hypertext*, which Apple commercialized with a Macintosh product known as HyperCard™.

To understand how hypertext is used, let's go back to our discussion of the CODASYL network database model. You will recall how application developers could choose an entry point into the data network and traverse one or more of a multitude of pointer types to retrieve information (and, of course, to insert new information and update or delete previously stored data as well). Conceptually, hypertext is very similar to the traversing of a CODASYL database, without the need to have a host program (such as a COBOL or Fortran program) and a complicated data manipulation language (DML) to perform the linkage traversals. In a hypertext environment, you might choose some *card* as your entry point into the information management system. Your screen will prompt you with the appropriate links and traversal paths available to you. You might choose to follow a particular path, which would in turn lead to other branching possibilities. At some given decision point, you can return to your starting position and follow some other path.

In Chapter 18 we'll discuss further the principles of hypertext and the future directions of that area of information management.

1.5.7 Database Languages

Earlier in this chapter, we mentioned that relational databases received a tremendous boost from two fronts: the minicomputer/mid-range system and the desktop. Each of these frontal assaults on database dominance took a different approach to database languages.

On the minicomputer front, the early relational DBMS vendors took divergent paths. Relational Technology, Inc.'s Ingres product, for example, used a language known as QUEL (which was based on a foundation known as *relational calculus*), whereas Oracle Corporation used a language initially developed at IBM known as SQL. When IBM commercialized their relational products, they too chose SQL, as did the early leaders in the UNIX DBMS market (Unify Corp. and Informix Corp., for example). Eventually, Ingres Corp. (as RTI was later known) added SQL support to the Ingres product. SQL became the dominant relational language among mid-range and mainframe relational DBMS products, and this dominance was acknowledged by the publication of a series of ANSI and ISO standards for SQL (SQL-86, SQL-89, and SQL-92, the last one published as ANSI X3.135-1992 and ISO/IEC 9075:1992).

On the PC front, however, a different picture emerged. Many of the mid-range vendors downsized their products to run on desktop microcomputers, and the SQL language went along with the product. The dominance of Ashton-Tate's dBASE family, however, led to a corresponding predominance of the dBASE language itself. Competitors such as Fox Software and Nantucket Software adopted variants of the dBASE language, and, as the 1990s began, a new category of relational database languages (in addition to SQL) was recognized: the Xbase language. In 1992 the major vendors of dBASE-like products and languages began efforts to standardize the Xbase language in much the same way as SQL variants had been formally standardized. (Interestingly, all three industry leaders, Ashton-Tate, Fox, and Nantucket, were later acquired by other vendors—Borland, Microsoft, and Computer Associates, respectively.)

In Part IV of this book, we'll discuss the future directions of database languages, including SQL (Chapter 12), Xbase (Chapter 14), and the Object Database Management Group, or ODMG, language standard (Chapter 13).

We'll look at major trends in each language; for example, in the SQL chapter we'll take a look at the SQL3 definitions and language extensions for object-oriented databases.

1.6 Into the 1990s

Research and future-oriented thinking about database and information management continued throughout the 1980s. Most of the areas we'll discuss, from extensions to the relational database model and from object-oriented databases to security, received a great deal of attention during the eighties. Then, from 1989 to 1990, three events occurred that might be considered representative of the major schools of thought within database technology as a new decade dawned.

In this section, we'll discuss in detail two of these events, the publication of the "Third-Generation Data Base System Manifesto" and the National Science Foundation (NSF) workshop on database futures, and briefly mention the third, the publication of "The Object-Oriented Database System Manifesto," as a prelude to further consideration of OODB trends.

It's important to understand that the two Manifesto documents represent the two major camps of object-oriented database and DBMS thinking. Both were produced by groups that favored a particular approach to OODBMSs, so neither should be thought of as the product of a bipartisan effort. (In contrast, the NSF workshop attendees represented more of a cross-section of DBMS experts from different backgrounds and with different philosophies.)

Further, neither Manifesto document could currently be considered as driving the technology because of the approach it advocates, both having been supplanted by language standards and commercial products that advocate one approach or the other.

It is worth briefly discussing the three group efforts, though, since database decision makers and planners often need to choose among alternative approaches to a particular problem, whether it be alternative OODB architectural approaches or different ways to achieve distributed database processing to cite a few examples. Having some idea of the roots of the candidate solutions helps in making informed decisions.

1.6.1 Third-Generation Data Base System Manifesto

In July 1990, the Committee for Advanced DBMS Function (a group consisting of many leading database researchers and practitioners[13]) published a paper for a conference in Windermere, England, entitled "Third-Generation Data Base System Manifesto."[14] The authors categorized database evolution as having occurred in two generations to that point:

- *The first generation:* Hierarchical and network systems, which were the first systems to unify data definition and data manipulation language facilities for collections of records.

- *The second generation:* Relational DBMSs, the major evolutionary step being the use of nonprocedural data manipulation language and provision of a substantial degree of data independence.

As the authors pointed out, the second-generation relational systems were oriented toward business data processing applications and were generally unsuitable for classes of applications like CASE, CAD, hypertext, and multimedia. Further, the authors argued, the second-generation relational systems weren't that suitable for the business applications they were oriented toward. If business applications were to follow true models of the work they represented (the committee used the example of insurance claims processing), then multimedia and other format data that are difficult to represent in and access from relational DBMSs should really be part of the application. Therefore, the following premise was put forward:

The correct statement is that *everybody* requires a better DBMS.[15]

In the Manifesto, the authors put forth three tenets and 13 propositions dealing with third-generation DBMSs.

The Tenets

TENET 1 Third-generation DBMSs will provide services in three areas:

- Data management
- Object management
- Knowledge management

TENET 2 Third-generation DBMSs must subsume second-generation DBMSs, meaning that the major contributions of the relational world—nonprocedural access and data independence—must not be compromised by third-generation systems.

TENET 3 Third-generation DBMSs must be open to other subsystems. Products claiming third-generation status must have 4GLs, decision support tools, remote data operations, and distributed capabilities.

The Propositions

The first five propositions deal with the object-oriented nature the authors felt was necessary for third-generation systems.

PROPOSITION 1.1 A third-generation DBMS must have a rich type system. In short—and this is one of the major premises of the Third-Generation Manifesto in contrast with the Object-Oriented

Manifesto—general features of object orientation are proposed as *extensions* to the relational (second-generation) systems rather than as replacements. To put it more precisely, object-oriented features are thought of as facilitators of entirely new DBMS architectural considerations, rather than as extensions to existing models.

PROPOSITION 1.2 Inheritance is a good idea.

PROPOSITION 1.3 Functions (methods, database procedures) and encapsulation are a good idea.

PROPOSITION 1.4 *Unique identifiers* (UIDs) for records should be optionally assigned by the DBMS.

PROPOSITION 1.5 *Rules* (triggers) will become a major feature in future systems. They should not be associated with a specific function or collection.

The next group of propositions are concerned with increasing the functions of the DBMSs, ensuring that the second tenet of preserving the integrity of second-generation systems is considered.

PROPOSITION 2.1 Navigation to desired data should be used only as a last resort. In other words, don't go back to programmer-specified data access as occurs in hierarchical and network DBMSs.

PROPOSITION 2.2 There should be at least two implementations for collections, one using enumeration of members and one using the query language to specify membership.

PROPOSITION 2.3 Updateable views are essential.

PROPOSITION 2.4 Clustering, UID indexes, buffer pools in user space, and the like are physical rather than logical issues and have nothing to do with the data model. The authors seem to be supporting the ANSI SPARC 3-schema—separating the physical model from upper layers—in the course of specifying third-generation characteristics.

The final group of propositions deals with the aspects of open systems.

PROPOSITION 3.1 Third-generation DBMSs must be multilingual.

PROPOSITION 3.2 A closer match between the type systems of the third-generation systems (as specified in Proposition 1.1) and languages is necessary, but should avoid the impedance mismatches of the SQL world. (See Chapter 12 for more on the future of SQL.)

PROPOSITION 3.3 Despite the many perceived shortcomings of SQL, it's here to stay, and it will have a role in the third-generation world.

PROPOSITION 3.4 Queries expressed in SQL and their resulting answers should be the lowest levels of communication between a client and a server.

Since the publication of the Third-Generation Manifesto, these tenets and propositions have played an important role in the world of relational databases extended with object-oriented capabilities. We'll discuss this particular hybridization in Chapter 9.

1.6.2 The Object-Oriented Database System Manifesto

Several months before the publication of the Third-Generation Manifesto, another group of database luminaries published a different document, this one entitled "The Object-Oriented Database System Manifesto."[16] Just as the Third-Generation Manifesto formed the backbone for future directions of the hybrid model (e.g., relational and object-oriented), the Object-Oriented Database System Manifesto did the same for "pure" object-oriented databases (OODBs). This document presents 13 "thou shalt" commandments regarding mandatory features of object-oriented databases. We'll discuss these in Chapter 8.

1.6.3 The National Science Foundation Workshop

In February 1990, roughly coinciding with the publication and presentation of the two Manifesto documents (1989 to 1990 was a *busy* time for the thinkers in the database world!), the National Science Foundation convened a workshop in Palo Alto, California, to identify the "technology pull factors that will serve as forcing functions for advanced database technology and the corresponding basic research needed to enable that technology."[17] Not surprisingly, the attendees included members who had been on the roll call for the Third-Generation Manifesto as well as some individuals who had contributed to the Object-Oriented Manifesto.[18]

Just as the efforts of each of the Manifesto documents produced major "must haves" for their respective database areas, so did the NSF workshop. There were three primary conclusions about the future of database and information management:[19]

1) Many of the advanced technologies that will underpin industrialized economies in the early twenty-first century will depend on *radically new database technologies* that are currently not well understood and that require intensive and sustained basic research. (This item certainly puts a new light on the *importance* of database technology, not just for the increased performance, new models, or improvements for the sake of improvements, but because a direct link was drawn from database technology to the success of twenty-first century industrialized economies!)

2) The next generation of database *applications* will have little in common with the business processing applications of today. (You might recall this premise from the Third-Generation Manifesto discussion in section 1.6.1.)

3) The cooperation among different organizations in scientific, engineering, and commercial areas will require *large-scale, heterogeneous, distributed databases.* However, very difficult problems lie ahead in specific areas within that domain. (We'll discuss these problems later in this section and in Chapter 2.)

The focus of the workshop wasn't so much on the next round of commercialization in the database and information world as it was on future directions of database research. It was asserted that the "solutions to the important database problems of the year 2000 and beyond are not known."[20] Two areas in particular were identified as candidates for heavy research:

1) Next-generation DBMS applications

2) Heterogeneous distributed databases

In the area of next-generation DBMS applications, the workshop report identifies several areas of concern or uncertainty:[21]

1) *Storage:* NASA would need storage for 10^{16} bytes of data to accommodate several years' worth of satellite images scheduled for collection during the 1990s, and the data would need to be retained for future scientific use.

2) *Interdependence of applications:* Increasingly, database applications featured interdependence among application components since databases are the backbone of those systems. Applications, supported by the database structures and capabilities, would need to compensate for these interdependencies more than in the past (the example cited was a civil engineering system with hundreds of subcontractors working on a project, where the actions of one affected the overall structure of the project).

3) *Data mining:* Applications, such as department store executives running ad hoc queries on historical databases of every cashier action to discern buying patterns, would tax current disk capacities, and the storage problem would get worse as the amount of historical data grew.

4) *Multimedia applications:* The growing area of multimedia applications introduces new problems in storage management and transaction control. We'll discuss multimedia and image database issues in Chapter 17.

5) *New kinds of data:* Complex objects, the ability to effectively manage components of those objects, flexible type systems, and other data issues would surface above the simple data typing of most current database systems.

6) *Rule processing:* Capabilities of "knowledge-base systems," such as embedding declarative and imperative rules within the database systems themselves rather than through other software systems such as expert system shells, would be commonplace.

7) *New data models:* To support new classes of applications, specialized data models have come into play. We'll discuss several of these—spatial and temporal (time-oriented) databases—in subsequent chapters.

8) *Scalability of DBMS algorithms:* Many search, connection, indexing, and other algorithms that operate efficiently on typical-sized databases would not necessarily scale effectively for terabyte-sized databases. The report specifically notes that backup and recovery time of a one-terabyte database is unacceptable if the algorithms applicable to much smaller databases are used.

9) *Parallelism:* We'll discuss parallel database issues in Chapter 5, noting for now that different models of parallelism are necessary depending on data and organization characteristics.

10) *Tertiary storage:* As more and more archive-based data (as contrasted with memory-based or disk-based data) comes into play within a database framework, algorithms must be adjusted to account for such environments.

11) *Long-duration transactions:* The models useful for relational and other "typical" database transactions don't necessarily apply to transactions for object-oriented databases and other environments that occur over much longer periods of time.

12) *Versioning:* The ability to maintain multiple versions of objects is related to both temporal databases and many types of object-oriented applications, and the maintenance and access of multiple versions is an area that must be considered.

The other area that the workshop participants recommended for concentrated research is heterogeneous distributed databases, our subject in Chapter 6. The report notes that areas such as security, incompleteness and inconsistency of global schemas, transaction management, and name services were among those that would need a great deal of investigation to bring the state of the art of distributed databases from the turn of the decade to the turn of the century.[22]

Finally, the workshop concluded that the twin problems of next-generation applications and heterogeneous, distributed databases would present tremendous research opportunities that would help to focus the future directions of information management.[23]

1.7 A Perspective on Future Directions

Before we begin our exploration of future directions of database and information management in Chapter 2, we should pause for a moment to understand some realities about the concept of future directions and trends.

Many of the subjects we'll discuss have proponents in opposing camps who claim that their particular model of whatever-technology-in-which-they're-experts is the correct or at least the best paradigm. At the time of writing, one of the most visible debates is the one in the object-oriented database discipline. Few would argue that the principles of object-oriented databases are desirable; properties such as inheritance, encapsulation, and methods are valuable tools for nearly every type of environment.

There is, however, great dispute as to the "right" model of object-oriented database management. As we briefly mentioned earlier, some claim that the dominance of the relational database model and the resultant number of commercial products based on this model demand that object-oriented database capabilities be realized through extensions to an underlying relational engine and to relational languages. Others claim that the baggage of relational implementations is undesirable for the object-oriented database paradigm, and OODB capabilities are best achieved from a clean slate.

Similar dissension exists in areas such as transaction management, distributed database management, and many other areas we'll discuss. The nature of database research—indeed, information systems research as a whole—is that new approaches are constantly being explored by graduate students, professors, industry researchers, and others. Nearly every discipline of information management has new approaches being explored at any given time leading to some degree of imprecision in determining what models or technologies will emerge as dominant.

This controversial approach to research and future directions is not confined to database and information management, nor is it new. Witness the Ethernet vs. Token Ring competitions of the mid-1980s regarding local area networks. We discussed the roots of the network DBTG and relational models in section 1.5.2. In 1975, the Association for Computing Machinery (ACM) Special Interest Group for the Management of Data (SIGMOD) conference was the site of "the great debate," in which E. F. Codd of relational fame and Charles Bachman, the pioneer of network databases, debated the relative merits of their respective database models.[24]

According to Michael Stonebraker, "The debate was significant in that it highlighted once again that neither camp could talk in terms the other could understand. . . . Both talks and the resulting discussion left the audience more confused than ever."[25]

With this perspective, we embark on our discussion of the database and information management future. The goal of our discussion is to give you sufficient grounding in the following:

- The historical background of each specific discipline
- The state of the art
- Major research directions and trends
- Some idea as to the likely directions of each discipline

We reference the uncertain future in the preface to this book; however, subject-by-subject collection can help remove some of the uncertainty about your organization's information systems environment. Some boldly stated predictions turn out to be incorrect. As an example, a prominent research area of the late 1970s was in database machines, special-purpose processors that served the back-end data management needs of an information system in much the same way that the traditional front-end processor served communications needs. A paper written in 1983, "Database Machines: An Idea Whose Time Has Passed? A Critique of the Future of Database Machines,"[26] predicted the demise of database machines.[27] However, the success of highly parallel database systems (discussed in Chapter 5) "refutes [the 1983 paper] predicting the demise of database machines."[28] External factors, such as the dominance of the relational database model (which hadn't been envisioned in 1983, when relational products were first starting to appear) and the suitability of relational queries to parallel execution, helped counter the predicted demise of database machines.[29]

Finally, quirks of fate often alter the future. Michael Stonebraker points out "two little-known facts that might have dramatically altered the events (of database management) of the last several years."[30] He notes that IBM once attempted to put an SQL interface on top of IMS (we discussed IMS in section 1.5.2), an effort that was abandoned in the late 1970s. At that point, IBM embarked on building a relational system from the ground up, choosing from among several prototype and research engines and candidate languages (including SQL). If, say, IBM had selected Chris Date's Universal Data Language (UDL)[31] rather than SQL (and Stonebraker states that UDL offered a cleaner coupling with PL/I than SQL did), then database technology may well have evolved differently.[32]

So keep these three things in mind about the future:

1) The future is uncertain.
2) The future often takes a different path from the obvious because of external factors that couldn't be foreseen at a particular point in time.
3) The direction the future takes is often dictated by factors other than "pure technological merit."

1.8 Conclusion

Our purpose in this introductory chapter has been to set the stage for our discussion of the database and information management future. In order to have some idea of where the disciplines are headed, it's important to know where we are now and how we got to that point.

More than just the historical aspects of information management are important, though. It's critical to understand that databases and information management systems do not operate in a vacuum but are heavily influenced by major information systems trends, such as heterogeneity and distribution of resources. They are also heavily dependent on other service areas of information systems, such as user interfaces (for collection of instructions and data as well as the presentation of the data and other results), communications (enabling distributed systems to talk with one another), and system services (providing the basic low-level facilities on which higher-level information management functions may be built).

While exploring brave new worlds of information management and other technology is exciting for developers, the reason computer technology is being used within a particular business should always be kept in focus, and that reason is to support the mission of a given organization. Whether for operational support (such as transaction processing) or informational needs (such as decision support and executive information systems), there is often a price to pay for venturing into new, unproven technology while seeking support for business ventures. Whatever the type of database, the *real* benefits, as well as the *real* difficulties and shortcomings, should be thoroughly understood before pursuing costly, time-intensive ventures. Part of the goal of this book is to provide you with a comprehensive framework from which you can determine when your organization should begin experimentation with or full-scale deployment of particular technologies.

Finally, keeping a somewhat critical eye to exactly what "future directions" means is crucial to our discussion in subsequent chapters. Factors other than business needs and technical merit affect the direction that any discipline, including information management, takes at critical junctures.

Let's now go on to look at trends and future directions. Our first stop will be in the area of distributed information management.

Outlook

Short-term

- Maturation of relational technology
- Extension of relational technology with object-oriented capabilities
- Specialized database models for certain applications

Long-term

- Solutions to identified problems
- Commercialization of those solutions
- Identification of new problems
- New information management models

Additional Reading

- P. J. Pratt and J. J. Adamski, *Database Systems: Management and Design* (Boston: Boyd & Fraser Publishing Company, 1987).
- A. Silberschatz, M. Stonebraker, and J. Ullman, eds., "Database Systems: Achievements and Opportunities," *Communications of the ACM* (October 1991).
- M. Stonebraker, ed., *Readings in Database Systems,* Second Edition (San Francisco: Morgan Kaufmann Publishers, 1994).
- "Third-Generation Data Base System Manifesto," *Proceedings IFIP WG2.6 Conference on Object Oriented Databases*, Windermere, England, July 1990.

Endnotes

1. J. Melton and A. Simon, *Understanding the New SQL: A Complete Guide* (San Francisco: Morgan Kaufmann Publishers, 1992), 16.

2. *NIST Special Publication 500–187, Application Portability Profile (APP), The U.S. Government's Open System Environment Profile OSE/1 Version 1.0*, April 1991.

3. P. J. Pratt and J. J. Adamski, *Database Systems: Management and Design* (Boston: Boyd & Fraser Publishing Company, 1987).

4. D. M. Kroenke, *Database Processing: Fundamentals, Design, Implementation* (New York: MacMillan Publishing Company, 1992), 406. IMS contains facilities not only for database management (IMS/DB, which implements DL/I databases) but also communications.

5. Pratt and Adamski, *Database Systems.*

6. Pratt and Adamski, *Database Systems.*

7. Kroenke, *Database Processing*, 407, 437.

8. Portions of this section adapted from Melton and Simon, *Understanding the New SQL*, 6–7.

9. E. F. Codd, "A Relational Model of Data for Large Shared Data Banks," *Communications of the ACM* (June 1970).

10. See T. Teorey, "Normalization," Chap. 5 in *Database Modeling and Design: The Entity-Relationship Approach* (San Francisco: Morgan Kaufmann Publishers, 1991), for a discussion of normalization.

11. E. F. Codd, "Extending the Database Relational Model to Capture More Meaning," *ACM Transactions on Database Systems* (December 1979), 397–434.

12. Dr. Codd's later work included yet another version of the relational model, RMV2.

13. Committee members included Michael Stonebraker of the University of California, Berkeley; Larry Rowe of the University of California; Bruce Lindsay of IBM Research; Jim Gray, then of Tandem Computers; Mike Carey of the University of Wisconsin; and David Beech of Oracle Corporation. Their names are cited within the body of the Manifesto document.

14. "Third-Generation Data Base System Manifesto," *Proceedings IFIP WG2.6 Conference on Object Oriented Databases*, Windermere, England, July 1990. (Note: throughout the paper, the authors use the phrase "data base" instead of the single word "database.")

15. "Third-Generation Data Base," 2.

16. M. Atkinson, F. Bancilhon, D. DeWitt, K. Dittrich, D. Maier, and S. Zdonik, "The Object-Oriented Database System Manifesto," *Proceedings of Deductive and Object-Oriented Databases*, Kyoto, Japan, December 1989.

17. A. Silberschatz, M. Stonebraker, and J. Ullman, eds., "Database Systems: Achievements and Opportunities," *Communications of the ACM* (October 1991), 111.

18. The workshop attendees included Michael Brodie, Peter Buneman, Mike Carey, Ashok Chandra, Hector Garcia-Molina, Jim Gray, Ron Fagin, Dave Lomet, David Maier, Marie Ann Niemat, Avi Silberschatz, Michael Stonebraker, Irv Traiger, Jeff Ullman, Gio Wiederhold, Carlo Zaniolo, and Maria Zemankova.

19. Silberschatz, Stonebraker, and Ullman, eds., "Database Systems."

20. Silberschatz, Stonebraker, and Ullman, eds., "Database Systems," 114

21. Silberschatz, Stonebraker, and Ullman, eds., "Database Systems," 115–118.

22. Silberschatz, Stonebraker, and Ullman, eds., "Database Systems," 118–120.

23. Silberschatz, Stonebraker, and Ullman, eds., "Database Systems," 120.

24. M. Stonebraker, ed., "The Roots," *Readings in Database Systems*, Second Edition (San Francisco: Morgan Kaufmann Publishers, 1988), 1.

25. Stonebraker, ed., "The Roots," 2.

26. H. Boral and D. DeWitt, "Database Machines: An Idea Whose Time Has Passed? A Critique of the Future of Database Machines," *Proceedings of the 1983 Workshop on Database Machines*, eds. H.-O. Leilich and M. Missikoff (New York: Springer-Verlag, 1983).

27. D. DeWitt and J. Gray, "Parallel Database Systems: The Future of High Performance Database Systems," *Communications of the ACM* (June 1992), 85.

28. DeWitt and Gray, "Parallel Database Systems."

29. DeWitt and Gray, "Parallel Database Systems," 86. The authors do state that the "trendy" hardware aspects of database machines all failed to fulfill their promises; it was the *principles* of parallel database systems which survived and thrived.

30. Stonebraker, ed., "The Roots," 3.

31. C. J. Date, "An Architecture for High-Level Language Database Extensions," *Proceedings of the 1976 ACM-SIGMOD Conference on Management of Data*, San Jose, CA, June 1976.

32. Stonebraker, ed., "The Roots," 3.

PART II

Distributed Databases and Information Management

CHAPTER 2

Principles of Distributed Information Management

A Note to the CIO

Chances are that you are constantly bombarded by phrases and terminology in which the word "distributed" is prominent. Likewise, the word pervades your discussions of information management for your organization. "Distributed databases are a must," the chant goes. "Centralized environments are out; you must downsize your information systems environments to stay competitive, and your information assets must become distributed as well."

2.1 Introduction

The term "distributed database" (DDB) is one of the most overloaded computer phrases, with almost as many meanings as that popular buzzword of the early 1990s, "open systems." In the simplest sense, a distributed database might involve an application running on one computing system which accesses data from several remote databases at different times (though most, of course, would consider the definition of such a model as a DDB as quite a stretch).

In general, this is true. Centralized architectures, at least in the traditional sense, are rapidly being replaced by environments in which distribution of computing resources is key. In this spirit, the philosophy behind distributed databases—or, more accurately, distributed information management environments—is a valid one.

What is difficult to determine, however, is to what extent distribution should be applied to information management, and that is our focus throughout this part of the book. This chapter will give you some grounding in the basic principles of distributed database technology, which will be valuable if the information systems under your control are still mostly centralized. The principles discussed here will reappear in other chapters throughout this book.

Another view of DDBs focuses on grandiose multidatabase configurations, which incorporate databases of all models (legacy hierarchical and network systems, relational databases, and newly developed object-oriented databases) under a single global schema. This configuration would allow transparent access for all applications to the underlying data, regardless of location and format.

Still others view DDBs as client applications running on desktop machines (PCs or workstations), opaquely accessing data from multiple databases through the standards-based middleware of the future (for example, Microsoft's Open Database Connectivity, or ODBC, API); this DDB would work in concert with remote procedures, rather than accessing and manipulating remote data themselves.

Expanding the focus from distributed *databases* to distributed *information management systems* (in which paradigms other than "the classical database" are important in the distribution and access of data), we add various models of data warehouses to the picture. In short, distributed information management, our focus for this and the following five chapters, is one of the most complex areas of the database and information management discipline.

In Chapter 1, we discussed the irreversible trends of heterogeneity and distribution for information systems. While tremendous advances have been made in the area of connectivity (e.g., bridges and gateways, communications media, protocols), the "islands of information" problem is yet to be solved. *The emergence and eventual maturity of distributed information management technologies and models are the keys to building information bridges among those islands.*

Each of the subjects we'll discuss, from basic remote database access and middleware through heterogeneous multidatabase frameworks, is evolving toward solving the distributed information management problem. Before we

Executive Summary

Distributed databases (DDBs) are a collection of multiple, logically interrelated databases that are distributed over a computer network, and a *distributed database management system* (DDBMS) is the software system through which distributed databases are managed and through which the distribution is transparent to the user. There are varying degrees of transparency, though, ranging from a single data model covering an entire enterprise with all applications running against this global data model to, on the other end of the spectrum, distribution controlled through client/server architectures and a hard-coding of location information within data server facilities.

discuss each of these areas and where they are headed in the next few years, we'll focus in this chapter on the basic underlying principles of distributed information management. We'll define and classify distributed database management systems, and we'll take a close look at the basic principles of such environments, including location transparency, partitioning, and replication. This material will provide a foundation for subsequent discussions.

We'll also take a look at the progress to date in distributed information management, as well as widely recognized problems. Finally, we'll introduce some of the alternative opinions about the "right" direction for distributed information management to follow.

2.2 Definition and Characteristics of Distributed Database Systems

At the heart of distributed information management is the distributed database (DDB) and distributed database management system (DDBMS). Let's define these terms.

A *distributed database* is a collection of multiple, logically interrelated databases that are distributed over a computer network.[1] A *distributed database management system* is the software system through which distributed databases are managed and through which the distribution is transparent to the user.[2]

These definitions can be expanded by looking at the various characteristics of DDBs and DDBMSs. In 1987, C. J. Date published Date's Rules for Distributed Databases.[3] These 12 rules are

A set of guiding principles define the characteristics of distributed databases, but to date these principles have remained mostly unfulfilled in commercial products. At the very least, a trade-off must be made among different principles, since today's underlying technology means that some are often at odds with others.

Some DDB/DDBMS environments are homogeneous, meaning that the local data managers are comprised of a single DBMS product. Others are heterogeneous in nature, with different DBMS products (sometimes different data models, including flat file systems) making up the local data manager group.

1) *Location autonomy:* Local data should be locally owned and managed; this includes the functions of security, integrity, and storage representation. Exceptions occur when integrity constraints must span multiple sites and distributed transaction management must be controlled by some external site.

2) *No reliance on a central site for any particular service:* Adherence to this rule helps prevent bottlenecks due to the inherently decentralized nature of all DDBMS functions.

3) *Continuous operation:* No forced halt in operations should occur as a result of adding sites to or removing locations from a distributed environment, making metadata changes, or (this is tricky) upgrading DBMS releases at an individual site.

4) *Location independence:* Users or applications don't need to know where data are physically stored.

5) *Fragmentation independence:* The fragments (partitions, in our terminology) may be stored and managed by the DDBMS without user or application awareness. Additionally, the DDBMS is responsible for avoiding processing requests against irrelevant fragments (that is, the DDBMS must be smart enough to recognize that a particular fragment or partition need not be accessed if the relational columns stored within aren't referenced in the query or update statement).

6) *Replication independence:* The same independence and transparency applies to replicates, which we'll discuss later.

7) *Distributed query processing:* The query processing itself should be carried out in a distributed fashion. In the next section, we'll discuss some of the architectural constructs of DDBMSs and different models under which queries may be processed in a distributed manner.

Some environments are constructed in a *top-down*, "from scratch" manner, but, more typically, the inclusion of legacy systems requires a *bottom-up* construction. Bottom-up construction is far more complex, since data redundancy, inconsistency, and structural mismatches typically make up the underlying environments which need to be brought together.

In some systems, different models of partitioning (also known as fragmentation) permit data to be distributed among different systems yet allow the data to be treated in a global sense as if they were still centralized. Another distribution model involves the replication of some or all data on multiple systems, the goal typically being to improve overall systems throughput and data availability.

8) *Distributed transaction management:* The principles of transaction management and concurrency control must be applied to distributed database operations. These include deadlock detection and resolution, timeout management, distributed commits and rollbacks, and other areas.

9) *Hardware independence:* The same DDBMS software should run on different hardware systems and should participate as an equal partner in the overall system. In reality, as we've discussed, this is extremely difficult because many vendors support multiple platforms. This limitation is overcome by the multiple-product framework model.

10) *Operating system independence:* This is closely related to hardware independence, and the same framework-based arguments in that discussion apply.

11) *Network independence:* Sites may be connected over a wide variety of network and communication environments. The layering model inherent in most information systems today (such as the OSI 7-layer model, the TCP/IP model, the layers of SNA and DECnet) provides a grounding for achieving this goal not only in DDB environments but in information systems in general.

12) *DBMS independence:* It should be possible for local DBMSs to participate in a DDBMS environment.

An examination of Date's rules reveals that while a system capable of supporting all 12 rules would be highly desirable, achieving this within a single product release or even within a short period of time would be impossible. And, indeed, this has been the case in the years since the rules were first defined by Date.

What This Technology Can Do for You

The following five chapters discuss distributed database and information management technology in more detail. Given the fact that
distribution and heterogeneity are rapidly becoming facts of IS life for
every organization, cooperative management of dispersed information
is essential to prevent total chaos. This chapter discusses the fundamental principles. Subsequent chapters will discuss various technologies
and Chapter 7 will cover trade-offs.

In part for that reason, database vendors targeting the DDBMS market
have taken a multiphase approach to the incorporation of distribution in their
products. One of the more highly publicized statements of direction came
from IBM, which in 1989 outlined a four-phase approach toward distributed
database management. These steps were[4]

1) *The Remote Request:* This is analogous to a basic remote access model. A
   connection is made to a remote site, and data at that site are read or
   updated. Results are returned to the originating site, and transactions are
   completed. Nearly every commercial DBMS now supports remote requests, and has done so for some time.

2) *The Remote Unit of Work:* This occurs when a group of requests can be
   executed as an atomic unit (a transaction) at a remote site. An application
   can then access or modify data at multiple sites, but each transaction
   must reference data from one site only.

3) *The Distributed Unit of Work:* This occurs when each request can be
   executed against a single site, and the requests within a distributed unit
   of work (a transaction) *collectively* can execute on multiple sites. The
   requests can then be committed or recovered as a unit.

4) *The Distributed Request:* This final state occurs when a request can
   involve multiple database objects at multiple sites. Several of these distributed requests can then be grouped as a transaction.

We can extend the last of the four steps—the distributed request—to an even
greater degree of heterogeneity and distribution, as we'll discuss in the next
section.

2.3 Distributed Information Management: The Ultimate Scenario

The scenario for the best use of the distributed database typically goes something like this: Following an endless series of corporate mergers and subsequent restructurings over the past decade, your organization—which once had a grand total of ten mainframes (all from the same vendor) based at three locations to handle worldwide business operations—now has literally tens of thousands of computers, from a PC or workstation on nearly every employee's desk to departmental mid-range systems (from eight different vendors) to those mainframes that are still there. These systems are scattered across hundreds of business locations around the world, all connected via a state-of-the-art series of local area networks (LANs) and a wide area network (WAN). Your global electronic mail system is considered to be among the most robust in the world; almost anyone can communicate with anyone else in your entire company.

Unfortunately, this communications uniformity is not true of your informational assets. The desktop systems, mid-range and minicomputer systems, and mainframes all have their own databases and file systems in which billions—perhaps trillions—of bits of information are stored. Your PC systems have several different DBMS products that manage databases (all relational). Several databases are Xbase products (dBASE IV, FoxPro, and so on), but Paradox for Windows and Microsoft Access databases are also scattered among the PCs.

The mid-range and mainframe computers have a total of ten different DBMS products, mostly relational but also including other database models. Many applications still use flat files as their main information storage mechanism. Additionally, two departments at a remote site are experimenting with object-oriented DBMSs for multimedia applications (such as voice and video), and management has expressed a desire to have access to whatever data will eventually reside there for traditional informational queries.

In addition to an applications backlog at the data center (which, though much lighter than it had been only three years before due to the placement of applications in departments, is still present), a major new human resources program is under development. The hardware and operating systems for this new system are still to be determined, but the environment will almost certainly be heterogeneous in nature, further complicating the information management picture.

Existing applications often need data from other sources, and in the few cases where online access is available, obtaining such data is typically done through a series of read-only data extractions using interoperability tools. The integrity of the data, once replicated across the environments, is somewhat suspect, and timeliness is typically a problem in accessing this data and in subsequent uploads.

Even newly developed applications require distribution of data, with a global schema having underlying data managers operating against portions of the data that reside on various independent computer systems. The information will be a combination of relational, table-based data, multimedia objects (some stored within object-oriented databases, others within hybrid relational/object-oriented databases), and perhaps some hypertext information. Also, the information management environment should be secure.

Taking all of this into account

- You want to put an "information management umbrella" on top of your existing environment to eliminate redundancy and improve data consistency and integrity. Applications should be able to access remote data as needed and modify or delete remote data as well, in accordance with appropriate privileges.

- You want to do all of the preceding actions within the context of "proper" distributed processing principles, such as transaction and concurrency control, controlled security and access, coordinated disaster recovery methods, and so on.

- You also want to be able to develop new applications against some global picture of their data, and *subsequently* distribute the instantiated objects and user data according to business rules, technical considerations, and other factors. That is, you don't want to start worrying about physical remote access during the design and early development stages of your applications.

- Those new applications will also need access to existing data and newly created data objects.

- You want the capability to use an appropriate information management model for different components of an application environment. That is, you would like to be able to use object-oriented databases in some places, hypertext environments in others, and so on, and have information from each model available as necessary to other applications, even if those applications are built around a different information management model.

The technical requirements of the distributed information environment we just described would include

- Operations that access—and update—distributed data should be optimized to most efficiently perform their mission. This may entail extracting data remotely and sending it to some intermediate stopping point where it is combined with other data and then sent elsewhere; or whole blocks of data being shipped to the requester, at whose site processing then takes place; or other possible alternatives. These decisions should be made on a case-by-case basis or according to some predictable cost algorithms.

- All of the traditional database functions (concurrent access control, locking, security, and others) must be expanded to take into account the distributed nature of the data.

- The DBMSs themselves should be distributed in an intelligent manner across the overall environment.

- The metadata should most likely be distributed, and the distributed information principles for user data applied to the metadata as well.

- Cost algorithms should be employed according to network and transportation capabilities and costs, and other factors. Given the likely dynamic nature of network and communication environments, these cost algorithms should be constantly updateable.

These certainly are lofty goals. The pursuit of a global information management layer on top of the collective whole of a company's data assets, providing transparent operational and decision support access to any and all components regardless of location, is an admirable one.

As we'll discuss in Chapter 6, some members of the database and information management discipline are dedicated to the advancement of global, transparent access. *However, a consensus has not been reached on the merits of this approach as the optimal solution for the management of company-wide data assets.* As we make our way through the possible distributed information management solutions, we'll explore the relative merits of each with respect to technical issues *as well as business needs*.

First, though, let's discuss the ways in which distributed databases might be characterized, since our subsequent discussion of trends and future directions will require a thorough understanding of various classes of DDBs.

2.4 Distributed Database Models

It's instructive to look at basic definitions of distributed databases and distributed DBMSs, and at goals of DDBs as outlined in Date's 12 Rules (see section 2.2). You may have noticed from our scenario in the previous section, though, that user and organizational business models from which the need for data distribution arises, exist at different ends of several spectrums. Specifically, DDBs might be either homogeneous or heterogeneous, and they might be created using either a top-down or a bottom-up approach.

Additionally, distributed data may take alternative forms. In some cases, data are partitioned, or divided, among multiple physical resources. In other cases, they are replicated, or duplicated, among multiple sites. We'll discuss different models of partitioning and replication.

Let's look at each of these areas in more detail, setting the stage for our analysis of trends and future directions.

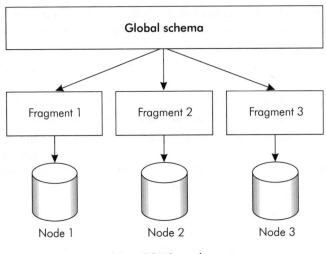

Figure 2-1 Homogeneous Distributed Database Architecture

2.4.1 Homogeneous versus Heterogeneous Systems

Homogeneous distributed database systems are relatively easy to understand; they involve a single DBMS product, typically with a single database language (e.g., SQL with distributed extensions). The distributed DBMS supporting homogeneous distribution is very tightly coupled, and internal search engines and query processing facilities are optimized and maximally tuned to improve performance and throughput. Figure 2-1 illustrates a typical homogeneous distributed database environment.

There are variations on the theme of homogeneous DDBMSs. Simply put, a single globally accessible "main DBMS engine" might exist at one site, with linkages to local data access components co-located with the databases themselves around the company (or department, depending on the scope of distribution). More complex models might allow the DBMS itself to be widely distributed, with components at any location capable of accessing distributed data from other locations in a peer-to-peer fashion. From the database side, though, we have identical storage area models, index structures, and data formats across the span of distribution. Homogeneous distributed databases are usually designed in a top-down manner[5] (which we'll discuss in section 2.4.2).

The flip side to homogeneous DDBs is, of course, heterogeneous DDBs. *Heterogeneous distributed databases* include two or more data management products that are distinct from one another in a significant way (e.g., relational DBMSs from different vendors, such as Oracle and Digital Equipment; or DBMSs from one vendor that operate on different platforms with different

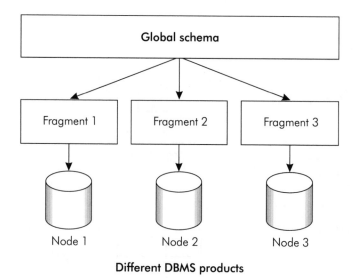

Figure 2-2 Simple Heterogeneous Distributed Database Configuration

database structures, such as IBM's DB2 and SQL/DS). Figure 2-2 illustrates a typical heterogeneous distributed database configuration. As we'll discuss in Chapter 6, heterogeneous databases can be further broken down into a wide range of classifications, from federated databases to different types of multi-database systems; in fact, a formal taxonomy exists for different heterogeneous models.

Earlier, we mentioned that homogeneous distributed databases are typically created in a top-down fashion; heterogeneous DDB environments, however, are usually the result of a bottom-up effort to create some type of common management environment on top of previously disjointed information resources. We'll discuss bottom-up distributed database creation next.

2.4.2 Top-Down versus Bottom-Up Distributed Databases

Let's first look at top-down models for creating distributed databases, because they are conceptually the simplest to understand. *Top-down* DDB design is accomplished in much the same way as the design of centralized databases: ideally, it is some type of formal methodology involving the creation of a conceptual data model, the mapping of that model to a logical data model, and the creation (and tuning) of implementation-specific database structures (e.g., Rdb/VMS tables).

In top-down distributed database design, though, the database objects will not reside at the same location, but rather will be distributed among different computer systems (Figure 2-3). This distribution can occur either through partitioning or by replication.

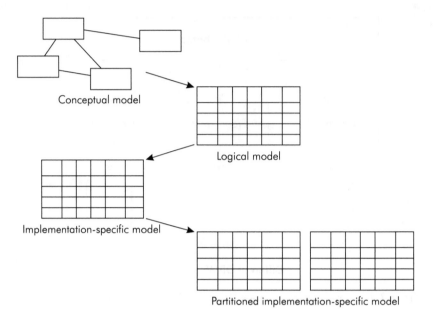

Figure 2-3 Top-Down Distributed Database Creation

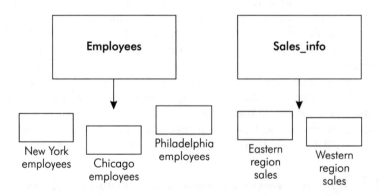

Figure 2-4 Horizontal Partitioning

Partitioning involves the decomposition of database objects such as relational tables into two or more parts that are then divided among multiple computer system resources. The classic examples used to describe partitioning usually involve employee tables or sales order information divided according to a geographical or other discerning characteristic, as shown in Figure 2-4.

The example in Figure 2-4 illustrates horizontal partitioning, in which a horizontal "slice" is made within the relational table according to, say, the values within a particular column of the table. Employee data might be

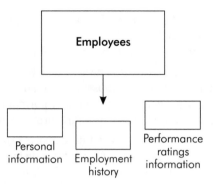

Figure 2-5 Vertical Partitioning

partitioned according to work location, sales data according to the store at which sales occurred. Alternatively, the partitioning might be done on a round-robin basis rather than on some type of value-based algorithm.

An alternative model is to vertically partition the data, slicing the table along column lines instead of by row (Figure 2-5). Certain information about an employee might be stored at one location, other information (but still from the same table) stored at some other location.

Regardless of whether horizontal or vertical partitioning is employed, a global schema exists that reconstitutes the partitions back into a logically centralized table or other database structure.

Before we go on to discuss replication, we should think about partitioning with respect to real-world distributed databases. While the classic examples of top-down integrated DDBs based on partitioning might appear to make sense, they actually have little benefit in real-world environments, at least in the ways originally envisioned. If you consider an application environment with an architecture like that of Figure 2-4, you might envision operations such as

- Payroll processed for Tucson employees by Tucson-based applications.
- Payroll processed for New York by applications residing on the New York system.
- The capability for authorized Tucson managers to query information about video rental and sales statistics, not only for the Tucson store but companywide.

At first glance, the idea of a global schema residing on top of partitions to support these and other operations seems to be a sensible solution. Yet, consider the following:

- For Tucson applications processing payroll for Tucson employees, there is no need to go through any type of global schema. That is, the payroll

application would not do a SELECT * FROM ALL_EMPLOYEES_EVERY-
WHERE WHERE JOB_LOC = "Tucson", but would proceed in a locally
autonomous manner to do those types of operations.

- A Tucson manager has little or no need to update personnel information
for New York employees (or for those working anywhere else within the
company); therefore, updates to personnel information at a remote site
via a global schema would indeed be a rare, probably nonexistent, event.

- Similarly, a New York manager doesn't need update capabilities for Tucson-
based video rental and sales data. Of course, a district manager or some
other company official who works in New York might want a read-only
query capability for Tucson sales activity data, in order to combine that
data with those of Chicago and Dallas and other sites for comparative and
summary reports. However, the granularity at which that sales activity
information (and similar data from other applications areas) would be
retrieved and returned to the application and the district manager would
be much finer than necessary. That is, a company official would most
likely not be interested in a complete list of every video and rental from
every store but rather summary information (e.g., sales by month by city,
compared against those of the previous month as well as the same month
from the previous year).

While a well-run business organization should truly have this type of reporting capability, *it is arguable that a partitioned data model with a global
reconstitution capability is* not *the best way of achieving it*. A growing school
of thought within the information management field claims that it makes
sense to maintain a distinction between operational databases and other
databases to be used strictly for decision support and similar informational
purposes. One such paradigm is through the use of data warehouses, which
we'll discuss in Chapter 4.

Taking all of this into account, then, it's arguable that having a global
schema sitting on top of widely distributed data partitions *may be less
valuable than previously believed*. Update operations tend to be clustered
against locally managed data, not remote data; dynamic retrieval operations
against widely distributed data for the purposes of informational reporting
could conceivably choke an operational system's performance and throughput
by repeatedly bringing large amounts of data back to some other location (or
locations) merely for the purpose of summarization. While homogeneous
DDBs with top-down data distribution through partitioning could conceivably apply intelligence to the formation of query graphs (e.g., perform the data
grouping at remote sites and then bring back summary information), the
usefulness of this approach to distributed information management is questionable.

Does this mean that implementation of homogeneous distributed databases is an outmoded idea? Not quite. Parallel database systems (one of our

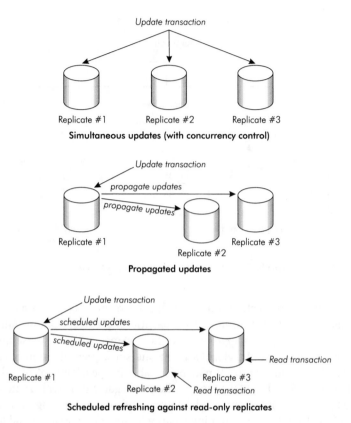

Figure 2-6 Database Replication Models

topics in Chapter 5, in which data partitioning occurs in closely coupled environments as contrasted with the DDB approach of partitioning over networked environments) may be the most promising forum partitioning models to achieve DDB goals of high performance and data throughput.

Let's turn our focus from partitioning to its counterpart, replication. *Replication* involves the creation of replicates (as you could probably guess). *Replicates* are a set of distinct physical copies of some database object (typically a table) that is kept in synchronization with the "main" copy according to the database's rules.[6] In the purest sense, all replicate-based database object values should be automatically and immediately kept in synchronization with one another. (Practical solutions usually dictate some relaxation of that goal.) In some environments, replicates are used exclusively on a read-only basis, and replicate-based values are refreshed according to a scheduling mechanism. In other environments, updates might be permitted to certain data values, with updates propagated elsewhere according to scheduling and coordination procedures. Figure 2-6 shows a variety of database replication models. We'll discuss replication models in more detail in Chapter 5.

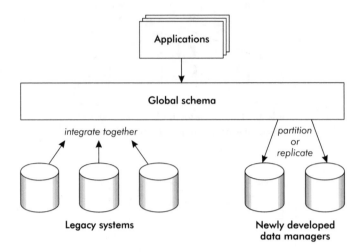

Figure 2-7 Bottom-Up Distributed Database Integration

So far in this section, our focus has been on a top-down approach to distribution of data, through either partitioning or replication. Again, the top-down philosophy is appropriate to homogeneous DDBs, those involving the initial definition of a global schema and subsequent division of database objects. While this approach may be suitable for development of a database environment for a brand new application, an organization will far more likely need to create an interconnected database environment through the integration of existing databases and information managers, possibly in addition to newly developed database components. *Such environments do not have the luxury of starting with a top-down approach with no legacy to be considered.* Rather, a *bottom-up* approach, which focuses on integrating the schemas of existing databases to provide new and existing applications with access to new and existing data assets, is more appropriate for these types of environments (Figure 2-7). Thus we have the discipline of multidatabase systems, which we'll discuss in Chapter 6.

As we'll note in Chapter 6, the process of creating some form of multidatabase environment is certainly a non-trivial process. Among the many difficult technical issues that must be addressed are

- Intermodel mappings (e.g., having some type of global access to multiple information forms, say flat files, hierarchical databases, relational databases, and object-oriented information).
- Metadata management.
- Resolving impedance mismatches (e.g., different representations of the data object type in different databases, such as numeric representation of MOVIE_TYPE in one database and character-based representation in some other database).

2.5 Conclusion

Our goal in this chapter has been to set the stage for discussions in the next several chapters of present trends and future directions in distributed information management. Much has been written about distributed database technology over the past 15 to 20 years, and a great deal of progress has been made in many areas.

Most importantly for our purposes, though, is that wide research and real-world experiences have caused a rethinking of some basic premises and their applicability in corporate information management environments. As we discussed, it may be technically feasible to partition a homogeneous distributed database over some type of network, but it offers little concrete benefit to an organization's information systems functionality. The implementation of a data warehouse in conjunction with autonomous databases may, in fact, be a better alternative to achieve the mixture of local update operations with global query-oriented information access.

With these fundamental principles behind us, let's next take a look at the future directions of client/server technology in the database world, as the developments in this area will certainly influence decisions about data distribution and reconstitution.

Outlook

Short-term

- Distribution becoming a "pervasive attribute" of database and information management environments, though implemented in many different ways

- More products with distribution as an inherent quality rather than through gateways and specialized interfaces

- New understandings of old concepts (e.g., partitioning, replication) and deployment in new ways

Long-term

- Solutions to identified problems (such as scaling, global schema management, distributed query optimization)

- Capabilities to handle a high degree of heterogeneity in the underlying components with greater ease than in today's systems

Additional Reading

- M. W. Bright, A. R. Hurson, and S. H. Pakzad, "A Taxonomy and Current Issues in Multidatabase Systems," *IEEE Computer* (March 1992).
- R. Hackathorn, *Enterprise Database Connectivity* (New York: John Wiley & Sons, 1993).
- M. T. Özsu and P. Valduriez, *Principles of Distributed Database Systems* (Englewood Cliffs, NJ: Prentice-Hall, 1991).
- M. T. Özsu and P. Valduriez, "Distributed Database Systems: Where Are We Now?," *Computer* (August 1991).

Endnotes

1. M. T. Özsu and P. Valduriez, "Distributed Database Systems: Where Are We Now?," *Computer* (August 1991), 68.

2. Özsu and Valduriez, "Distributed Database Systems," 68–69.

3. Date's 12 DDB Rules are different from E. F. Codd's 12 Rules for Relational Databases. The latter applies to relational databases in general, while the former deals with distributed databases and, in theory, can be applied to non-relational information.

4. "Inside IBM's Database Strategy," *DBMS* IBM-sponsored supplement 2, 9 (1989). Quoted in S. Khoshafian et al., *A Guide to Developing Client/Server SQL Applications* (San Francisco: Morgan Kaufmann, 1992), 531.

5. M. W. Bright, A. R. Hurson, and S. H. Pakzad, "A Taxonomy and Current Issues in Multidatabase Systems," *IEEE Computer* (March 1992), 51.

6. D. McGoveran, "Two-Phased Commit or Replication?," *Database Programming and Design* (May 1993), 36.

CHAPTER 3

Client/Server Databases and Middleware

A Note to the CIO

Client/server technology is valuable to your organization. Chances are that your dabblings to date have been on a departmental level, with LAN-based servers meeting the needs of PC database users. The products you have been using, whether commercially purchased or developed in-house, have likely used proprietary interfaces between client systems and the back-end database and information management servers. While the early experiences of many organizations have undermined the idea that client/server computing automatically equals immediate cost savings (the jury is still out), compartmentalization of

3.1 Introduction

The concept of client/server technology, whether applied to computer systems in general or specifically to information management, is extremely simple. *Client/server* computing divides the labor within a companywide or department-level system (or within a small business computing system). *Client systems*, with which users interact, communicate with *servers* that provide some formal set of services (communications, database management, repository services, global naming services, and so on). Division of labor is chiefly accomplished by keeping user-oriented functions within client systems (typically, desktop PCs or workstations). Here are some examples of user-oriented functions:

client and server functions irrefutably helps an organization develop distributed, heterogeneous systems.

Key for the future, and important to your organization, is the emergence of *standards* in the client/server world, which will be one of our primary focal points in this chapter. As is typical in the world of standards, we have multiple candidates from which to choose. Many of these standards are just emerging, so comparing, say, the relative merits of SAG and DRDA or ODBC and IDAPI (which are discussed in this chapter) is difficult, because much will be determined by future directions and enhancements, compliant commercially available products, and the like. This chapter provides an overview of the emerging client/server information management standards so they may be tracked and analyzed.

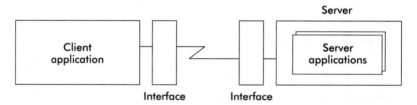

Figure 3-1 A Basic Client/Server Environment

- Creating and validating a database query or update operation.
- Receiving information from a server and, according to predefined screens or other templates, presenting the results to the user.
- Fielding statistical information provided by the system as a whole (e.g., operational statistics) and presenting that information to users in accordance with templates or other presentation rules.

Figure 3-1 shows a conceptual view of a typical client/server environment.

Client/server configurations can exist within local area networks (LANs), over metropolitan or wide area networks (MANs and WANs, respectively), or they can reside on the same processor (e.g., one process performs client functions, another server functions). We'll focus on the distributed aspects of client/server computing in this chapter.

Information management was one of the first areas in which client/server computing made serious inroads. As PCs became widespread in the mid-1980s, they were used as analysis tools for corporate- or department-level data

Executive Summary

Client/server computing typically involves the division of information systems functions among different computer systems. The classic model that has evolved features desktop *client systems* (usually personal computers or workstations) in which user-oriented functions occur; examples of such functions include forms and screen management and data presentation. *Server systems*, which can vary from high-powered PCs on a small local area network (LAN) to the corporate mainframe, provide "back-end" functions such as database management.

The first generation of client/server systems involved proprietary interfaces, and the majority were built to support client/server database operations. Ideally, client/server computing should promote a mix-and-

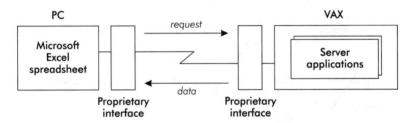

Figure 3-2 Mid-1980s Client/Server Environments

stored in a LAN server, a mid-range system, or on the corporate mainframe. Architectures and products were developed to make this access possible. For example, a user could request particular data from the departmental VAX/VMS system to the PC, then further analyze that data using a spreadsheet product such as Microsoft Excel or Lotus 1-2-3 or a PC-based DBMS such as dBASE III+ or FoxPro (Figure 3-2).

This client/server environment had one drawback, however: the interfaces were all proprietary, provided either by a single vendor or a small vendor consortium that wanted to promote the use of their product in a client/server environment. This configuration could not meet the growing need for *portability* and *interchangeability* in client/server computing.

The emphasis on a "plug and play" model of interchangeable hardware and software (the "open systems" concept that began in the late 1980s) brought portability and interchangeability to the forefront. As illustrated in Figure 3-3, *portability* means being able to move either client or server or both to new platforms without disrupting the application environment in

match approach to corporate computing, including the capability to switch to new hardware platforms, operating systems, and/or applications software, as business needs dictate. Such switching should occur without disrupting the operations of the entire information system.

In the area of database management, standards are emerging that promote mix-and-match capabilities. A growing trend is the use of *middleware*, or standards-based units that provide abstraction of system-specific functions away from both client and server components. While architecturally more complex than simple point-to-point client/ server connections, standards-based middleware is expected to help promote the long-term evolution of information systems, as well as provide a framework through which legacy systems transition can occur.

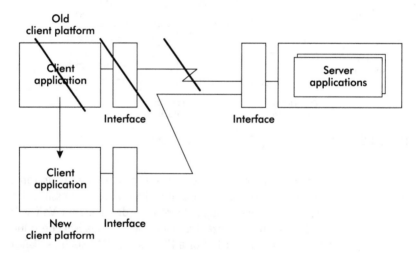

Figure 3-3 Portability within a Client/Server Environment

place. *Interchangeability* is the capability to replace either the client or the server with some other product but still keep the interface in place. For example, a database server is switched from Product X to Product Y, but client applications running against that server remain unchanged (Figure 3-4).

The incorporation of standards makes portability and interchangeability possible, and standards will affect the future of client/server information management as we'll discuss in this chapter. Efforts to standardize, such as

What This Technology Can Do for You

Client/server computing has many benefits for information systems organizations. First, bringing computing power to the desktop is crucial for the productivity of workers, as has been demonstrated throughout the personal computer revolution. Second, linking corporate data via client/server technology can provide consistent views of data to the user.

Rather than pursue programs that involve proprietary, custom-developed interfaces, the approaches discussed in this chapter will bring standardized, evolvable technology to corporate client/server computing.

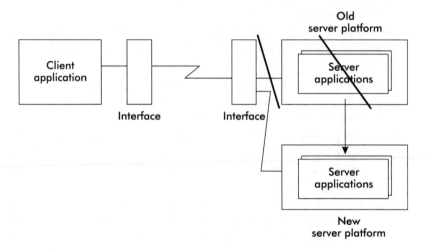

Figure 3-4 Interchangeability in Client/Server Environments

Remote Database Access (RDA), Distributed Relational Database Architecture (DRDA), Integrated Database Application Programming Interface (IDAPI), Data Access Language (DAL), and Open Database Connectivity (ODBC), will drive client/server computing for the rest of the 1990s. Before we discuss these specific standards, let's take a brief look at some of the guidelines that have developed as client/server computing has matured since the mid-1980s.

3.2 Client/Server Guidelines and Evaluation Criteria

In *A Guide to Developing Client/Server SQL Applications,*[1] the authors present a checklist of 12 criteria that should guide the development of client/server products and services:

1) *Preservation of server autonomy:* Clients should follow all rules set by servers, should not impact the availability of servers (e.g., shouldn't unnecessarily lock excessive amounts of data), and should not violate any server data integrity.

2) *Preservation of client autonomy:* Clients should not act any differently whether connected to a remote database server or a local database server; users should be isolated from data location issues.

3) *Support for server-independent applications:* Clients should operate the same regardless of which server (of several possible) is being accessed, and what remote hardware, operating systems, and services are used (but see #4 following).

4) *Accessibility to server-specific features:* Clients may require some server-specific functions to best perform a job; these functions should be accessible.

5) *Support for live data access:* Unlike a file server configuration, client/server data access and updates should be based on the data themselves in the server, not files of data uploaded and downloaded.

6) *Minimal workstation impact for adding server access:* Client software should not be resource-intensive; for example, PC-based systems destined to be used as clients should not require a doubling of RAM or hard disk capacity merely to access servers.

7) *Completeness of connectivity options:* Client software should not require additional programming to complete a connection to a server, though, of course, connections to the database servers themselves may be made through communications servers or other layers. An end-to-end connection should be available.

8) *Local prototyping opportunity:* The remote nature of information should not affect the capability to prototype applications for users.

9) *A complete set of end-user tools:* Screen development tools, query generation toolboxes, and other tools should be part of the environment.

10) *Completeness of the application development environment:* In addition to the tools listed in #9, the development environment should include the means to establish and manage network connections, access to global naming and location services, and so on.

11) *An open-host language environment:* Programming capability to extend end-user tool capacities and predefined access services should be available.

12) *Adherence to standards:* The greater the support for standards, the fewer problems there will be with interoperability among components.

3.3 Client/Server Information Management Standards

The good news is that the database interface for client/server connection is rapidly undergoing standardization. The bad news is that many different standards exist, which, some cynics might claim, leaves us only slightly better off than we were in the world of proprietary client/server database interfaces. Instead of three or four vendors supporting a particular standard API or protocol set, we now have twenty or thirty or perhaps one hundred companies . . . but certainly not every vendor who offers such products.

Actually, having multiple standards isn't such a bad thing. A common criticism of the standardization process is that in trying to provide a complete solution set for as many different environments as possible, certain features that might be advantageous to a particular environment are omitted or left to vendor-provided extensions. By having several different standards options, organizations incorporating client/server technology into their data management environments can choose the one(s) best suited for their particular needs.

3.3.1 SQL Access Group and DRDA

The standardization process for client/server database access became very active in the late 1980s and early 1990s. The SQL Access Group (SAG) was formed in 1989, its membership consisting of a consortium of 42 companies, including most major database engine and tool vendors.[2] One of the roles of SAG was to define a formats and protocol (FAP) specification for client/server database communication based on the International Standards Organization (ISO) Remote Database Access (RDA) specification. The RDA standard is defined in ISO/IEC 9579, *Information Technology—Database Languages— Remote Database Access,* which consists of two parts: "Generic Model, Service and Protocol" and "SQL Specialization."[3] "SQL Specialization" was the basis for SAG's FAP specifications.[4]

FAP specifications include the structure of messages and the control information protocol among components exchanging information, for example, control structures that tell one site that a data unit with a particular block number is being transmitted, or that a particular message number is being acknowledged.

Around the same time, IBM, the only major database vendor not a member of SAG, introduced the Distributed Relational Database Architecture (DRDA), which is unrelated to the ISO RDA (despite the common three initials, note that "R" and "A" represent different words in the two standards).

SQL Access Group
- Based on ISO RDA
- Goal: de jure standard
- "Open" components (e.g., ASN.1)

DRDA
- Original goal: IBM-based database access under SAA
- May evolve to de facto standard
- Utilizes IBM components

Figure 3-5 SQL Access Group and DRDA Client/Server Efforts

The initial goal of DRDA was to provide database integration under IBM's Systems Application Architecture (SAA). SAA was originally envisioned as a master integration and interoperability program for four of IBM's platforms (MVS, VM, OS/400, and OS/2). Using DRDA, SAA would bring together the database managers from those platforms (DB2, SQL/DS, the OS/400 Data Manager, and the OS/2 Extended Edition Database Manager, respectively) in one client/server model.[5] Figure 3-5 compares the client/server efforts of the SQL Access Group and DRDA.

IBM's 1991 announcement of its Information Warehouse architecture placed DRDA in a key role of integrating interproduct client/server databases, and a number of database vendors announced their support for DRDA. By early 1992, two camps competed in the field of client/server database access: SQL/Access Group with its RDA roots, and DRDA with its IBM enterprise computing focus.

Because SAG was and is a multiple-vendor initiative, working through the standardization process, SAG results will be a *de jure*, or formal, standard, established by a standards organization through a formal process. In contrast, even though vendors other than IBM are involved in DRDA, that effort is first and foremost an IBM-driven standard. DRDA standardization will be a *de facto* standard, similar to SNA, 3270 terminal communications, and other efforts with roots in the IBM corporation.[6]

Technical differences exist between SAG and DRDA specifications. Because SAG FAPs are based on ISO RDA, ISO components, including the ASN.1 abstract syntax and the basic encoding rules (BER) for ASN.1, are used as the transfer syntax (though the syntax of the actual messages are negotiated on a per-connection basis). In contrast, DRDA uses the IBM Distributed Data Management (DDM) Architecture—specifically Level Three, which defines an abstract syntax and encoding for commands and responses. For data and metadata, DRDA uses the IBM Architecture FD:OCA, which is also used for compound documents.[7]

Other distinctions between SAG and DRDA are addressed in detail in Newman and Gray's article, "Which Way to Remote SQL?"[8] Now, let's turn our attention to derivative efforts based on the work by the SQL Access Group, specifically ODBC and IDAPI.

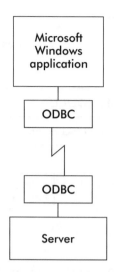

Figure 3-6 ODBC Architecture

3.3.2 SAG CLI-Based Standards

In 1992, two competing efforts surfaced, each with roots in the Call-Level Interface (CLI) of the SQL Access Group: ODBC and IDAPI. The first effort, Open Database Connectivity (ODBC), was introduced and driven by Microsoft. Microsoft's goal was to allow Microsoft Windows applications to access SQL databases through a standards-based client/server interface (Figure 3-6). The primary purpose of ODBC was to take the SAG CLI and move it from a somewhat abstract, generic standard into an environment in which it would be immediately usable through PC applications.

Several months later, in November 1992, a group of four companies led by Borland (and including IBM, Novell, and WordPerfect) announced a similar client/server database standard, also based on the SAG CLI, known as the Integrated Database Application Programming Interface (IDAPI) (Figure 3-7). IDAPI is conceptually similar to ODBC in that both are client/server interfaces based on SAG CLI, but IDAPI initially supported other platforms aside from Microsoft Windows and provided navigational access to database servers in addition to SQL-based access.[9] IDAPI replaced another Borland program, the Object Database API (ODAPI), which had been part of Borland Object Component Architecture (BOCA).[10]

IDAPI provides support for dBASE servers (see Figure 3-7). A large number of dBASE programs (written in the Xbase programming language, which we'll discuss in Chapter 14) use navigational data access for system databases (e.g., a master table-vs.-transaction table update model, bidirectional browsing of tables of information, and so on) rather than SQL-like set operations. Therefore, IDAPI includes a navigational component in its interface

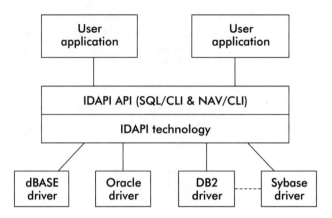

Figure 3-7   IDAPI Technical Architecture[11]

known as NAV/CLI[12] that allows existing dBASE databases (the legacy data-bases of the PC world) on the server side of newly developed application environments. The same is true for other drivers on the server side of IDAPI, such as Borland's Paradox.

Figure 3-8 shows IDAPI and ODBC, both today and in a possible future. When IDAPI was announced, the SQL Access Group chairman stated that SAG would investigate IDAPI extensions to the basic SAG CLI standard, which means that navigational capabilities may eventually find their way into the SAG CLI.[13]

At the time of this writing, the IDAPI Working Draft specification includes 149 pages of call-level statements as part of the API. The statements are divided into several categories, including the following:[14]

- *Environment and connection:* Opening and closing connections to servers, handles management, and cursor management.

- *Resources and capabilities:* Configuration file management.

- *Catalogs and schemas:* Path management for schema information.

- *Statement preparation and execution:* Functions for direct execution of SQL statements, preparation and subsequent execution of statements, obtaining row counts for those rows affected by some SQL statement, and similar tasks.

- *Data definition:* Table creation and modification, index creation, dropping tables and indexes.

- *Data manipulation:* Updating and deleting rows, managing locks of rows and tables, binary large object (BLOB) management, and opening cursors.

- *Transaction control:* Commits and rollbacks, as well as a function that attempts to cancel an SQL statement.

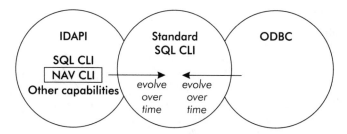

Figure 3-8 IDAPI and ODBC, Today and Tomorrow

- *Diagnostic handling:* Returning error information.
- *DBMS/operating system–specific extensions:* Password management, file and directory management, and other system-specific items.
- *Composite:* One statement is currently included that finds and positions the cursor on the first row matching some key value (such as an Xbase FIND or SEEK statement).

Readers interested in examining the types of statements included within a standards-based specification are directed to the IDAPI Working Draft, available from IDAPI, or the counterpart document for ODBC, available from Microsoft Corporation.[15]

3.4 Middleware

Standards-based client/server interfaces have, in recent years, fallen under the term middleware. Middleware applies to nearly every service area of computer systems, including database and information management. *Middleware* is defined as "any set of routines or functions that allow[s] two dissimilar programs to interoperate."[16] In short, middleware is glue. Commercial or home-grown products based on IDAPI, ODBC, DRDA, or other standards, and that provide client and server interface capabilities, fall into the middleware category.

Standardization of middleware is of particular interest for its impact on the future direction of client/server information management. Similarly, the standardization is making its way into communications, object management, electronic mail, and other areas.[17] As tomorrow's information management systems are constructed, they will inevitably contain not only client/server database access (network and communications services) but also electronic mail and other components. Therefore, a coordinated analysis of middleware requirements will be necessary.

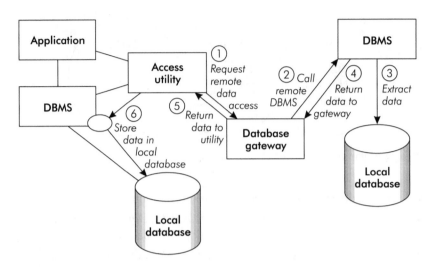

Figure 3-9 A Simple Database Gateway Architecture

3.5 Database Interoperability

We shouldn't leave this chapter without discussing what the future holds for other database integration mechanisms, specifically database gateways. We noted in section 3.1 that the client/server paradigm involves not only a distribution of computing resources but also a formal division of function among those resources. The real-world issue of legacy systems and the vast amounts of data they manage must be considered, as organizations attempt to implement client/server environments.

The traditional database integration mechanism was the gateway (Figure 3-9), with interoperability over that gateway ranging from simple data extraction to application-drive read/write capabilities. Middleware usage was sporadic and varied, from attempts to provide some layer of abstraction to direct management of the gateway access from the applications.

The number of client/server interface paradigms will increase in the coming years, but the gateway is not obsolete. Many organizational information systems are not easily transitioned to a client/server environment, for reasons ranging from closed application architectures to insufficient supporting hardware. But the desire for increased levels of database integration remain. Therefore, gateway solutions will still play a role in many organizations, if only as a continuing stopgap until client/server solutions are implemented later.

A variation on the theme of handling legacy applications during the transition to client/server systems is the use of a client/server-based *Object Request Broker (ORB)*, in which an object-oriented wrapper is placed around

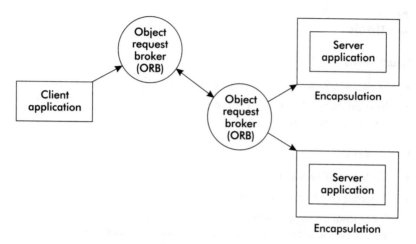

Figure 3-10 The Object Request Broker (ORB) Approach to Client/Server Information Management

client application components and existing or newly developed applications. The client and servers communicate via object-oriented methods. Figure 3-10 shows how the ORB works. We'll discuss object request brokers in Chapter 11.

3.6 Conclusion

In this chapter, we focused on recent developments in client/server database and information management, particularly standards-based middleware. If in the future a typical company has an "any client may connect to any server" environment, then standards will be the key to that interchangeability.

Even the emergence of multiple standards should not be a problem, for several reasons. First, regarding IDAPI and ODBC, the roots of those two standards are both in the SAG CLI world. Interstandard interoperability, therefore, will not be a problem in cases such as IDAPI-to-ODBC connections, because "mini-gateways" or dual-middleware-support clients and servers can be used. Even intermiddleware connectivity between incompatible systems, such as ODBC to DRDA, will be trivial, possibly handled through *metamiddleware* (middleware for middleware) or through clients and servers supporting multiple standards.

Regardless of the directions taken in client/server database architectures, the other areas we'll discuss in upcoming chapters, from data warehouses to multidatabase systems, will all be affected by client/server technology. DRDA, ODBC, IDAPI, and other standards that emerge will play an important role in distributed information management.

Outlook

Short-term

- Widespread use of client/server architectures for database applications
- Incorporation of emerging standards (e.g., DRDA, IDAPI, ODBC) into newly developed and existing client/server applications

Long-term

- Evolution of standards
- Emergence of new standards
- Incorporation of client/server database middleware with middleware from other service areas (e.g., communications, operating systems)

Additional Reading

- *American Programmer* (November 1994). Issue devoted to client/server technology.
- IDAPI Working Draft, Version 1.00, February 1993.
- S. Khoshafian, A. Chan, A. Wong, and H. K. T. Wong, *A Guide to Developing Client/Server SQL Applications* (San Francisco: Morgan Kaufmann Publishers, 1992).
- B. Marion, *Client/Server Applications* (New York: McGraw-Hill, 1993).
- S. Newman and J. Gray, "Which Way to Remote SQL?," *Database Programming and Design* (December 1991).
- A. Tang and S. Scoggins, *Open Networking with OSI* (Englewood Cliffs, NJ: Prentice-Hall, 1992).
- Regular articles about client/server computing and standards appear in publications such as *Software Magazine*, *Datamation*, and *Data Based Advisor*.

Endnotes

1. S. Khoshafian, A. Chan, A. Wong, and H. K. T. Wong, *A Guide to Developing Client/Server SQL Applications* (San Francisco: Morgan Kaufmann Publishers, 1992), 603–614.

2. S. Newman and J. Gray, "Which Way to Remote SQL?," *Database Programming and Design* (December 1991), 46.

3. A. Tang and S. Scoggins, *Open Networking with OSI* (Englewood Cliffs, NJ: Prentice-Hall, 1992), 500.

4. Newman and Gray, "Remote SQL," 48.

5. SAA is discussed in A. Simon, *Enterprise Computing* (New York: Bantam Books/Intertext, 1992), Chap. 7.

6. Newman and Gray, "Remote SQL," 48–49.

7. Newman and Gray, "Remote SQL," 51.

8. Newman and Gray, "Remote SQL," 46–54.

9. D. Richman, "Borland Group Offers Bold Plan on SQL Access," *Open Systems Today* (November 23, 1992), 1.

10. Richman, "Borland Group."

11. "Enterprise Computing," 2.

12. "IDAPI: Delivering Enterprise Computing to the Desktop," IDAPI Technical Overview, 3.

13. Richman, "Borland Group," 1.

14. IDAPI Working Draft, Version 1.00, February 1993, 4–9.

15. Interested readers should contact Microsoft Corporation or Borland International for the most current specifications for ODBC and IDAPI, respectively.

16. J. Louderback, "Making Sense of Middleware," *Proceedings of the June, 1993 DCI Database World*, Vol. II, E26-2.

17. Louderback, "Middleware," E26-6–E26-11.

CHAPTER 4

Data Warehouses

A Note to the CIO

Satisfying both the operations and information needs of your company (those information needs probably include decision support systems [DSS] or executive information systems [EIS]) can be difficult. Databases structured to meet operations needs are often incapable of adequately performing information analysis, while attempts to provide information often hamper the performance and throughput of your operations.

Data warehouses, some claim, will be increasingly important in information management throughout the 1990s. Varying degrees of summarization of operational data, maintenance of historical information,

4.1 Introduction

Data warehouses combine old and new approaches as a component of distributed information management. Conceptually, the process of extracting information from operational databases for decision support analysis has been around for a number of years. In the past, though, centralized databases that were typically based on mainframes provided the source for such data extraction. As distribution has become pervasive in corporate data management, the challenges in creating and managing what has become known as a data warehouse have increased.

consolidation of a variety of information sources, and other capabilities may solve the problem of managing data for information applications. More importantly, data warehouse trends, specifically in the area of distributing information with DSS/EIS applications that can access a variety of "mini-warehouses," will affect the use of data warehouse technology over the next few years.

Executive Summary

A *data warehouse* is a logically integrated source of data for decision support systems and executive information systems applications. The warehouse can be centralized, but future implementations will be distributed among multiple underlying systems.

A data warehouse is *not* a database. Though data warehouses may be implemented using DBMSs or DDBMSs, this is not necessarily a

In this chapter, we'll look at the principles of data warehousing. We'll discuss why the model has become such a hot topic in recent years, and we'll examine the outlook and future of the data warehouse.

4.2   Principles of the Data Warehouse

"Data warehouse and the underlying support for informational processing will emerge as a growing trend in the '90s. With the advent of data warehouse, some basic ideas about data management will change."[1]

The preceding quote is from a consultant whose information management focus is on data warehouses. A tremendous surge in interest in data warehouse models and technology has caught the attention of corporate managers responsible for information management.

A data warehouse is a logically integrated source of data for decision support systems (DSS) and executive information systems (EIS) applications. We say *logically* integrated because even though some of the simple data warehouse environments we'll discuss are based on a centralized warehouse (whether or not the warehouse's sources of data are themselves distributed), a distributed architecture will likely be desirable as the popularity of data warehouses grows. It may even become a necessity due to factors such as storage capacity.

Figure 4-1 shows a very basic data warehouse architecture. Information from an operational information management environment (typically one or

requirement. Because the purpose of a data warehouse is to support informational decision making—and not an organization's operations or transactions—many of the principles that underlie database and DBMS technology are unnecessary.

Data warehouses have a subject orientation, and are organized around a particular subset of the operational database. They are built on data extracted from different applications, which may reside on different platforms, requiring integration capabilities. Further, data is summarized to varying degrees rather than brought in instance by instance (as in the operational database).

Once data have been brought into the warehouse environment, they are *nonvolatile*, meaning that updates are propagated on a "stocking" basis (i.e., planned, regular extractions from the operational databases into the warehouse), rather than updated piecemeal as in operational databases.

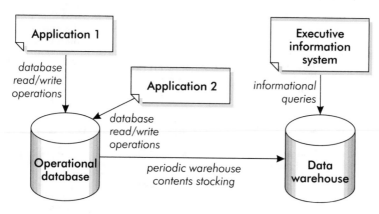

Figure 4-1 A Basic Data Warehouse Architecture

more databases) is extracted according to certain principles (which we'll discuss in a moment) and loaded into the warehouse. A more complex architecture, with multiple databases serving as the source for the warehouse, is shown in Figure 4-2.

It's important to understand, though, that a data warehouse is *not* a database, distributed or not. Though data warehouses may be implemented using DBMSs or DDBMSs, this is not necessarily a requirement. Because the purpose of a data warehouse is to support informational decision making and not an organization's operations or transactions, many of the principles that underlie database and DBMS technology are unnecessary. Specifically, tradi-

The stocking process usually involves sophisticated reconciliation of inconsistencies in the areas of data types and sizes, coding, and other data properties. Algorithms similar to those used in heterogeneous bottom-up distributed database environments can be used for this process.

Once the warehouse has been stocked with data, a variety of executive information system and decision support system applications can be run against it. Such applications may involve *drill-down* processes, in which successive levels of detail are invoked to answer "how come"–oriented questions.

Finally, the properties of data warehouses are useful in long-term information management areas such as digital libraries and data stores on forthcoming information highways.

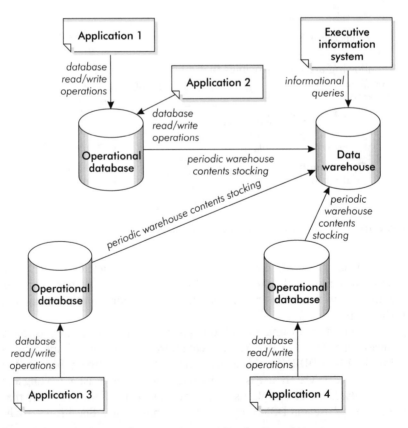

Figure 4-2 Multiple Databases as Sources for the Data Warehouse

What This Technology Can Do for You

One of the most frustrating problems facing many corporate and government decision makers is the inability to receive online, timely, consolidated, and flexible reports based on corporate data. Decision makers need accurate and timely information that, for the most part, already exists within the corporation, but extracting that information from many different operational databases and data stores is problematic. The data warehouse approach, while not revolutionary, provides a framework for decision support and executive information systems to remain competitive in the global economy of today and the future.

tional database update operations do not occur within a data warehouse. We'll discuss this later.

Following are four principles that guide the formulation and organization of the data warehouse:[2]

1) *Subject orientation:* Operational information systems contain a number of subject areas that are candidates for groupings within the data warehouse. For example, a retail video and music store could have the following subject areas:

- Customers
- Videotapes
- CDs and tapes
- Employees
- Suppliers

You could draw an analogy between data warehouse subject areas and object classes in an object-oriented database environment. Indeed, object-oriented database design and modeling techniques can be very valuable in creating the subject areas for a data warehouse.

2) *Integration capability:* Consider our discussion in Chapter 2 of the challenges of data integration in building a global schema for federated or multidatabase distributed environments. Recall that identical concepts may have dramatically varying representations among existing databases and applications, and that a common representation must be mapped. The same principle applies to data warehouses that receive

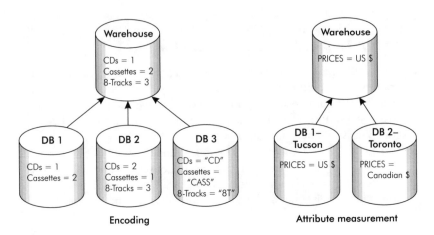

Figure 4-3 Integration Requirements of Data Warehouses

information from multiple applications and operational databases, especially those shown in Figure 4-2.

Some of the types of mismatches that must be resolved through integration are shown in Figure 4-3.

3) *Nonvolatile data:* Earlier in this section, we mentioned that data warehouses do not process traditional database updates. Figure 4-4 shows a typical operational database, regardless of the underlying model (object-oriented, relational, other). Different database environments have different levels of volatility for their data. For example, in relational databases, rows are added, values in columns are changed, and rows are deleted, all on a more or less regular basis. The data warehouse, though, is a "mass load" model that is populated at a given time according to the extraction rules supported. The mass load can be from a centralized database residing on the same system as the warehouse, or it can involve simultaneous extractions and "stocking" operations from distributed databases (or even disjoint databases and information systems, those not under the control of any type of global schema). In short, the object-at-a-time model of traditional databases is not applicable to warehouses.

4) *Time variance:* For all its integration and information support capabilities, a data warehouse is little more than a "sophisticated series of snapshots"[3] that *always* has a temporal, or time-oriented, aspect to its contents. In Chapter 15, we'll discuss temporal databases as another emerging area of information management. The fundamental principle of temporal databases—that *time* is a key component of the database and its contents—applies to data warehouses as well.

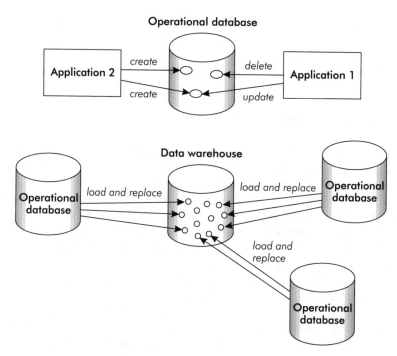

Figure 4-4 Different Update Models of Databases and Data Warehouses

4.3 Multiple Media

Consider a simple data warehouse environment, for example, one designed to support DSS applications for a small regional video and music store. (Given the predominant philosophy that "storage is free," with the proliferation of high-capacity PC-based disks and their logical connections via LANs, it's hard to imagine that a data warehouse environment could ever run into storage problems, at least for many years.)

Now take that same video and music store example and expand it to an international chain of franchised stores. Large corporations commonly use media other than magnetic disks for historical data, and archives are often managed through magnetic tapes or optical disks. The reason for using media other than magnetic disks is the cost of storage and its trade-off against access time. Less frequently accessed data is stored on slower but less expensive media.

As the international chain's data warehouse builds over time, older components of the warehouse inevitably will find their way to media other than magnetic disk. Even with the data summarization nature of warehouses (discussed in the following section), warehouses will eventually get very large. As a result, capabilities such as mixed-media indexes[4] will be necessary for large data warehouses as they evolve.

4.4 Data Summarization

The examples in Figures 4-1 and 4-2 are an oversimplification of the data warehouse concept. Operational data is extracted on a snapshot basis from one or more databases and/or other information sources, and the warehouse is built from the integration of those capabilities. But the data warehouse does *not* exist at the same level of granularity that operational data does.

Consider the differences between operational applications and applications for decision support and executive information management. Operational applications require a fine level of granularity, indeed the finest, in order to serve their role. Every customer is represented in the operational database, as is every employee, videotape, supplier, CD, and so on.

In contrast, DSS and EIS users are typically not interested in lists of every customer and a detailed report of every videotape rented or every CD purchased by that customer. Nor would your average high-level manager even be interested in a monthly or an annual summary of such information.

He or she might, though, want to see a report of average monthly rentals and sales per customer broken down by zip code within a specific company region or district. Likewise, a comparison of such summarized information against that of the previous month or the same month of the previous year or two years might be useful.

The key to the effectiveness of data warehouse–based applications is summarization. Conceivably, the DSS or EIS applications themselves could take highly granular data, whether stored within the operational database or at the same level of granularity in the data warehouse. But that course is impractical, since there is little reason to either 1) tax an operational database to repeatedly perform read-only summarizations, which would adversely affect database performance; or 2) accept the storage penalty within the data warehouse for data that won't be used individually.

Data warehouses could, of course, support multiple levels of granularity (e.g., lightly summarized and highly summarized[5]), which is desirable for drill-down analysis.[6] *Drill-down analysis* occurs when a DSS/EIS user of a data warehouse finds something of particular interest and at that point wishes to research the issue, causes, and foundations of that information further. Figure 4-5 shows the structures necessary for a typical drill-down analysis. As long as the data warehouse supports appropriate linkages from some level of summarization to other levels that feed it, the application software can traverse such linkages.

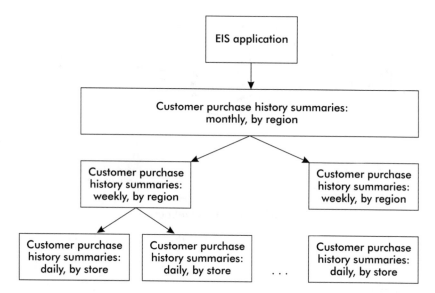

Figure 4-5 Drill-Down Analysis and Multiple Levels of Data Warehouse
Granularity

4.5 Distributed Data Warehouses

So far in this chapter, our focus has been on the underlying principles of data
warehouses. Little about the concept is new, other than having a formal name
and policies associated with periodically updated information bases. This
author designed and implemented a PC-based data warehouse in the mid-
1980s (it wasn't known as such at the time), where operational data from a
video and music store was periodically extracted, summarized, and placed in
separate read-only data structures with specialized reporting and decision
support software residing on top of the pseudo-warehouse.

So what is all the hoopla about data warehouses lately, and, more importantly, what are the directions in which warehouse technology is heading?

The keen interest in data warehouses arguably began with IBM's announcement in 1991 of its Information Warehouse architecture, a framework
the company thought would eventually reside on top of multiple *distributed,
heterogeneous* databases. Information Warehouse would ". . . provide the
tools and facilities to manage and deliver complete, timely, accurate and
understandable business information to authorized individuals for effective
decision making."[7]

IBM envisioned Information Warehouse as employing multiple forms of
middleware, including the Distributed Relational Database Architecture (DRDA)
(see Chapter 3), to support an increasingly complex environment of distributed

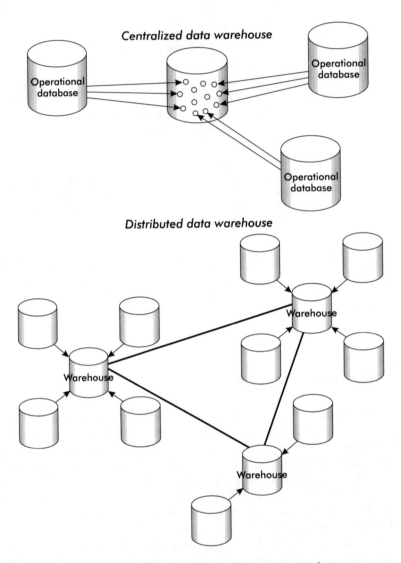

Figure 4-6 Centralized and Distributed Data Warehouse Architectures

data applications. If Information Warehouse was intended to manage the distributed data of large companies, then surely the data warehouse must evolve to include distribution.

Consider the data warehouse architectures shown in Figure 4-6. A centralized data warehouse may be appropriate for environments in which a mainframe is still the focal point of the company. However, it may not be advisable to retain informational applications under a centralized architecture while the operational applications (and underlying information) move toward distributed computing resources.

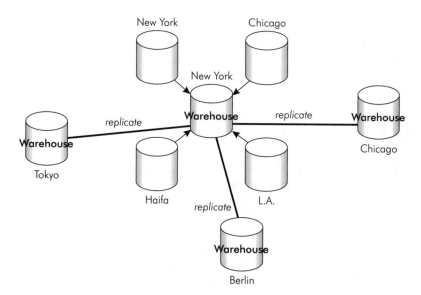

Figure 4-7 Replication and the Distributed Data Warehouse

If the distributed data warehouse in Figure 4-6 looks familiar, it should. In Chapter 2, we discussed the principles of distributed database partitions and managing those partitions via a global schema. Applications using the distributed data warehouse need not be concerned with distributed database issues such as update concurrency control, but many principles of DDBs are applicable to emerging distributed data warehouses. Figure 4-7 illustrates the replicated warehouse.

Just as databases, distributed or not, must have appropriate metadata to support access to and management of the contained information, so too must data warehouses. In the case of centralized data warehouses, the metadata structure is relatively simple. Indeed, if a warehouse is implemented through a relational DBMS, then the metadata of the DBMS is usually sufficient to support the necessary tables and other database objects. That metadata may be synchronized with the EIS/DSS applications that use the warehouse, and that synchronization would ideally occur in a high-capacity, high-perform-ance repository of the future (see Chapter 19).

Adding distribution to the warehouse may or may not complicate the metadata management. A distributed warehouse built on top of a distributed DBMS (DDBMS) would, of course, utilize the DDBMS metadata for the warehouse components. In other cases, such as a "home-grown" distributed warehouse, the designers and implementors of the warehouse may be respon-sible for defining and managing the appropriate metadata. As in centralized warehouse environments, this may also be done through repository capabilities.

Organizations that either utilize data warehouses today or plan to do so in the future will inevitably desire some degree of distribution to their warehouse, just as they will for operational databases. Therefore, data warehouses architects, designers, and implementors must *be aware* of the principles of distributed warehouses, as well as developments from vendors and other sources.

4.6 Rewriting History

This capability to change history in order to perform what-if analysis is one of the most interesting data warehouse concepts, and one that may affect future architectures and implementations.[8]

We've already mentioned that data warehouses are used not for operational applications, but rather for decision support and executive information applications. One of the characteristics of DSS and EIS applications is the capability to examine summarized historical information (and, as we discussed earlier, to drill down to finer levels of granularity to determine root causes); also, these applications should be able to ask questions such as "what if such-and-such happened instead of what actually occurred?"

In order to accomplish what-if analysis, the capability to *change data within the data warehouse* must exist. Having this capability, though, presents at least three problems:

1) Data warehouses are not meant to be updated beyond adding new snapshots of information to the existing contents; item-by-item updates are not part of the warehouse model. Concurrency control and other database issues could surface for data warehouses (e.g., one person performing historical analysis wouldn't want real values changed by someone else doing what-if analysis).

2) Because data warehouses are based on summarization (discussed in section 4.4), the warehouse may not have a sufficient level of granularity to perform the necessary changes. Changes could be made against summarized information (e.g., increase Tucson store gross revenues for the entire month by 10%), but an analyst could conceivably want to change the revenue only on certain days of the month for a particular analysis. If that level of detail doesn't exist in the warehouse, what-if analysis may be difficult to accomplish.

3) Any changes to data warehouse contents for the purpose of what-if analysis must automatically be rolled back once the analysis is completed; history may be changeable, but not permanently. However, a user performing such operations may wish to hold the results of a complicated series of warehouse changes without having to reenter each one later. Therefore, the data warehouse and the underlying structures will likely have to be extended to support a "personal analysis area" or some type of shadow database in which such processing may occur.

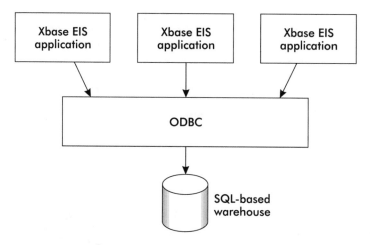

Figure 4-8 Simple Client/Server Data Warehouse Architecture

The full utility of data warehouses in the future will likely require capabilities such as what-if analysis. To achieve this goal, though, the underlying structure of data warehouses—indeed, some of the basic premises such as supporting update transactions—will need to evolve.

4.7 Data Warehouses and Other Information Management Technology

Let's take a brief look at how the future directions of other information management areas will likely apply to the data warehouses of the future. We've already discussed distribution among multiple sites (see section 4.5); now we'll look at some of the other areas.

4.7.1 Client/Server Databases and Applications

Client/server databases are a relatively minor jump for a data warehouse environment. Figures 4-8 and 4-9 show alternative data warehouse architectures based on emerging client/server models.

In Figure 4-8, EIS applications written in the Xbase language (see Chapter 14 for a discussion of Xbase) access a centralized SQL-based warehouse through the Open Database Connectivity (ODBC) Application Programming Interface (API), which we discussed in Chapter 3. In this environment, a basic client/server model with a single server supporting multiple clients can be implemented easily.

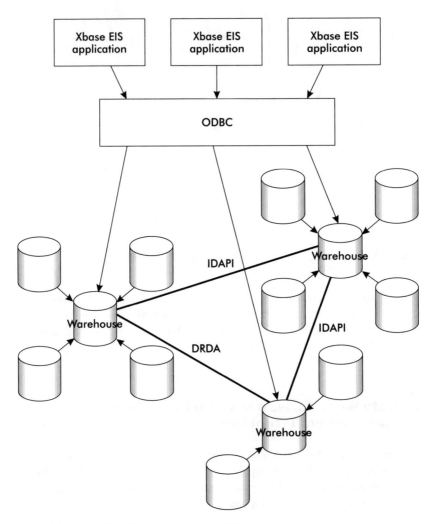

Figure 4-9 Complex Client/Server Data Warehouse Architecture

Figure 4-9 presents a more complex client/server architecture. A logically centralized data warehouse, distributed across multiple platforms (as we discussed in section 4.5), is accessed in the same way as in Figure 4-8. The data warehouse, though, uses a combination of IDAPI and DRDA APIs to access its components (partitions) from the distributed platforms. In this case, the application running on top of the data warehouse serves two roles: as a server for an EIS application suite, and as a client that accesses warehouse-based information from other servers.

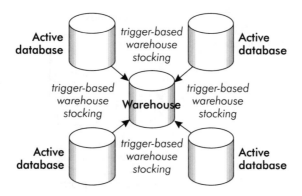

Figure 4-10 Active Databases as Data Warehouse Sources

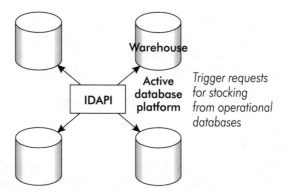

Figure 4-11 Active Database as a Data Warehouse Platform

4.7.2 Active Databases

In *active databases*, events, triggers, and similar capabilities are used to preemptively execute actions based on factors such as timers, database values, or other state changes.

As active databases become widespread, several likely uses for data warehouse environments appear. As shown in Figure 4-10, databases that serve as sources of information for the data warehouse may employ active capabilities in order to automatically transmit the current snapshot of appropriate information to the warehouse. In this model, "stocking the warehouse" might be a predetermined and stored action within the database itself, one not requiring invoking by any user or application.

Alternatively, the data warehouse itself could be built on top of an active database, and its "stock the warehouse" action might be a time-based querying of operational database servers (Figure 4-11).

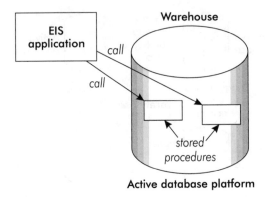

Figure 4-12 EIS Applications Trigger Stored Procedures

Of course, a combination of the environments shown in Figures 4-10 and 4-11 (active databases on both the source and recipient sides) could be used, if applicable. Additionally, EIS/DSS applications running against the data warehouse could also trigger stored procedures within the data warehouse itself (Figure 4-12).

We'll discuss active databases in Chapter 16.

4.7.3 Hypertext

One way in which hypertext might be used in the data warehouse is to support drill-down analysis within EIS applications on top of the warehouse. For example, a hypertext-based interface might be used as part of the platform for an EIS application. Hypertext environments allow users to follow one or more paths from the currently active screen, traversing further alternative paths but still having the option to return to a previous point. Conceivably, a hypertext-based path could be used to invoke the drill-down process for more detailed analysis of warehouse contents. Examining another portion of the warehouse might be desired at some level during the drill-down process. The hypertext interface could manage this, providing the return path to a previous point or proceeding to other paths.

In Chapter 18, we'll discuss the future directions of hypertext and hypermedia.

4.7.4 Temporal Databases

Briefly, *temporal databases* add a dimension of time to the basic structure of the database itself. In section 4.2 we discussed time variance in data warehouses. Historical information, or previous snapshots, is an important part of the data warehouse (the applications running on top of warehouses invariably perform cross–time-period comparisons of summarized results); therefore, a temporal database is a natural foundation for a warehouse. The contents of a data warehouse must have a relevant time (either a point in time or an interval) associated with the data, so a time structure built directly into the database model is desired, as opposed to requiring the warehouse applications and data structures to support the time variance.

We'll discuss temporal databases in Chapter 15.

4.8 Digital Libraries and Information Highways

The principles of the data warehouse are likely to play an important role in future trends such as digital libraries and access facilities over the much-hyped information highways. By bringing information from multiple sources into warehouses that can be accessed over nationwide fiber optic systems, a vast array of data can be provided to users in their homes or businesses.

4.9 Conclusion

In this chapter, we looked at the basic concepts and future directions of the data warehouse. As we discussed, the term "data warehouse" might be relatively new, but the concept is not. What is new, though, are increased data warehouse capabilities based on advances in underlying database technology. Distributed data warehouses are an inevitable outcome of the growth of distributed database technology. Distribution may be of a relatively simple nature, for example, multiple disjoint "subwarehouses" managed through client/server middleware (ODBC, IDAPI, DRDA, and others). Or it may be more complex, for example, providing a global data warehouse schema above component partitions on which EIS/DSS applications may run.

Finally, as we discussed in section 4.7, the distributed database is not the only development likely to affect data warehouses in upcoming years. Active databases, temporal databases, and hypertext may provide a number of expanded capabilities to the data warehouse environments of the mid- to late 1990s.

Outlook

Short-term

- More organizations incorporating data warehouses for informational applications
- Higher degrees of distribution for warehouse environments
- More robust EIS applications

Long-term

- Incorporation of advanced database technologies for warehouses (e.g., active databases, active repositories, live links)
- What-if capabilities
- A closer tie between warehouses and operational databases
- Base technology used in digital libraries and information highways

Additional Reading

- J. Bischoff, "Achieving Warehouse Success," *Database Programming & Design* (July 1994), 26.
- R. Cafasso, "Users Warehouse Data on the Cheap," *Computerworld* (December 1994), 1.
- E. U. Harding, "Parallel Technology Meets the Warehouse," *Software Magazine* (November 1994), 19–20.
- W. H. Inmon, *Building the Data Warehouse* (Wellesley, MA: QED Publishing Group, 1992).
- W. H. Inmon, "Should We Rewrite History?," *Database Programming and Design* (March 1992).
- P. Uhrowczik, "Information Warehouse Architecture," *Proceedings of DB/Expo 93*, San Francisco, May 5, 1993.

Endnotes

1. W. H. Inmon, "Making Sense Out of Chaos," *Database Programming & Design* (January 1993), 79.

2. W. H. Inmon, *Building the Data Warehouse* (Wellesley, MA: QED Publishing Group, 1992), 29–33.

3. Inmon, *Data Warehouse*, 32.

4. C. Kolovson, "Indexing Techniques for Historical Databases," in *Temporal Databases: Theory, Design, and Implementation*, ed. A. Tansel (Redwood City, CA: The Benjamin/Cummings Publishing Company, 1993), 418–432.

5. Inmon, *Data Warehouse*, 42–50.

6. Inmon, *Data Warehouse*, 160–167.

7. P. Uhrowczik, "Information Warehouse Architecture," *Proceedings of DB/Expo 93*, San Francisco, May 5, 1993, 107.

8. Discussed in W. H. Inmon, "Should We Rewrite History?," *Database Programming and Design* (March 1992), 70.

CHAPTER 5

Partitioning and Replication: The Next Generation

A Note to the CIO

Opinions vary on the topic of finding more efficient ways to manage very large databases other than using centralized, mainframe-based DBMSs. (In Chapter 6 we'll discuss the "traditional" approach to this problem, management by a distributed DBMS environment.) In this chapter, we'll look at the parallel database system approach to very large databases, an approach that uses massively parallel processing (MPP) architectures to manage partitioned corporate data. If your organization is currently experimenting with MPP systems, parallel database systems should be of interest to you. If you currently maintain a centralized database environment that is stretching your mainframe's

5.1 Introduction

In Chapter 2, we discussed the principles of partitioning and replication, the primary means of distributing data in a distributed database environment. As we defined it, *partitioning* involves the division of a data object, such as rows or columns within a relational table, among different resources within a computer system. The classic models of partitioning involve the horizontal or vertical fragmentation of a relational table according to values in a column (e.g., JOB_LOCATION used to determine in which physical node certain rows are stored).

capacity to the limits, then understanding parallel database technologies—a key future direction for nearly every major DBMS vendor—is critical. You will have to compare this approach against more traditional distribution models (of course, your organization may be able to pursue both options at various "suborganization" levels, depending on which is more appropriate for a particular set of applications).

Executive Summary

Traditional models of partitioning and replication in the distributed database environment are being reconsidered in the context of required support for business applications processing and underlying technologies. The approach to database research common since the early 1980s has proven, at present, to be of little value to most organizations.

Replication involves the creation of replicates (duplicate copies) of data objects among various nodes, to improve availability and/or access time to critical data.

We also showed in Chapter 2 that the classic view of partitioning, with data divided among nodes within a network, may not be the most effective model for data distribution, given the business rules and norms for accessing and updating objects by certain users and applications. But, as we also noted, partitioning is hardly passé in data distribution.

In this chapter, we'll focus on the use of partitioning models for implementing massively parallel processing (MPP) and parallel database systems. We'll take a brief look at MPP concepts and partitioned database models for MPP systems.

We'll also look at trends in replication, as organizations investigate and implement it as a primary database distribution mechanism.

5.2 MPP and Parallel Database System Concepts

The basic concept of *massively parallel processing* (MPP) systems is simple: decomposition of computing tasks into a large number of parallel operations. The MPP architecture, shown in Figure 5-1, is scalable to thousands of processors, with bottlenecks common to symmetrical multiple processing (SMP) systems removed by advanced interprocessor networks and memory access schemes.[1]

Instead, partitioning models are applicable to parallel database systems, built on top of massively parallel processing systems. Replication has been given new life as an alternative to distributed processing based on two-phase commit (2PC) models.

Database vendors are aggressively pursuing both parallel database systems and replication servers, and both trends are growing.

What This Technology Can Do for You

An understanding of where DBMS vendors are headed in these areas and the underlying foundations of different models of data placement and reconciliation can help provide a basis for efficient distribution of corporate data across department or corporation-wide environments. You need not understand the intricacies of MPP technology to realize

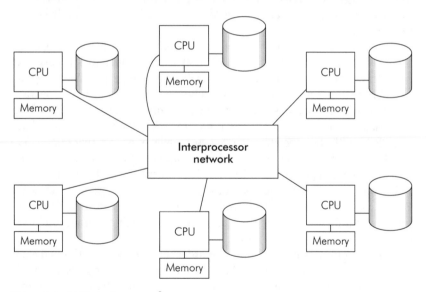

Figure 5-1 MPP Architecture[2]

In information management environments, MPP is a building block for highly parallel database systems that provide useful alternatives to centralized mainframe-based databases.[3]

As an aside, recall from Chapter 1 (section 1.7) that the specialized database machine, which was beginning to lose favor by the early 1980s, has

that parallel database systems present an alternative to the management of very large databases (VLDBs), superior to the mainframe-based solutions that have dominated the past.

Similarly, two-phase commit, while a technically viable solution in some environments, does not scale well to widely distributed environments with transactions covering many different systems. Understanding replication and, as we'll discuss in Chapter 20, complex transaction processing, can give planners and decision makers attractive, easily implementable distributed information management alternatives.

in fact triggered a tremendous amount of research through advances in parallel database systems. Part of this rebirth of interest in such systems is due to the emergence of relational DBMSs as the dominant force in information management, because relational queries are perfectly suited to parallel execution models.[4]

Consider the basic property of a relational model: that every operator produces a new relation. This means that a set of operators (a large set, perhaps) can be composed into highly parallel dataflow graphs. With *pipelined parallelism*, the result of operator A can be fed into operator B, one operator working after another. If, say, two database operators, SCAN and REPORT, are executing in a pipelined parallelism mode, the results of SCAN can be fed into REPORT, but the two operators can execute parallel to one another (Figure 5-2).

An alternative parallelism model, *partitioned parallelism*, allows division of an individual operator into independent operators, each working on an independent set of data and operating parallel to one another. As shown in Figure 5-3, each thread within the partitioned parallelism model can have pipelined parallelism, with the data sets eventually feeding into a recombinant operator (e.g., a MERGE operator).

There's only one catch, though. In order to implement partitioned parallelism, *data must be partitioned*. We'll discuss partitioning models for parallel database systems in section 5.3; for now, we'll leave partitioning as a prerequisite to parallel database systems using partitioned parallelism.

In the world of parallel systems, various hardware approaches are available to achieve parallelism. A simple taxonomy by Michael Stonebraker[5] classifies parallel systems into the following categories:

- *Shared-memory:* All processors can directly access a common global memory and all disks.

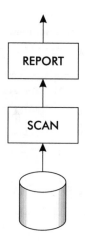

Figure 5-2 Pipelined Parallelism[6]

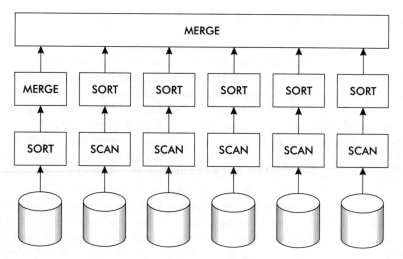

Figure 5-3 Partitioned Parallelism[7]

- *Shared-disks:* Each processor has its own private memory but can directly access all system disks.

- *Shared-nothing:* Neither disks nor memory are shared; all processors communicate with one another via an interprocessor network, as illustrated in Figure 5-1.

The consensus reached by the computer systems community is that shared-nothing hardware design is the *most* appropriate for parallel database

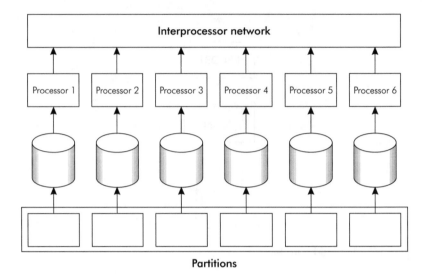

Figure 5-4 Generic Parallel Database System Partitioning Model

systems.[8] Such systems in both commercial and research installations are, for the most part, implemented on shared-nothing architectures, though the actual interconnection networks vary widely from one system to another.[9]

Parallel database systems based on shared-nothing architectures are obviously a good idea, but the true value of such an implementation becomes clear when one considers the trend towards large—no, make that *very large*— databases. As an example, the U.S. National Aeronautics and Space Administration (NASA) estimated in the late 1980s that 10^{16} bytes of storage would be needed for data collected by a single set of applications on satellite imaging.[10] Not too long ago, multigigabyte online databases were considered large databases; the 1990s has brought terabyte online databases to many large organizations. In addition to the obvious need for greater amounts of storage, parallelism is critical to achieving acceptable performance for very large databases.

5.3 Partitioning Models for Parallel Database Systems

As we mentioned in the preceding section, the key to partitioned parallelism is data partitioning, which we first introduced in Chapter 2. Figure 5-4 illustrates basic partitioning under a parallel database system.

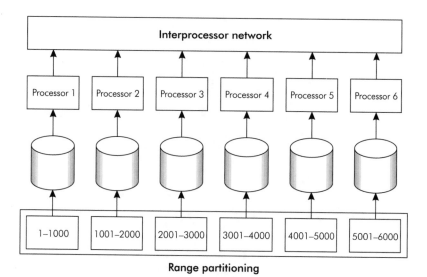

Figure 5-5 Range Partitioning for Parallel Database Systems

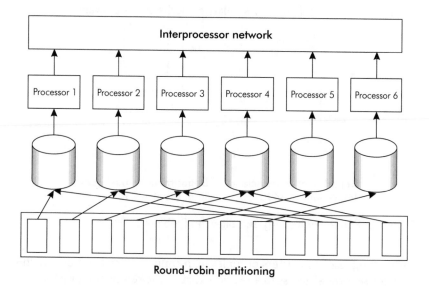

Figure 5-6 Round-Robin Partitioning for Parallel Database Systems

The three partitioning schemes are range partitioning, round-robin partitioning, and hashing.[11] Figures 5-5, 5-6, and 5-7 show an example of each of these.

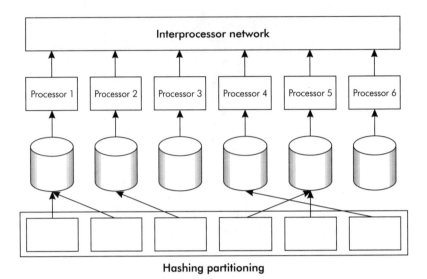

Hashing partitioning

Figure 5-7 Hashing Partitioning for Parallel Database Systems

Each of these schemes has relative merits and disadvantages. Range

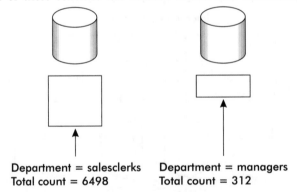

Department = salesclerks   Department = managers
Total count = 6498   Total count = 312

Figure 5-8 Range Partitioning and Skewing Problem

partitioning leads to clusters of tuples with similar characteristics, which is good for sequential access to a relation; that is, the results from each cluster can be brought back and merged and, if the requesting ordering of the output is the same as the basis for partitioning (e.g., ascending order by some job location code), then intermediate sorting may not even be necessary within each execution thread. Depending on the distribution of values across the range, though, you could wind up with skewed data, which would lead to execution skew (Figure 5-8). This skewing can be minimized by selecting criteria with a fairly uniform distribution.[12]

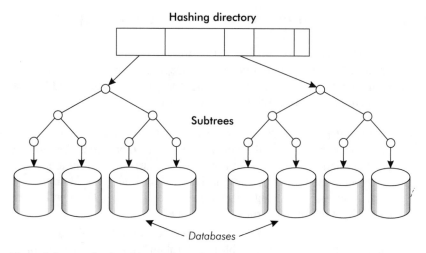

Figure 5-9 A Hybrid Index Structure for Parallel Database Systems

Data values play no role in round-robin partitioning. Instead, partitions are assigned to disks and processors on the basis of one tuple to one disk, another tuple to the next disk, and so on. Round-robin partitioning is less susceptible to skewing, as is hashing partitioning, that is, using a hashing function against a particular attribute for each row.[13]

5.4 Parallel Relational Operators and Index Structures

Once data partitioning has occurred, a parallel database system then processes relational operators against the partitions. While the traditional approach has been to use parallel data streams instead of newer parallel relational operators,[14] improved algorithms devised for most relational operators are finding their way into parallel database systems.[15] For example, a hash-join algorithm may supply join operator capability instead of a traditional sort-merge join. With a hash-join, a large join operator is broken into many smaller joins, resulting in linear speedup and scaleup of the join operation.[16]

Indexing techniques are also being researched to create optimal structures for parallel database systems. Because many relational database indexes are built on some type of tree structure (e.g., B-tree, B+-tree, B*-tree), the parallelism in the database won't help if the index structures are the scene of bottleneck-inducing access conflicts. One solution is a hybrid index structure (HBX) in which a tree structure is partitioned into several subtrees and access is controlled by a hashing function.[17] This hybrid index structure is shown in Figure 5-9.

5.5 The Future Direction of Parallel Database Systems

Many advances have been made in the area of parallel database systems: "standardization" on a shared-nothing conceptual architecture (if not the actual implementations), parallel-friendly relational operators, and others. However, among the areas still needing work are[18]

- *Mixing batch and OLTP queries:* Lock management and priority scheduling differ in batch and OLTP environments. To most efficiently process parallel relational operators in these two concurrent environments (e.g., batch operations running from the data center while ad hoc queries come from individual users), algorithms and models appropriate for both batch and OLTP environments must be developed.

- *Optimizing parallel queries:* Query optimizers need to be fitted with the capability to consider all possible parallel algorithms for each operator, in order to most efficiently produce partitioned and pipelined parallelism.

- *Application program parallelism:* While a few languages such as Ada have some degree of parallel execution capabilities (e.g., Ada's tasking model, which often needs additional tweaking for even today's multithreaded environments), languages such as COBOL have no means to express parallelism. Library routines will likely be the mechanism by which application programming-level parallelism will be invoked.

- *Physical database design:* Because three partitioning alternatives are available to support parallel database systems, tools for the physical design process could help analyze database composition and suggest appropriate partitioning strategies.

- *Online data reorganization and utilities:* Given the likely usage of parallel database systems on terabyte-sized databases, standard loading, reorganization, dumping, index creation and management, and other utility functions simply will not work well (in terms of required time for such operations) on databases of that size. Additionally, the partitioning of the data should be incorporated into utility functions such as selective backup and restoral functions.

Some database experts argue that parallel database systems are the key to supporting the extremely large databases that are becoming common in large corporations, particularly those that deemphasize mainframes in favor of downsized hardware. Implementing such an environment requires a combination of massively parallel processing (MPP) and partitioning, the latter with its roots in traditional distributed database theory and practice. As we discussed at the beginning of this chapter, classic data partitioning has found a home in an area not envisioned when original theories and algorithms were devised. Just as MPP has given the database machine concept a new lease (albeit using different technology than originally foreseen), MPP implemen-

Replication principles

- Full or partial replicates
- Variations of update policies
  - synchronized
  - asynchronous/propagated
  - scheduled/deferred
- Policies against replicates
  - all updateable . . . or
  - some are read-only

Figure 5-10 Principles of Replication

tation for parallel database systems has created a renewed interest in partitioning technology.

5.6 Revisiting Replication

In Chapter 2, we discussed the principles of replication, which are briefly
noted in Figure 5-10. Replication involves the distribution of data not according to a division-oriented model (e.g., horizontal or vertical partitioning) but
rather via duplication. Various models exist that govern applications' capability (or lack thereof) to update replicates, as well as synchronization policies
among replicates, within an environment.

If one were to take a long-term view, focusing on the optimal distributed
database environments of the future, then replication would appear to be little
more than a stopgap solution on the way to that "ultimate model" of multiple
databases containing easily accessible data partitions over a global area network (GAN). Or read-only replicates of infrequently updated data might be
placed at strategic locations within the global organization, for quicker access
by users and applications than a single copy of such data could provide.

However, just as the value of partitioning has changed over time, so too
have thoughts on the long-term value of database replication models. In this
section, we'll discuss the reasons for this change in thought, as well as future
directions of replication in distributed information management.

Replication has moved from its role as a sort of placeholder until "real
DDBMSs" came along and into the realm of distributed concurrency control.
Concurrency control in distributed databases depends on transaction processing capabilities such as two-phase commit (2PC), in which a global transaction manager coordinates the commit/rollback decision process of multiple
local database managers (or, more generically, local resource managers).[19]
Despite the presence of 2PC features in DBMS products and transaction
processing monitors, "two-phase commit has not been widely implemented."[20]

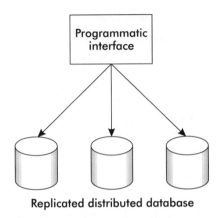

Figure 5-11 Programmatic Control of Replicates

Basically, the unwillingness of many organizations to implement 2PC or similar distributed concurrency control measures is very much connected with decisions to virtually ignore database partitioning capabilities in networked environments; while the technology is certainly there and is relatively mature, many business models that drive information systems architectures simply don't require such capabilities. DBMS vendors, while still supplying 2PC and other distributed concurrency control capabilities, seem to be backing away from 2PC features as a product differentiator, instead emphasizing replication technology.[21]

Traditionally, replication has been available to database environments through plug-in utilities such as Digital Equipment's VAX Data Distributor. Since about 1993, commercial DBMS vendors have moved replication models (several, as we'll discuss) into the DBMS engines themselves.

Replication can be achieved in several ways. In the simplest model, a programmatic interface is used so that the application program itself controls the establishment of replicates as well as the coordination and synchronization policies (Figure 5-11). Alternatively, in the more advanced declarative model (Figure 5-12), replication establishment and management rules are embedded in the database itself.[22]

Note in Figure 5-12 that the declarative handling of replication updates might be accomplished through an active database, which we'll discuss in Chapter 16. Briefly, an *active database* employs techniques such as triggers and stored procedures to automatically accomplish certain actions based on database rules, as opposed to application or systems software-based logic. In such an environment, an update to a replicate could fire a trigger, causing automatic propagation of updates to the other replicates.

Replication models based on deferred propagation of updates to remote replicates (with updates permitted only against a single copy of data) could easily accept a time-based propagation or one based on an as-updated scheme.

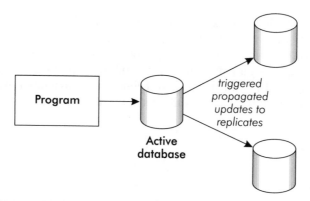

Figure 5-12 Declarative Replication Management Through Active Databases

When attempts are made to keep all replicates in real-time synchronization and updates are permitted against any replicate in the system, however, the process of maintaining data integrity becomes very difficult. Many research models have been proposed and investigated over the years, including the use of timestamps and locks to determine the true state of replicates at a resolution time.[23] These mechanisms will likely find their way into commercial products that support replication, to improve the level of consistency in replicated data.

5.7 Conclusion

Classic distributed database theory is evolving as 1990s' computing proceeds. Partitioning models, long assumed to be in the realm of databases distributed over networked environments, appear to be most valuable as parallel database systems come to prominence as managers of large databases. Likewise, the belief that real-time concurrency control in distributed database environments would be managed via two-phase commit protocols doesn't seem to be holding true for many organizations; replication models, once thought of as stopgap measures on the way to robust distributed database capabilities, appear to be the preferred concurrency control solution for many organizations. The basic concepts of partitioning and replication, introduced many years ago as a means of data distribution, will remain valid, but in different forms than those envisioned ten or even five years ago.

Next, we'll shift our focus to "the big one": distributed, heterogeneous, multiple-DBMS databases. With respect to Chapter 6 and our discussion of partitioning and replication in this chapter, it's important to note that the global approach to synthesizing a distributed database environment from previously autonomous components involves the creation of global partitions and/or replicates based on existing database contents. Therefore, even though "the big one" will remain an elusive goal, as degrees of heterogeneous DDBs are achieved over time (and assuming global schema models are a part of real-world implementations), partitioning and replication will play a role in such environments. Until then, the distributed implementation paradigms we've considered in this chapter will remain the dominant models.

Outlook

Short-term

- Widespread use of replication, with relaxed concurrency policies
- Dabblings into MPP architectures for parallel database systems, primarily on the department level
- Revisiting long-held notions of partitioning and replication in light of findings from researchers and practices in the real world

Long-term

- Widespread use of parallel database systems to handle very large databases (VLDBs)
- Advanced models for concurrency control among replicates

Additional Reading

- D. DeWitt and J. Gray, "Parallel Database Systems: The Future of High Performance Database Systems," *Communications of the ACM* (June 1992).
- S. Helle, "Massively Parallel: Reaching Critical Mass," *Database Programming & Design* (June 1993).
- P. Korzeniowski, "Replication Gains in Distributed DBMS," *Software Magazine* (April 1993).
- D. McGoveran, "Two-Phased Commit or Replication?," *Database Programming & Design* (May 1993).
- G. Schussel, "Database Replication: Playing Both Ends Against the Middleware," *Client/Server Today* (November 1994), 57–67.

Endnotes

1. S. Helle, "Massively Parallel: Reaching Critical Mass," *Database Programming & Design* (June 1993), 48.

2. Helle, "Massively Parallel."

3. D. DeWitt and J. Gray, "Parallel Database Systems: The Future of High Performance Database Systems," *Communications of the ACM* (June 1992), 85.

4. DeWitt and Gray, "Parallel Database Systems," 86.

5. M. Stonebraker, "The Case for Shared Nothing," *Database Engineering* 9, 1 (1986). Quoted in DeWitt and Gray, "Parallel Database Systems," 88.

6. DeWitt and Gray, "Parallel Database Systems," 86.

7. DeWitt and Gray, "Parallel Database Systems."

8. DeWitt and Gray, "Parallel Database Systems," 88.

9. DeWitt and Gray, "Parallel Database Systems."

10. A. Silberschatz, M. Stonebraker, and J. Ullman, "Database Systems: Achievements and Opportunities," *Communications of the ACM* (October 1991), 114–115.

11. DeWitt and Gray, "Parallel Database Systems," 92.

12. DeWitt and Gray, "Parallel Database Systems," 91–92.

13. DeWitt and Gray, "Parallel Database Systems."

14. DeWitt and Gray, "Parallel Database Systems," 92.

15. DeWitt and Gray, "Parallel Database Systems," 93.

16. DeWitt and Gray, "Parallel Database Systems."

17. T. Honishi, T. Satoh, and U. Inoue, "An Index Structure for Parallel Database Processing," *Second International Workshop on Research Issues on Data Engineering: Transaction and Query Processing* (Los Alamitos, CA: IEEE Computing Society Press, 1992).

18. DeWitt and Gray, "Parallel Database Systems," 96–97.

19. J. Gray and A. Reuter, *Transaction Processing: Concepts and Techniques* (San Francisco: Morgan Kaufmann Publishers, 1993), 562–574.

20. P. Korzeniowski, "Replication Gains in Distributed DBMS," *Software Magazine* (April 1993), 93.

21. Korzeniowski, "Replication Gains."

22. D. McGoveran, "Two-Phased Commit or Replication?," *Database Programming and Design* (May 1993), 42.

23. M. Carey and M. Livny, "Conflict Detection Tradeoffs for Replicated Data," *ACM Transactions on Database Systems* (December 1991), 704.

CHAPTER

6

Heterogeneous Federated Databases and Multidatabase Systems

A Note to the CIO

In addition to distribution, heterogeneity is likely to be a key characteristic of your data assets. This chapter will give you a rundown on different models of managing heterogeneity in the database. Keep in mind that many of the topics in this chapter have been under investigation since the early 1980s and solving many of their underlying problems has proven difficult (e.g., scaling distributed heterogeneous architectures among different sizes, from 20 to 30 nodes to hundreds

6.1 Introduction

In the last four chapters, we've discussed many areas of distributed information technology. In this chapter, we'll shift our focus to an area envisioned by many as the ultimate information manager: the system involving heterogeneous, distributed databases under a single control environment.

As we'll see, though, various levels of this type of environment exist; in fact, a formal taxonomy has been developed and will be presented in the next section. A number of variables factor into these different architectural levels, including the following:

or even thousands). In Chapter 7, we'll examine alternative solutions that utilize more available technology (e.g., client/server) to solve the distribution and heterogeneity problem.

Executive Summary

Despite all the excitement about large-scale global transparency in distributed database systems, it will take many years of research to make this a reality. The term "distributed database system" has multiple meanings; in fact, a taxonomy of different architectures exists, ranging from tightly coupled systems built around global information models (schemas) to loosely coupled, interoperable systems with distributed data managed by the applications themselves.

- Whether a single database model (e.g., relational) or multiple models (e.g., relational, flat file, object-oriented) are supported within the environment.

- The distribution policies of the underlying data.

- Whether or not a global schema for the purpose of transparent access to the underlying distributed data is used.

- The homogeneity or heterogeneity of the DBMS products involved.

- The degree to which database constructs such as security, referential integrity, and other areas are enforced or supported across distributed environments.

We'll look at these variables, as well as existing problems in these classes of environments. It's important to note that our discussion in this chapter is oriented toward a survey of technological approaches discussing advances in the multidatabase/federated database area, as well as problems and issues. In Chapter 7, we'll conclude our discussion of distributed information management with an analysis of Chapters 2 through 6.

6.2 Distributed Database Systems Revisited: A Taxonomy

In Chapter 2, we introduced some of the variables that characterize different types of distributed database systems. Specifically, we discussed homogeneous versus heterogeneous systems, as well as whether the distributed environment was created in a top-down or bottom-up manner. In this section, we'll

Many different problems in this area are under active research, including resolving conflicts among different underlying systems in data representation and formatting (similar to our discussion in Chapter 4 on data warehouses), varying degrees of site autonomy, transaction processing, cross-database integrity, and security.

What This Technology Can Do for You

The prospect of distributed databases with a global schema providing transparent access to companywide data is an attractive one, if not totally realizable with today's technology. A number of approaches will meet the operational mission of business, and this should be the goal of whichever distributed database approach you pursue. In the mean-

provide formal definitions of the different types of distributed database systems, focusing on various combinations of the heterogeneity/homogeneity and top-down/bottom-up variables, and other factors.

Figure 6-1 lists a taxonomy of different types of multidatabase systems. A multidatabase system is a "distributed system that acts as a front end to multiple local DBMSs or is structured as a global layer on top of local DBMSs."[1] Comparing this definition and the distributed database definition in Figure 6-1, note that the common term "distributed database" actually has a more restrictive meaning than its casual usage suggests (i.e., as a substitute for "multidatabase systems").

Further, the classifications in Figure 6-1—and the nomenclature—are not universally accepted. An alternative taxonomy[2] distinguishes between two approaches, the first a *unified schema* approach (with a global schema architecture, as we'll discuss) and the second a *multidatabase* approach (no global schema); in this taxonomy, "multidatabase" has a specific meaning instead of the generic meaning "all types of multiple databases."

With this in mind, let's look at the different classes of multidatabase systems listed in Figure 6-1. At the axis with the tightest coupling and integration, we have distributed databases, which are homogeneous in nature and operate on a global schema (which in turn is mapped to the schemata of the underlying databases). Functions internal to the DBMS system itself are used to provide mapping and interfacing. As we discussed in Chapter 2, this model of distribution has gained favor in recent years and will continue to do so, primarily in the realm of parallel database systems. While there is still some applicability across LAN- and WAN-based environments, these architectures will make few further inroads into corporate and organizational environments, primarily due to their inability to handle heterogeneity (that is,

time, it is probably just a matter of time before base technology (e.g., processors, wide area networks) and algorithms make some of the dream come true. You can use the information from this chapter to pursue different approaches to distributed information management on department and other suborganization levels with the goal of evolving toward corporatewide information management over time.

tight
coupling

- **Distributed databases**
  – Homogeneous
  – Global schema
  – Internal DBMS for global-to-local interface
- **Global schema multidatabase**
  – Heterogeneous
  – Global schema
  – DBMS user interface for global-to-local interface
- **Federated database**
  – Heterogeneous
  – Partial global schema
  – DBMS user interface for global-to-local interface
- **Multidatabase language system**
  – Heterogeneous
  – Access language functions
  – DBMS user interface for global-to-local interface
- **Homogeneous multidatabase language system**
  – Homogeneous
  – Access language functions
  – DBMS user interface, plus some internal DBMS functions, for global-to-local interface
- **Interoperable systems**
  – Multiple types of data sources
  – No global integration
  – Applications used for global-to-local interface

loose
coupling

Figure 6-1 A Taxonomy of Multidatabase Systems[3]

multiple products or models, as we'll discuss next). Consult Chapter 2 for further discussion on the issue of homogeneous distributed database architectures in parallel database systems.

The next level of multidatabase systems adds heterogeneity to the picture, while still utilizing a global schema; hence the name *global schema multidatabase*. As with homogeneous distributed databases, client applications are written against the global schema as if it represented one large, centralized database; all mappings to the underlying databases and their contents are handled via the capabilities of the global layer.

Unlike homogeneous distributed databases, though, global schema multidatabases do not have internal DBMS functions available for mapping and interface between the global and local layers, primarily because heterogeneity precludes such internal mapping (i.e., DBMS interfaces are external to the DBMS and must be established and managed as necessary, since internal DBMS facilities don't exist). This is partially because preexisting local DBMSs and databases can be plugged into a global schema multidatabase environment without having to modify the local levels.[4]

Although the global schema approach looks conceptually simple (a complete set of global objects mapped to their underlying physical implementations), it actually has a great deal of complexity. Specifically, creating an all-encompassing global schema is far from a trivial task; in fact, it is rather complex, because it needs to ensure that 1) the global schema represents the entire universe of data elements within the environment, and 2) all changes to the underlying databases (e.g., data relocation, subsequent replication) are propagated to the global schema to ensure correct mapping from the global to local level.

In fact, upon further examination, this approach is more complex than at first glance. The "classic" conceptual architecture for multidatabase systems (discussed in section 6.3) looks relatively simple, with directory services responsible for the global-to-local mappings. Consider, though, that the client applications *themselves* are distributed across the environment among multiple nodes. This means that *each* application must be capable of accessing the global schema before any local database operations can be accomplished, which introduces a decision point to the architecture of the global schema itself. In one sense, the global schema could be centralized and stored in a single location (or possibly lightly replicated across a node or two within the company), and all accesses by any client application anywhere within the company would first go to the "directory node" in order to access the global schema. The disadvantages to this approach are fairly obvious; a major reason for the existence of distributed information management environments is to alleviate bottlenecks, and routing all applications from a widely distributed environment into a small number of clearinghouse stations is likely to introduce traffic jams, especially in environments with a high transaction volume.

Recall our argument from Chapter 2 (section 2.4.2) in which we made two points. First, a large percentage of the processing of a given application is likely to take place against locally stored data. Second, following this logic, there is little reason to process local requests against a global schema; such operations are more effective against the local schema that manages the database. With this access paradigm, the mandated access against a global schema for local data not only introduces unnecessary mapping into the processing picture but also creates additional, unnecessary network access if that client application is located at a node in which a global schema instance is not resident.

Alternatively, the global schema could be widely distributed to all sites within the company where client applications might be executed, precluding the need for remote access by an application to mapping and directory services offered by the schema. The downside to this approach is that changes to the global schema now must be propagated across the entire company, which is certainly not a trivial task. Depending on the volatility of the distribution within a given environment (ranging from relatively few updates to the global schema on the low end to highly volatile, rapidly changing schemata at the high end), wide distribution of a global schema could conceivably introduce to the environment throughput impediments and integrity problems (the latter occurring when changes are not propagated to one or more nodes in a timely manner as part of a redistribution or schema adjustment process).

One might envision an environment in which a client application is equipped with the ability to know whether or not it needs to access a global schema. That is, the global schema approach might be suitable for access by client applications of remote data, but it introduces unnecessary overhead and potential performance impediments when accessing local data. There is actually a great deal of merit to an environment in which different types of accesses are handled in different manners. This brings us to the next class of multidatabase system, the federated database.

A *federated database*, unlike a global schema multidatabase, does *not* have a complete global schema against which applications are processed. Rather, a local import/export schema is maintained (e.g., a directory of accessible information elsewhere in the company).[5] A federated database makes use of a *partial* global schema; only the information from remote sources that is applicable to the business processing functions at a given node is maintained in the partial global schema at that source.

Note that some of the complications in global schema multidatabases are still present; changes to global schema information must still be propagated to appropriate places within the information systems environment (not necessarily organizationwide in all cases, but rather to a subset of the organization). An additional drawback is that a determination must be made as to *what* data from the organization as a whole is applicable to the processing inherent to the applications at a given node, and that information must be modeled and represented in the import/export schema appropriately. In short, the "everything is represented in the global schema, just go there and get it when you need it" approach doesn't apply to the federated database model, making that approach a sort of midpoint between the client/server-based model of distributed information management and a global schema multidatabase. Of course, subsequent determination that applications at a given site need to access some remote node, or changes in the metadata at a remote node in which the local site's applications are interested requires updates to the local site's import/export schema.

The advantage of this approach is that it hones in on what is actually needed instead of capturing everything. In extremely large environments capturing everything may very well be an unmanageable process; the federated approach might be easier to model and implement.

The next level in the taxonomy, more oriented toward loose coupling than the federated database approach, is the multidatabase language system, in effect, a distributed information management environment based on client/server access. We discussed the principles and directions of client/server computing in Chapter 3, and in Chapter 7 (specifically, section 7.2) we'll compare the multidatabase language system (e.g., client/server-based) approach to distributed information management to that of the global schema multidatabase environments. For our purposes here, we'll note that the multidatabase language approach—whether heterogeneous or homogeneous in nature—involves no global schemata at all but rather uses "access language functions" (an API) to request data from remote sources. As with federated databases and their partial global schemata, it is necessary to predetermine and adjust accordingly the data objects from remote sources needed by applications at a given site that run client applications, in order to know which nodes to access to retrieve information.

Finally, with the loosest coupling, we have interoperable systems, in which applications running on top of DBMSs are responsible for the interface among multiple data management environments, whether homogeneous or heterogeneous. Interoperable systems are primarily oriented toward data exchange rather than database-oriented processing[6] and represent more of the past of distributed information management than the future.

6.3 A Conceptual Architecture of a Multidatabase System

In section 6.2, we referred to the global schema multidatabase as the classic conceptual architecture that has been the directional beam for vendors and research projects since the early 1980s. Figure 6-2 illustrates this classic global schema–based architecture, with mappings from the global schema level to the DBMSs and local schemata of the underlying nodes.

Several items are worth noting about this architecture and approach, in addition to the complexities and potential drawbacks noted in the previous

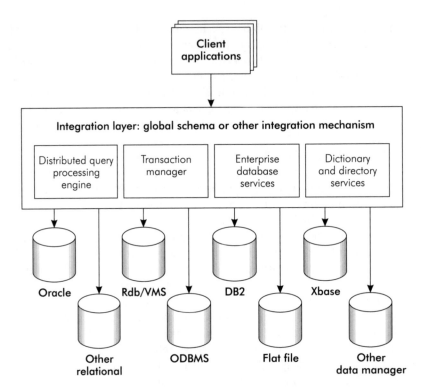

Figure 6-2 The Classic Global Schema Multidatabase Architecture

section. The information model in which the global schema is represented can, in theory, be whatever is most appropriate for a given environment. Of the 16 prototype and research systems listed in the table in Bright et al., "A Taxonomy and Current Issues in Multidatabase Systems,"[7] the majority (11) featured a global data model based on the relational database model; the rest utilized a conceptual data model, such as the entity-relationship or "abstracted conceptual" approach, for their global schemata.

Until recently, utilizing a relational-based global schema made sense, because the underlying databases were usually relational themselves; even if non-relational systems were integrated into the environment (e.g., an IMS- or CODASYL-based system), well-defined mappings from a relational global layer to the underlying hierarchical or network model could be utilized, and applications could be written as if they were accessing relational databases exclusively.

The advent of object-oriented databases, and their capability to capture a richer set of semantic information (as we'll discuss in Part III of this book), calls into question the relational-oriented approach to global schemata (regardless of the merits of this approach in general when contrasted with other multidatabase models as shown in Figure 6-1). As more and more object-oriented DBMSs and databases are incorporated into global schema multidatabases over the next few years, a conceptual layer capable of capturing more semantic information may be more desirable than a basic relational model. Whether that semantically rich global model is an extended relational one (see Chapter 9), based on a well-established conceptual modeling technique such as entity-relationship, or on an emerging object-oriented database model (e.g., ODMG, discussed in Chapter 10), implementations of the architecture shown in Figure 6-2 will likely move away from relational global schemata.

6.4 Database Services

In section 6.3, we discussed the incorporation of non-relational databases into heterogeneous, multimodel (e.g., a mix of relational and object-oriented systems) multidatabase environments. What about the opposite end of the information model spectrum, non-DBMS data managers such as flat file systems or documents? In this section we'll discuss work being done to extend the scope of database services to non-DBMS resident sources.

The motivation for this work is that only a small portion of all organizational data is stored under the control of DBMSs.[8] To allow non-database data managers such as flat file systems to "play" in multidatabase environments, database services that are not part of non-DBMS environments must be included on such systems. These services include the following:[9]

- *Data independence:* This service separates the data from the applications to which they are closely coupled (e.g., the files were created as part of a specific application programming set).

- *Transaction properties:* In Chapter 20, we'll discuss the principles of transaction processing, specifically the ACID properties of atomicity, consistency, isolation, and durability. We doubt that all of these properties could be provided for a non-DBMS environment (e.g., emulate full transaction processing capabilities on top of a flat file system as if it were a DBMS), but some of them might be provided to the underlying data stores.

- *Interoperability among unstructured and semistructured data:* Databases provide a means by which data objects may be related with one another for appropriate processing, regardless of the model of that database (e.g., pointers in hierarchical and network systems, or relational operators in relational systems). Non-DBMS data doesn't possess this inherent attribute, but in order to be incorporated into a multidatabase environment, such characteristics must be provided. Interrelationship tools and utilities, coupled with a finely grained high-capacity repository (see Chapter 19) in which metadata for non-DBMS data is stored, will likely be available to provide relationship information among data objects.

- *Information filtering:* Query capabilities common to database environments, such as SELECT . . . WHERE (with appropriate predicates) can operate against basic flat file systems (e.g., VSAM or RMS files) with relatively little modification, but extending this filtering capability to documents, spreadsheets, graphics, or other very unstructured information is a tricky proposition. It is important to provide ad hoc query capabilities against graphics (e.g., DISPLAY ALL PICTURES OF EMPLOY-EES WITH A MOUSTACHE) or documents, along with the means to access these capabilities from a global schema or a remote database application. Note that emerging spatial, image, and text databases (see Chapter 17) will provide these types of capabilities, but against an underlying *database* environment rather than an unstructured file-based system. Until data can be transitioned completely from file systems to future image and text databases (which will likely be never), filtering will continue to be a necessity.

- *Activity management:* The trend toward providing databases with activity management capabilities (triggers and stored procedures in relational systems, methods in object-oriented environments) has resulted in pushing application programming logic into the data storage manager. For this to take place in file-based systems, additional services must be added. Perhaps the most common way activity control is provided to underlying traditional systems is through *encapsulation*, as in the Object Request Broker (ORB) approach discussed in Chapter 11. By providing a wrapper through which behavior-oriented information may be coupled with data themselves, non-database systems can receive activity-oriented capabilities in much the same way that DBMSs are evolving.

Database services for non-DBMS environments are important for the future direction of information management, because whatever integration mechanism is chosen to create amd manage distributed environments (traditional client/server, ORB-based client/server, global schema multidatabases, or some other variation), data not resident in databases or under DBMS control will inevitably need to be incorporated into a non-DBMS environment. Today's integration mechanisms for these non-database environments are typically based on either batch-oriented import/export or, when some type of global schema layer is used, read-only access. To promote the level of interface paradigms to real-time, read-write access on a par with database-resident information and the extended services already described are necessary.

6.5 Conflict Resolution

In Chapter 4, we discussed one of the problems that must be overcome when using data warehouse environments, specifically the need to account for mismatches in data types, sizes, usages, and other properties as rollups are made to a logically centralized warehouse. This same problem is present in multidatabase environments, particularly when 1) a global schema approach and 2) a bottom-up approach are used when creating the multidatabase system.

The mismatch problem is arguably more serious in multidatabase environments than in warehouse systems because of the need for real-time or near real-time access against the environment, the processing time of which includes all mappings to the underlying "real locations" of the data. In the data warehouse environment, access by executive information system (EIS) applications is actually against the warehouse itself rather than the operational databases from which the data are extracted, and resolving conflicts may be done on a case-by-case basis, and (depending on the specific environment) not necessarily in real time.

Multidatabase systems capable of adequately handling such conflicts must first formalize the types of situations likely to be encountered; such understanding will be helpful in providing a rule-based approach toward handling these resolution processes. Specifically, one might look at two different types of conflicts: *schematic* and *data*.[10] Schematic conflicts include the following:

- *Table-versus-table conflicts*, which may be broken down further into one-to-one or many-to-many table conflicts. One-to-one table conflicts might be different names for equivalent tables in multiple local databases, or the same name for different tables. Even tables with the same name and semantic equivalence might still present conflict problems, such as a missing attribute in one or more local instances (which would make UNION operations particularly difficult). In order for client applications to operate against a global schema and to have requests mapped properly to multiple underlying databases, the multidatabase system must identify and provide conflict resolution processing.

  Many-to-many table conflicts are common in relational environments, due to the normalization and denormalization processes. Specifically, n number of tables in one local database might be used to represent a collection of information (e.g., about a videotape inventory), but another local database uses x number of tables. In order to operate successfully against these different databases with the understanding that the information managed within each is the same, conflicts in this area must be resolved.

- *Attribute-versus-attribute conflicts*, which include situations parallel with table-versus-table conflicts (e.g., different names for equivalent attributes in local databases, or the same name used to represent different attributes), plus other cases such as default value conflicts and constraint conflicts. Likewise, many-to-many conflicts may exist at the attribute level, such as one attribute used with a local database *a* to represent information while two or more attributes used in another local database *b* represent that same information.

- *Table-versus-attribute conflicts*, which occur when one local database uses a table to represent a concept while another local database uses attributes within another table to represent the same concept. This conflict commonly occurs when a local database doesn't fully enforce third normal form (no non-key dependencies) and might, for example, feature the following:

```
video_employee (emp_id, emp_name, emp_address,...
                dept_id, dept_name, dept_revenue_YTD,...)
```

In this example, the normalization process would typically create a separate table for department information with the primary key DEPT_ID, followed by the rest of the department attributes. If that were the case on a different local database instance, any attempt at semantic reconciliation to resolve the conflict would need to take into account the table-versus-attribute conflict described.

Data conflicts, the other conflict type, are similar to those discussed in Chapter 4, with some additional classes. These classes include different representations for the same data (e.g., data types, sizes, and so on) among local databases, and also factors such as the following:

- *Obsolete data*, such as different rental prices for the same videotape stored within local stores' databases.

- *Incorrect-entry data*, which is similar to obsolete data in that different values exist that actually should be the same; in the case of incorrect-entry data, one or more of the values are just plain wrong, for some unexplained reason.

Note that these data conflicts are particularly important in multidatabase environments that make use of replication; a distributed database operation processed against one replicate *c* would return a different result than another operation processed against the other replicate *d*, even though the results should be identical.

As noted in Kim and Seo, "Classifying Schematic and Data Heterogeneity in Multidatabase Systems,"[11] several of these conflict types still "require significant additional research," indicating that we are still several years away from a fully functional, robust conflict resolution process for global schema multidatabases. Organizations pursuing this aspect of distributed information management therefore need to follow this area closely.

6.6 Mediators

Another approach to conflict resolution is the use of mediators.[12] A *mediator* is a software module that "simplifies, abstracts, reduces, merges, and explains data"[13] between workstation applications and the databases of an environment. Mediators border on artificial intelligence/knowledge-base concepts as well as the database and information world. In addition to conflict resolution, mediation functions include the following:[14]

- *Gathering the "appropriate amount" of data:* Depending on the type of database operation requested, a varying amount of data from one or more sources will be needed. The mediator, by virtue of its "intelligence," can help with this determination.

- *Support for abstraction and generalization:* Mediators can assist with the summarization process, which we discussed in Chapter 4 in the context of data warehouse environments and informational databases.

- *Text-to-data integration:* In section 6.3, we mentioned that a large percentage of corporate and organizational data assets were maintained in pictorial or textual form (primarily the latter). A mediator, acting as a front end to such information classes, can help "regularize" text and image data for further processing and mediation with other data forms.

- *Maintenance of interim data results:* Even though summarized or derived data may be the most appropriate for a particular database operation sequence, interim knowledge must be maintained for a "proof of concept" approach (e.g., EIS applications seeking the answer to a "WHY DID *XYZ* HAPPEN?" type of question). Mediators can function in this realm as well.

With respect to multidatabase systems, mediators might play a role through the layered architecture approach, as discussed in section 6.3. Any other multidatabase class from our taxonomy in Figure 6-1, however, could conceivably make use of mediators for partial global schema or client/server interfaces as well. In effect, the mediator would "exploit encoded knowledge about certain sets or subsets of data to create information for a higher layer of applications"[15] and would reside at the middle layer of a three-layer architecture, between the user (client applications) and base (multiple database). Specific to multidatabase environments using global schemata, mediators would assist with *location* (where is the data I need for this database operation?), *mapping* (how do local databases map to the global schema?), and *conflict resolution* (as a result of mapping and consolidation, what inconsistencies must be resolved?).

Extending the mediator approach from global schema to client/server, we have a three-level architecture not unlike that of an Object Request Broker (ORB), as mentioned in Chapter 3 and discussed in more detail in Chapter 11. In effect, mediators may be distributed according to network cost and other parameters, making them accessible by client applications and providing different types of services to underlying distributed local databases.[16]

At first, mediators seem to be only a slightly different implementation of distributed information management. What makes mediators unique, though, is that because they border both the artificial intelligence and database management disciplines of information systems, they may someday embody AI techniques such as knowledge maintenance and learning abilities. If AI and information management converge (as some practitioners and researchers have predicted for many years and which we'll discuss further in Chapter 16), the resulting knowledge and intelligence could certainly help overcome many of the difficult problems still facing distributed multidatabases.

6.7 Cross-Database Integrity

As database languages and specifically SQL evolved into the 1990s, one of the areas greatly enhanced was database integrity support. Specifically, features such as referential integrity constraints have helped solve much of the integrity problem in application programming, creating a more declarative, database-resident-and-enforced model.

These gains in integrity, though, fall apart in multidatabase environments, specifically in heterogeneous environments created from the bottom up. Even if a global schema exists against which cross-database integrity requirements could be specified, none of the local DBMSs would be capable of enforcing those requirements in cooperation with each other, at least in their "native operating mode." Some form of global constraint management and enforcement must be added to the multidatabase environment to maintain the degree of declarative integrity management that exists in the database world.

One approach is to provide syntax and semantics at the global level, using *polytransactions*—global-level transactions capable of generating "a series of related transactions that maintain mutual consistence among interrelated databases."[17] For example, if components of two different local databases were designated to have an interdatabase dependency, maintained through a type of *interdatabase dependency schema*,[18] transactions at the global level could automatically map to the underlying local transactions to control cross-database integrity.

This approach presents difficulties that must be resolved, including the following:

- Local database transactions that ordinarily would not involve the global schema may be subject to interdatabase dependencies. How is this problem handled? Do we go back to everything forced against the global schema? Does each site have a lookup schema in which cross-database dependencies are noted, so that each local transaction must first determine if any interdatabase dependencies are applicable, and *then* operate against the global schema?

- If no global schema (e.g., a distributed information environment based on client/server access) is used, how are the interdatabase dependencies handled? Are they hard-coded within the server logic?

Cross-database integrity is an extremely important area that needs a great deal more work. The multidatabase properties we've discussed in this chapter (e.g., mappings against local databases, resolving conflicts) should not, when sufficiently resolved, be compromised by a lack of integrity management capabilities across a distributed heterogeneous environment.

6.8 The Role of Standards in Heterogeneous Information Management

The role of standards in distributed heterogeneous information management environments should be fairly obvious. As we discussed in Chapter 3 with respect to client/server architectures, standards help mitigate the problems encountered when heterogeneity is introduced to an environment. This holds true for multidatabase environments as well. If, for example, a global schema layer uses accepted standards such as IDAPI or ODBC (see section 3.3.2) to map from the global schema to local databases, the mapping problems for that environment need not be handled on a case-by-case basis with new formats and protocols developed each time a new DBMS product is added; rather, standards-based interfaces can be used to accomplish that mapping. If global schema multidatabases ever become widespread in commercial environments, they will make extensive use of standards.

6.9 Problems and Issues with Multidatabase Environments

In this chapter, we've discussed some issues and challenges for multidatabases (e.g., mappings, global schema architecture, conflict resolution). Not surprisingly, many more challenges are under active research and must be overcome before multidatabase environments can become widespread. Let's look at some of them:[19]

- *Site autonomy and database administration:* Local database administrators (DBAs) may not be heavily affected if they are required to participate in a distributed multidatabase environment (though, of course, they face additional burdens and tasks). However, the "global DBAs" responsible for tasks such as global schema maintenance, cross-database integrity specification, and redistribution of data, must often resolve intersite conflicts as well as conflicting local and global needs. The management and control of widely distributed multidatabase environments is not well understood, considering that factors such as security enforcement, user IDs, and other items must be handled in a more complex manner than they would in a single-site, single-DBMS environment.

- *Global query processing and concurrency:* The distributed database query optimization problem becomes more complex when heterogeneity is introduced to the environment; likewise, widespread distribution invalidates most of the transaction models (e.g., a single, monolithic control level in which the ACID properties are enforced) common to centralized environments. In Chapter 20, we'll discuss advanced transaction models and ACID properties; for now, we'll just note that query processing is extremely complex and often unpredictable (with respect to response times) in distributed, heterogeneous, multidatabase environments.

- *Security:* Advances in areas such as supporting multiple levels of security with a single database are much more difficult in distributed environments, especially as cross-database integrity constraints blend into cross-security constraints. Enforcement can be extremely difficult, and "little work has been reported on the specific security requirements of the multidatabase environment."[20] In Chapter 21, we'll discuss trends in database security.

6.10 Conclusion

Multidatabase environments, the subject of research and development for many years, continue to be highly desired by information managers. A great deal of progress has been made since the early 1980s, in many areas.

A big question, though (as we'll discuss in detail in Chapter 7) is the form in which these environments are most likely to be successfully implemented. If you think of the term "multidatabase" in the generic sense (see Figure 6-1), meaning "many different databases within an environment," then surely any sizable organization will implement a multidatabase environment.

As we will discuss in Chapter 7, the question is whether global schemata with transparent access to underlying local databases will play any role in the multidatabase picture, considering the inherent difficulty in implementing such architectures. If all its technical, performance, and procedural problems could be overcome, such an environment would provide the highest degree of transparency possible, but it is questionable *if* these problems will ever be overcome to the extent needed to implement such environments. At the very least, we still have a number of years until such environments (e.g., those based exclusively on transparent access) are commercially practical, and the need for distributed information management (multidatabase environments, in the generic sense) exists *right now*. Therefore, let's carry our discussion into Chapter 7 and talk about the outlook for distributed information and database management.

Outlook

Short-term

- Continued research into transparent global distribution of data assets
- Establishment of transparency-based environments at the department level
- Investigation into identified and not-yet-identified problems
- Continued growth in the extraction-only heterogeneous market

Long-term

- Possible expansion of global transparency to larger scales of computing assets
- Heterogeneous information models (e.g., relational and object-oriented) in an updateable environment
- Identification of new problems and challenges

Additional Reading

- M. W. Bright, A. R. Hurson, and S. H. Pakzad, "A Taxonomy and Current Issues in Multidatabase Systems," *IEEE Computer* (March 1992).
- R. Hackathorn, *Enterprise Database Connectivity* (New York: John Wiley & Sons, 1993).
- W. Kim and J. Seo, "Classifying Schematic and Data Heterogeneity in Multidatabase Systems," *IEEE Computer* (December 1991).

- M. T. Özsu and P. Valduriez, *Principles of Distributed Database Systems* (Englewood Cliffs, NJ: Prentice-Hall, 1991).

- S. Ram, "Heterogeneous Distributed Database Systems," *IEEE Computer* (December 1991).

Endnotes

1. M. W. Bright, A. R. Hurson, and S. H. Pakzad, "A Taxonomy and Current Issues in Multidatabase Systems," *IEEE Computer* (March 1992), 52.

2. S. Ram, "Heterogeneous Distributed Database Systems," *IEEE Computer* (December 1991), 8.

3. Bright et al., "Taxonomy and Current Issues," 51.

4. Bright et al., "Taxonomy and Current Issues," 51.

5. Bright et al., "Taxonomy and Current Issues," 52.

6. Bright et al., "Taxonomy and Current Issues," 52.

7. Bright et al., "Taxonomy and Current Issues," 56.

8. D. Barbará, "Extending the Scope of Database Services," *SIGMOD Record* (March 1993), 68.

9. Barbará, "Extending the Scope."

10. W. Kim and J. Seo, "Classifying Schematic and Data Heterogeneity in Multidatabase Systems," *IEEE Computer* (December 1991), 14.

11. Kim and Seo, "Classifying Schematic and Data Heterogeneity," 17.

12. G. Wiederhold, "Mediators in the Architecture of Future Information Systems," *IEEE Computer* (March 1992), 38–49.

13. Wiederhold, "Mediators," 42.

14. Wiederhold, "Mediators," 43.

15. Wiederhold, "Mediators," 44.

16. Wiederhold, "Mediators," 45–46.

17. M. Rusinkiewicz, A. Sheth, and G. Karabatis, "Specifying Interdatabase Dependencies in a Multidatabase Environment," *IEEE Computer* (December 1991), 47.

18. Rusinkiewiez, Sheth, and Karabatis, "Specifying Interdatabase Dependencies."

19. From Bright et al., "Taxonomy and Current Issues," 52–54.

20. Bright et al., "Taxonomy and Current Issues," 54.

CHAPTER

7

Conclusions: Future Directions of Distributed Information Management

A Note to the CIO

The discussion in this chapter provides an analysis of many of the subjects covered in Part II of this book. We can discuss the fundamentals of, say, multidatabase systems in a heterogeneous distributed environment, but chances are that your information environment may

7.1 Introduction

We've taken a comprehensive look at many aspects of distributed information management, from basic client/server DBMS models (and emerging standards in that area) to full-scale multidatabase systems capable of supporting transparent access to underlying heterogeneous data.

In this chapter, we'll summarize our discussions on these topics, to understand the directions being taken in the distributed information management discipline. We'll look at where we are today, as well as at a number of problems that remain. Finally, we'll focus on the most promising areas of distributed information management and their usage in the information systems of the near future.

not be able to wait for commercially available technology to catch up with what is envisioned in many of these areas. We have, however, alternative solutions that you may be able to employ to meet certain distributed information management goals now while waiting for new technologies to emerge. This chapter will focus on these areas.

Executive Summary

Following several years of research, in the mid-1980s a general understanding of the characteristics of distributed databases was reached. Despite this general agreement on DDB properties, many aspects have yet to be realized in real-world implementations.

Many organizations have scaled back grandiose distributed database plans based on globally transparent access to widely dispersed data assets. Rather, they are relying on proven technologies or new generations of those technologies. Examples include replication servers and client/server systems that make extensive use of stored procedures to provide data services to remote requestors.

One only has to consider common functions, such as how automated teller machines (ATMs) work, to gain a realistic perspective about the

7.2 Where Are We Today?

One statement sums up the state of distributed databases and information management in the mid-1990s:

> Long-held notions about the "correct" way to distribute data across an organization's computing resources are undergoing a philosophical shift, based on over a decade of experimentation, research, and development.

In Chapter 2, we discussed Chris Date's 12 rules for distributed databases, originally proposed in 1987. Compliance with Date's 12 rules results in a full-function distributed DBMS (DDBMS) environment, making it reasonable to measure the state of the art against those rules.

David McGoveran did an analysis of this type in early 1993, and he concluded that "today's commercially available distributed database management systems do a poor job of supporting all of Chris Date's Twelve Objectives of Distributed Databases."[1] Specifically, McGoveran noted that the objective most lacking was data and location independence, primarily due to the absence of a global naming scheme capable of mapping logical assets to

capabilities and limitations of distributed information technology. At the same time, envisioning how an ATM might work in the future (e.g., enabling a user to enter a transaction such as "Withdraw $250 from whichever account I have [of five checking accounts at different banks across the country] that has the largest balance, but only if a deposit has been made in the past week") shows us how global transparency might work, once underlying technology and distributed processing algorithms catch up with the ideas.

What This Technology Can Do for You

This chapter is a summary of the previous five chapters, and it puts the finishing touches on distributed information management alternatives. Whether you are a decision maker or technical implementor, understanding the trade-offs and the realities among the many implementation choices available is essential. Pay close attention to the discussion in section 7.2.1 on business needs as they apply to technical alternatives, whether based on today's or tomorrow's technology. As mentioned in Chapter 1, business needs should dictate technical implementation.

physical names (e.g., mapping entity-relationship diagram objects to tables, columns, constraints, and other components of implementation DBMSs).[2] This lack of transparency is echoed by M. Tamer Öszu and Patrick Valduriez, who noted in early 1992 that "most commercial DBMSs do not provide a sufficient level of transparency."[3]

7.2.1 Multiple Models of Information Distribution

The question that begs asking, though, is whether transparent access to distributed data, regardless of the location or form of those data, is really such a good thing. A counterargument to the value of transparent access was proposed in 1987 by Jim Gray, then at Tandem Computers, in his paper "Transparency in Its Place: The Case Against Transparent Access to Geographically Distributed Data."[4] In this paper, Gray offers a contrary view of the value of transparent access to data, arguing that 1) transparency was hardly used in homogeneous environments where it had been available for many years, and 2) transparency introduces severe manageability problems when widely used. One could extend his argument from the homogeneous DDBMS to heterogeneous, multidatabase systems (as discussed in Chapter 6); viewed on the corporationwide scale, the manageability problems become even more serious.

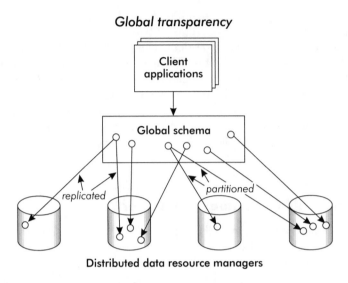

Global transparency

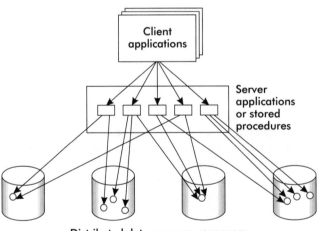

Client/server-based access

Figure 7-1 Two Approaches to Distributed Information Management

And so we come to this critical juncture with respect to DDB and DDBMS future directions: just where are they headed? Gray proposed that a requester-server model—now more commonly called client/server, which we discussed in Chapter 3—is the "right" solution to the distributed information management problem. Figure 7-1 summarizes the distinctions between transparently accessible data and client/server-based access.

One of Date's 12 objectives, location autonomy, is preserved with a client/server model (Figure 7-2). Any site may reorganize its database, even replace the DBMS, if desired, and as long as the client systems' access

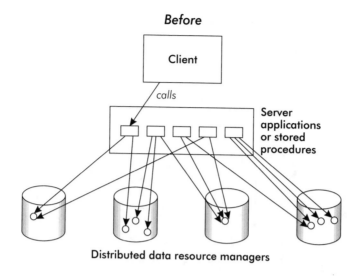

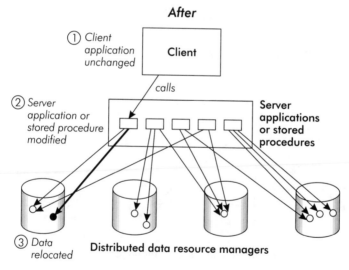

Figure 7-2 A Client/Server Model of Local Autonomy

procedures remain unchanged, then applications remain unchanged.[5] Correspondingly, such local autonomy under a transparently accessible model would, when implemented correctly, also permit the applications to remain unchanged (Figure 7-3). With transparent access to the data, though, the global schema *would* need to be adjusted to reflect the new mappings to underlying data managers and data models, an additional environment management step that is unnecessary with a client/server-based model.

Conceptually, global transparency offers a lot of "nice" things for an information systems environment, particularly the unification of all of the

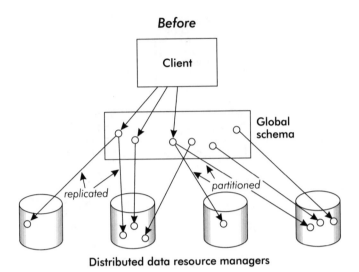

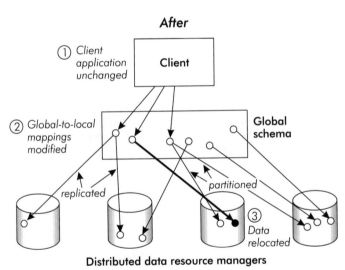

Figure 7-3 Transparency Access Model and Local Autonomy

data and information within that environment under a single global schema. With access to this global schema, applications developers can pick and choose among the millions of data objects common to a large corporation and access or update the ones appropriate to the business functions of their applications, subject to appropriate permissions. The magic of transparency will do the rest, or so the argument goes.

The counterargument is that as we move towards consolidated corporation-wide information management environments, transparency does *not* scale well from department-class up to corporation-class. Consider this example, as

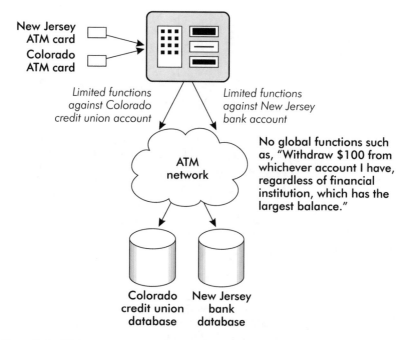

Figure 7-4 ATM Access to Databases without Global Schema

illustrated in Figure 7-4. I carry two cards in my wallet capable of accessing automatic teller machines (ATMs); card #1 is from a credit union in Colorado, card #2 permits access to a bank in New Jersey. If I insert card #1 into an ATM at a supermarket, I can perform a limited number of predetermined functions: get cash, make a deposit, and obtain balance information. If I insert card #2 into that same ATM, I can do the identical functions, except against a different account. That ATM, through a consistent interface, permits me to perform specific functions, for which I am authorized, against at least two different back-end databases (one in New Jersey, the other in Colorado).

How are my transactions routed from that supermarket ATM, which may be in Pittsburgh, to either New Jersey or Colorado? I can assume that some network will connect to another network, which may connect to another network, and so on, and that a set of parameters obtained from the ATM access card I use for each transaction is passed along that network route. Do I know the precise route of either of those accesses or exactly what parameters are passed along the way? No, nor do I really care. For my purposes as a user, I have transparent access from a single location to a global information environment. As mentioned earlier, I can perform a predetermined set of operations (e.g., get cash, obtain balance) in a consistent manner against different back-end sources of information.

Now consider this: if that ATM in Pittsburgh—let's call it the client system—permits me to access either New Jersey–based or Colorado-based

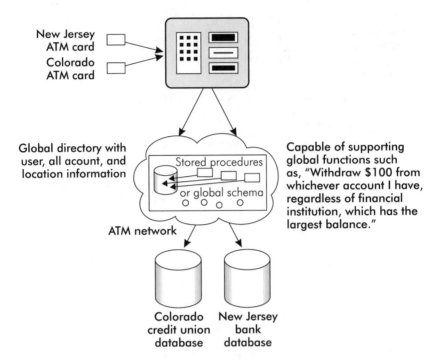

Figure 7-5 ATM Access to Databases with Global Schema

banking information, then from a single card I should be able to do the following:

- Get a consolidated account balance report, with the sum total of my balances in the Colorado and New Jersey checking accounts, all savings accounts, all CDs, and so on.
- Perform additional operations (ad hoc queries, perhaps), such as "Give me the last five ATM withdrawals I have made anywhere in this network, from any account, sorted in descending order by date of withdrawal."

But I can't. The information to support the above classes of operations, and many more, is there. If I can get to the databases of my bank in New Jersey and my credit union in Colorado with two separate cards through a rigidly controlled, proceduralized interface, and if a network infrastructure exists between the ATM in Pittsburgh and both back-end systems (which it must, if I can get to either system), then why can't I do those other procedures?

Actually, I could, under certain conditions. Chief among those "conditions" would be the creation of a global schema for banking/financial institution information (Figure 7-5). Global objects such as PERSON and ACCOUNT could be partitioned (or possibly replicated) among underlying remote databases, with the mappings from the global schema to underlying data managers in place to support transparent access.

Once such a global schema is in place, that ATM in Pittsburgh could be given far superior capabilities to the limited set of functions it can perform today. Perhaps through a graphical user interface or some sophisticated help facility, I could enter queries such as, "Of all my checking accounts, which has the largest balance?" as well as operations based on such queries (e.g., "Withdraw $150 from my checking account with the largest balance"). Such queries and update operations could then be processed against the global schema, which would support the mappings of those requests to the underlying data managers for processing.

Following the principles of global transparency, I could, say, open three new checking accounts over the next month, and if I were to issue the request, "Withdraw $150 from the checking account with the largest balance," all mappings would be in place to include the new accounts during that operation. This means, though, that some extremely large, always-consistent directory structure with all current mappings must exist (e.g., the directory would contain sufficient information so that the ad hoc query would be able to determine that my checking accounts are located at Point X in Colorado and Point Y in New Jersey, as well as new Points A, B, and C). Or, in the absence of such a directory, the distributed query engine must exhaustively search all back-end databases (through requests to the local database managers) to see if I have a checking account there and, if so, to return my balance. Given the likely number of back-end local database managers, such an exhaustive search—just one—would consume a tremendous amount of network, processing, and database management resources.

I'm not the only one making changes to my overall financial structure by adding new accounts; millions of other people add new accounts, change accounts, add new owners to accounts, and perform simple account maintenance functions. Likewise, I'm not the only one who will make such queries against that global schema, which inevitably means one of two possibilities:

1) With a directory structure in place, we have a management nightmare, requiring a significant number of updates (e.g., new account information) to the global-to-local mappings. Such a directory structure would likely be replicated as well to avoid bottlenecks, introducing a consistency issue (the directory structures must be consistent with one another, subject to the definition of "consistency" in such an environment).

2) Without a directory structure, we have a significantly large number of very expensive (in terms of resources consumed) simultaneous queries, with obvious effects on overall systems performance.

To sum up, we might make the following observation about global transparency to distributed data: it is technically possible to base a distributed

DBMS architecture on a global schema approach, with applications running against that global schema. This is true whether the local data managers underneath are homogeneous (meaning that the environment was likely designed in a top-down manner) or heterogeneous (indicating a bottom-up creation of a federated database). But is such an architecture suitable for a particular environment? A particular system, such as our ATM example, might very well have a certain number of commonly used functions that are better handled through a client/server model than through a global schema that supports transparent access to underlying data.

Even current plans for "major enhancements" to ATM systems focus on single-site functions, such as transferring money from certificates of deposit into checking accounts, or opening all new accounts at a single institution. Basically, new canned (stored) procedures are being added to augment the functionality that already exists, but no major architectural changes (e.g., ad hoc cross-institution access) are planned for the near future.

Note that the principles of distributed data are still sound; the implementation, though, may vary from one environment to another. No one programming language is optimal for every software development effort; the same statement can be made for distributed data management. As we pointed out, some degree of application transparency exists, regardless of the model used; clients are insulated from local data management changes (such as rehosting or reformatting of data objects) whether through a global schema or a server interface. Of course, events such as adding new data objects or deleting others do require application changes, but this is true whether the global schema or client/server approach is implemented. In short, today (and for the foreseeable future) we have two choices for distributed data management with multiple local data managers; depending on the specific environment, one or the other may be identified as the more appropriate solution.

7.2.2 Parallel Database Machines

Let's take another quick look at parallel database systems (see Chapter 5) and where they are heading. Parallel database systems "will take a large piece of the large systems database market," according to consultant Richard Winter, who also notes that database vendors "have a big challenge to overcome in achieving operational robustness in [high-end] applications."[6] Most major DBMS vendors, including Oracle, Informix, Sybase, Teradata, and others,[7] are working on parallel database systems—as of mid-1993, IBM was working on at least six efforts for different platforms.[8]

One interesting area in which parallel database systems show promise is in decision support queries against operational databases (in contrast to the database warehouse approach, which we discussed in Chapter 4). Because decision support and executive information systems (DSS and EIS) overtax operational database resources in traditional architectures, the informational database concept, physically separate from the operational database, has grown in favor. With massively parallel processing (MPP) architectures for parallel database systems, DSS/EIS processing could conceivably occur against an operational database through use of a subset of the processing capacity of the overall system, without a substantial impact against operational performance.[9] While problems such as impedence mismatches among data and other warehouse/multidatabase issues would still need to be resolved, at least the processing overload problem in mixed informational/operational environments would be partially (if not completely) overcome.

Summarizing, terabyte-sized databases, involving perhaps billions of relational rows, are a prime candidate for parallel database systems. As with multidatabase environments (transparently accessible or not), the premise of data distribution among computing resources remains valid, particularly as organizations struggle to comprehensively manage all of the information under their control.

7.3 Problem Areas in Distributed Information Management

The database and information management industry has made great strides in several areas, from basic technology to gaining a better understanding of users' needs for distributed information management. Obviously not all problems are resolved. So what are the "hot" research areas in this field over the next few years?

The report from the 1990 National Science Foundation workshop on advanced database technology (which we discussed in Chapter 1, section 1.6.3), determined that "very difficult problems lie ahead in the areas of inconsistent databases, security, and massive scale-up of distributed DBMS technology."[10] Other papers and articles written in the 1990s have also identified DDBMS problem areas that require further research. Because these areas form a large portion of the topical research in distributed information, let's look at some of these current problems under investigation.

7.3.1 Semantic Inconsistency

In Chapter 4, we discussed the problem in data warehouse environments of handling mismatches among different data representations or formats from multiple sources. Encoding of values, data types and sizes, and similar issues were mentioned, along with the simplistic declaration that "the warehouse environment must handle these inconsistencies."

The problem goes deeper than simple differences in representations, though; when multiple sources of information must interact, either in a warehouse environment or through operational multidatabase systems, we often have problems of semantic inconsistencies. An example cited in the NSF workshop report illustrated that a global database schema with connections to every Ph.D.-granting institution in the United States would still be unable to provide an accurate answer to the question "How many computer science Ph.D. students are there in the U.S.?"[11] The reason is that some of those databases may include every student currently enrolled, whether actively attending classes or not; others might only include students currently taking some minimum number of core hours. Some databases might not include foreign students; other databases would disregard students with dual majors; and so on. In short, the inconsistency problem goes far deeper than simple data typing and representation mismatches, which can usually be handled through mapping algorithms. The very *meaning* of the information in component local databases—the semantics—often differs among those sources, and ways must be found not only to resolve those semantic inconsistencies but also to communicate the underlying semantics of the databases from one to another to determine *what* must be done to achieve semantic consistency.

7.3.2 Browsing

When database components are rolled up or consolidated, possibly through some global schema, inconsistencies might still occur. Users must be able, somehow, to interrogate the structure of the database itself, as well as the process(es) that created the consolidated set of data; the interrogations determine how the consolidated database arrived at the state it is in. Capabilities are needed to filter out information that invalidates a global query (e.g., by ignoring part of the "stuff" one is given in order to make something meaningful out of the rest). Global queries are expensive enough in terms of computing resources; we don't want to just give up because of inconsistencies.[12]

7.3.3 Security

In Chapter 21, we'll discuss database security, which poses its own problems when multiple levels of information (e.g., SECRET, UNCLASSIFIED, TOP SECRET) are to be handled together in the same database environment. Add a little distribution to the architectural mix, throw in some heterogeneity, and security becomes nightmarish. In section 21.6 we'll discuss approaches to the distributed database security problem.

7.3.4 Site Scale-Up

In section 7.2.1 we mentioned that one of the major problems with the global schema approach to distributed information management is that algorithms (e.g., query processing, searching, updating) that work very well with a small number of sites simply do not scale as 1,000 or even 10,000 sites become commonplace.[13] As we'll discuss in Chapter 22, this problem becomes even more complex when mobile computing devices and their databases are added to the equation. For a global schema approach to ever be practical, scalability of all algorithms must be available to handle tens of thousands of sites in an organization.

7.3.5 Transaction Processing

In Chapter 20, we'll discuss the present trends and future directions of transaction processing. Assuming that a multidatabase environment will incorporate database managers from different vendors (and support different models, such as relational and object-oriented), different concurrency control algorithms will be used by each product.[14] Even different transaction models will be in use, perhaps classic chained or nested transactions for relational information (discussed in section 20.3) combined with long-running transactions for the object-oriented data. Clearly, transaction processing mismatch will cause problems in heterogeneous environments.

One possible solution is the emergence of standards-based transaction processing (e.g., X/Open DTP), which we'll discuss in section 20.5 of Chapter 20. Eventually (probably in the late 1990s) enough database and information management vendors will incorporate DTP into their transaction processing environments to enable standards-based transaction processing across heterogeneous environments.

7.3.6 Distributed Design

Designing distributed information management systems also becomes very complex as large-scale environments are created. For classic homogeneous distributed database environments, with distribution occurring over a limited number of nodes, a top-down modeling approach (coupled with an additional step of distributing data objects according to network cost and political and other factors) is often sufficient to accomplish the distributed design, though the allocation of partitions and replicates to various nodes can itself be a fairly complex process.[15] When bottom-up approaches are needed for federated environments, the design process becomes very complex.

Even a top-down homogeneous approach for parallel database systems involves extremely complex design. Determining the type of partitioning (round-robin, hashing, or range—see section 5.3 of Chapter 5) among the processing components requires new design models not yet formalized. This is another area in which further research is required.

7.3.7 Distributed Query Processing

In section 7.2.1, we discussed the problem of query processing against a global schema. Öszu and Valduriez note that a trade-off must be made between the costs of optimizing queries and the usefulness of the results from such optimization.[16] Costly optimization processes for repetitive queries may be acceptable, but not for ad hoc queries. Even if one were to accept that repetitive queries are worth the costs of optimization, changes in underlying local database structures (e.g., adding or deleting nodes, making major changes in data volumes or changing the schema structure at one or more nodes), network infrastructures, and other components that comprise the inputs to optimization algorithms could radically shift the optimal data access paths. With *static optimization*—global query optimization performed prior to execution of the query[17]—such changes may very well invalidate the optimization that had been performed.

Therefore, we have two problems in query processing. The first is ad hoc queries against large-scale distributed databases (with heterogeneity complicating the process, because different DBMS products have different individual characteristics that must be considered in the process of global optimization); we discussed this issue earlier. The other problem, also mentioned earlier, is that dynamically shifting underlying components require revisiting the optimization process itself. There must be a way to determine the optimal intervals at which query recompilation and reoptimization should be accomplished, according to the dynamics of the underlying distributed infrastructure.[18]

7.4 Promising Areas in Distributed Information Management

So there are still problems to be solved in distributed information management; that in itself is hardly shocking, since every area of computing and communications is constantly going through a discovery and rediscovery process, with old problems being solved and new ones identified.

To focus on the more positive aspects, as we wrap up our discussion, let's briefly revisit two areas we identified earlier as among the most promising in helping manage distributed organizational data.

The first is parallel database systems, which we've discussed several times. For emphasis, we'll again note that large distributed databases may, in many environments, eventually include MPP systems handling terabytes of data much more efficiently than either centralized database environments or classic variations on the distributed database theme (e.g., distribution over a local, metropolitan, or wide-area network).

Second, we have client/server-based distributed information management. As we discussed in section 7.2.1, we may soon see global schemas providing transparent access to widely distributed heterogeneous data in an effortless, highly efficient process. Newly discovered technologies, highly advanced algorithms, and other factors may overcome the problems identified today with the global schema approach.

Until such time, though, client/server environments, particularly the emergence of standards such as those based on SQL Access Group CLI (IDAPI and ODBC, as we discussed in Chapter 3), may very well fill the distributed information management needs of most organizations. While ad hoc queries and update operations across a distributed environment can't be done through the formalized procedures of such environments, we still must determine the true value of such capabilities—that is, is the cost of providing an information system capable of such ad hoc operations *really* worth the benefit?

Such issues aside, client/server technology, not only in information management but in other service areas of information systems, has undeniably made great strides in recent years and will continue to do so in the future.

7.5 Conclusion

We wrap up six chapters of discussion on many different areas of distributed information management, from the basic principles to new thoughts on old concepts (e.g., partitioning and replication). We've also discussed different models of multidatabase environments and associated technical problems and opportunities.

In this chapter, we've concluded our discussion with some thoughts on remaining technical problem areas (or perhaps we should optimistically call them "challenges"), as well as business models that represent different approaches to the discipline (such as client/server contrasted with global transparent access).

Outlook

Short-term

- Multiple ways of achieving data and information distribution
- Client/server to play a very important role
- Global transparency still considered "a future technology" (at least in real-world implementations, though many prototypes and experimental systems exist)

Long-term

- Global transparency possible, subject to overcoming technical challenges for widely distributed data
- Advances in all of today's technologies, in capacity, performance, and standardization
- Distribution of data will be a given

Additional Reading

- J. Gray, "Transparency in Its Place: The Case Against Transparent Access to Geographically Distributed Data," *UNIX Review* (May 1987).

- M. T. Özsu and P. Valduriez, "Distributed Database Systems: Where Are We Now?," *Database Programming & Design* (March 1992).

- A. Silberschatz, M. Stonebraker, and J. Ullman, "Database Systems: Achievements and Opportunities," *Communications of the ACM* (October 1991).

- A. Simon, "What Happened to Our Dream House?," *Database Programming & Design, Special Supplement* (December 1994).

Endnotes

1. D. McGoveran, "State of the Distributed DBMS Art," *Network World* (May 1993), S5.

2. McGoveran, "Distributed DBMS."

3. M. T. Özsu and P. Valduriez, "Distributed Database Systems: Where Are We Now?" *Database Programming & Design* (March 1992), 49.

4. J. Gray, "Transparency in Its Place: The Case Against Transparent Access to Geographically Distributed Data," Tandem Technical Report TR89.1, Tandem Computers, rev. February 1989. Originally published in J. Gray, *UNIX Review* (May 1987), 42–50.

5. Gray, "Transparency," 4.

6. B. Francett, "Business Community Primes for Parallel," *Software Magazine* (July 1993), 63.

7. Francett, "Primes for Parallel," 67.

8. Francett, "Primes for Parallel," 67–71.

9. Francett, "Primes for Parallel," 67.

10. A. Silberschatz, M. Stonebraker, and J. Ullman, "Database Systems: Achievements and Opportunities," *Communications of the ACM* (October 1991), 111.

11. Silberschatz, Stonebraker, and Ullman, "Database Systems," 118.

12. Silberschatz, Stonebraker, and Ullman, "Database Systems," 119.

13. Silberschatz, Stonebraker, and Ullman, "Database Systems," 120.

14. Silberschatz, Stonebraker, and Ullman, "Database Systems."

15. Özsu and Valduriez, "Distributed Database Systems," 49–50.

16. Özsu and Valduriez, "Distributed Database Systems," 51.

17. Özsu and Valduriez, "Distributed Database Systems."

18. Özsu and Valduriez, "Distributed Database Systems."

PART III

Object-Oriented
Databases

CHAPTER 8

Principles of Object-Oriented Databases

A Note to the CIO

As with client/server technology (discussed in Chapter 3), you are probably bombarded by variations on the object-oriented database (OODB), from programming languages ("the wonders of C++") to operating environments and databases. This chapter will provide background on database and information management as they relate to object-oriented technology, with discussions on principles and general future directions. Alternative approaches to OODB will be discussed in subsequent chapters.

8.1 Introduction

Although the future direction of object-oriented database (OODB) implementation is marked by questions and disagreements, the majority of the database and information management experts agree: object orientation is here to stay.

In this chapter, we'll set the stage for our future-oriented discussion over the next three chapters. We'll look at the principles of OODBs and object-oriented database management systems (OODBMSs), including the following:

- The characteristics and rationale behind OODBMSs and OODBs.
- Architectural issues and considerations.
- Strengths and shortcomings of today's OODBMS products.

Executive Summary

Two major camps compete in object-oriented database management systems (OODBMS): extended relational DBMSs, discussed in Chapter 9, and "pure" OODBMSs, discussed in Chapter 10. For the most part, both models are driven by the same motivations, principally to support complex applications that closely represent real-world objects.

Fundamental concepts, even terminology, have varied in object-oriented databases since the paradigms first surfaced. In recent years, efforts within both camps have brought some degree of standardization to terminology and concepts, to provide a stable base from which technology and products can grow.

8.2 Rationale and Characteristics of Object-Oriented Databases

The rationale behind object-oriented databases and DBMSs, as well as object orientation in general (e.g., including programming languages, design methodologies, operating systems) is rather simple. Recall in section 1.3.4 of Chapter 1 we mentioned that one of the dominant trends in computing was how to forge a closer relationship between information systems and the real-world systems they support or represent. Figure 8-1 illustrates the traditional implementation model that has dominated computing since the early days. Semantic loss characterizes the process; that is, at a point in the conversion from some real-world system to a computer-based representation, some degree of semantics, meaning, is lost, usually resulting in a mismatch between the real-world system and its information systems counterpart.

Semantic loss has long been a problem for the developers of computer systems, particularly those dealing with business applications. Consider that one of the primary purposes of commercial information systems is to perform business transactions and functions that traditionally have been done manually. The automation of these transactions and functions is designed to improve throughput (i.e., a greater number of transactions processed by fewer people). Because all of the semantics of real-world processing (that is, the ways in which the functions have been done) inevitably elude capture in their entirety in traditional computer systems, there is a risk that the developed system "just doesn't fit right" and either will meet with resistance from users or cannot do the job.

Figure 8-2 narrows the scope of this transformation process and the accompanying semantic loss to the data. Typically, real-world objects have

What This Technology Can Do for You

As with distributed information management (discussed in Part II of this book), you should keep in mind that object-oriented databases and information management systems are simply tools through which systems and applications can be developed; object orientation is *not* a cure-all for the ills of data management or of information systems technology in general.

Powerful client/server applications (systems that support complex data structures, large in-memory data representations, and so on), such as computer-aided design (CAD), may be built using object-oriented databases as the information management layer. The power of these applications comes not only from the data service support (e.g., using

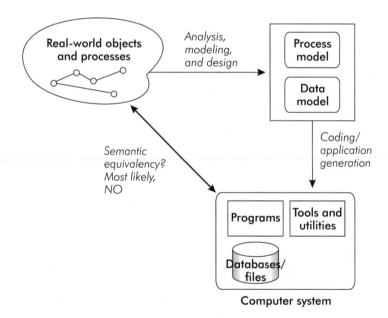

Figure 8-1 Semantic Loss in Traditional Systems Development

properties and applicable functions that provide definition and classification. Objects are related to one another, either on an interobject basis according to "business" rules (e.g., an employee works in a video store; a video store contains videotapes and laser disks; an employee sells videotapes and laser disks to customers; a customer shops in a video store; and so on); or possibly

OODBMSs) but also from high-powered desktop client systems. The increased computational power, memory capacity, and other performance characteristics of today's (and tomorrow's) desktop systems have brought complex applications development to the desktop, and such development often requires data management support that is better provided by OODBMSs than by relational DBMSs (RDBMSs).

One reason for this marked distinction between OODBMSs and relational DBMSs is that RDBMS vendors developed their base products in a time frame characterized by lack of high-powered desktop computing performance and capacity (e.g., early-generation PCs and workstations); therefore, the vendors poured their resources into server functionality.

by some type of *inheritance* of properties (e.g., an employee may be a manager, store employee, or headquarters employee; all three of these categories share some properties, such as name and address, but also have certain properties and operations that make them different from one another). Further, certain operations and functions apply to real-world objects (e.g., an employee may be hired, fired, or given a raise; a videotape may be purchased, returned damaged by a customer, or discontinued; and so on).

As those real-world objects are modeled and eventually translated into computer-based data structures (such as relational tables), semantic loss occurs. Even attempts to counteract this information loss problem through the use of data modeling techniques capable of capturing semantics (e.g., extended entity-relationship modeling, functional data modeling,[1] or semantic data modeling[2]) still suffer from one persistent problem: database implementations themselves are incapable of maintaining and using any model-based semantics that have been captured.

Certain classes of applications that came to prominence in the 1980s, particularly computer-aided design (CAD) and computer-aided software (or systems) engineering (CASE), highlighted this deficiency, as CAD, CASE, and similar applications proved extremely hard to run on top of relational database systems. Or, more specifically, applications developers had tremendous difficulty mapping the structures needed for the CAD or CASE systems to table-based structures of RDBMS engines.

The first natural step in the evolution, then, to object orientation in the database was to create application-specific structures capable of capturing the semantic meaning; these structures would be used by applications as a sort of surrogate data manager, simplifying the program development and maintenance. As shown in Figure 8-3, information managed at these layers would

By contrast, OODBMS vendors have worked during the age of the powerful desktop system, permitting client support for robust and complex applications.

The power of the OODBMS approach has not come free, however; a good deal of the data independence found in relational environments has been lost. OODBMSs feature in-memory data structures that are equivalent to stored representation; in single-application environments this feature is valuable and efficient, but in multiple-application environments some degree of flexibility is sacrificed. Coordinates of class libraries and other object-oriented constructs must occur among applications, ensuring adequate support in the object representations for all candidate client applications.

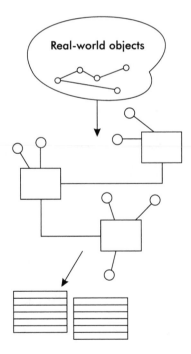

Figure 8-2 Semantic Loss in the Data Realm

then be transformed into underlying relational tables according to mapping rules and algorithms, to preserve as much semantic information as possible while simplifying application development.

Again, it's important to keep these (and other) trade-offs and issues in mind as you swim through the mass of hype from vendors, the computer trade press, and even the general business press. View object orientation not only in information management and databases, but also in other areas such as programming languages, as one tool in your toolbox in the 1990s, not as a cure for all of your database ills.

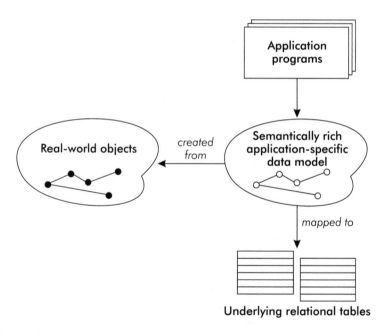

Figure 8-3 Surrogate Object-Oriented Layer

Even though the application programming process could be simplified using this type of layered approach, the fundamental problem remained; the underlying relational engines and data structures typically were incapable of maintaining all of the semantics needed by the applications. This problem existed in the following areas:

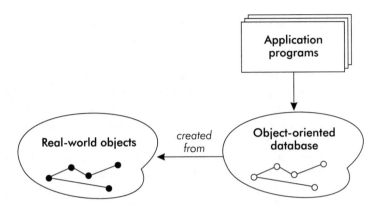

Figure 8-4 A Simple OODBMS/OODB Environment (No More Mappings)

- *Data types:* Relational DBMSs supported a limited set of data types (character, integer, floating point, dates, and a few others); the real world—and the intermediate representation models—typically featured abstract, user-defined data types (e.g., type of movie).

- *Operations:* The applications programs still needed to support all procedural logic within the system, because the underlying relational systems couldn't handle business rules representation, declaration and execution of object-specific operations (e.g., couldn't give an employee a monthly bonus if he or she reached some system-defined goals), and similar operations.

The next logical step (this was the motivation for object-oriented databases and DBMSs) was an attempt to push the semantics into the database engine itself. Part of the rationale for this was to break the bonds of the relational database world, creating a fourth database model (along with the hierarchical, network, and relational models).[3] The goal of OODBs and OODBMSs was to eliminate the intermediate mapping levels that had been developed and to have an environment similar to the one shown in Figure 8-4.

The characteristics of an object-oriented database (or object orientation in general) include the following:[4]

- *Highly efficient type-specific representations:* Instead of having to map real-world constructs into awkward table-based representations, the representations themselves would be *efficiently* managed within the OODBMS environment.

- *Use of encapsulation:* Encapsulation is used to insulate applications from changes in the previously mentioned representations. In encapsulation, a system is a collection of modules, each accessible through a well-defined interface.[5] That interface—the specification—is independent of the implementation techniques. Implementations may be modified without affecting the specification, that portion visible to other encapsulated components of the system.

- *High degree of consistency:* Operations of a given object are consistent regardless of what application invokes that operation, subject to support within specific OODBMS projects. When the applications themselves must procedurally maintain and execute the business rules applicable to an object, they are soon out of synchronization with one another with respect to the steps within an operation. For example, one application, ReplaceBrokenVideotape, may have procedural rules for putting a new videotape copy into the store's inventory, while another application, OrderJustReleasedVideotape, might have similar rules. Any changes in the procedures for stocking a tape (such as adding bar coding to the existing steps, or having to print a NewTapeInStock label for in-store advertising) must be maintained and updated in both applications as well as any others in the system. By maintaining these rules with the Videotape objects themselves, the changes may be made against the object rather than in the procedural applications code.

- *Cost reduction for new application development through code/object reuse:* Definitions registered in a class library may be reused by newly developed applications or functions. In section 8.3 we'll discuss the use of class libraries in object-oriented development libraries.

The rationale behind object-oriented databases, and the characteristics that have evolved since initial experimentation in the 1980s, are primarily based on the goal of real-world representation. In the next section, we'll take a closer look at the concepts that have evolved.

8.3 Concepts of Object-Oriented Databases

A number of concepts have grown out of the characteristics of object-oriented databases, namely[6]

- Object identity
- Attributes
- Methods
- Classes
- Class hierarchies and inheritance

Let's take a brief look at each of these.

8.3.1 Object Identity

Every object within an object-oriented system has a unique identifier, typically called an *object ID*, or *OID*. The uniqueness of OIDs must be maintained even in distributed object environments, which we'll discuss in Chapter 10. OIDs permit you to change the value of any attributes of an object, including those that would constitute a primary key, without corrupting the reference to the object.

Note that the concept of unique OIDs is a departure (some would claim backward step) from value-based uniqueness in the relational model. In any case, one of the fundamental premises of OODBs is the presence of a unique OID that is immutable (no operation may ever change the association between an object and its identity).[7]

It's important to note that the OID may not actually be used by the OODBMS users and applications to access object instances; queries of the relational type (e.g., "Find all videotapes with a current rental price less than $1.00") may utilize value-based searches. For interinstance associations, though, the OID(s) of related object instance(s) may be stored in the instance to which those other instances are related.[8] Even though this is a throwback to pointer-based persistent data structures such as those of the CODASYL network database model, application performance is often dramatically improved by this OID-based association model.

8.3.2 Attributes

A given object always has two properties: state and behavior. The state of an object is defined by the set of values of its *attributes* (or properties, or instance variables, or fields—a number of terms are used).[9] In object-oriented environments, the value of any given attribute must obey certain rules related to the data type (which may be user-defined or abstract), ranges and lists of values, whether a single value or multiple values may be present, and so on. Behavior is discussed in the next section.

8.3.3 Methods

Just as attributes describe the state of an object, *methods*, also known as procedures or operations, describe their behavior.

If our object is a CD, these methods apply:

- Method 1 = Before insert, check to make sure CD-ID being entered is unique.
- Method 2 = Update sales price. Get value from authorized employee, make sure it's within valid range, update database value.

- Method 3 = Cut-out. Decrease price of every CD of this type currently in stock by 40% now, and 20% more next week for those left; don't order any more.

Through explicit message passing among system objects, encapsulated methods and attributes of a given object are invoked or accessed according to the rules of the OODBMS.

8.3.4 Classes

Classes, also known as types, are constructs into which objects that share the same set of attributes and methods are grouped.[10] Classes may be primitive (all integers, or all string objects), in which case they have no attributes. Or, they may be given attributes and methods, in which case all objects within that class have those same set attributes and methods (though most likely not the same attribute values).

8.3.5 Class Hierarchies and Inheritance

Recall our example in section 8.2 about employees and merchandise. Figure 8-5 illustrates a simple *class hierarchy*, in which subclasses inherit attributes from a superclass (or subtype/supertype, depending on the terminology used) and have new object-specific attributes as well. For example, Merchandise has a set of attributes (title, number on hand, and so on) that apply to both CDs and videotapes. The subclass CDs, however, also has attributes, such as the number of tracks, the artist, and the primary distributor. The subclass Videotapes doesn't share the attributes of CDs, but instead has other attributes, such as regular and current rental price, if the movie is a sequel, and so on.

8.4 Persistence

Unlike relational databases, which originated in data management of information systems, object-oriented databases are largely rooted in programming languages.[11] The OODBMS environment has the following features:

- The host programming language is also the data manipulation language (DML).
- The in-memory and storage models are merged.
- No conversion code between models and languages is needed.[12]

To create this type of environment, the concept of *persistence* is applied to the programming environment. By using statements such as[13]

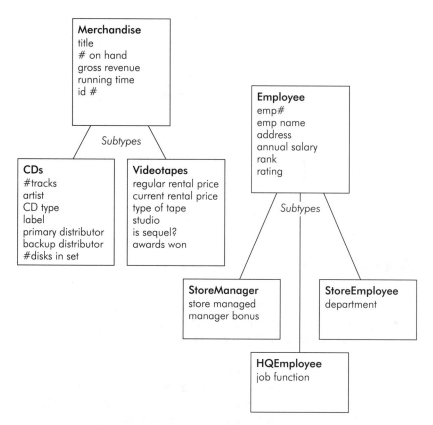

Figure 8-5 A Simple Class Hierarchy

```
Point * p3 = new Persistent Point ( 5,5 );
```

values may be placed into database objects. In effect, persistence of data within programming bounds is provided by the OODBMS capabilities. Recall from Figure 8-4 that the database model and implementation are the same, with no mappings required (including the real-world objects as well). Creating a new persistent object within the programming language introduces a database object that may be used directly within the program without the need to map it to language memory structures.

One of the advantages of programming language–based persistence is that it eliminates impedance mismatches between the database language and the programming. Consider that the typical relational DBMS has an SQL-based data manipulation language that supports basic data types such as integers and characters (though, as we'll discuss in Chapter 12, SQL3 will incorporate abstract data types). Most OODBMSs are hosted within either the C++ or Smalltalk object-oriented programming languages (OOPLs). With all

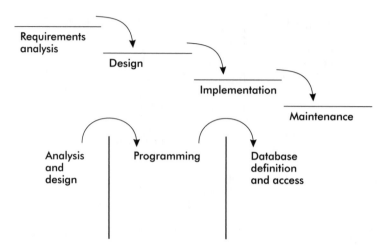

Figure 8-6 Traditional Development Methodology[14]

of the abstract data typing of OOPLs, the mappings we discussed with respect to semantic loss would have to occur whenever data requests are made, resulting in performance problems as well as the information loss we discussed earlier.

As we noted in section 1.5.5 of Chapter 1, some OODBMS proponents claim that the programming of data management languages is one of the major OODBMS contributions, in contrast to relational, network, and hierarchical models (but, as we noted, this paradigm has also been present in the PC database world, particularly in the Xbase language, since the early 1980s).

In the next section, we'll discuss the development environment of OODB applications in more detail. For now, we'll just state that persistence within the programming language allows the OODB environment to exist.

8.5 Development Methodology and Programming Languages

In addition to the unification of the semantically rich data model with the implementation database model (which we discussed in section 8.2), persistence, encapsulation, and the other capabilities we've discussed in this chapter, the system development methodologies applicable to OODBMS environments have significant advantages over their more traditional counterparts. Figure 8-6 illustrates two different views of traditional development methodologies in which the output of one stage is passed to the next phase as input.

In an OODBMS environment, requirements related to conceptual (e.g., class definitions) and physical databases are semantically equivalent (or at

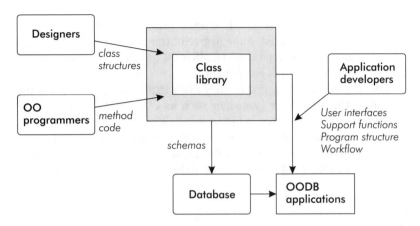

Figure 8-7 Object-Oriented Methodology and Development Roles[15]

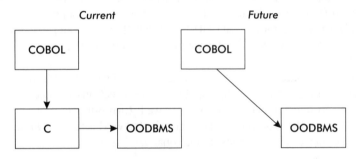

Figure 8-8 Language-to-OODBMS Interfaces, Today and Tomorrow

least that's the goal). Further, Figure 8-7 shows the different roles of development staff members interacting with a common class library. Unlike traditional methodologies, in which requirements definers (functional analysts), database designers, process designers, and programmers use different tools and rarely share information through a common repository, object-oriented methodology enforces the sharing of information among various development roles.

In section 8.4 we mentioned that most OODBMSs are hosted within Smalltalk or C++. Other languages, such as COBOL and Ada, are capable of accessing many OODBMSs through the C programming language, because 1) most 3GLs can call C programs, and 2) most OODBMSs have a C API in addition to C++ and/or Smalltalk. As shown in Figure 8-8, C currently can act as an intermediary between non-OOPLs, such as COBOL, and OODBMSs.

It's important to note that even though it's desirable to call OODBMS facilities from COBOL or FORTRAN or some other language, the advantages of the close coupling between OOPLs (C++, Smalltalk) and the OODBMS facilities that we discussed in this chapter may be lost due to impedance mismatches. Or, at the least, some degree of translation similar to using an object-oriented layer on top of an RDBMS must be achieved to match COBOL data structures with OODB components.

Looking to the future, it is entirely likely that bindings will appear (near the end of the 1990s) for languages such as COBOL and FORTRAN with OODBMS facilities, as shown in Figure 8-8. Talk of "object-oriented COBOL," for example, means that non–object-oriented programming languages will likely be fitted with abstract data types and other object-oriented capabilities to better match the programming and database models with one another.

8.6 Conclusion

Object orientation is pervasive in emerging information system trends, including information management. In this chapter, we've looked at the rationale and basic characteristics of OODBs and OODBMSs, as well as architectural and methodology issues. Finally, we discussed some of the shortcomings of today's OODBMSs.

All of the material in this chapter has provided some background for our discussion in Chapters 9, 10, and 11 on the directions of object-oriented information management. In Chapter 9, we'll turn our attention to various ways in which the relational and object-oriented worlds are merging, including object-oriented extensions to relational databases.

Outlook

Short-term

- OODBMSs will continue to be used in certain classes of applications
- Relational databases will continue to be extended with object-oriented capabilities
- Standardization will come to the OODBMS world

Long-term

- Standards will be extended with new capabilities
- The relational and object-oriented worlds will converge even more than in the short term

Additional Reading

- *Journal of Object-Oriented Programming*, Focus on OODBMS, Special Issue, 1992.
- D. Shipman, "The Functional Data Model and the Data Language DAPLEX," in *Readings in Object-Oriented Database Systems*, eds. S. Zdonik and D. Maier (San Francisco: Morgan Kaufmann Publishers, 1990).
- S. Zdonik and D. Maier, eds., *Readings in Object-Oriented Database Systems* (San Francisco: Morgan Kaufmann Publishers, 1990).

Endnotes

1. D. Shipman, "The Functional Data Model and the Data Language DAPLEX," in *Readings in Object-Oriented Database Systems,* eds. S. Zdonik and D. Maier (San Francisco: Morgan Kaufmann Publishers, 1990), 95–111.

2. M. Hammer and D. McLeod, "Database Description with SDM: A Semantic Database Model," in *Readings in Object-Oriented Database Systems*, eds. S. Zdonik and D. Maier (San Francisco: Morgan Kaufmann Publishers, 1990), 123–140.

3. In reality, there are hundreds of database models, but the widespread adoption by vendors and implementors of hierarchical, network, and relational models led to the general acceptance of those three as the primary alternative data models.

4. T. Atwood, "An Introduction to Object-Oriented Database Management Systems," *Journal of Object-Oriented Programming,* Focus on OODBMS, Special Issue, 1992, 2.

5. S. Zdonik and D. Maier, "Fundamentals of Object-Oriented Databases," in *Readings in Object-Oriented Database Systems*, eds. S. Zdonik and D. Maier (San Francisco: Morgan Kaufmann Publishers, 1990), 13.

6. W. Kim, "Architectural Issues in Object-Oriented Databases," *Journal of Object-Oriented Programming:* Focus on OODBMS, 13–21.

7. Zdonik and Maier, "Fundamentals," 9.

8. Zdonik and Maier, "Fundamentals."

9. Kim, "Architectural Issues," 13.

10. Kim, "Architectural Issues," 14.

11. P. Butterworth, "OODBMSs as Database Managers," *Journal of Object-Oriented Programming*, Focus on OODBMS, Special Issue, 3.

12. M. Loomis, "Principles of Object Databases," *Proceedings of DCI CASEWorld,* Vol. II (September/October 1992), D22-21.

13. Loomis, "Principles," D22-22.

14. The second part of Figure 8-6 is from Loomis, "Principles," D22-3.

15. From Loomis, "Principles," D22-11.

CHAPTER 9

Hybrid and Extended Relational Forms of Object Management

A Note to the CIO

Information system planners today are concerned with balancing the desire to incorporate new technology into their environments with the preservation of an already installed technology and applications base. One approach to this dilemma is to incorporate object-oriented database capabilities through a relational foundation in the form of relational databases with object-oriented extensions. This chapter and Chapter 12, which describes the MOOSE (Major Object-Oriented System Extensions) portions of SQL3, will give you a good understanding of how the convergence of relational and object-oriented technologies may take place.

9.1 Introduction

In section 1.6.1 of Chapter 1, we discussed the "Third-Generation Data Base System Manifesto," a document published in 1990 that outlined a vision for the next generation of DBMS products (that is, the next generation after the relational systems, which had achieved prominence by that time and are still the platform of choice for most new development today). The Manifesto presented three tenets, or guiding principles. The second tenet states, "Third-generation DBMSs must subsume second-generation DBMSs."[1]

This tenet has proven to be a driving force for one of the strongest trends in information management, the unification of relational DBMSs with object-

Executive Summary

One approach to object-oriented databases that many organizations are seriously studying brings object orientation to underlying relational technology. In contrast to "pure" OODBMSs (products and environments constructed from scratch without considering relatively mature relational technology), this unified approach attempts to marry the best of both approaches by providing environments that support both traditional MIS applications (e.g., transaction processing systems) and object-oriented applications.

This unification can be achieved in two ways: the *hybrid* approach, in which an object-oriented layer is "grafted" onto an underlying relational database system, and the *extended relational approach*, in which

oriented principles and constructs. Unlike OODBMSs created from scratch, which are a strong force in their own right (we'll discuss them in Chapter 10), the primary motivation for the unified approach is to avoid the problem that arose when relational DBMSs first became commercially available in the early 1980s. This was the extreme difficulty in migrating corporate and organizational mission-critical applications from hierarchical database, network database, or flat file environments into the newer relational technology. In fact, as noted in Chapter 1, the vast majority of organizational data center information is still stored in IMS, VSAM files, or similar non-relational structures (and usually managed through heavily patched COBOL, FORTRAN, PL/I, and assembly language programs).

By incorporating the next generation of information management paradigms—object orientation—into an existing, accepted database model, the argument goes, the migration path toward full utilization of the new technologies will be significantly easier than past paradigm shifts (e.g., hierarchical or network to relational).

It should be noted that the merits of this unifying approach are the subject of a great deal of debate among DBMS authorities. Some argue that relational DBMS engines are ill suited for object-oriented extensions, that the baggage of relational systems impedes performance and the ability to incorporate object-oriented capabilities, such as inheritance and encapsulation.

The counterargument is that while "pure" OODBMS products may indeed offer a cleaner base on which to build a DBMS engine, the lessons learned from the paradigm shift of the mid-1980s to relational systems (which, as we noted, is still occurring) have forced the information systems community to avoid technology implementations that require discarding a large portion of an installed computer and communications base. That is, the unified relational object orientation is pushed into the database server. The latter option is achieved by facilities such as adding abstract data types (ADTs) to the primitive data typing common to most relational systems. Database language support is expected to be provided primarily by the SQL3 Major Object-Oriented SQL Extensions (MOOSE), discussed in section 12.4.2 of Chapter 12.

What This Technology Can Do for You

There are many reasons why typical information systems organizations cannot simply forsake extensive investments in relational technology in favor of object-oriented databases and information management. For one thing, the OODBMS market is relatively immature in comparison

object-oriented approach is more suitable than its pure OODBMS counterpart to phased migration and transition efforts from a relational base.

With this background in mind, we'll turn our attention to object-oriented information built onto a relational base. First, we'll look at two different approaches to unifying the two data management models. Next, we'll look at the technologies and issues of this unification. Finally, we'll look at other ways in which object orientation and relational database technology are merged (e.g., accessing relational databases from object-oriented languages such as C++ and Smalltalk).

9.2 Hybrid Versus Extended Relational Approaches

Figure 9-1 illustrates two different approaches to relational/object-oriented unification.[2] *Hybrid DBMSs* incorporate a relational DBMS engine just as regular relational products do but provide an object-oriented front-end layer against which applications can interact as if they were working with a pure OODBMS product.

The other approach, more technologically advanced and favored by most relational DBMS vendors today, is the *extended relational* approach in which the DBMS engine itself is extended with object-oriented capabilities (e.g., inheritance, abstract data types, and so on). Within hybrid DBMSs, mapping algorithms from the objects at the front end to underlying relational tables must be accomplished, and the objects must be reconstituted from their table-based storage when requested by users or applications (Figure 9-2).

to the relational database market; engine technology, tools and utilities, and other aspects still need to evolve.

Further, many "traditional" types of applications may very well be best served through relational database server technology. Such applications include MIS systems where high-throughput transaction processing occurs (e.g., banking, inventory management).

The norm for most organizations today is a multiple data manager, multiple data model environment. The bulk of the legacy applications still run on IMS databases or in VSAM files, while department systems use relational technology. By attempting to "extend" the relational systems with object-oriented capabilities, organizations can avoid supporting yet another data model that has little in common with its ancestors.

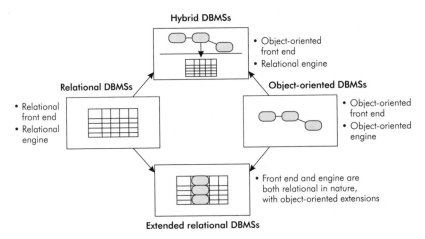

Figure 9-1 DBMS Approaches: Relational, Object-Oriented, Hybrid, and Extended Relational[3]

While hybrid DBMSs provide applications with an object-oriented view of the underlying database environment (and help with the application development and maintenance productivity problem), run-time performance often suffers because of the constant need for mapping algorithms from the front end–based objects to underlying "real" table-based information. Nevertheless, this approach was popular in the late 1980s, not so much in commercial DBMS products (though some systems did reach the market with this type of architecture) as in CASE, CAD, repositories, and similar environments that

Though the unified approach seems to provide the most straightforward evolutionary path from relational technology to object-oriented systems for applications that require complex data types and so on, many questions remain regarding the effectiveness of this unification. OODBMS vendors claim that relational technology is ill-suited for engine-based extension, that in fact database engine development from scratch is the best way to achieve OODB functionality. Many relational proponents decry the "corrupting" of the relational model with object-oriented capabilities, arguing that extensions in the relational model should conform to the spirit and mathematical foundations of that model. Quite simply, then, this seemingly benign, "wonderful" approach is not universally acclaimed as the next great advance in data management.

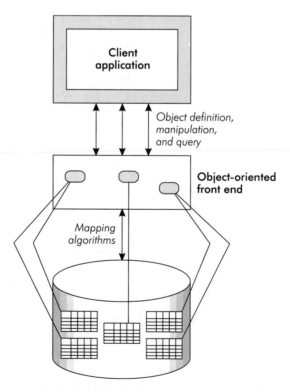

Figure 9-2 Object Management and Reconstitution under a Hybrid DBMS Approach

The hybrid approach discussed in this chapter (providing a mapping layer between the programming language and the underlying relational DBMS) may present the best opportunity for organizations to dabble in the unified approach, helping them determine not only what database characteristics are best suited for their future information needs but also what types of applications are needed.

A number of technical problems still need to be solved in the extended relational approach, but as solutions are found, products based on the resulting models may provide the foundation for much of the high-speed multimedia storage and transmission envisioned in the Information Highway of the year 2000.

utilized a relational storage manager and provided users and applications with non-relational interfaces.

On the other hand, the extended relational approach is *not* achieved simply through the incorporation of capabilities such as BLOBs (*binary large objects*, or large-capacity data types with no structure), triggers, stored procedures, and other advanced relational features. While one could argue that the capability to handle irregular data types (e.g., something other than character, integer, floating point, dates, and similar standard data types) and to attach procedural logic to a database is a strong step toward object orientation, it is still far away from abstract data types and database operations— "real" object-oriented capabilities (Figure 9-3).

Figure 9-4 illustrates a database structure suitable for an extended relational database environment.

9.2.1 Uses and Trends of the Hybrid and Extended Relational Approaches

At first glance, the hybrid and extended relational approaches appear to offer the same solutions, bringing object-oriented capabilities to relational data stores. There are some differences, though.[4]

While extended relational databases are a more sophisticated approach (object functionality is pushed into the server), problems still exist in getting "objectified" data into and out of client memory when traditional programming languages are used. Absent programming language or other application development constructs capable of handling complex data types, server-based objectification provides only a minimal level of incremental benefits.

Initial Extended Relational Capabilities

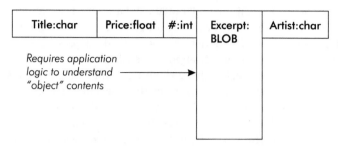

Title:char	Price:float	#:int	Excerpt: BLOB	Artist:char

Requires application logic to understand "object" contents ⟶

Extended Relational with Object-Oriented Capabilities

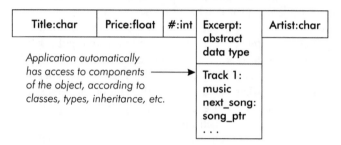

Title:char	Price:float	#:int	Excerpt: abstract data type	Artist:char

Application automatically has access to components of the object, according to classes, types, inheritance, etc. ⟶

Track 1:
music
next_song:
song_ptr
. . .

Figure 9-3 Different Levels of Extended Relational Capabilities

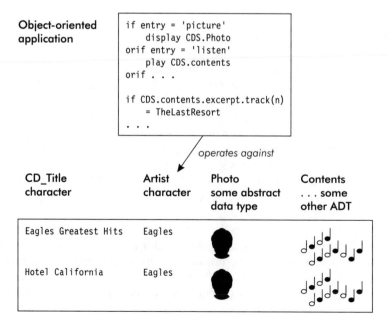

Object-oriented application

```
if entry = 'picture'
     display CDS.Photo
orif entry = 'listen'
     play CDS.contents
orif . . .

if CDS.contents.excerpt.track(n)
    = TheLastResort
. . .
```

operates against

CD_Title character	Artist character	Photo some abstract data type	Contents . . . some other ADT
Eagles Greatest Hits	Eagles		
Hotel California	Eagles		

Figure 9-4 Example of Extended Relational Database

The hybrid approach (using an object-oriented layer between a programming language and a traditional relational database server) serves an important purpose in one area in particular. Throughout the 1990s, we are likely to see environments in which developers need to do sophisticated systems programming in object-oriented languages such as C++ or Smalltalk. By "sophisticated" we mean that such development cannot be done in a 4GL or traditional MIS language (e.g., COBOL), and the object orientation of C++ and Smalltalk provides far greater productivity than C, Ada, or other languages. However, in many of these environments the developers *must* use an underlying relational data store. The hybrid approach provides (or attempts to provide) the transparent layer between an object-oriented programming language (OOPL) and the relational data store, even when object-oriented capabilities aren't available in the database server.

Products for the hybrid approach will likely evolve in the following direction: object-oriented layers under which many different relational database servers can reside (e.g., mix-and-match middleware) will dominate, probably from independent third-party (e.g., non-DBMS vendor) suppliers. It is *possible* that the market may fade near the end of the 1990s as extended relational systems become more commonplace, but the realities of legacy systems handling lead us to believe that many organizations will still be relying on hybrid layer middleware to provide converged OODBMS and RDBMS capabilities in their organizations.

9.3 Extended Relational Languages

Providing an extended relational engine, capable of supporting not only traditional data types and database operations but also complex data types and objectlike operations, is just the first step. There must also be a way to access these capabilities from application programs or in a querylike manner from the command line (or from a graphical user interface). As hybrid solutions entered the marketplace in the late 1980s, object-oriented extensions to SQL were provided by vendors. Like the original incarnations of SQL among relational products, or the object manipulation and definition facilities of pure OODBMS products, these extensions were proprietary in nature, varying from product to product.

In Chapter 12, we'll discuss the future directions of SQL, particularly the Major Object-Oriented SQL Extensions (MOOSE) of the SQL3 standard currently under development. The primary purpose of MOOSE is to provide a standards-based framework for RDBMS vendors as they add object-oriented capabilities to their SQL-based products; rather than allowing each vendor to do this independently, the extensions would be standardized in language syntax and underlying concepts. In section 12.4.2 of Chapter 12, we'll discuss MOOSE in detail, giving examples of data definition and manipulation statements as proposed for the SQL3 standard.

9.4 Object-Oriented Languages and SQL

So far, our discussion has focused on relational databases and languages as the legacy side of an organization's information management environment, the goal being the incorporation of object-oriented databases into that environment. The flip side to this model is applicable to organizations that have made heavy use of pure OODBMS products in their environment and subsequently wish to utilize SQL.

In an object-oriented program (written in a language such as C++ or Smalltalk), a series of classes may be declared that can subsequently be mapped into relational tables, as in the following:[5]

```
Merchandise (MNum, MTitle, MCost, MPrice, MDescription,...)
Store (StoreID, StoreName, StoreAddress, StoreManager,...)
Employee (EID, EName, ESalary,...)
```

Within the body of an object-oriented program, EXEC SQL embedded statements may be used, through which standard SQL statements (e.g., SELECT ... INTO ...) provide the data manipulation capabilities. Methods may be invoked by putting SQL statements within a function, as in[6]

```
void add_inventory (int num, char* title, float cost,...)
{
SQLTable MerchandiseTable (SchemaInfo (db,"MERCH_TABLE"));
MerchandiseTable["MNUM"]=num;
MerchandiseTable["MTITLE"]=title;
MerchandiseTable["MCOST"]=cost;
...
MerchandiseTable.Insert();
}
```

With this code sequence, a method ADD_INVENTORY can be created to add a new row to the relational database table MERCHANDISE. In terms of functionality, this is equivalent to the capabilities of an OODBMS.

Note that as object-oriented capabilities are added to the engines of relational databases, the object-oriented language-to-RDBMS interfaces will achieve greater robustness (Figure 9-5). With basic RDBMS engines, classes

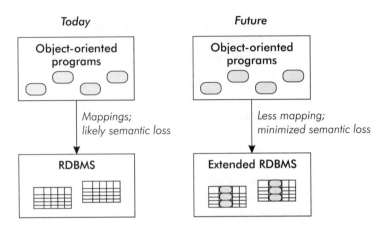

Figure 9-5 Likely Evolution of Object-Oriented Language-to-RDBMS Interfaces

declared and used within the object-oriented programming language must be mapped to the underlying relational tables, which often results in semantic loss due to the inability of the RDBMS to adequately represent hierarchies, inheritance, methods and operations, and other object-oriented capabilities (we discussed semantic loss in section 8.2 of Chapter 8). As the RDBMSs themselves add these capabilities, the degree of mapping will be reduced, resulting in a *higher* degree of semantic equivalence (but probably not 100%) than we have today between the OOPL and the RDBMS. Some degree of semantic loss is inevitable when the underlying database has to serve multiple needs and views. An inherent tension exists between flexibility (the ability to serve multiple needs) and the semantic loss that is inevitably present, unless the entire application, absent screen and display components, is pushed into the database through stored procedures and the like.[7]

9.5 Conclusion

In this chapter, we've taken a look at one of the directions object-oriented databases are heading, in which object-oriented capabilities are added to relational DBMS engines. The first attempts at this relational/object-oriented unification was hybrid in nature, based on the coupling of an object-oriented front end with a traditional RDBMS. It is only in recent years that the engines themselves have been extended with inheritance, encapsulation, methods, and other object-oriented capabilities. This second, later trend will no doubt continue, as nearly every RDBMS vendor (as of 1993) is working on extending primitive object-oriented capabilities (e.g., BLOBS, triggers, and stored procedures) into abstract data types and other object-oriented facets.

Finally, we looked at a third model of unifying relational and object-oriented technology, which uses object-oriented programming languages with underlying RDBMSs. This approach has some limitations today that are basically the same as in the hybrid approach to model unification: whether the object-oriented layer is incorporated into the programming language (e.g., C++) on top of a standard RDBMS, or a standard 3GL (e.g., C or COBOL) is used to interface with an object-oriented layer which in turn is mapped to a standard RDBMS, a degree of mapping and likely semantic loss is involved. For the relational world to truly approach (some would say "encroach") the object-oriented world, the products themselves must be given engine-based object-oriented capabilities. This effort has begun in earnest among vendors and in standards-based languages (via SQL3 and MOOSE), and it will be a dominant trend throughout the rest of the 1990s.

Outlook

Short-term

- Relational database engines will incorporate abstract data types, stored procedures, triggers, inheritance, and other objectlike capabilities
- Object-oriented programs will further incorporate access to relational databases
- SQL will incorporate object-oriented constructs (see Chapter 12)

Long-term

- A closer coupling of relational and object-oriented technologies; relational engines tuned for object-oriented performance

Additional Reading

- M. E. S. Loomis, "Moving Objects into Relational Systems," *Proceedings of the Database World & Client/Server World,* Vol. I (June 14, 1993).
- "Third-Generation Data Base System Manifesto," *Proceedings IFIP WG2.6 Conference on Object Oriented Databases,* Windermere, England, July 1990.
- S. Varma, "An OODBMS Venn Diagram," *Database Programming & Design* (May 1993), 63.

Endnotes

1. "Third-Generation Data Base System Manifesto," *Proceedings IFIP WG2.6 Conference on Object Oriented Databases*, Windermere, England, July 1990. See section 1.6.1 of Chapter 1 for a complete discussion of this document.

2. S. Varma, "An OODBMS Venn Diagram," *Database Programming & Design* (May 1993), 63.

3. Varma, "An OODBMS Venn Diagram."

4. J. Stein, private communication, November 1993.

5. M. E. S. Loomis, "Moving Objects into Relational Systems," *Proceedings of the Database World & Client/Server World*, Vol. I (June 14, 1993), D5-7.

6. Loomis, "Moving Objects."

7. J. Stein, private communication, November 1993.

CHAPTER

Object-Oriented
Engines and Models

A Note to the CIO

An alternative approach to object orientation involves OODBMS products "started from scratch," apart from a relational foundation. You may be in the position of choosing between the "pure" and unification approaches as object-oriented technology is added to data management; therefore, you need to understand not only the roots of this "pure" OODBMS approach but also where the discipline is headed, including Object Database Management Group efforts and advanced OODB capabilities.

10.1 Introduction

In Chapter 9, we discussed what is arguably the most significant future direction of OODB: unifying object-oriented models with their relational predecessors.

This doesn't mean, though, that "pure" OODBMS products—which grew out of the research stage into commercial systems without accounting for a legacy of relational applications or database structures—can be considered old technology that will eventually fade from the scene. Rather, several interesting trends in this area are occurring, including the following:

- Standardization
- Enhanced levels of distribution
- Incorporation of relational facilities (e.g., SQL interfaces)

Executive Summary

In contrast to the relational/object-oriented unification approach discussed in Chapter 9, the other OODBMS approach has focused on development of OODBMS engines from scratch. Historically, the roots of this approach are in the "Object-Oriented Database System Manifesto," a scholarly document that advocated the "pure" OODBMS approach and attempted to consolidate terminology and concepts for OODBMS development.

Arguably the most noteworthy event from a commercial standpoint is the publication of the ODMG-93 standard by the Object Database Management Group (ODMG), a group of OODBMS vendors. This document is expected to become a de facto standard for products, both new and evolving.

In this chapter, we'll discuss the standardization efforts under the guidance of the Object Database Management Group (ODMG) as well as developments in the area of distribution models for object-oriented systems. First, though, let's take a brief look at the history of this "member" of the OODB/OODBMS family.

10.2 The Object-Oriented Database System Manifesto

Recall that in section 1.6.2 of Chapter 1 we introduced the 1989 publication "The Object-Oriented Database System Manifesto."[1] The appearance of this document occurred around the same time as the "Third-Generation Data Base System Manifesto" (discussed in section 1.6.1), which views the incorporation of object orientation into the database environment as an extension of second-generation (e.g., relational) DBMS products and architectures.

"The Object-Oriented Database System Manifesto," in contrast, takes the view that object-oriented databases and DBMSs need not be constrained by a relational legacy, that in fact the research systems under development and their eventual successors should utilize the most appropriate technological foundations possible, regardless of concerns for existing systems and environments.

At the time the paper was written (August 19, 1989), it was noted by the authors that[2]

1) Unlike the relational model, which had been introduced with Dr. E. F. Codd's 1970 paper and which had a formal mathematical foundation, the

What This Technology Can Do for You

Many organizations will likely choose to develop complex department-class information systems using OODB technology, using "pure" OODBMS products rather than extended relational systems (see Chapter 9). Therefore, an understanding of where the OODBMS market is headed is important for long-term systems maintenance and evolution. Particularly, an understanding of the ODMG-93 standard, both in its current form and in stated goals, will help decision makers in this area. See Chapter 13 for further discussion of the ODMG-93 standard.

object-oriented model had no common data model or formal foundation (a point we noted in section 8.6 and which we'll discuss in this chapter in the context of standardization efforts).

2) OODBMSs at the time were primarily based on experimental activity. The paper's authors noted that even though this meant theoretical concepts were actually put into practice, there was an associated risk that whichever system was first on the commercial market would become the de facto standard, regardless of long-term technical merits.

The stated goal of the Manifesto was to refine terminology rather than standardize languages.[3] That is, unlike the ODMG authors, who concentrated on both terminology (e.g., concepts) and languages, the Manifesto authors thought it appropriate in 1989 to stem the divergence of concepts from one experimental system to another. They believed language standardization could come later, just as SQL as a standard language with multivendor support came years after relational databases began appearing in research laboratories.

The Manifesto established three categories of OODB characteristics:[4]

1) *Mandatory:* These characteristics must be satisfied in order for a system to "deserve" (the authors' word) the label of an OODB.

2) *Optional:* These improve the basic functionality of the system but aren't mandatory.

3) *Open:* A designer could choose from among equally acceptable alternatives.

The mandatory features were further grouped into two classifications:

1) The system must be a DBMS, which means that it must support

   • Persistence
   • Secondary storage management
   • Concurrency
   • Recovery
   • Ad hoc query facilities

   (These are well-defined functions with which readers of this book should be familiar, so no further discussion is presented.)

2) The system must be an OODBMS, which means that it must have the following eight features:

   • Complex objects
   • Object identity
   • Encapsulation
   • Types or classes
   • Inheritance
   • Overriding combined with late binding
   • Computational completeness
   • Extensibility

We have discussed the first five features; in the sixth, *overriding and late binding*, the same name might be used for different operations (e.g., *display* will operate differently for voice, video, still image, or text data). By overriding, or redefining, names, different operations for these different data types could still be given the same name. To support this, compile time binding of operation names to programs is not suitable; it must be done at run time (*late binding*).

Computational completeness means that the data manipulation language (DML) of an OODBMS must be capable of expressing any computable function, instead of passing such functions to a host language.

Finally, *extensibility* means that any set of predefined types must be capable of supplementation by user-defined types, with no difference between the predefined and the user-defined types (at least to the application developer).

The optional features are further classified into object-oriented (multiple inheritance, for example) and other, more general, aspects. These include[5]

1) *Multiple inheritance:* Multiple inheritance was deemed optional because of the lack of general agreement on two points: whether multiple inheritance should be supported by an OODBMS product, and, more importantly, how conflicts should be resolved in such environments. An example of a conflict is the inheritance of two like-named operations, each with different semantics (Figure 10-1).

- The *Register* operation means different things for an employee and some outside person

- Since both employees and outside people (customers, suppliers) may shop at the video store, and different policies (discounts, return policies, etc.) may be in effect for people of different types, the *Register* operation conflict must be resolved

- Not all operations are inherited by the subclass, and these conflicts must be resolved as well

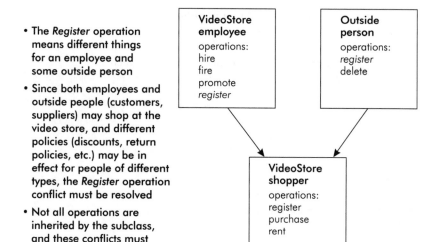

Figure 10-1 Multiple Inheritance and Conflicts

2) *Type checking and type inferencing:* The more type checking that occurs at compile time, the better the environment is. However, the Manifesto leaves open whether this occurs and the degree to which such compile-time type checking is accomplished.

3) *Distribution:* The discussion of distributed database technologies in Part II of this book applies to object-oriented databases too.

4) *Design transactions: Design transaction* is the term used by the Manifesto authors to mean either long transactions (discussed in Chapter 11) or nested transactions (discussed in Chapter 20); basically, short-duration, flat transactions common to today's information systems aren't suitable for many OODB environments (though they can be used for some).

5) *Versions:* A means to maintain multiple versions of objects is highly desirable.

Finally, the open features for which multiple options exist include[6]

1) *Programming paradigm:* A developer should be able to utilize any paradigm he or she wishes to, whether procedural, declarative, rule-based, and so on.

2) *Representation system:* The atomic types (from programming languages) and constructors (set, list, and tuple constructors) may be extended in many different ways to support the object orientation.

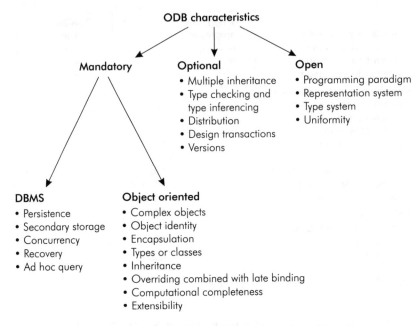

Figure 10-2 Summary of Object-Oriented Database Manifesto Features

3) *Type system:* Aside from encapsulation, "type formers" such as generic types and type generators, restriction, union, and functions are all optional.

4) *Uniformity:* The Manifesto proposes a three-level architecture (implementation, programming language, and interface) at which questions such as "Is a type an object?" may be given different answers, depending on the context in which the question is asked.

And so we have the turn-of-the-decade effort to apply some degree of formality and commonality to OODBs and OODBMSs; Figure 10-2 summarizes the highlights of the Object-Oriented Database System Manifesto. Where have these efforts led? In the next section, we'll discuss the efforts of the Object Database Management Group (ODMG).

10.3 The ODMG Standardization Effort

In the previous section, as well as in section 8.6 of Chapter 8, we noted that the lack of standards and model formality has been a hindrance to the widespread adoption of OODBMS technology among users (estimates for 1992 total industry revenue range from $25 million to $33 million).[7] This fact was noted by vendors, and an organization known as the Object Database Management Group (ODMG) came into existence in late 1991 to resolve these problems. The ODMG goal was to provide portability for[8]

- Data schemas
- Programming language bindings
- Data manipulation languages
- Query languages

In short, applications portability is a goal of the ODMG effort. The ODMG expects its member companies (Versant, Objectivity, Servio, and others) to support its standard in their respective products, which makes the ODMG proposal a de facto standard for the OODBMS industry.

The ODMG effort is not intended to result in identical OODBMS products,[9] any more than standardization of SQL as the "official" RDBMS language resulted in identical RDBMS products from Ingres, Oracle, IBM, Digital Equipment, and the many other relational product vendors. Indeed, just as RDBMS vendors' respective products differ dramatically from one another in terms of language extensions and similar areas, in the late 1990s OODBMS vendors will conceivably need their own version of the SQL Access Group (see Chapter 3)—perhaps the ODMG Access Group?—to reconcile product differences that will have evolved.

So what is in the ODMG standard? In the next section we'll look at the basics and characteristics.

10.4 ODMG Contents

The ODMG defines an OODBMS as "a DBMS that integrates database capabilities with object programming language capabilities."[10] With an OODBMS, database objects are indistinguishable from programming language objects; the OODBMS is used to extend the language with transparently persistent data, concurrency control, associative queries, and other database capabilities.[11]

ODMG defines an object model, conceptually similar to the relational model on which RDBMSs are based (the terminological and conceptual differences among products and systems noted in Chapter 8 are unified under the ODMG object model).

As might be expected, the basic modeling primitive is an object, and objects can be categorized into types. Object behavior is defined by a set of operations, and the state of any given object is defined by the values of a set of properties. Properties, in turn, may be either attributes of that given object, or relationships between that object and one or more other objects. Figure 10-3 summarizes the object model.

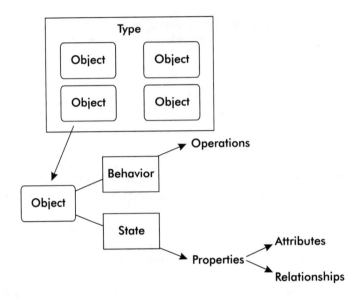

Figure 10-3 ODMG Summary

Each type has one interface, as well as one or more implementations. The *interface* is used by external agents (e.g., an application program) to get and store values, traverse relationships, and perform other object-oriented functions. *Implementation* defines the actual physical representation of a type instance, as well as the methods (operations) that operate on those data structures.[12]

ODMG types are objects as well, and they may have attributes and participate in relationships. The interfaces of types specify values of *type properties*, such as supertypes and extents.[13]

Supertypes are part of the "standard" object-oriented model, in that subtypes inherit relationships, attributes, and operations from a supertype. An *extent* is the "set of all instances of a given type"[14] and provides a means by which the developer ("type programmer" in ODMG language) can request that a current index to all members of a set be maintained by the system. Extents are optional and may be specified (or not) depending on whether such set maintenance is deemed useful to the applications and users of that system.

In the ODMG model, the supertype/subtype system is used to supply inheritance from a supertype to objects of a declared subtype. An instance of a subtype may be treated in the same manner as an instance of each of its supertypes; that is, all state and behavioral information of the supertype is inherited by the subtype.[15]

Abstract types, which define the characteristics but *not* the implementations inherited by their subtypes, are not directly instantiable. Abstract types might be viewed as templates; a type programmer who wants to instantiate a subtype of that abstract type must first define an implementation that supports the inherited characteristics.[16] Alternatively, some types are directly instantiable. In the base ODMG model, only object types have user-definable implementations; property and operation types do not.[17] Such a user-definable implementation (which has a name, unique within the scope defined by that type) consists of the following:[18]

- A *representation*, which is a set of data structures.

- A set of *methods*, or procedure bodies; one method is assigned for each operation defined in the specification.[19]

Taken together, the type interface specification and *one* of the implementations defined for that type (multiple implementations may be defined, in accordance with mixed-language and mixed-system environments[20]) are known in ODMG as a *class*.

In accordance with basic object-oriented principles of object identity, an immutable *object identifier* is used to distinguish any given object from all other objects within the object's domain.[21] To meet one of the goals of object orientation—to readily represent the real world—an object name may be assigned to an individual object; in fact, more than one symbolic name may be given to an object, if so desired.[22]

The ODMG model supports three different lifetimes of an object:[23]

- *Coterminus_with_procedure:* Objects with this lifetime have storage allocated when a procedure is invoked, but that storage is released when the procedure returns to its caller.

- *Coterminus_with_process:* Objects with this lifetime are allocated by a programming language run time for the duration of a process.

- *Coterminus_with_database:* Objects with this lifetime come from the OODBMS run time.

The many other characteristics and properties of the ODMG model are discussed in some of the books recommended for additional reading at the end of the chapter.

10.5 ODMG Languages

The ODMG standard includes recommendations for three different types of object-oriented languages:

- *An Object Definition Language*, or ODL, which is conceptually identical to a relational or CODASYL data definition language (DDL).

- *An Object Manipulation Language*, or OML, which is like a data manipulation language (DML) in a relational or network DBMS.

- *An Object Query Language*, or OQL, which addresses one of the major shortcomings of OODBMSs—the lack of query language facilities in most systems and products.

In Chapter 13, we'll look at an example of each of these three ODMG languages. Again, for more detail, refer to the list of additional readings at the end of this chapter.

As a final note, although ODMG is separate from the Object Management Group (OMG, discussed in Chapter 11), much of the ODMG work is being done in the context of OMG efforts.[24] Decision makers and information system planners keep current with the efforts of both groups.

10.6 Conclusion

In this chapter, we've traced the background and evolution of standards for pure OODBMS environments, from its roots in the academic community (the "Object-Oriented Database System Manifesto" of 1989–1990) to the vendor-based standardization effort called ODMG that will drive its progress for the rest of the 1990s.

Significantly, the relatively small market for OODBMS products (compared to networking and communications products and relational DBMSs) has motivated OODBMS vendors. Many of these vendors have been around in one form or another since the mid-1980s, and they are anxious to see growth in their own shares of the OODBMS market and the market as a whole. Learning from the lessons of the early 1980s about relational DBMS products and the effects of "pseudo-standardization" in that market (one RDBMS was conceptually similar though not identical to another RDBMS product; the terminology was mostly the same, and SQL-based products came from the same roots), OODBMS vendors no doubt look at the market size and see the merits of cooperation, unifying the concepts and interfaces from one product to another. Even if OODBMS vendors wished to take a more proprietary approach to their marketplace, they could ill afford to do so. The incorporation of object-oriented capabilities into SQL (discussed in more detail in Chapter 12) and relational/object-oriented databases would likely have forced OODBMS vendors into cooperative arrangements anyway.

To survive in the tough information management marketplace of the 1990s, ODMG will have to play an important role in the development of nearly every OODBMS product in the marketplace. One of the goals of the ODMG is to construct a common framework for OODBMS products that will increase the usability—and the underlying technology— of the product for prospective users. This is especially important now that a shakeout, of the kind seen in nearly every other information systems area since computer systems became commercially viable, will likely occur, leaving a relatively small number of OODBMS vendors in the marketplace by the end of the 1990s. Hopefully, ODMG compliance will help protect any applications bases that are developed using the OODBMS product of a vendor who stops manufacturing that product. At least some portion of the application code base and data structures should be salvageable to be ported to another ODMG product.

RDBMS vendors have recognized that their products are increasingly used as commodities, and their tools, utilities, interfaces, and applications are successful in the marketplace today for reasons beyond raw performance, storage efficiency, or similar mid-1980s' "buying factors." OODBMS vendors similarly realize that their products are edging toward commodity status. By the end of the 1990s, if not sooner, the OODBMS vendors will be commodity-driven, with one OODBMS engine virtually indistinguishable from another *from the user's perspective.* Storage models, benchmarking figures, and the like will play a minor role only, in contrast to provided type libraries, interfaces with development tools and generators, and other more important decision factors.

Outlook

Short-term

- ODMG standard will influence the direction of OODBMS products
- C++ and Smalltalk will be extended with ODMG-driven constructs for more robust development environments (see Chapter 13)
- Distribution will be more pervasive in OODB environments

Long-term

- ODMG will be extended; additional compliant products will appear in the commercial marketplace
- Distributed ODMG-compliant databases will be commonplace

Additional Reading

- M. Atkinson, F. Bancilhon, D. DeWitt, K. Dittrich, D. Maier, and S. Zdonik, "The Object-Oriented Database System Manifesto," *Proceedings of Deductive and Object-oriented Databases*, Kyoto, Japan, December 1989. This document will provide some historical perspective on the OODBMS camp's directions.

- B. D. Bowen, "Staking Out the OODBMS Territory," *Open Systems Today* (July 5, 1993).
- R. G. G. Cattell, ed., *The Object Database Standard: ODMG-93* (San Francisco: Morgan Kaufmann Publishers, 1994).
- S. Varma, "Objects and Databases: Where Are We Now?," *Database Programming & Design* (May 1993).

Endnotes

1. M. Atkinson, F. Bancilhon, D. DeWitt, K. Dittrich, D. Maier, and S. Zdonik, "The Object-Oriented Database System Manifesto," *Proceedings of Deductive and Object-Oriented Databases*, Kyoto, Japan, December 1989.

2. Atkinson et al., "Object-Oriented Database," 2.

3. Atkinson et al., "Object-Oriented Database."

4. Atkinson et al., "Object-Oriented Database," 2–3.

5. Atkinson et al., "Object-Oriented Database," 12–13.

6. Atkinson et al., "Object-Oriented Database," 13–14.

7. S. Varma, "Objects and Databases: Where Are We Now?," *Database Programming & Design* (May 1993), 63. B. D. Bowen, "Staking Out the OODBMS Territory," *Open Systems Today* (July 5, 1993), SF8.

8. R. G. G. Cattell, ed., *The Object Database Standard: ODMG-93* (San Francisco: Morgan Kaufmann Publishers, 1994), 2.

9. Cattell, ed., *ODMG-93*.

10. Cattell, ed., *ODMG-93, 3*.

11. Cattell, ed., *ODMG-93*.

12. Cattell, ed., *ODMG-93, 12*.

13. Cattell, ed., *ODMG-93*.

14. Cattell, ed., *ODMG-93*.

15. Cattell, ed., *ODMG-93, 14*.

16. Cattell, ed., *ODMG-93*.

17. Cattell, ed., *ODMG-93, 15*.

18. Cattell, ed., *ODMG-93*.

19. See Chapter 13 for examples of ODMG Object Definition Language (ODL) specifications.

20. Cattell, ed., *ODMG-93, 15*.

21. Cattell, ed., *ODMG-93, 17*.

22. Cattell, ed., *ODMG-93*.

23. Cattell, ed., *ODMG-93*, 19.

24. F. Manola, private communication. And Cattell, *ODMG-93*, 5, Appendix A.

CHAPTER 11

Other Issues in Object-Oriented Information Management

A Note to the CIO

This chapter will deal with corollary issues in object-oriented information management, such as transaction management, object request broker architectures, and other topics that must be considered in your decision to incorporate object-oriented technology into your environments. For example, you may find yourself utilizing object-oriented

11.1 Introduction

In Chapters 8, 9, and 10, we've looked at the background and directions of object-oriented information management, specifically object-oriented databases. In this chapter, we'll discuss a few other topics related to object-oriented information management:

- Transaction models
- Security
- Object request brokers (ORBs)

We'll wrap up our discussion by taking a look at the future directions of object-oriented information management.

wrappers, which may be CORBA-compliant, to encapsulate legacy applications and permit intercomponent communications in an object-oriented manner. Further, the transaction models applicable to OODBMSs may be different in terms of duration and other characteristics than those of hierarchical, network, or relational systems. In short, determining an object-oriented information management strategy for your organization will include making decisions about the topics discussed in this chapter.

Executive Summary

In addition to the two major camps of OODBMS engines (discussed in Chapters 9 and 10), other areas in object-oriented information management must be considered, including the following:

11.2 Transaction Processing for Object-Oriented Environments

In Chapter 20, we'll discuss the future of transaction processing in information management. In object-oriented environments, transactions tend to be of a longer duration than in traditional database or file system environments (Figure 11-1). This characteristic is primarily due to the types of operations that use object-oriented databases: computer-aided design (CAD), computer-aided software engineering (CASE), repository management, and so on. Transactions performed within an OODBMS environment might be of as short a duration as those in relational environments; nothing precludes such a paradigm, particularly if "relational-like" data (e.g., salary information, inventory control) are stored within the OODB. Object-oriented environments, though, must be capable of supporting a wider variety of transaction durations than their relational counterparts, due to the likelihood of complex data being managed within such an environment.

Vendors and research programs have tried many different approaches to manage long transactions, just as they have used different OODBMSs. The exact direction that transaction models for object-oriented environments will take is unclear, though surely some robust, extended transaction model will play a role in this area. For example, at Brown University,[1] research focuses on the development of a *cooperative transaction model*, in which the transaction principle of *atomicity* (the all-or-nothing illusion of a transaction, discussed in section 20.3 of Chapter 20) is relaxed, forming groups of transactions that can then be nested into a *cooperative transaction hierarchy*.

- *Transaction processing models:* The complex applications for which OODBMSs might be used typically involve cooperative workgroup and workflow paradigms; further, commit protocols, object visibility rules, and other characteristics would likely require modification to adequately support such environments.

- *Security models:* The same principles of multilevel security developed in relational database environments have made their way into object-oriented databases, although state of the art in the OODBMS arena lags somewhat behind that of relational databases for reasons we will discuss in Chapter 21.

- *Distributed object management:* This topic includes the use of object request brokers (ORBs) to encapsulate legacy system components and provide object movement among department- or corporationwide systems.

Traditional transaction processing environment

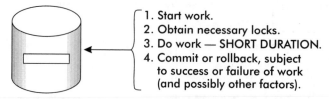

1. Start work.
2. Obtain necessary locks.
3. Do work — SHORT DURATION.
4. Commit or rollback, subject to success or failure of work (and possibly other factors).

Long transactions in an object-oriented environment

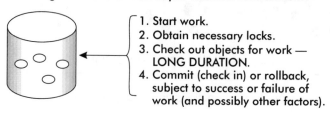

1. Start work.
2. Obtain necessary locks.
3. Check out objects for work — LONG DURATION.
4. Commit (check in) or rollback, subject to success or failure of work (and possibly other factors).

Figure 11-1 Transaction Processing in Traditional and Object-Oriented Environments

    Here's an example of a cooperative transaction model.[2] A typical design environment might have three, four, or some other number of individual module types (e.g., *Customer_Mg, Inventory_Mg,* and *Storage_Mg,* in a video store system under development). Designing a system can be a time-consuming process, so a cooperative transaction for each major design change over the

What This Technology Can Do for You

Though many database planners who want object orientation focus on object-oriented DBMS products (we discussed the two approaches in Chapters 9 and 10), object-oriented information management encompasses much more than OODBMS engines. The work of the Object Management Group (OMG) on object request brokers (ORBs) will likely provide facilities to encapsulate and deliver legacy systems into an environment of distributed object sharing.

Likewise, as we'll discuss further in Chapter 20, traditional transaction processing (TP) models that have matured in centralized environments don't scale well to distributed environments, particularly widely distributed ones. Therefore, long-held notions of classic transaction processing will have to evolve to support environments with a high degree of cooperative workgroup and workflow processing, where traditional

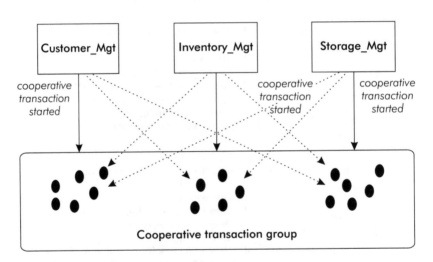

Figure 11-2 Cooperative Transactions and Groups

life of the development may be started by the developers involved. These cooperative transactions are members of a *transaction group*, which may read and modify uncommitted object versions of other members (Figure 11-2).

Members of a transaction group work together to do some logical unit of work—known as a *task*—which may be further decomposed into *subtasks*. A given cooperative transaction is responsible for a particular subtask, and it must maintain local state information about that subtask. Since atomicity is relaxed, a given cooperative transaction need not preserve the global consis-

locking algorithms, commit protocols, and other TP components don't function well.

Finally, database security, an area in which commercial relational systems are finally catching up with the government's visions from the mid-1980s, must make its way into object orientation. As we'll note in Chapter 21, decade-old notions from the U.S. Defense Department will likely be modified as commercial security concerns overtake military ones. Given the time frame, new database and information management security models will no doubt take object-oriented databases into account.

tency in the database, which is handled by the overall set of cooperative transactions in the group. That is, once a *write* operation within a group is issued and an object written by a given cooperative transaction, the new version may be read by other cooperative transactions of that group. *Checkpoints* are used to make the effects of an operation visible outside the group; an explicit sequence of operations (known as a *pattern*) defines "correctness" for each transaction group. Once that pattern-defined correctness has been achieved, a checkpoint is issued (and may not be revoked), again making the object state changes visible outside the group. This dynamic is illustrated in Figure 11-3.

The complexity of the process of being able to define correctness shouldn't be underestimated. One technique is to use a rule-based approach; for example, if a particular interface file is modified, the implementation must also be modified; until that point, the state of the group is not correct as defined by the pattern.[3] *Conflicts* might be defined to detect such inconsistencies or even to ensure that some pair of operations occur in synchronization with one another; for example, we may modify the implementation at the time the interface is modified, but if an implementation is modified first, the interface may not need to be changed.

Additionally, automating these areas may very well prove to be necessary because conflicts occur in *semantics* (meaning) rather than *syntax*.

Regardless of the particular approach, or what types of transaction models evolve to be common, or standard, in the object-oriented information environment, it is a safe bet that some advanced level of robustness will be commonplace in this arena as OODBMSs evolve.

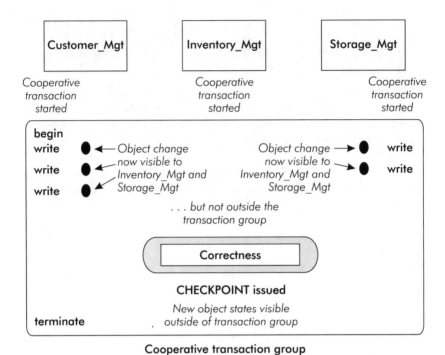

Figure 11-3 Cooperative Transaction Groups and Visibility of Changes

11.3 Distributed Object Management and Object Request Brokers

For the most part, the issues discussed in Part II of this book about distributed databases and information are directly applicable to object-oriented environments, particularly those taking the extended relational approach (as we discussed in Chapter 9). Client-server environments, partitioning and replication, and distributed warehouse environments may all utilize object-oriented models, as distribution (and possibly heterogeneity) are added to department- or corporationwide systems.

Less clear is whether object-oriented platforms are applicable to parallel database systems; as we noted in section 5.2 of Chapter 5, relational DBMSs are particularly applicable to massively parallel processing (MPP) environments. Complex data of an object-oriented variety might be less suitable to parallel query processing; further investigation needs to be done in this area.

A number of distributed object management programs are currently being researched, and many of these technologies will likely enter the commercial sector near the end of the 1990s (though CORBA-compliant products are available now). A number of these research areas were presented and discussed at the International Workshop on Distributed Object Management

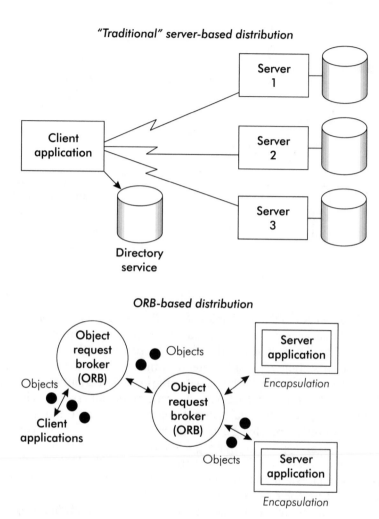

Figure 11-4 Evolution from Server-Based Distribution to ORB-Based Distribution

held in August 1992.[4] This workshop was exclusively devoted to distributed object management, and over 50 papers were received by the program committee,[5] signifying the level of interest in distributed object management.

Perhaps the most important area in distributed object management is that of object request brokers (ORBs), which we introduced in Chapter 3 in our discussion of object-oriented client/server computing. The concept of object distribution has spread not only to OODBMS environments but to nearly any information systems environment imaginable, primarily due to the work done under the direction of the Object Management Group (OMG). OMG is a nonprofit organization with nearly 300 member companies,[6] which developed the Common Object Request Broker Architecture (CORBA).

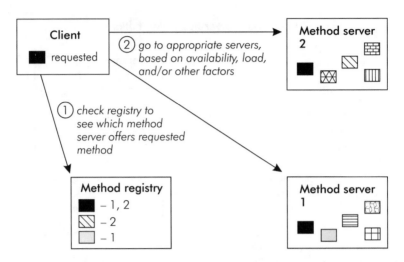

Figure 11-5 Method Registry

Before we discuss the mechanics of CORBA and its influence on distributed object management, we should draw a parallel between the principles of an ORB and the server-based model of distributed information management introduced in section 7.2.1 of Chapter 7 (which was an alternative to the approach based on a global schema with transparent distribution on top of underlying heterogeneous databases). A strong argument can be made for a server-based approach to data distribution, the advantage being a tighter degree of control of underlying data assets and implementations (in contrast to a global schema approach). That argument can be further extended into the object-oriented world via the ORB approach; that is, the basic distributed server model gives way to a semantically richer one, with encapsulation of methods under an object-based model (Figure 11-4).

The dominant architecture supporting distributed object "brokerage" is OMG's CORBA. CORBA components have been derived from Digital Equipment Corporation, Hewlett-Packard, HyperDesk, and Sun Microsystems.[7] Under a CORBA-based implementation, a server registry (basically, a directory structure) is used to match a method requested by a client application to one or more *method servers* that can supply that method (Figure 11-5).

Note that the ORB approach, in which applications are encapsulated within an object-oriented framework, is applicable not only to newly developed applications but also helps achieve the goal of incorporating legacy applications into an environment under development, either before a migration effort is completed (e.g., an interim basis) or for some longer, undetermined period (e.g., until the hardware gives out ten or more years from now). Through this approach, data management environments may be integrated with one another in much the same way as the server-based approach discussed in Chapter 7, except that the object-oriented layering through the ORB provides a pseudo–object-oriented feel not only to underlying OODBMSs but also to RDBMSs, hierarchical systems, flat file environments, and other data resource management architectures. In effect, an environment built around ORBs and method servers provides a distributed object management paradigm to the system, regardless of underlying implementations.

For organizations that have aggressively pursued server-based distributed information management, moving toward an ORB-based environment is the next logical step. Instead of traditional interfaces with demarcations between data and operations, the object paradigm implicit in an ORB system brings all of the merit of OODBMS and object-oriented programming (OOP) environments (e.g., inheritance, encapsulation, methods) to a distributed client/server environment. Even if initial implementations under such an environment take a bit longer than more traditional methodologies and techniques, subsequent development, and more importantly, system maintenance, could be accomplished much more easily in an ORB environment than in procedural client/server models, and significantly more easily than in a centralized mainframe-based environment.

11.4 Security in OODBMS Environments

In Chapter 21, we'll discuss database security at length, focusing on the trends and directions in that very important discipline of information management. For now, we'll simply state that much of the work done in the mid- and late 1980s on database security in relational environments is applicable to object-oriented environments as well.

The directions database security will take in the commercial world are unclear, however, and this is true for relational environments as well as OODBMSs. The stringent guidelines from the U.S. Department of Defense (DOD) have proved extremely difficult to implement in data management environments, and the commercial vendors will likely look at modifications of standards, such as the DOD Trusted Database Interpretation (TDI). This issue will carry over as well into object-oriented information management, which requires a great deal of further research into OODBMS security models. Because OODBMSs have been mostly absent from defense-oriented applications, vendors have had little incentive to look at security models other than basic authorization systems (e.g., the methods that a user has permission to invoke). As commercial information management security increases in importance, vendors will be forced to turn their attention to such matters, in addition to ODMG standardization and other ventures.

11.5 A Final Look at Object-Oriented Information Management

The future is object-oriented; that much is inevitable. The relational and object-oriented models are converging, as we discussed in Chapter 9. "Pure" OODBMSs have gone from objects of curiosity in research and academic institutions (with only sporadic usage in commercial organizations for special kinds of projects) to a stage positioned for tremendous growth, partially due to agreement among vendors on the importance of standardization (as we discussed in Chapter 10).

Object orientation is also growing throughout the computing world, from tremendous interest in C++ (and a resurgent interest in Smalltalk) in object-oriented programming (OOP) to operating systems, where the IBM–Apple Computer cooperative effort under the Taligent banner is dedicated to producing an object-oriented operating system.

Even legacy applications and environments aren't "safe" from object-oriented technologies, thanks to the Object Request Broker that can encapsulate existing environments to legacy environments with newly developed applications through an object-oriented interface.

In short, then, the rise of object-oriented information management through the rest of the 1990s is assured. Unclear, though, is whether the hybrid relational/object-oriented approach or the outgrowth from the OODBMS market (driven by the ODMG standardization efforts) will be the winner. In fact, one may argue that both approaches may flourish, each offering strengths to different environments.

Organizations with substantial investment in relational technology (especially those that have made the painful trek from hierarchical databases and flat files, through the transition efforts of the past) have little incentive to again forsake their information system environments and embark on expensive and time-consuming architectural shifts. These companies will more likely be interested in an evolutionary approach, one that incorporates the wonders of object orientation into their relational environments in the ways discussed in Chapter 9, rather than the more revolutionary approach of moving their information management infrastructure to "pure" OODBMS engines.

Other companies, though, that don't already have significant investment in legacy relational databases and applications may prefer not to be burdened by hybrid environments, shifting instead to ODMG-compliant products. Indeed, the server-based approach to distributed information management discussed in Chapter 7 provides organizations with the means to utilize ODMG-compliant systems for certain classes of applications while still maintaining a relational (or even extended relational) corporate information infrastructure (Figure 11-6).

Finally, object-oriented information management capabilities are key to many of the emerging technologies in the discipline, as we'll discuss in subsequent chapters (see Chapter 17, on image, multimedia, and spatial data management). Image management, for example, is far more difficult in a

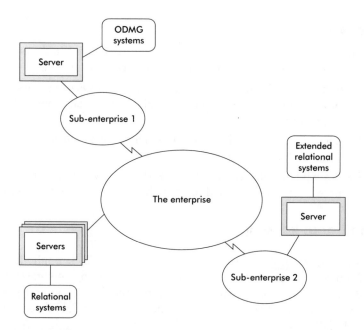

Figure 11-6 Multiple OODBMS Architectures Within an Organization

relational environment than in an object-oriented framework. We can safely state that OODBMSs of one variety or another will be increasingly important in the future.

11.6 Conclusion

In this chapter, we've taken a final look at the subject of object-oriented information management, focusing on related topics such as transaction models and object request brokers. We also took a consolidated look at the whole area of object-oriented information management, concluding that the future of databases and information management in general will contain some degree of object orientation, regardless of implementation.

Outlook

Short-term

- CORBA-compliant servers will bring OODB capabilities to many classes of applications
- Security will continue to be investigated for OODB environments

Long-term

- Transaction models for OODBs will become more formalized than today, allowing the creation of heterogeneous OODB environments
- A degree of security will become commonplace for OODB environments as they become more a part of "mainstream" corporate database environments over time
- Transaction models should be developed that will permit easy mixture of relational and object-oriented environments
- The CORBA architecture will be extended and enhanced, helping to promote code reusability and prolong the life of legacy applications

Additional Reading

- M. H. Nodine, A. H. Skarra, and S. B. Zdonik, "Synchronization and Recovery in Cooperative Transactions," *Implementing Persistent Object Bases: Principles and Practice, 4th International Workshop on Persistent Object Systems* (San Francisco: Morgan Kaufmann Publishers, 1991), 329–342.
- M. T. Öszu, U. Dayal, and P. Valduriez, "Workshop Report: International Workshop on Distributed Object Management," *SIGMOD Record* (March 1993), 40–52.
- M. P. Roy, "Developing Reusable Client/Server Applications Using an ORB," *Proceedings from Database World & Client/Server World*, Vol. II, (June 1993) E9-7.

Endnotes

1. Described in M. H. Nodine, A. H. Skarra, and S. B. Zdonik, "Synchronization and Recovery in Cooperative Transactions," *Implementing Persistent Object Bases: Principles and Practice, 4th International Workshop on Persistent Object Systems* (San Francisco: Morgan Kaufmann Publishers, 1991), 329–342.

2. Based on the description in Nodine, Skarra, and Zdonik, "Synchronization and Recovery."

3. Nodine, Skarra, and Zdonik, "Synchronization and Recovery," 333.

4. Described in M. T. Öszu, U. Dayal, and P. Valduriez, "Workshop Report: International Workshop on Distributed Object Management," *SIGMOD Record* (March 1993), 40–52.

5. Öszu, Dayal, and Valduriez, "Distributed Object Management," 40.

6. M. P. Roy, "Developing Reusable Client/Server Applications Using an ORB," *Proceedings from Database World & Client/Server World*, Vol. II, (June 1993) E9-7.

7. A. Simon, *Implementing the Enterprise* (New York: Bantam Books/Intertext, 1993), 201.

PART IV

Database and Information Management Languages

CHAPTER

12

SQL Futures

A Note to the CIO

SQL is undoubtedly an important part of your organization's database picture. You should understand where the language is headed with respect to the just-released SQL-92 standard as well as SQL3. Further, the problems of noncompliance with standards (either product extensions or deficiencies, or both) are addressed in this chapter, permitting you to formulate a long-range strategy for the continued incorporation of SQL into your applications and database environments.

Although the features, performance, and other properties of SQL-based products used in your organization (or those that you might be contemplating using) are important, the developments and future directions of SQL in the context of the database language standard are also important.

12.1 Introduction

SQL is one of the two dominant languages used in relational databases (the other is the Xbase language, which we'll discuss in Chapter 14). SQL has existed in various forms since the mid-1970s and gained tremendous popularity in the 1980s as relational databases became widespread on mainframes and mid-range systems. In this chapter, we'll look at the future direction of SQL, including the SQL-92 standard and ongoing work on the next generation of SQL, known as SQL3.

First, let's briefly discuss the history and background of SQL, including its various incarnations as a research and a commercial language.

Executive Summary

From its roots in IBM research laboratories in the 1970s to its role as one of the most dominant information system standards, SQL has provided the base language technology for a generation of DBMS products based on the relational model.

Though introduced commercially in the early 1980s in a handful of products, SQL arguably came into its own with the publication of the SQL-86 standard by ANSI and ISO. A later enhancement to the standard (SQL-89) provided additional features to the language.

The SQL-92 standard, which had been under development for a number of years, was published in 1992 and will provide the primary guidelines for the next generation of SQL-based DBMS products.

12.2 SQL History

The roots of SQL can be traced to the birth of the relational data model (described in E. F. Codd's paper, which was discussed in Chapter 1).[1] Though SQL-like languages didn't appear for several more years, the research projects started at IBM after the publication of Codd's paper emphasized the need for languages to interface with the databases being built, to examine the capabilities of the relational model.[2] Figure 12-1 shows the history of SQL's development.

In 1974, Donald D. Chamberlin of IBM's San Jose Research Laboratory defined a relational language known as SEQUEL, and a prototype was built over the next two years.[3] A revised version (SEQUEL/2) was developed in 1976 and 1977, and the name was eventually changed to Structured Query Language (SQL).

One of the relational databases under IBM research and development was System R, which evolved into the commercial product SQL/DS (initially for DOS/VSE environments, later for VM/CMS). As might be guessed from the product name, SQL/DS featured a database language based on earlier SEQUEL/Structured Query Language work at IBM. The primary IBM relational database for the commercial world, DB2 (for MVS environments) followed, also featuring SQL, though, in an ominous sign for the relational world, the SQL languages of IBM's two mainframe DBMSs differed from each other.

Even before IBM's commercial products hit the market in the early 1980s, Relational Software, Inc. (now known as Oracle Corporation) introduced a relational database based on SQL that through its evolution has become one of the dominant commercial DBMS products: ORACLE. As a preview to the multiple-platform standardization of SQL, Oracle Corporation proceeded over the years to port their flagship product to dozens of hardware and operating system platforms, from desktop PCs to mainframes.

At the same time, the SQL3 standard is underway; this effort represents another significant increase in SQL functionality, particularly through the inclusion of object-oriented extensions to support the unification of the relational and object-oriented data models (discussed in Chapter 9).

Criticism of SQL from database luminaries is not uncommon, but there is no doubt that SQL is here to stay. Most DBMS vendors have staked their entire product line code base (for their run-time engines, at least) on SQL-based DBMS products. To switch to some other, as-yet-unspecified language base would require retooling to an extent that no vendor would undertake, and no customer with a substantial investment in SQL-based products would tolerate.

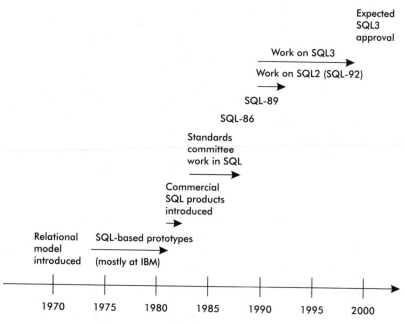

Figure 12-1 History and Roots of SQL

As other commercial products based on the relational model came to market, a number of other languages appeared. For the PC, the language used by Ashton-Tate's dBASE family of products (dBASE II and III, and later III+

What This Technology Can Do for You

Alhough the features, performance, and other properties of SQL-based products used in your organization (or those that you might be contemplating using) are important, the developments and future directions of SQL in the context of the database language standard are also important. We have no guarantee that every feature of either the SQL-92 or SQL3 standard will eventually find its way into a commercial DBMS product, yet an understanding of those standards can help guide your future database applications development.

Understanding SQL directions is also helpful if you wish to influence the kinds of features to be added by major DBMS vendors, which is particularly likely if you are a decision maker and strategic planner with

and IV) became the dominant database language. Even as SQL was introduced to the PC world in the mid-1980s, the dBASE language (now known as Xbase, as discussed in Chapter 14) remained the primary language on the desktop.

The ORACLE product with its SQL language faced competition in the mid-range/minicomputer world from a number of fronts, including Relational Technology, Inc. (now ASK/Ingres) and the QUEL language for its Ingres database, and Digital Equipment Corporation's Rdb/VMS with its RDML language. As many readers probably know, both Ingres and Rdb/VMS now have SQL interfaces, which shows the growth of SQL in database products.

One of the reasons why SQL succeeded was the formation by the American National Standards Institute (ANSI) of the X3H2 committee, chartered to develop standards for database languages. After earlier work in the area of network databases (such as CODASYL, discussed in section 1.5.2 of Chapter 1), the committee turned its attention to languages for relational databases. The IBM representative submitted a proposal based on IBM's earlier work on SEQUEL/2 to replace preliminary work on a relational language specification, and the world of standards development went to work. The document, entitled "SQL," was basically a treatise on the various forms of SQL in the marketplace.

The International Standards Organization (ISO) also was working to develop a standard for relational database languages through the TC97 technical committee, now known as ISO/IEC JTC1, and both ANSI and ISO approved SQL standards in the mid-1980s (ANSI in 1986, ISO in early 1987).

The first SQL standard, due to the manner in which it was developed, was rather incomplete regarding database functionality, and most vendors continued to provide a large number of extensions to the standard in their products. Some of the primary enhancements were in the area of referential integrity,

a large, influential corporation or governmental organization. It may come as a surprise to some readers, but as a former product manager with the database systems group of a major computer systems vendor, this author can certify that input from influential customers is considered when planning and prioritizing features for product release cycles. By knowing what is possible within the bounds of standards compliance, you can plan a road map of product features you'd like to request in conjunction with the strategic direction of your information systems applications development.

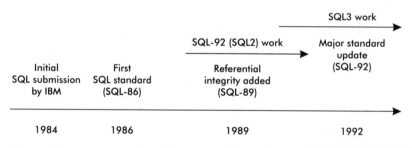

Figure 12-2 History of the Various SQL Standards

and a revised SQL standard was introduced in 1989 that differed from the 1986 standard primarily in its incorporation of referential integrity capabilities.

Even before 1989, though, work had commenced in both ANSI and ISO to add dramatic enhancements to SQL. The work, initially identified as "SQL2," began in 1987 and, five years later, was approved as SQL-92, which we'll discuss in the next section.

To add to the confusion, work in SQL2 overlapped work in SQL3, the next generation of SQL, which is still under development. In 1990, SQL3 work commenced parallel to SQL2, mostly as a kind of "holding tank" for features thought to be outside the scope of SQL2 for one reason or another.[4] As we'll discuss in section 12.4, SQL3 includes object-oriented extensions to the language, as well as additional relational features that didn't find their way into SQL2.

Summarizing, Figure 12-2 shows the respective timelines of the various SQL standards.

Before we continue, we should discuss SQL standards in the context of the language capabilities of commercially available products. As we consider the future of SQL, we should understand that it has two parts. The first concerns the standard, currently consolidated under the framework of SQL3 (no, there's *not* an SQL4 underway in parallel, at least not yet). We will discuss this in section 12.4.

The second part concerns the language features of SQL-based DBMS products. This area hints at a more complicated future for SQL.

For example, let's look at the database language feature known as a trigger. A *trigger* is a schema object that tells a DBMS what other actions to perform after certain SQL statements have been executed.[5] Triggers might be used to insert rows into a log table after every update of prices in a database table of CDs, to track who is making price changes. Unlike the "traditional" database application method of handling such functions through the procedural applications code, the DBMS itself provides the capabilities to define triggers (typically through a CREATE TRIGGER statement) and to declaratively specify the actions that will occur.

Nearly all commercial SQL-based DBMSs available in the early 1990s have trigger capabilities. However, the SQL-86 and SQL-89 standards do not cover the capabilities of or include the syntax for triggers. More important, *neither does the recently approved SQL-92 standard.* Not until the SQL3 standard, currently under development and not expected to be approved until the mid-1990s, is that particular feature addressed.

In short, you can't generalize that the features of SQL-based products follow the specification of those features within a standard. Nor can you assume that popular features such as triggers are included in the next—or any—version of a standard. In some cases, product features lead to elements of standards; in other cases, inclusion of certain capabilities in standards will lead to the inclusion of those capabilities within products. Both situations occur.

How does this bidirectional path between standards and SQL language features affect computer developers, planners, and users? There is no simple answer, but here are some guidelines.

If your database environment is monolithic in nature—a single product, possibly used on multiple classes of platform, with no interoperability and integration requirements—then one might say that although standards should not be ignored, they have a secondary importance compared to product functionality and capabilities.

If, however, your database environment comprises multiple DBMSs, a need for distributed database capabilities, and transactions that span multiple databases and multiple DBMSs (discussed in Part II of this book as a major trend in information management), the standards take on increased importance. Using our earlier example of triggers, you may find yourself faced with a dilemma: do you use the triggering capabilities of a portion of your overall database environment (i.e., some DBMS products, but not others), despite the fact that not all of your DBMSs have those capabilities, and despite having nonstandard syntax for those capabilities from DBMS to DBMS?

Following are some of the factors that will help with your decision:

- The anticipated inclusion of that particular feature in the SQL standard (in the case of triggers, its inclusion in SQL3 is scheduled for several years down the road).
- The anticipated incorporation of that particular capability in the products you use (since features sometimes appear before incorporation in standards) *and* syntactic compatibility with those in your other DBMSs.
- Your system's transaction environment (e.g., might a transaction with triggering capabilities need to incorporate those features from multiple DBMSs within the same transaction, or are the operations on the DBMSs disjoint from one another?).

Other factors will probably influence your study and analysis of the future of SQL. Keep in mind, though, that your study needs to incorporate not only the future of the standard but also the future of SQL-based products that are important to your particular environment, either now or in the future.

12.3 The SQL-92 Standard

As we mentioned earlier, SQL-92 work began in 1987 and was approved in 1992. Unlike the relationship between SQL-86 and SQL-89, where the primary difference between the two was the addition of referential integrity, SQL-92 represents a major enhancement over its predecessors in terms of capabilities. Much has been made in the computer press of the comparative sizes of the SQL-92 standard and its immediate predecessor—about 115 pages for SQL-89, 580 pages for SQL-92.[6] However, after adjusting for 1) the inclusion of features that had already been implemented by most vendors, and 2) more careful specification of existing features within the SQL-92 document, then the actual size of SQL-92 is not quite double that of SQL-89.[7]

Even after "scaling down" the size difference between the standards, note that many SQL-92 features will not find their way into products for several years to come.

12.3.1 Leveling

That leads us to the topic of SQL-92 "leveling," an important consideration in understanding the future of SQL. SQL-92 is divided into three different levels:[8]

1) *Entry SQL:* This level was designed to be very similar to SQL-89, with some minor distinctions such as new programming language interfaces for Ada, C, and MUMPS; SQLSTATE status variables; and other small items.

2) *Intermediate SQL:* Designed to cover approximately half of the remaining differences between SQL-89 and SQL-92, this includes such items as dynamic SQL, schema manipulation statements, domain support, and other items we'll take a brief look at later.

3) *Full SQL:* This is the entire SQL-92 standard. The differences between it and Intermediate SQL include deferred constraint checking, self-referencing updates and deletions, scrolling cursors, temporary tables, assertions, and other capabilities.

Achieving compliance with Entry SQL is expected to be a relatively minor process for most DBMS vendors, typically within a release or two after 1992. Intermediate SQL and Full SQL compliance, however, are expected to be *major* efforts. As we mentioned in the previous section, many vendors already have some SQL-92 features in their products (as well as SQL3 features such as triggers and Boolean and enumerated data types), so we can't assume that every intermediate-compliant feature will be a new addition for every vendor. There is talk within the SQL community of adding an "Implementors' Level," somewhere between Intermediate and Full SQL, with a "manageable" set of SQL-92 features that may be implemented in the near term at a point sometime before compliance with Full SQL is achieved.

12.3.2 Implementation Issues

Another important item regarding the future of SQL involves implementation issues.[9] Specifically, the SQL-92 standard uses two terms that sound similar and at first glance seem to be interchangeable. But they aren't. The two terms are implementation-defined and implementation-dependent. *Implementation-defined* items are those that must be documented within the scope of a product. For example, INTEGER data types may have different precisions from one product to another, and implementation-defined means that the precision is defined by the implementation, and that it must be documented. SQL-92 has 149 implementation-defined items, in these areas:

- Data types
- Metadata
- Sessions, transactions, and connections
- SQL statements
- Literals, names, and identifiers
- Value expressions and functions
- Diagnostics
- Information schema
- Embedded SQL and modules
- Miscellaneous (other areas, or general concepts)

Implementation-dependent applies to the physical representation of a value of a given data type. This would vary from implementation to implementation, but it does *not* need to be documented. There are 75 implementation-dependent items, spread among most of the areas that also contain implementation-defined items.

12.3.3 SQL-92 Language Features

Let's take a brief look at some of the features and enhancements that were added to the SQL language in the SQL-92 standard. We'll concentrate on the language features that might be viewed as "future-oriented," that is, those not widely used in today's SQL-based commercial products. A complete discussion of the SQL-92 language, along with supplemental material, may be found in *Understanding the New SQL: A Complete Guide.*[10]

12.3.3.1 Table manipulation. In addition to the necessary capability to create tables via the CREATE TABLE statement, capabilities were added to get rid of tables (DROP TABLE) and modify the contents of a table (ALTER TABLE). Note that these statements and the underlying ideas are far from revolutionary and are found in most commercial SQL DBMS products; they are examples of commonly found "extensions" to the basic SQL language that, through commercial necessity, found their way into the standard.

12.3.3.2 Domains. SQL-92 added domain definition capability to the language. For example, you could write

```
CREATE DOMAIN names_and_titles CHAR (35)
 CHECK (VALUE IS NOT NULL) ;
```

This domain definition, which creates a domain called NAMES_AND_TITLES that is 35 characters long and not null, can then be used in a CREATE TABLE statement, as follows:

```
CREATE TABLE cds_and_tapes
    ( music_title names_and_titles,
      year_released DATE,
      ....                  -- rest of columns for that table
    )
```

This table definition would then replace the "more traditional" direct usage of a data type, as in

```
CREATE TABLE cds_and_tapes
    ( music_title CHAR (35) NOT NULL,
      ...
    )
```

One of the advantages to the usage of domains is that any changes to the domain definition is propagated to all column definitions in all tables that use that domain definition, so you don't have to go through a prolonged search and change numerous definitions. Conceptually, this is similar to the use of type definitions for variables in certain programming languages, which we'll discuss in the next section in the context of SQL3 and object-oriented capabilities.

12.3.3.3 New data types. The following data types were added to SQL-92:

- DATE
- TIME
- TIMESTAMP
- BIT string
- variable-length characters and bit strings
- NATIONAL CHARACTER strings

Most commercial DBMS products support a DATE data type, because a great deal of application processing is oriented toward dates and the relationships between those of various entities (e.g., values in the same column in different rows of a table; values in different columns in the same row of a table; values in columns of different tables; and so on). In addition to the raw data type, most commercial products also provide a number of DATE manipulation and extraction functions; the SQL standard is just catching up in this area.

NATIONAL CHARACTER strings are the same as those of a CHARACTER data type, except that an implementation-defined character set is used (primarily for international applications).

12.3.3.4 New status parameter. The SQLCODE status code was supplanted by SQLSTATE, which offers much more diagnostic information. Additionally, a diagnostics area was added; this diagnostics size is specified through the SET TRANSACTION statement by the user, or is implementation-defined if the user doesn't explicitly specify a size.

12.3.3.5 Transaction statements. Minor syntax changes were made in the COMMIT and ROLLBACK statements (both used to terminate transactions). In SQL-89, the correct syntax required the use of the word WORK with either (e.g., COMMIT WORK and ROLLBACK WORK). In SQL-92, the word WORK was made optional. Unlike some commercial DBMS products, transactions do not start via a type of START TRANSACTION statement, but rather implicitly (i.e., executing a statement that requires the context of a transaction, though no transaction is currently alive). Note, however, that SQL3 will have a START TRANSACTION statement.

12.3.3.6 Additional language bindings. In the previous section, we mentioned that Entry SQL is basically the same as SQL-89, with minor enhancements. One of those enhancements was the language bindings for Ada, C, and MUMPS.[11]

12.3.3.7 New functions. One of the areas in which the SQL standard seriously differs from most implementations is functions. SQL-92 added a number of new functions, such as TRIM (remove leading or trailing blanks from a character string); obtaining the current date, time, or timestamp; and extracting positions from string variables in which a particular substring begins. Consider these two issues with respect to SQL-92 functions and commercial products:

- Most commercial products support far more functions than SQL-92.
- Even functions that are similar often have different syntax.

As an example of the first issue, we might look at ORACLE7, which has functions such as LEAST and GREATEST, to determine which of a list of dates is "greatest" or "least" (later in the year or earlier in the year, respectively).[12] Other functions are available in ORACLE7 for adding and subtracting months (ADD_MONTHS), determining the date of the next named day of the week after a given date (NEXT_DAY, which may be used, for example, to determine the date of the first Monday after the second day of each month), and dozens more,[13] none of which are included in the SQL-92 standard.

An example of the second issue, functions that may be similar in meaning but that have different syntax, is the LTRIM and RTRIM functions of ORACLE7, used to trim leading and trailing occurrences of a particular character from a string.[14] In SQL-92, these functions are both handled by the TRIM function:

```
TRIM (LEADING ' ' FROM ' Batman Returns ')
TRIM (TRAILING ' ' FROM ' Batman Returns ')
TRIM (BOTH ' ' FROM ' Batman Returns ')
```

As one might guess, the results of the above three statements, in order, are

```
'Batman Returns '
'  Batman Returns'
'Batman Returns'
```

Because product function statements are used to manipulate and extract information about strings, numbers, dates, and other database objects, this area will likely be one in which the products will stay far ahead of the SQL standard in terms of functionality. For single-DBMS environments, this may not present too much of a problem (though applications that make extensive use of nonstandard functions risk being locked into a single product or facing painful migration efforts). For heterogeneous distributed database environments, however, which utilize a global layer over underlying local DBMSs, decisions must be made as to how nonstandard functions will be used (e.g., whether the global layer will support ones that aren't handled by an underlying DBMS, or should represent an intersection of the functions common to underlying products). We discussed this decision in Chapter 7.

12.3.3.8 The Information Schema. SQL-92 provides a formal means to manage database metadata. The Information Schema provides base tables in a DEFINITION_SCHEMA and viewed tables built on them and managed in an INFORMATION_SCHEMA, as a formal method of metadata management.

The base tables of the DEFINITION_SCHEMA aren't accessible by applications programs through SQL statements, because they aren't "real." Implementations are given the latitude to handle the information in the base tables any way that is most advantageous. As long as that information is available through the views of the INFORMATION_SCHEMA in accordance with the standard, then the metadata management is compliant with the SQL-92 standard.

Base tables are specified through a series of CREATE TABLE definitions, all of which are specified in the SQL-92 standard. Table definitions are provided for

- USERS
- SCHEMATA
- DOMAINS
- DOMAIN_CONSTRAINTS
- TABLES
- VIEWS
- COLUMNS

A total of 24 "objects" have table definitions. The INFORMATION_SCHEMA views, all built on one or more DEFINITION_SCHEMA tables, include

- SCHEMATA
- DOMAINS
- TABLES
- VIEWS
- COLUMNS
- TABLE_PRIVILEGES

- COLUMN_PRIVILEGES
- TABLE_CONSTRAINTS
- REFERENTIAL_CONSTRAINTS
- TRANSLATIONS

This is only a partial list; there are 23 in all.

As with most other aspects of SQL related to commercial DBMS products, the INFORMATION_SCHEMA will likely undergo transformation to suit the architecture of the product. For example, object-oriented extensions to SQL databases will require base tables and views dealing with concepts such as abstract data types (the SQL3 information schema contains such tables, as we'll discuss in section 12.4.2). DBMSs that support triggers require base tables and views for triggers, and so on.

As distributed DBMS products and SQL-92 converge, you will likely see information schema tables and views dealing with distributed features, such as replicates and partitions, supporting metadata for such configurations. For example, a DBMS that supports horizontal partitioning (fragmentation) may have a base table HORIZONTAL_PARTITIONS, in which a key-based relationship to a "parent" table is identified, and viewed tables (in the INFORMATION_ SCHEMA) such as the following:

- HORIZONTAL_PARTITIONS: To see the base table information, such as the method of partitioning (value-based, round-robin, or some other type).
- PARTITION_PRIVILEGES: To join information between user privileges and given partitions.
- PARTITION_CONSTRAINTS: Any constraints particular to a partition.

Similarly, DBMSs that support temporal (time-oriented) extensions to the language would likely have DEFINITION_SCHEMA and INFORMATION_ SCHEMA tables and views to support the temporal constructs. (Temporal databases will be discussed in Chapter 15, and part of that discussion will propose temporal extensions to the SQL language.)

The point is that just as product features differ from one DBMS to another—and will continue to do so—so will the metadata contained within that DBMS. DBMSs that will claim compliance with SQL-92 will have base tables and viewed tables similar to those described in the standard, with extensions (both in terms of the columns within "standard" tables such as TABLES and COLUMNS, and additional tables and views).

As organizations continue to build heterogeneous distributed information management environments, the metadata managers of the underlying DBMSs will play an important role in extracting and managing information about the location and contents of organizational data spread throughout the organization. Convergence on a more or less standard metadata management architecture, such as SQL's INFORMATION_SCHEMA, would lead to a reduced amount of inter-DBMS translation and conversion among metadata objects. Therefore, even though the metadata management exemplified in the SQL-92 INFORMATION_SCHEMA may appear at first to be of lesser importance than the overall language features themselves, the "higher-level view" of creating federations and multidatabase environments may be very dependent on INFORMATION_SCHEMA capabilities.

12.3.3.9 Security. In SQL-89, security properties were provided for tables, columns, and views. SQL-92 added protection and access control capabilities for domains, character sets, collations, and translations.[15] Protection capabilities are provided in these areas:

- Viewing (SELECT)
- Creating (INSERT)
- Modifying (UPDATE)
- Deleting (DELETE)
- Referencing (REFERENCES)
- Using (USAGE, for domains, character sets, collations, and translations)

Privileges are allotted via the GRANT statement. In SQL-89, privileges could never be revoked; SQL-92 added that capability through the REVOKE statement. Additionally, privileges may be GRANTed and the recipient may be allowed to pass on that specific privilege; this is accomplished by tagging the GRANT statement with a WITH GRANT OPTION.

Here's an example of SQL-92 security:

```
GRANT DELETE
  ON movie_transactions
  TO AUDITOR
  WITH GRANT OPTION;
```

This statement will allow a user with the authID (authorization identifier) of AUDITOR to delete rows from the table MOVIE_TRANSACTIONS.

Here's another statement:

```
GRANT UPDATE (movie_rental_price)
  ON movies
  TO BUYER;
```

This will allow the user with the authID BUYER to update the rental price in the MOVIES table.

SQL-92 supports the concept of PUBLIC, in which anyone may be granted permissions regardless of authID. For example,

```
GRANT SELECT
  ON movies
  TO PUBLIC;
```

This statement will allow anyone to browse the table with information about the movies. In real-world applications, however, such a privilege would more likely be granted on a view, say, PUBLIC_MOVIE_INFO, which allows only certain columns for PUBLIC browsing.

Complete privileges may be granted through a single statement by using ALL PRIVILEGES:

```
GRANT ALL PRIVILEGES
  on MOVIES
  to NEW_MANAGER;
```

While security properties have been greatly enhanced in SQL-92 over earlier versions of the SQL standard, they still lack a great number of the capabilities necessary for even the most basic security-sensitive applications. You may have noticed that all of the privileges discussed in this section deal with data manipulation language (DML) statements; none deal with any data definition language (DDL). The rules for CREATE, ALTER, and DROP within the SQL-92 security model are as follows:[16]

- You can perform any and all DDL operations in a schema that you own.
- You *cannot* perform any DDL operations in a schema that you don't own, which also means that no one else can perform any DDL operations in any schema that you own.
- These rules *cannot* be overridden.

These rules provide constraints that require extensive planning as to schema ownership and possibly workarounds to bypass restrictions. Many commercial DBMSs provide additional security permissions for DDL operations to be granted (e.g., ORACLE provides for ALTER privileges[17]), so we have yet another area in which standards diverge from commercial realities.

It's important to note that REVOKE, while seemingly a straightforward command, has some complications. The underlying DBMS must maintain a privilege graph (as in graph theory) in which links are maintained within each specific privilege combination (the privilege, who granted it, to whom was it granted, and whether a WITH GRANT OPTION was specified). As privileges are revoked, the system must determine any propagations of privilege granting that occurred as a result of someone who received WITH GRANT OPTION granting privileges. A detailed example, with multiple steps of granting and revoking privileges and the resulting actions, may be found in *Understanding the New SQL: A Complete Guide.*[18]

12.3.3.10 Temporary Tables. SQL-92 added support for the explicit creation of temporary tables within the context of a transaction. They avoid the overhead associated with permanent tables but may be used for storage of intermediate operation results or other purposes.

Many more SQL-92 additions were not discussed here, of course. Again, the important thing to understand is that no direct relationship exists between commercial features and the components of the SQL standard. Planners of single-DBMS environments can simply use the standard to see what features may be coming from vendors several years from now. For most organizations, though, the multiple-DBMS nature of their information environments places increased importance on the SQL standard and makes incompatibilities among SQL products a subject of lasting concern.

12.4 The SQL3 Standard

In section 12.2, we mentioned that work on SQL3 actually began in 1990, at the same time SQL2 (which became SQL-92) was being developed. The primary motivation for SQL3 was to have a "holding tank" for several classes of features that for one reason or another were not considered for SQL2.

SQL3 can be viewed as comprising three parts, though, as we'll discuss, the demarcations are not quite so clean. These parts are[19]

1) SQL-92 (the entire standard).
2) Advanced relational capabilities that didn't find their way into SQL-92, such as triggers and additional basic data types (Boolean, enumerated).
3) Object-oriented concepts.

SQL3 also has capabilities under consideration for addition to the SQL language, which arguably fall not in the realm of any of the above three parts but into the general category of database and information management architectures. For example, savepoints (see section 20.3.2 of Chapter 20) are included in the mid-1993 draft of the standard, and statements for chained transactions (see section 20.3.3) are actively being considered for inclusion as well.[20] A procedural language, with honest-to-goodness procedural logic statements (IF, CASE, loop control, and so on), is also part of the SQL3 standard. In addition there are other extensions and related standards activities which we'll examine later.

For now let's look at some of the advanced relational concepts or, more generally, advanced relational-like database concepts, including primitive data types, that will likely be in SQL3.

12.4.1 SQL3 Advanced Relational-Like Database Concepts

Arguably, the most desirable language feature in SQL3 outside the realm of object-oriented extensions is triggers. Earlier, we cited triggers as an example of a feature commonly used in commercial SQL-based DBMS products that had not been included in any version of the standard to date, including SQL-92.

Triggers play an important role in active databases (discussed in Chapter 16), where rules of processing are embedded in the database itself rather than in procedural applications logic.

The syntax may differ slightly in the final standard, as the mid-1993 versions of the CREATE TRIGGER statement differ between ANSI and ISO, but the basic syntax of triggering is as follows:

```
CREATE TRIGGER trigger-name
   trigger-action-time trigger-event
   ON table-name
   REFERENCING some-action
```

The "trigger-action-time" is either BEFORE, AFTER, or INSTEAD OF (the last one is currently an ANSI-only option), and the "trigger-event" is either INSERT, DELETE, or UPDATE. Some of the combinations of the trigger-action-time and the trigger-event are as follows:[21]

- BEFORE INSERT—The specified "some-action" is performed before the INSERT is executed; note that in the "action," a granularity of FOR EACH ROW or FOR EACH STATEMENT can be specified, meaning that the given action is executed either for every row that is inserted or once only, respectively. (The latter is the default if neither is specified.) An example statement might be

  ```
  CREATE TRIGGER new_movies_added BEFORE INSERT
     ON movies
     INSERT INTO new_movies_log VALUES (.......)
  ```

  where any INSERT into the MOVIES table will cause an entry into the NEW_MOVIES_LOG table to be made, with the specified values.
- AFTER INSERT: The action is performed after the INSERT.
- BEFORE UPDATE: The action is performed before the specified columns are UPDATEd.

In section 12.3.2, we mentioned that SQL-92 introduced a formal INFOR-
MATION_SCHEMA, in which viewed tables built on top of the DEFINI-
TION_SCHEMA base tables may be accessed and managed by authorized
DBMS users. We also discussed how DBMSs implementing extensions (e.g.,
additional features and capabilities) to the basic SQL-92 would likely need to
add new INFORMATION_SCHEMA viewed tables for the management of the
metadata necessary for those capabilities.

In SQL3, additional capabilities such as triggers have appropriate views
in the INFORMATION_SCHEMA. In the case of triggers, the TRIGGERS,
TRIGGERED_ACTIONS, and TRIGGERED_COLUMNS views provide management of the metadata for the various aspects of triggering.

SQL3 also includes capabilities for RECURSIVE UNIONs, in which a
"limited amount of recursion"[22] may be invoked to perform recursive operations (such as building lists of parts) without having to use several cursors to
scan a table; traditionally, these "bill of materials" problems were handled in
much the same way as on navigational (network, hierarchical) databases, with
program logic used to construct such results. With the RECURSIVE UNION
statement, and a host of options such as search, cycle, and limit clauses to
control the degree of recursiveness, such operations become embedded in the
database logic.

One of the major trends in databases, thanks to client/server computing
(discussed in Chapter 3), is the placement of much or even all of an application
in the server. To support such an architectural split, SQL3 introduces a set of
control statements—a *procedural language*—with the capabilities to perform
the following tasks:[23]

- CALL a procedure (a subprogram). Parameters may be declared within
  the routine, in much the same way that they are for high-level languages.
  Routines may be either within the scope of SQL (compound statements)
  or external to SQL, such as high-level language functions or procedures.
  In short, we can now not only call SQL from C or COBOL or another
  high-level language, but also do the opposite.

- RETURN values from SQL functions (see above).

- Manage EXCEPTIONs through handlers, as in the Ada language.

- Declare SQL variables.

- Assign values to SQL variables via the SET statement.

- Create a NEW instance of an abstract data type (for the object-oriented
  extensions, which we'll discuss in the next section).

- Destroy an instance of an abstract data type (again, for the object-oriented
  extensions).

- Have CASE . . . END CASE block statements for logic control.

- Have IF . . . END IF statements, also for logic control.

- Have a LOOP . . . END LOOP statement and a WHILE "loop iteration scheme," for repeated execution.
- Have a LEAVE statement, to jump out of a block or loop statement.
- Have FOR . . . END FOR statements, to execute a statement for each row of some query expression.
- Have SIGNAL and RESIGNAL statements, to signal and resignal (obviously) exception conditions.

In short, the traditional programming constructs are provided in SQL3: branching logic (CASE, IF-THEN-ELSE), looping (DO-WHILE, DO-UNTIL), even jumping out of loops.

We mentioned earlier that SQL3 provides additional data types like TRIGGERS, which were common in commercial DBMSs but hadn't made their way into SQL. The first is the BOOLEAN data type, as in

```
CREATE TABLE movies (
  movie_title    CHAR (30),
  in_stock       BOOLEAN,
  ...
)
```

In this case, the column IN_STOCK may be assigned the values of TRUE or FALSE; no longer is a character-based "pseudo-Boolean" data type needed for such situations.

Another example is enumerated data types. In SQL-92, you could specify something like

```
CREATE TABLE movies (
  movie_title    CHAR (30),
  ...
  movie_type     CHAR (10),
  ...
  CHECK (movie_type IN
    ( 'Romance', 'Children', 'Western', 'Adventure',
      'Horror', 'Comedy', 'Musical', 'Other' ) ) )
```

The CHECK clause provided an accurate list of values that could be assigned to the column MOVIE_TYPE, but the data type was still character-based. In the implementation-specific sense, not having every row use ten bytes (or more, for multi-octet character sets) is favorable for storing the actual characters for "Romance" or "Musical"; encoding would be much cleaner and would take much less space. Even aside from implementation-specific issues such as storage, enumerated data types are extremely valuable to good programming practice and are hardly new; the JOVIAL language, introduced in the late 1950s, provided for previous examples, as do most high-level languages—and many SQL-based DBMSs.

In SQL3, enumerated data types finally make an appearance; the above example could be handled as follows:

```
CREATE DOMAIN types_of_movies (Romance, Children, Western,
    Adventure, Horror, Comedy, Musical, Other)
...
CREATE TABLE movies (
  movie_title      CHAR (30),
  ...
  movie_type       TYPES_OF_MOVIES,
  ... )
```

Values could then be assigned to MOVIE_TYPE by

```
INSERT INTO movies VALUES
  ('Camelot', ..., types_of_movies::musical,...)
```

The transaction model of SQL3 has been enhanced over SQL-92. Savepoints can be used to control partial rollback of an SQL transaction (that is, a transaction in the formal SQL sense, as defined in the standard) to a specified point—in effect, a nested transaction. As we mentioned earlier, capabilities are being considered for chained transactions as well.

Of course, many other capabilities in SQL3 fall within the domain of "advanced relational." A scan through the SQL3 standard will give you some idea of the direction certain areas are taking. For our purposes, though, let's turn our attention to MOOSE—the object-oriented capabilities within SQL3.

12.4.2 MOOSE

The concept of object-oriented SQL has grown with the convergence of relational and object-oriented databases (see Chapter 9). A presentation by Michael Stonebraker in 1990 at Digital Consulting Inc.'s Database World conference was entitled "Database Trends: The Interaction Between SQL and Object-Oriented Databases."[24] As we discussed earlier, the ANSI and ISO standards committees consciously deferred all object-oriented SQL capabilities and features to the SQL3 effort; none made it into SQL-92.

The object-oriented portions of SQL3 fall under the umbrella of MOOSE: Major Object-Oriented SQL Extensions. One of the concepts behind the MOOSE components of SQL is that some classes of applications will require access to both relational and object-oriented data with relative ease of management (i.e., not forcing the data together through glue layers). An example is a gas and electric utility company, which would likely require traditional, relational-based data about customers and their accounts in conjunction with data from a geographic data system with spatial database characteristics (see Chapter 22); transactions such as management of outages and service interruptions would ideally require access to both types of data within the same transaction.[25]

The SQL3 standard, since near its inception, had a "skeleton of 'user-defined datatypes'" from which the foundations for object identity and abstract data types (ADTs) were built.[26]

The language is still evolving, and in addition to new capabilities, the differences between the ANSI and ISO versions are being worked out by the two committees. As with triggering, data types, recursive unions, transaction management, and the other capabilities we discussed in the previous section, a scan through the 1,000-page SQL3 document will satisfy anyone's appetite for MOOSE syntax.

Before we leave our discussion of SQL3, let's take a look at some of the issues regarding the release and adoption of the standard.

12.4.3 Issues

No doubt about it, the SQL3 standard is big. Consider that many of the criticisms of SQL-92 centered on its size and the anticipated difficulty of vendors implementing the higher levels (Intermediate and Full). SQL3 has the same three levels (Entry, Intermediate, and Full), as well as a still higher, unnamed level, and vendors will continue to face a daunting task.

Conformance by vendors to any of the SQL-92 levels is an all-or-nothing proposition; there is no such thing as an optional feature that defines each level. For SQL3, the standards committee has decided that "a monolithic document will be a serious problem and that a simple leveling model for conformance to a monolithic language will be a bigger problem."[27]

Because the committee wants to make some of the SQL3 features official (that is, adopted by the standards approval process) as soon as possible (recall our earlier discussion of triggers, with many vendor implementations but no standard to which they could conform), earlier thoughts of moving away from the three-year cycle (1986, 1989, 1992) to a four- or maybe five-year cycle have been dismissed.

All this has led to a consensus that both the language and the standards document will be partitioned. Compartmentalization of the language is not an easy task, however. While it might appear fundamental that one part would comprise SQL-92 plus some advanced relational features, another even more advanced relational features, and another part would represent MOOSE, even this isn't easy. As an example, the abstract data type material is very closely integrated with the SQL3 relational specifications, so a clean demarcation is all but impossible.[28]

The thinking as of mid-1994 is that the SQL3 language will be divided as follows:[29]

1) A core language with SQL-92 Intermediate-level (and possibly some Full-level) features.
2) Additional "packages" that may or may not exhibit interdependencies with one another.

As for the document itself, a nine-part breakdown is being considered, with the following parts:[30]

1) A framework, featuring a road map to the other documents and the basic conformance clauses
2) Concepts and DML
3) Information and definition schemas
4) Schema definition and manipulation language
5) Command language interface (CLI)
6) Stored SQL
7) Control language
8) Transaction, session, and connection management statements
9) Language bindings

Regardless of how the actual divisions of the language and the document turn out through the mid-1990s, the basic concepts of SQL3 remain: advanced relational DBMS capabilities, plus an important role in the convergence of relational and object-oriented database technologies. As with triggers and Boolean data types (and other capabilities), an object-oriented feel to SQL has already begun to appear in hybrid or extended relational products, before any official adoption of syntax and concepts by the standards committee. Those who use OOSQL capabilities in their applications should carefully track the development of the MOOSE aspects of SQL3.

12.4.4 Related Standards Efforts

It's worth noting that the standards developers are involved in other efforts related to extended database capabilities. ISO has authorized a project for development of a standard for multimedia data in SQL, tentatively known as SQL MM.[31] Those organizations with interest in multimedia databases should track the efforts of SQL MM.

Additionally, the Air Transportation and Airline Industry Associations are working on the Structured Full-Text Query Language (SFQL), another SQL extension. The IRDS repository standards committee is also interested in pursuing closer cooperation between the SQL3 object model and IRDS.[32]

The point worth noting is that even within what appears at first to be a monolithic standards community (SQL) there are a number of corollary efforts and relationships with other efforts, most coming to life due to the movement of SQL from exclusively relationally oriented to 1990s' data and applications.

12.5 Conclusion

SQL is here to stay. Though the language has many vocal critics, SQL has become the dominant multiple-platform language for databases using the relational model. The Xbase language is still dominant in the desktop realm, but SQL continues to make inroads into the personal computer, which began in the mid-1980s with PC versions of minicomputer DBMS products from vendors such as Oracle and Unify. As the role of PCs in the corporate environment changes from stand-alone systems or small LAN environments (dedicated to an application or two) to critical client roles, the use of SQL will likely continue to grow, along with Xbase and windows-based DBMS interfaces, as we'll discuss in Chapter 14.

The SQL-92 standard, a significant accomplishment after many years of development, provides a challenging target for DBMS vendors seeking compliance. Compliance with even the Intermediate level, let alone the Full level, is certainly an effort that will take most vendors several years to complete. At the same time, the development of the SQL3 standard, expected for completion and approval sometime betweem 1995 and 1997, will present additional capabilities for vendors to consider, even before approval by the ANSI and ISO committees. We discussed such popular features as triggers and Boolean data types; as DBMS products with object-oriented extensions to their relational foundation continue to come to market, the MOOSE components of SQL3 (or at least "work-alikes") will probably emerge well before the adoption of that standard.

Because of user demand for standards compliance (whether or not they really *need* compliance for their particular environments is another issue), vendors claiming compliance with standards such as SQL-92 or one of the levels of SQL3 will provide capabilities such as extension flaggers. *Extension flaggers* are compiler or other options that flag any nonstandard product features that developers may use (many vendors provide such facilities already). So organizations with multiple-vendor and multiple-DBMS environments will have assistance in their often frustrating attempts to maintain a degree of standardization within their heterogeneous environments.

But keep one very important lesson in mind: while standards are generally a dominant force in information systems and information management, they have never been a guaranteed impetus for intervendor and interproduct compatibility; nor will standards ever fill that role. Database vendors, like all vendors, will continue to jockey for primacy through product extensions and features that provide (at least in the eyes of their marketing managers) competitive advantages over other vendors.

Outlook

Short-term

- DBMS products with SQL-92 features will begin appearing soon (though some capabilities are already in some commercial products)
- SQL3 features will also begin to appear, including MOOSE characteristics

Long-term

- SQL3 features will find their way into commercial products by the end of the decade
- Will there be an SQL4? If so, when?

Additional Reading

- J. Celko, *Joe Celko's SQL for Smarties: Advanced SQL Programming* (San Francisco: Morgan Kaufmann Publishers, in press).
- J. Melton and A. Simon, *Understanding the New SQL: A Complete Guide* (San Francisco: Morgan Kaufmann Publishers, 1992).

Endnotes

1. E. F. Codd, "A Relational Model of Data for Large Shared Data Banks," *Communications of the ACM* (June 1970).

2. Portions of this section are adapted from J. Melton and A. Simon, *Understanding the New SQL: A Complete Guide* (San Francisco: Morgan Kaufmann Publishers, 1992), 9–10; and J. Melton, "Inter-Galactic Dataspeak?" *Database Programming and Design* (January 1993), 35–37.

3. As J. Melton points out in "Inter-Galactic Dataspeak?," there is some dispute about the exact place and date of origin of SQL predecessors. Regardless, it is safe to state that pre-SQL languages were developed at IBM in the early 1970s.

4. J. Melton, "Changing of the Guard," *Database Programming and Design* (March 1993), 31.

5. Melton and Simon, *New SQL,* 388.

6. Melton and Simon, *New SQL*, 12.

7. Melton and Simon, *New SQL*.

8. Melton and Simon, *New SQL*, 461–463.

9. Melton and Simon, *New SQL*, 445–461.

10. Melton and Simon, *New SQL*.

11. According to Melton and Simon, *New SQL*, ANSI had specified Ada and C support in an interim (pre-SQL-92) standard that ISO didn't have.

12. G. Koch, *ORACLE7: The Complete Reference* (Berkeley, CA: Osborne/McGraw-Hill, 1993), 174–176.

13. Koch, *ORACLE7*, 175–177.

14. Koch, *ORACLE7*, 110.

15. Koch, *ORACLE7*, 273–274.

16. Koch, *ORACLE7*, 275.

17. Koch, *ORACLE7*, 728.

18. Melton and Simon, *New SQL*, 284–291.

19. J. Melton, "The Structure of SQL3," *Database Programming & Design* (June 1993), 65.

20. Melton, "SQL3."

21. Discussed in Melton and Simon, *New SQL*, 389.

22. ISO-ANSI working draft—Database Language SQL (SQL3), February 1993, 260.

23. ISO-ANSI, draft—SQL3, 581–608.

24. The presentation was cited in F. Pascal, "Sharpening Our Perceptions," *Database Programming & Design* (October 1990), 75.

25. Example from J. Melton, "The MOOSE is Loose," *Database Programming & Design* (May 1993), 71.

26. Melton, "MOOSE."

27. Melton, "SQL3," 65.

28. Melton, "SQL3," 66.

29. Melton, "SQL3."

30. At publication time, this breakdown was being revised somewhat, but will be mostly the same as listed.

31. Melton, "SQL3."

32. Melton, "SQL3."

CHAPTER 13

ODMG Languages for Object-Oriented Databases

A Note to the CIO

One of the problems with the OODBMSs has been their lack of standardization, in terms of not only languages and application programming interfaces (APIs) but also terminology and basic concepts. The ODMG-93 effort, introduced in Chapter 10, should result in some degree of standardization of OODBMSs in definition, manipulation, and query languages, much as SQL helped standardize the relational environment. Any long-term OODBMS strategy should take ODMG efforts in these areas into account.

13.1 Introduction

In Chapter 10, we discussed the efforts of the Object Database Management Group (ODMG) to create standards for object-oriented databases and languages. In this chapter, we'll take a closer look at proposals by the ODMG in the various language areas, including

- Object definition language (ODL)
- Object query language (OQL)
- Object manipulation language (OML)

Executive Summary

The ODMG-93 object database standard represents the efforts of many leading OODBMS vendors to develop a common language for products. As with relational databases and SQL, the goal is not 100 percent language compatibility among OODBMS products but rather adoption of a common language base on which products can build their own extensions. Additionally, OODB vendors have long disagreed on fundamentals (e.g., the definition of an *object*) and terminology, so the ODMG-93 effort addresses this area as well.

Syntax and semantics are provided for an object definition language (ODL), object manipulation language (OML), and object query language (OQL). Bindings are specified for the C++ and Smalltalk object-oriented programming languages.

ODL and OML may be viewed as parallels to the traditional data definition languages (DDLs) and data manipulation languages (DMLs) that are institutions in existing network (CODASYL/DBTG) and relational[1] database architectures. OQL, unlike OML, is language-independent and performs querying for interactive queries.

This chapter gives a brief overview of the various language capabilities provided for by the ODMG, but it is certainly not a complete reference work. Our purpose is to look at where OODB standardization efforts are headed with respect to language support, because the future of OODBs and OODBMSs will inevitably be heavily influenced by such standardization work. A more complete discussion of the entire ODMG-93 standard, including the various language facilities, can be found in *The Object Database Standard: ODMG-93.*[2]

13.2 Review of ODMG Principles

You may recall from our discussion in Chapter 10 that one of the driving forces behind the ODMG-93 effort has been the desire to bring standardization, which has been lacking, to OODBMSs. In addition to the general object model of ODMG, which we'll briefly review, the standardization of OODBMS language components is also important to the future of object-oriented databases.

The ODMG model features an object as the basic modeling primitive, and objects can be categorized into types. Object behavior can be defined by a set of operations that can be executed on objects of a given type. Object states are

What This Technology Can Do for You

Any organization that has already deployed OODBMS products, or is considering doing so, must be aware of the ODMG-93 standard and the intentions of OODBMS vendors to comply with the standard. Early relational products that used database languages other than SQL scrambled to catch up as SQL gained dominance in relational systems (at least on mid-range and mainframe systems); similar developments will occur in the OODBMSs.

As with SQL, strategic customers of OODBMS vendors can influence not only the direction of the standard but also which features receive high priority for incorporation into commercial products. An understanding of the standard can help you make smart choices.

defined by the values of a set of properties, and those properties can be either attributes or relationships to another object (or more than one other object).[3]

A typical environment in which an ODMG-compliant OODBMS is used is shown in Figure 13-1. Objects are declared through the ODL, which may be language-independent, or through facilities in a programming language such as C++ or Smalltalk. Following preprocessing activities, metadata for the objects are stored within the OODB, and the compiler for the specific programming language has access to the output from the preprocessor. The compiler also receives as input application source code, which contains not only object-oriented programming (OOP) constructs but also OML extensions. Following the traditional compilation process and bindings with the OODBMS, an application is created which then runs against the OODB.

With this background in mind, let's take a look at the ODMG languages, starting with the ODL.

13.3 Object Definition Language (ODL)

ODL proposals are intended to be as language-specific as possible; that is, ODL can be declared through text files fed into the preprocessor or through programming languages themselves. However, implementations may choose to provide graphical front ends or other tools to permit developers to automatically generate ODL from object-oriented design techniques, as is commonly done with front-end design tools for relational or other databases.[4]

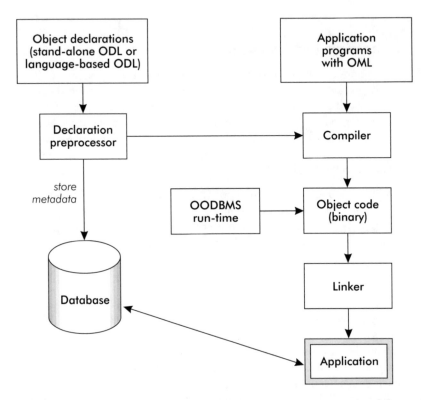

Figure 13-1 Language Usage in an ODMG-Compliant Environment[5]

Additionally, the ODMG-93 standard defines ODL in a language-independent manner, but it is also intended to provide mappings to and/or from common languages, including SQL3, which we discussed in Chapter 12 in connection with the Major Object-Oriented SQL Extensions (though, as any systems integrator or migration specialist will testify, interoperability among different language systems is rarely effortless or as simple as intended). As illustrated in Figure 13-2, SQL3 object definitions can be mapped into ODMG ODL, which then can be mapped into C++ or Smalltalk.

The purpose of ODL is to provide syntax so the ODMG object model can be specified, which is to say that ODL syntax can support not only object type declarations but also specifications of operations, attributes, and relationships. ODL is based on the IDL from the Object Management Group's (OMG's) object request broker (ORB), which we discussed in Chapter 11.

Class declarations (known as interfaces, in ODL terminology) are key-worded by the term INTERFACE. Figure 13-3 shows a simple object diagram, with the appropriate type hierarchies and relationships noted.

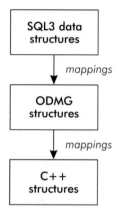

Figure 13-2 ODL and Mappings

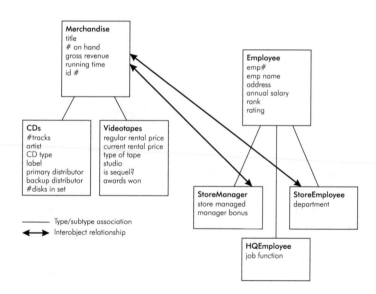

Figure 13-3 Simple Object Database Model

The ODL for the database model of Figure 13-3 is shown below. You might determine from the syntax that attributes, relationships, and operations are declared within the body of an interface.

```
interface merchandise{
     attribute          string<32>      title;
     attribute          short unsigned number_on_hand;
     attribute          float           gross_revenue;
     attribute          float           running_time;
     attribute          short unsigned id_number;
     relationship       set{store_manager}
                        ordered_by      inverse orders;
     relationship       set{store_employee}
                        stocked_by      inverse stocks;

     }

interface cds:merchandise{
     attribute          short unsigned number_tracks;
     attribute          string<32>      artist;
     attribute          string<32>      cd_type;
     attribute          string<32>      label;
     attribute          string<32>      primary_distrib;
     attribute          string<32>      backup_distrib;
     attribute          short unsigned num_disks_in_set;
     void               reorder_merchandise;
     }

interface videotapes:merchandise {
     attribute          float           reg_rental_price;
     attribute          float           curr_rental_price;
     attribute          string<32>      type_of_tape;
     attribute          string<32>      studio;
     attribute          string<32>      sequel;
     attribute          string<32>      awards_won;
     }

interface employee{
     attribute          short unsigned emp_number;
     attribute          string<32>      emp_name;
     attribute          string<32>      emp_address;
     attribute          float           annual_salary;
     attribute          string<32>      emp_rank;
     attribute          string<32>      rating;
     void               do_performance_report;
     }
```

```
interface store_manager:employee {
    attribute           string<32>      store_managed;
    attribute           float           mgr_bonus;
    relationship        set{store_employee}
                            manages inverse managed_by;
    relationship        set{merchandise}
                            orders inverse ordered_by;

}

interface hq_staff:employee {
    attribute           string<32>      job_function;
}

interface store_employee:employee {
    attribute           string<32>      department;
    relationship        set{merchandise}
                            stocks inverse stocked_by;
    relationship        set{store_manager}
                            works_for inverse managed_by;

}
```

The ODMG plans to provide future versions of the ODL standards proposals, with appropriate syntax for concepts expected to be introduced to future
versions of the object database model itself, such as n-ary relationships and
object versioning.

13.4 Object Query Language (OQL)

Let's shift our attention to the ODMG OQL. OQL is similar in syntax to SQL
(discussed in Chapter 12). Primitives are provided for sets of objects, as well
as structures and lists. OQL is exactly what it says: a query language. Update
operators are not explicitly provided, but rather are left to operations defined
on the objects.[6]
   Let's take a brief look at some sample OQL queries. To obtain a result of
all store managers with a bonus of greater than $10,000 last year, a query is
made against the extent (the set of all instances of a given type) of the form

```
select e.emp_name
  from e in store_managers
  where e.mgr_bonus > 10000
```

You should note several things about this OQL query. If you look back at
the ODL syntax in the previous section, you will see that STORE_MANAGER

is a subtype of EMPLOYEE, and the attributes EMP_NAME and MGR_BONUS were declared for the supertype and subtype, respectively. An OQL query automatically takes into account the inheritance of a supertype's attributes by a subtype; therefore an OQL SELECT query can be offered against a set of objects with all attributes from its supertype considered.

The previous query can be slightly extended to return a structure (similar in concept to a multiple-column relational projection, as compared with a single-column projection), as in

```
select struct (name: e.emp_name, bonus: e.mgr_bonus)
  from e in store_managers
  where e.mgr_bonus > 10000
```

Queries can also be formally defined through query definition expressions, and further queries can be offered against those definitions. These are conceptually similar to SQL view definitions and subsequent SELECT operations against that view. For example,

```
define sale_video as select v from v in videotapes
    where v.curr_rental_price < v.reg_rental_price;
select v.title from v in sale_video;
```

In this example, the query definition expression is used to determine what videotapes are on sale by comparing the current and regular rental prices. The subsequent OQL query will produce the TITLE (as with our earlier examples, provided by the subtype inheritance from MERCHANDISE).

Queries may also be defined against ODMG elements, in which case the single object from the database satisfying the query will be returned (or, if there is not a single result, an exception will be raised):

```
define term2 as element (select v from v in videotapes
    where v.title = "Terminator 2");
```

OQL also provides facilities to create objects using a type name constructor. For example,

```
videotapes(title: "Last Action Hero", number_on_hand: 35,
    gross_revenue: 45,235, running_time: 135.5,
    id_number: 2456, reg_rental_price: 2.99,
    curr_rental_price: 2.99, type_of_tape: "Adventure",
    .....)
```

OQL also includes facilities for constructing objects, sets, and lists, as well as *expressions*, such as membership testing (e.g., if an element belongs to a collection) and existential quantification. A sort-by operator may be used for the ordering of query results, along with a group-by operator, which works much like to its SQL namesake. For example, the group-by operator may be used to combine all videotapes into groups based on current rental prices, from which appropriate summaries and averages may then be derived.

Summarizing, OQL provides a means by which queries may be presented against an ODMG-compliant database. OQL in its present form has far fewer querying capabilities than, say, SQL-92 or SQL3, though as ODMG-compliant databases become commonplace in the future the language will likely have its capabilities extended, not only by the ODMG committee but also by vendor implementations of the standard.

13.5 ODMG and C++

In section 13.3, we defined the object definition language (ODL) as a stand-alone language that may be run through a preprocessor to create object definitions in an ODMG-compliant database. In Figure 13-1, we noted that ODL need not come exclusively from an external source; it may also be included within a C++ program (or a Smalltalk program, as we'll discuss in the next section).

A C++ program may process OQL as well (see section 13.4). Object manipulation language (OML), which we haven't seen yet so far in this chapter, also has C++ bindings in the ODMG standard. Let's look at each of these.

13.5.1 C++ and ODL

C++ ODL is very similar to basic C++ class definitions, with several new keywords defined (in the example below, EXTENT and KEYS). For example,[7]

```
class merchandise : Object
{
        extent all_merchandise;
        keys id_number;
    public:
        // properties:
            char*       title;
            int         number_on_hand;
            float       gross_revenue;
            float       running_time;
            int         id_number;
```

```
set<ref<store_manager> ordered_by inverse orders;
     // operations:
          initial_order ();
          reorder ();
          take_inventory ();
          report_sales ();
          close_out ();
       ...
     }

class cds:merchandise
     {
        ...
```

The C++ ODL, as shown above, allows the definition of attributes, relationships, and operations, similar to the capabilities of the stand-alone ODL that we saw earlier.

13.5.2 C++ and OQL

OQL capabilities can also be used from C++, in two ways. The first is via a query method defined on the generic class COLLECTION, as in[8]

```
set<videotapes> romance_movies;
romance = videotapes.query (
          " . . . an OQL query for romance movies . . ."
```

The second way is through the OQL function, as in

```
set <videotapes> romance_movies;
oql ( romance_movies, "select . . . OQL query for romance movies
. . .")
```

13.5.3 C++ and OML

The C++ bindings provide capabilities for the creation, deletion, and modification of objects through OML.

The OML syntax for object creation allows objects to be designated as either PERSISTENT or TRANSIENT, as in

```
ref<videotapes>tape1 = new(persistent) videotapes;
```

An implementation-specific *clustering* argument may also be used, which specifies object placement as "near" some other object (the definition of "near" is the implementation-specific aspect).

Objects are deleted by the DESTROY operator, as in

```
ref<some type>videotape_ref;
videotape_ref.destroy();
```

The third major OML operation after creation and deletion is modification. Following the updating of object properties or running an operation against an object, the MARKMODIFIED operation is used to communicate the state changes to the OODBMS.

```
videotape_ref.markModified();
```

OML also provides capabilities to create, traverse, and break relationships among instances of objects (the relationships having been defined earlier in ODL). A number of methods are used to perform such operations, and a complete list may be found in the ODMG-93 standard.[9]

Note that the various C++ bindings for the languages depend on some degree of transparency to support ODL and OML within the body of the language. Either C++ technology (e.g., the language itself plus supporting environments) must evolve to support this transparency, or a preprocessor will be required to do so. The ODMG bindings are based on the principle that the treatment of persistent and transient objects should be the same within the body of C++ programs. The ODMG committee's ideas is that the path to "the C++ environment of the future" is either 1) through the evolution of the definition of operator overloading within the C++ language definition or 2) a C++ preprocessor that can handle C++ method bodies in addition to C++ class declarations.[10]

In anticipation of more robust C++ environments, the ODMG-93 standard includes a section that outlines the proposed *future* bindings for ODL and OML, with capabilities beyond those we discuss in this section. While it may seem a bit overzealous to consider future bindings to a standard which has not been implemented yet, information system planners who decide to commit to ODMG-based technology for their OODB/OODBMS environments should carefully track the future of such bindings (in much the same way that implementors of the 1993 version of SQL should track the progress of SQL3). This way, their environments may be positioned to take advantage of future capabilities as they arrive.

13.6 Smalltalk and ODMG

The Smalltalk-to-ODMG language bindings are different than those of C++ to ODMG-compliant languages.[11] Because Smalltalk is an untyped language and inherently dynamic, as contrasted with the strong typing of ODL and the compiled nature of OML, an impedence mismatch not unlike that of SQL to 3GLs exists.[12]

As of this writing, the ODMG was still working on its proposals for Smalltalk bindings. Some decisions have been made (e.g., operation declarations are not included with attributes and relationships in object type declarations, because Smalltalk is a dynamic language). Those readers with Smalltalk environments who have plans for ODMG-compliant databases and languages should track the efforts in the area of bindings, preparing for whatever eventually emerges from standards committees and vendors.

13.7 Conclusion

The ODMG effort represents agreement by OODBMS vendors that standards are key to the future of the OODB world. Recall that it took a number of years for relational vendors to agree to bring SQL to the forefront of the relational languages. As the SQL/relational-based world "encroaches" on object-oriented databases (through the MOOSE capabilities we discussed in Chapter 12), resistance to standards by OODBMS vendors would be counterproductive, causing the OODB camp based on "pure" object-oriented engines to fall far behind extended-relational vendors in terms of market share.

Fortunately, OODBMS vendors are aware of this fact, even explicitly stating such in the ODMG-93 standards proposal.[13] Therefore, OODB standardization is an irreversible course. By the mid-to-late 1990s, compliance with ODMG models and languages will be a given, much as SQL and basic relational model support are standard for RDBMS products. We will see product differentiation in the areas of feature extensions, interfaces, and the like.

Finally, it's important to note that the efforts of the ODMG, while representing a meeting of the minds of OODBMS vendors, do not by themselves constitute an *official* standardization effort. Recall our discussion in section 3.3.1 of Chapter 3 with respect to SQL CLI and DRDA, and the differences between de jure, or official, and de facto standards, which are based on general agreement rather than official edicts. The ODMG efforts fall into the latter category, though of course their research is likely to be presented to standards-making bodies (such as ANSI and ISO) as the foundation for an official standard.[14]

Outlook

Short-term

- As ODMG compliance occurs among commercial products, OQL, ODL, and OML facilities will be incorporated into database programming environments
- C++ and Smalltalk will be extended with ODMG-driven constructs
- Likely submission of "final" ODMG-93 de facto standard to standards-making bodies for formalization

Long-term

- Further language extensions to ODL, OML, and OQL will appear
- Interfaces to other object-oriented languages (including SQL3 MOOSE) will appear

Additional Reading

- R. G. G. Cattell, ed., *The Object Database Standard: ODMG-93* (San Francisco: Morgan Kaufmann Publishers, 1994).

Endnotes

1. There are underlying differences, however. ODL, like SQL DDL, is translated into host language data constructs subject to data type matching and other reconciliations. Under the OODBMS principle of unifying the programming and database languages, OML is handled in much the same way; SQL DML, by contrast, is converted to a "call" to a database procedure not expressed in that host language.

2. R. G. G. Cattell, ed., *The Object Database Standard: ODMG-93* (San Francisco: Morgan Kaufmann Publishers, 1994).

3. Cattell, ed., *ODMG-93*, 11.

4. The source of material for this section, and reference for more information, is Cattell, ed., *ODMG-93*, Chap. 3.

5. Cattell, ed., *ODMG-93*, 6.

6. The source of material for this section, and reference for more information, is Cattell, ed., *ODMG-93*, Chap. 4.

7. Based on the example in Chap. 5.

8. Adapted from the example in Cattell, ed., *ODMG-93*, 111.

9. Cattell, ed., *ODMG-93*, 96–98.

10. Cattell, ed., *ODMG-93*, 119–121.

11. Cattell, ed., *ODMG-93*, 131.

12. Cattell, ed., *ODMG-93*.

13. According to Cattell, ed., *ODMG-93*, 1, "To date, the lack of a standard for object databases has been a major limitation to their more widespread use."

14. This is a common occurrence in the IS world. Another example is in the area of computer-aided systems (or software) engineering (CASE) in which de facto standardization efforts for control integration like CASE Communique and the CASE Interoperability Alliance were merged in 1993 and presented to the ANSI X3H6 Committee for formal, de jure standardization efforts. Discussion of these efforts may be found in A. Simon, *The Integrated CASE Tools Handbook* (New York: Van Nostrand Reinhold/Intertext, 1993), Chap. 12.

CHAPTER 14

Xbase and Other Desktop Databases

A Note to the CIO

If your organization has made liberal use of desktop PC technology over the past ten years or so, you most likely have a large set of personal and department applications written in some dialect of the Xbase language, either from the original dBASE family of products or from others such as FoxPro or Clipper. The PC database is undergoing attempts to standardize Xbase and movement toward graphical user interfaces as the primary PC DBMS API. Understanding these two areas of research and where they are headed is important. Further, desktop databases in general are growing up rapidly in terms of performance, capabilities, and capacity, primarily due to the tremendous advances in memory and disk capacity as well as processor performance on the desktop. Products such as DB2, long the exclusive property of the most powerful mainframes, are shrinking to the desktop, and it's a good idea to understand the trends in this area as well.

14.1 Introduction

To many database professionals and a large number of end users, particularly in small and medium-sized businesses, SQL, object-oriented databases, and "professional" databases have little or no meaning. Their database experience is primarily on PC platforms, and a great deal of that experience is with Xbase products. In this chapter, we'll look at the future of the Xbase language and other interfaces to desktop databases, and at the directions of desktop databases themselves. Traditionally, the languages, work areas, and engines of

Executive Summary

Many in the data center think of PC and desktop databases as mere toys, useful only for small personal productivity applications such as mailing lists. But the incorporation of desktop DBMS products into client/server environments, together with the ever-increasing computer power and storage capacity of the desktop, makes such systems extremely viable for real-world applications.

Several major trends will affect the desktop database future:

- Standardization of the Xbase language, the dominant program development system on the desktop.

- Incorporation of graphical user interface (GUI) and object-oriented programming (OOP) technologies into desktop DBMS products.

desktop databases have been much more closely connected than those of mainframe and mid-range database environments, including the SQL and relational database pairing (discussed in Chapter 12). In fact, the desktop database resembles object-oriented databases more than SQL-based relational databases in the close coupling of languages and databases, even though the dominant database paradigm on the desktop has been the relational model. Therefore, no discussion of desktop database language would be complete without examining its close relationship to the underlying database engines— and how that relationship is changing and will continue to do so.

14.2 Desktop Databases and Xbase: A Brief History

14.2.1 dBASE and Related Products

During the early days of the personal computer, a quartet of horizontal applications emerged, common to nearly every organization, regardless of their business mission. Word processing, spreadsheet, graphics, and database software fulfilled the information management needs of hundreds of thousands, perhaps millions, of organizations and small businesses around the world.

Many different vendors vied for dominance in the early days of the PC. For a short period of time, PCs running the CP/M operating system had a strong presence in the small business and department market, and the database

- Bringing "real DBMS" functionality (transaction models, security, more robust multiuser models) to PC products that have traditionally operated in stand-alone or small-scale LAN environments.

- New commitments to PC DBMS products from vendors who dominate the mid-range and mainframe realms.

What This Technology Can Do for You

Many applications in your organization can be developed using desktop DBMS products. The marriage of desktop DBMS functionality with client/server standards and technologies (discussed in Chapter 3) provides organizations with additional options for deploying distributed processing in database environments. An understanding not only of today's products and technologies but also of the trends and directions of desktop databases is essential for long-range strategic decisions.

product that dominated in that environment was dBASE II from Ashton-Tate. Recalling our definition of database management from section 1.2 of Chapter 1, dBASE II wasn't a true DBMS product, falling short in many areas, particularly transaction management; nor could it be considered a "real" relational product despite its table and column orientation. Small businesses and department users, however, were enthralled by the capability to store and manipulate table-based data on the desktop outside the control of the data center, creating and using millions of customer mailing lists, employee rosters, and similar files.

When the IBM PC and its clones, all powered by the MS-DOS operating system, achieved dominance in the early 1980s, Ashton-Tate introduced dBASE II for DOS-based systems. The DOS version basically had the same capabilities as the CP/M version, including the latter's limitations such as having a maximum of only two files open at a given time, which made applications development difficult for anything other than simple list or file management. In 1984, though, Ashton-Tate introduced a major new product called dBASE III. Many of the restrictions of dBASE II were removed, and powerful language, function, and query enhancements were introduced. While some limitations remained, dBASE III became the dominant database manager for PC systems.

Around 1986, an enhanced version known as dBASE III Plus was introduced. At the same time, other software vendors introduced work-alike products that utilized the basic dBASE language. Vendors claimed product supremacy in areas such as sort times, reindexing operations, index-based record seeks, and other features that could be competitively measured. Other products, particularly Nantucket Corporation's Clipper, functioned as compilers for the interpreted dBASE language, staking their primary market claim on compiled application performance versus the interpreted code that was part of the dBASE environment.

This trend toward product work-alikes, paralleled in the PC spreadsheet market with work-alikes for Lotus 1-2-3, is arguably the single most important event leading to the standardization efforts for the Xbase language, an important future direction for desktop databases.

In the 1987–1988 period, the first attempts were made to standardize what is now known as the Xbase language. A committee of vendors, including then-independent Fox Software (FoxPro) and Nantucket Corporation (Clipper), began work on standardization efforts which eventually came under the control of the Institute of Electrical and Electronic Engineers (IEEE); these attempts were short-circuited by legal action from Ashton-Tate under claims of proprietary rights to the dBASE language.[1] That put the standardization effort on hold until 1992, although vendors of dBASE-compatible products periodically made public statements of eventual conformance with whatever standards would emerge.

As the 1990s approached, the dominance of the PC database market remained with Xbase products, while the dBASE family began to lose market share to other vendors. Ashton-Tate introduced a new version of their flagship product, dBASE IV, which was followed several years later by a "point release product," dBASE IV version 1.1, to correct perceived product shortcomings. By this time, though, other Xbase products, particularly FoxPro and Clipper, had gained a tremendous market share.

The Xbase market was rocked by a rapid series of acquisitions of the major players by much larger software companies—in fact, some of the largest software companies in the United States. Microsoft acquired Fox Software, Computer Associates acquired Nantucket, and Borland acquired Ashton-Tate. Within a short period of time, the Xbase market had changed dramatically.

Following the acquisitions, talk about Xbase standardization began to surface again, though this time it was Xbase *developers* rather than vendors who spearheaded the effort.[2] In mid-1992, Xbase standardization came to life; we'll discuss it in section 14.3. A timeline of the events discussed in this section is presented in Figure 14-1.

14.2.2 Other PC Databases

Before we go on to discuss Xbase standardization efforts, it's important to note that the history and current events of the PC database are not exclusively within the context of Xbase. Although many of the early competitors of dBASE II and dBASE III became "also-rans" in the marketplace, at least one, Borland's Paradox, has survived and thrived into the mid-1990s. When Borland acquired the dBASE family in 1992, it began pursuing a two-database product strategy.

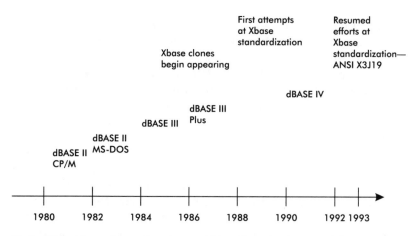

Figure 14-1 Major Events Leading to Xbase Standardization Efforts

Interestingly enough, the rash of acquisitions we discussed in the previous section have led Microsoft, Borland, and Computer Associates into a situation often dreaded by software vendors: having two or more products within the same application on the same platform. Though this book isn't a forum for discussions on product management philosophy, pursuing a dual-product strategy within a specific market (in this case, personal computer databases) makes product differentiation tricky to handle. At the time of writing we have the following lineup:

Vendor	PC Database Product
Borland	dBASE IV
	Paradox
Computer Associates	CA-Clipper
	CA-dBFast
Microsoft	FoxPro
	Access

Note that the above list does not include variations of each product for different PC platforms (e.g., FoxPro for Windows and FoxPro for MS-DOS), nor does it include other areas, such as databases for the Apple Macintosh or database products for non-desktop platforms (Borland's Interbase or Computer Associates' CA-IDMS and CA-DATACOM). Gauging vendors' commitments to their product suites will be interesting as standardization, advances in object-oriented capabilities, and other events occur in the next few years.

Speaking of the Apple Macintosh, one of the curious occurrences from the time the Macintosh was first introduced in 1984 until the early 1990s was the lack of interest in DBMS software of many Macintosh users. As we discussed in the previous section, the MS-DOS PC world and even earlier CP/M-based systems were dominated by applications targeted at personal productivity: word processing, spreadsheets, databases, and graphics (and later, desktop publishing). As the Apple Macintosh entered corporate environments, database software didn't become as firmly entrenched on that platform as the other horizontal applications (though it eventually did, functioning as a client front end to database servers). DBMS software for the Macintosh certainly existed. For whatever reason, possibly that the GUI environment of the time wasn't particularly suitable to database applications (even those of the desktop), databases for Macintosh systems were much less common than on their MS-DOS competitors. The two major branches of the PC world—Macintosh, and systems rooted in MS-DOS but now running Microsoft Windows or OS/2—will converge in the mid-1990s. As that happens, the distinctions between these branches will vanish, and new hardware, such as Digital Equipment's Alpha AXP processor, and new operating systems, such as Microsoft Windows NT, will appear; the confinement of desktop databases to DOS will also inevitably disappear.

Even though Xbase emerged as the dominant database language for the desktop, SQL was not totally absent. Many of the DBMS vendors with SQL-based products in either UNIX or VAX/VMS environments introduced PC versions of their products in the mid-1980s. PC versions of ORACLE, INGRES, Informix, Unify, and others were available but for the most part never achieved the degree of penetration into the desktop DBMS market that their makers had envisioned, mostly due to the relative ease of using Xbase products over SQL-based products. Likewise, IBM introduced an SQL product for OS/2, known originally as the OS/2 Extended Edition Database Manager. We'll discuss how the desktop database market is evolving with respect to IBM software products in section 14.7.2.

It's also interesting to note that late 1980s' attempts to put Xbase on mid-range systems, typically coupled with underlying relational database engines, also received less than stellar market share. It seems that the demarcation lines drawn from 1983 to 1984—SQL on mid-range systems, Xbase on PCs—remained in effect even as vendors moved SQL and Xbase outside their traditional homes.

Finally, even though relational-like products, whether SQL or Xbase, dominated the PC database market, the network data model (described in Chapter 1) made appearances, and at least one product has survived into the mid-1990s using the network model as its underlying paradigm.

14.3 Xbase and ANSI X3J19

A proposal to the American National Standards Institute (ANSI) in May 1992 resulted in approval by the Standards Planning and Requirements Committee

(SPARC, now known as the Operations Management Committee, or OMC) for X3 to proceed with Xbase standardization.[3] As we discussed in section 14.2.1, this effort was a user-driven movement.[4] However, noting the motivations of Xbase users and eager to promote their particular language nuances as the basis for the standard, the major vendors (Microsoft, Borland, Computer Associates), other Xbase vendors,[5] developer organizations, the U.S. Department of Defense, the National Institute of Standards and Technology (NIST), and the NASA Jet Propulsion Laboratory (JPL) all joined the effort.[6] In short, it was clear that this movement was receiving serious interest from all involved.

Interestingly, the standardization effort occurs within the programming language group of ANSI rather than the database group. (Within ANSI, programming language committees are prefaced by the letters "X3J," while database committees always begin with "X3H"—for example, X3H2, discussed in Chapter 12 on SQL.) By placing the standardization efforts within the area of programming languages, those involved sought to put Xbase in the realm of COBOL, C, Fortran, and other languages, *regardless of the underlying database engine*. As we'll discuss in section 14.7.1, Xbase systems have typically been run on top of the .DBF file format, with the language and file formats closely coupled within product environments. By explicitly distinguishing Xbase as a programming language independent of the underlying database engine, many other future directions, such as client/server front ends and interfaces to standards-based middleware, will be easier to achieve.

The technical committee for Xbase, which was assigned the classification X3J19, began meeting in late 1992, and efforts are continuing. One of the first official decisions was the adoption of the name *Xbase* as the formal language name.

It's important to note that because of the relative newness of X3J19 and its work at the time of writing, many outstanding issues in procedures are still unresolved, including the following:[7]

- Whether the standard would be developed by U.S. attendees only or with international participation. One option is to create an ANSI standard through U.S. participation only, which would then be submitted to ISO as a candidate for an ISO standard. Another option is to have international voting-level participation from the beginning, with eventual ISO adoption supposedly "greased" through this participation.
- Unresolved legal issues remain with respect to language ownership.
- Scoping and leveling of the Xbase document, as in SQL-92 and SQL3 (see Chapter 12). General thought at present (mid-1993) is that a Level I must take into account the thousands of Xbase applications that currently exist and should reflect the state of current implementations as it provides a "proper subset" for the development of Level II.

14.3.1 Standardization Efforts

And what exactly are the major areas for X3J19? Main efforts are targeted toward stemming the divergence among major products in the Xbase market. Xbase has decisively "won" the PC database language market in much the same way that SQL won dominance in mid-range and mainframe DBMS languages. With SQL, though, major vendors have merrily gone their own ways in the language syntax of their products. X3J19 will attempt to walk the tightrope between letting existing applications remain executable under a product compliant with the standard, and allowing for the degree of innovation and product capabilities that have driven the Xbase market to date.

As with most committee efforts, numerous papers have been submitted that deal with various language features. This typically results in disagreement between the least-common-denominator approach (i.e., finding the intersection of capabilities from current products and establishing that as the standard) and those who favor robust standards which often get ahead of most or all products for whose sake the standards are being developed.

As an indication of the general thoughts of the committee, let's take a look at the following items:[8]

- The trend favoring Xbase as a compiled language as opposed to its interpreter-based dBASE roots means potential problems with *interactive commands*, which can be built and submitted dynamically within the body of an Xbase program. Xbase systems have traditionally been closely coupled environments, involving not only the language and the database engine, but utilities and development environments as well. One idea is to have a separate interactive development environment for Xbase programs and preprocessors as necessary.

- The original dBASE language is devoid of data typing for variables. Variables may be created at any time "on the fly." Because many Xbase programs currently exist without any data typing and data typing has been deemed important for the Xbase standard, the current thought is that compilers will be capable of performing type inferencing. *Type inferencing* distinguishes the data type of a variable from how it's used within a program (what values are assigned to it, whether it's used for mathematical operations, and so on). This way, Xbase compilers could have data typing without "breaking" existing programs that don't utilize those constructs. Many programs written without data typing reuse variable names in different contexts, which often dynamically changes the data type associated with a particular variable name.

- dBASE III introduced a degree of modularity to Xbase programming. Variables could be declared as PUBLIC, which meant they would act as if they belonged to shared memory. The absence of PUBLIC declaration meant that their scoping would be limited to the program file (the "subroutine") in which they were used. X3J19 is trying to strengthen the modularity of the Xbase language, believing that team developments for large programs will become the norm as Xbase moves into corporation-class applications (as opposed to just the desktop). One possibility is to adopt a four-class scoping for variables, as proposed by CA for CA-Clipper and the Aspen "future language":[9]

- *Public:* Globally visible, dynamically allocated, with data type established by how a variable is first used.

- *Private:* Visible in the function or procedure that owns it, as well as in any function called by it. Private variables are also dynamically allocated with data typing established by first usage.

- *Global:* Visible over the entire application, statically allocated, and strongly typed.

- *Local:* Visible only in the function or procedure that owns it, statically allocated, and strongly typed.

- The work areas of Xbase are closely tied to the relational base of the underlying files, that is, a row-and-column paradigm. As we'll discuss in section 14.5, the future of PC databases, including those using the Xbase language, is undoubtedly headed toward object orientation. Therefore, separation of the data manipulation language of Xbase from the work areas could lead to object orientation in underlying implementations.

The list goes on. The most important thing to remember is that X3J19 is focused on the following objectives:

- Halting the divergence among Xbase products.

- Preserving the installed code base of as many Xbase applications as possible, for all products.

- Allowing for future developments, such as Windows-based interfaces and incorporation of an object-orientation model, as we'll discuss shortly.

What can the Xbase world expect from X3J19? In addition to the items we have discussed, the agenda includes interfaces with SQL, both in terms of SQL embedded within Xbase procedural code and in the area of SQL interfaces.[10] The SQL interfaces will possibly be through a standard based on SQL/CLI, such as IDAPI or ODBC (see Chapter 3 for further discussion of those standards).

14.3.2 Xbase Standardization Concerns

Despite the attention given to X3J19, some say that Xbase standardization matters not in the least; it is old technology, and the desktop database world is rapidly passing it by. Many argue plausibly that the appropriate time to pursue standardization was when it was originally attempted, from 1987 to

1988. The divergence of the major products since that time, as well as paradigm shifts in user interfaces and underlying data models, mean that Xbase standardization through the mid-1990s is little more than a futile effort. As we'll discuss in the next section, most major desktop database product announcements from 1992 to 1993 have been directed at two major concepts:

1) A graphical user interface (GUI) as the primary interface paradigm, coupled with object-oriented programming and development characteristics.

2) Object orientation in the underlying data model.

However, Xbase is not dead, for one simple reason: it has been the primary development tool for PC applications for over a decade, and the need to incorporate legacy systems into database environments of the future demands its continued life.

COBOL too has been pronounced dead (or at least outmoded) many times by its critics who point to C, C++, Ada, and other modern languages as far superior in terms of functionality. But the fact remains that having millions of COBOL applications that will effectively never go away demands continued work in the area of language standardization and enhancements (including early 1990s' discussion of object-oriented COBOL), compiler technology, tool and utility development, and other related areas. This exact argument can be made of Xbase as a language.

Therefore, even with continuing talk of development and enhancement—GUI-based object-oriented extensions to both the programming practices and the database-stored information, and decoupling of PC database languages from the underlying data managers—Xbase is here to stay. And because of the persistence of the language, the standardization efforts will continue.

14.4 Graphical User Interfaces (GUIs) to PC Databases

If Xbase and its standardization are not futile efforts, then, what is to be made of the argument that the future of desktop database interfaces will be based on GUIs (closely coupled with object-oriented methodologies, which we'll discuss in section 14.5) rather than procedural languages such as Xbase?

Before we answer that question, let's take a quick look at the historical roots of windowing interfaces to user databases. The roots of the Xbase language, as we discussed, have been in most PC database products since the dBASE II days: a procedural, programmatic interface to user data, coupled with command line query capabilities, to obtain database results (Figure 14-2).

```
* program sample.prg
public emp_name, emp_salary
emp_name = spaces (30)
emp_salary = 0.0

use videoemps index videonme

do while trim(emp_name) <> "xxxx"
    @ 5,5 say "Enter name, xxxx to exit" get emp_name
    @ 7,5 say "Enter employee salary" get emp_salary
    read

    if trim(emp_name) <> "xxxx"

        append blank
        replace name with emp_name, emp_salary
    endif
enddo
```

Figure 14-2 Traditional Xbase Interface

dBASE III Plus introduced an ASSIST mode, in which an interface featuring pull-down menus, assisted command executions, overlapping windows, and similar features could be accessed both by developers and end users. The ASSIST mode was *not* a graphical user interface; it was an attempt to provide GUI-like capabilities to a character-based interface mode.

As GUIs became widely used outside of the Macintosh systems (driven primarily by the success of version 3 of Microsoft Windows), database product vendors (indeed, nearly all commercial software vendors) labored to rehost their products to a GUI platform. This is no easy task, as is evident from vendor delays in the mid-1980s in the introduction of Macintosh versions of their DOS software and similar delays in the early 1990s in moving DOS-based applications to Microsoft Windows or other GUI environments. Capabilities such as event handling, incorporation of some degree of object-oriented thinking, and other GUI characteristics outside the scope of our present discussion often lead to difficulties in developing GUI-based software.

This developmental learning curve, however, is being conquered, not just by commercial software vendors but also by independent developers and consultants. This means

- Nearly all PC database products will have graphical user interfaces, both for end users querying databases and for developers of applications based on those products. Many products have already been rehosted for Microsoft Windows (Borland's Paradox and Microsoft's FoxPro in particular).

More importantly, new database products without MS-DOS roots are appearing (Microsoft's Access, for example). Even if traditional Xbase developers feel more comfortable in environments where they create and edit program files, giving their application users only the amount of data management and program control they deem is appropriate, they will nevertheless see this development model continue to fade from the desktop. End users will, through the GUIs, be given more powerful data access and manipulation capabilities than are currently available with today's crop of products. Application generators, based on screen designers and visually oriented programming, will create database programs with less procedural logic than is necessary in most Xbase environments. Finally, application developers themselves will find that they make extensive use of the appropriate GUI application programming interface (API) for managing windows, dialog boxes, menus, and other GUI properties.

- Database applications in PC environments have been developed with languages such as Xbase primarily due to the increased level of productivity over traditional third-generation languages (C and Pascal, for example), but this situation will change. As we discussed, one of the trends in the Xbase world is the decoupling of the Xbase language itself from the underlying database engines. As this occurs, the distinctions between Xbase, GUI-based programming, and other PC languages such as Visual Basic will shrink dramatically, causing an increase in the importance of the role that GUI APIs play in application development.[11]

Figure 14-3 shows the current distinctions between application development based on Xbase and on GUI environments (typically called from a language such as C). We also see how the incorporation of object-oriented development techniques into those environments, including visually oriented programming, will bring the two worlds closer together.

14.5 Object Orientation

Two aspects of object orientation are important in understanding the future of databases and PC database languages. The first, the development environment, is directly related to our discussion in the previous section. The second aspect of object orientation for PC databases is, of course, object-oriented databases themselves.

GUI environments are a natural fit for object-oriented development techniques, and as the role of Microsoft Windows and other GUI managers increases within the database world, so too will the use of object orientation. Creation and use of classes of dialogs, types of queries, and instances of those object classes for application development will become commonplace.

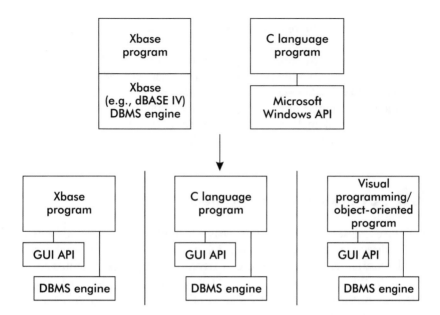

Figure 14-3 The Growing Role of GUIs for Application Development

Developers accustomed to object-oriented development, from design through coding, may support this move, but those more familiar with procedural coding (as used for Xbase programming, for example) may find the restrictions and rules of object-oriented development frustrating and difficult to learn. Even though a great deal of power can be pushed into an object-oriented framework that experienced developers can utilize (in contrast to having to procedurally design and code capabilities such as messaging and methods, event management, and so on), many programmers feel that the perceived loss of control of their applications is uncomfortable when compared to more traditional environments.

The above discussion falls somewhat outside our subject of the future direction of database languages and databases, although the developmental models used for the languages and databases of the future are an important topic as well. Development of software in an object-oriented language such as C++ or Smalltalk is generally believed to be extremely difficult if one were to utilize programming techniques learned from assembly language or even COBOL days. Therefore, as the desktop database environments evolve and advance, so too must the developmental methodologies and tools used to create database applications.

In Chapters 9 through 12 we discussed object-oriented database trends and future directions, including convergence and unification of the relational and object-oriented models. Object-oriented database capabilities are beginning to find their way to the desktop, initially by adding BLOB (binary large object) capabilities to relational-based engines, and later by full object-oriented capabilities, through either their addition to existing relational products or the downsizing of object-oriented engines to the desktop. In short, our entire discussion from our earlier object-oriented database chapters applies to PC databases as well. The work area of Xbase environments, with their row-column orientation, must be decoupled from the Xbase language (or, for that matter, GUIs) to provide a smooth movement toward object-oriented database capabilities under Xbase.

14.6 PC Databases and Architectures

Let's take a closer look at the PC databases themselves. So far, we've focused on the directions of interfaces to desktop databases, both in terms of Xbase standardization and the growing GUI trend utilizing object-oriented techniques. In this section, we'll look at the future of dBASE-rooted databases, how the downsizing of IBM's DB2 is affecting desktop databases, and database architectures in general.

14.6.1 The .DBF File Format

In addition to language compatibility (more or less), Xbase products also share a common file format to store the tables and columns of data (Figure 14-4). This is the .DBF format, so called because in the MS-DOS environments in which these products operate, the extension for those files is .DBF, as in MOVIES.DBF or VIDEOTAP.DBF.

While the .DBF format has provided much data compatibility over the years, it plainly is aging. In section 14.2.1, we discussed the history of Xbase products and their roots in department and small-business applications. For such applications, MS-DOS PCs have traditionally been the dominant developmental and operational environment, and a simple storage structure such as .DBF files was sufficient for many years. However, as PC databases play an increasingly important role in corporation-wide information environments including client/server (see Chapter 3) and multidatabase (see Chapter 6) systems, additional capabilities are clearly needed.

What are those capabilities? Chief among them is some degree of data dictionary/repository integration.[12] A metadata management model similar to SQL-92 and SQL3 (see Chapter 12) is a likely outcome, including features such as self-describing schemas and a formal interface between the database manager and a repository, such as one based on IRDSs (Information Resource Dictionary Systems), which we'll discuss in Chapter 19.

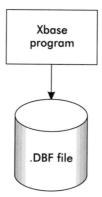

Figure 14-4 Traditional PC Database Architecture: the Xbase Language and the .DBF File Format

14.6.2 IBM Desktop Databases: Future Directions

No discussion of PC databases would be complete without taking a look at IBM's philosophy of unifying their various database environments, including those on the desktop. Xbase products and their GUI-based successors, along with Paradox for Windows and Microsoft's Access, will continue to be the dominant products in the Microsoft Windows environments (that is, systems rooted in an MS-DOS foundation). Meanwhile, IBM is concentrating its desktop areas in the OS/2 and AIX (UNIX) environments.

IBM had long pursued a multi-DBMS product strategy, with SQL/DS and DB2 for mainframe environments, the OS/400 Data Manager for AS/400 systems, and OS/2 Extended Edition Data Manager for desktop systems. The Distributed Relational Data Architecture (DRDA), which we discussed in Chapter 3, had been viewed as the unifying protocol among those various DBMS products under the auspices of the Systems Application Architecture (SAA) framework. The increased hardware and software power available on the desktop, when compared with that of even the recent past, seems to have given IBM the opportunity to downscale DB2 to OS/2 and AIX from its MVS origins, something unimagined in the recent past. This appears to be a response to frequent criticism of IBM for pursuing different product strategies on different hardware and operating system platforms.

For OS/2, IBM introduced DB2/2 in early 1993. DB2/2 is a 32-bit client/server database which can function as a server for DOS, Windows, and OS/2 applications and software.[13] It supports NETBIOS and the APPC and APPN (Advanced Peer-to-Peer Communications and Advanced Peer-to-Peer Networking, respectively) protocols.

DB2/6000 also functions as a server, not only for the three client types supported by DB2/2 but also for other AIX systems. It supports the TCP/IP and APPC protocols.

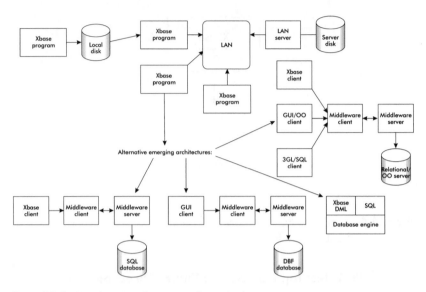

Figure 14-5 Trends in Desktop Database Directions

Given the accelerating trend toward downsizing information systems environments (discussed in Chapter 1), putting DB2 versions on server-capable desktop platforms such as OS/2 and AIX appears to be IBM's effort to avoid losing DB2 applications to other SQL-based desktop database products. Therefore, the future of PC databases (desktop databases, to be more accurate) will include far more than the DOS- and Windows-based focus discussed earlier in this chapter. Future enhancements to DB2 for MVS environments will likely be included in both DB2/2 and DB2/6000 and will bear watching.

14.6.3 Representative PC Database Architectures

We've mentioned that the Xbase language is rapidly decoupling from its underlying database engines. This trend, which started when dBASE-compatible products became front ends to SQL server databases, has accelerated. Some of the possible resulting architectures are shown in Figure 14-5. We can expect a mix-and-match environment, made possible by the growing acceptance of database middleware for client/server environments, as we discussed in Chapter 3.

14.7 Conclusion

As we conclude our discussion in this chapter, let's note several important points:

- As the computing power on the desktop continues to increase, traditional distinctions between PC databases (those typically built around Xbase) and "real" DBMS products will eventually vanish.

- The widespread adoption of client/server computing has led to the decoupling of desktop database languages and interface environments from the underlying database engine. This irreversible trend includes Xbase and interfaces built around GUIs and object-oriented capabilities.

- As a result of the two previous items, desktop databases and databases running on mid-range and mainframe environments will eventually be indistinguishable, at least in terms of languages, interfaces to middleware, SQL usage, and similar factors. Xbase will eventually become another standards-based programming language, though it more closely resembles (at least in its current product incarnations) fourth-generation languages than it does C, COBOL, or other 3GLs. Xbase evolution will result in developers commonly writing Xbase code with embedded SQL, as well as calls to a variety of APIs for service access (IDAPI or ODBC for connectivity, Microsoft Windows for GUI control, IRDS for repository management, and so on).

- It's important to reemphasize that even though the Xbase standardization process is getting what many feel is a late start, considering the product-based shift towards GUIs and object-oriented paradigms for software development, Xbase is still the dominant legacy language in the PC world, and continued maintenance of existing applications will remain as important to the desktop as COBOL applications are to mainframes.

- The decoupling of Xbase and other interfaces from engines will lead to the use of database formats other than the currently standard .DBF files. However, evidence indicates that the .DBF file format will eventually be greatly enhanced to permit production-level database and information management capabilities (e.g., dictionary and metadata management, security, transaction management).

Outlook

Short-term

- The X3J19 standard for the Xbase standard will be published
- To varying extents, commercial Xbase products will move towards X3J19 compliance
- More GUI-driven PC database environments will appear on the market
- Additional object-oriented capabilities will be incorporated into desktop database products

Long-term

- GUIs will become the predominant interface for desktop databases
- Usage paradigms from mobile computing information management (see Chapter 22) will be incorporated into personal database systems

Additional Reading

- Computer Associates, "CA-Clipper, CA-dBFast, and the Future of Xbase—Statement of Direction," June 1992.
- X3J19 documentation, available from PC DBMS vendors.

Endnotes

1. Xbase Institute, "Xbase News" (October 1992), quoted in *DB/Expo 93 Proceedings* (May 1993), 209.

2. John Hawkins, private communication, May 1993.

3. Xbase Institute, "The Xbase Language Standard—Summary of Proceedings, First and Second Meetings," *DB/Expo 93 Proceedings* (May 1993), 207.

4. The major proponents of the effort were Marc Schnapp, the author of the proposal and an independent Xbase consultant; Martin Rinehart, who had proposed the aborted 1987 standardization efforts; and Bill House. Further discussion about the proponents and their backgrounds may be found in Xbase Institute, "Language Standard," 210.

5. A complete list may be found in Xbase Institute, "Language Standard," 208.

6. Xbase Institute, "Language Standard."

7. Xbase Institute, "Language Standard", 223–225.

8. "Future Directions of Xbase," panel discussion, DCI Database World (June 1993).

9. Computer Associates, "CA-Clipper, CA-dBFast, and the Future of Xbase—Statement of Direction," June 1992, 14.

10. Computer Associates, "Statement of Direction."

11. The discussion in this section is based on comments by several speakers at the June 1993 DCI Database World, including Adam Green and a panel of Xbase vendor representatives.

12. Based on comments, June 1993 DCI Database World.

13. R. Hedges, "IBM OS/2 and UNIX Database Directions," *Proceedings of DB/Expo 1993* (May 1993), 235, 237.

PART V

Future Database and Information Management Models

CHAPTER

Time Is on Your Side: Temporal Databases

A Note to the CIO

In Chapter 4, we discussed the distinctions between operational and informational database needs as they applied to data warehousing architectures and implementations. Time-sensitive aspects, or temporal qualities, that are applicable to informational database needs may be instantiated through temporal database systems. Only certain classes of applications in your environment might need these qualities; to that end, an understanding of the subjects in this chapter (models, language extensions, and others) is important as you determine whether temporal technology is worth pursuing for certain subsystems within your corporation.

15.1 Introduction

Suppose you are a relational database designer, and you have been retained by a video and music store to design a database for a set of applications that not only will do "normal" database transactions (checking out customers, processing payroll, managing inventory, and so on), but will also support time-oriented queries. These _temporal_ queries can be processed against data that are current at the time the query is made (e.g., What is the average current rental price of all Eddie Murphy videotapes? What country album has the lowest sales volume in the past month?). The temporal queries can also request information such as

- The price change history of a given videotape.

Executive Summary

Temporal databases add the property of *time* to the underlying data. Nearly every DBMS product today requires user intervention to handle the temporal property (e.g., creating certain relational tables into which historical data is placed for subsequent access). Temporal systems move this property into the DBMS environment itself, automatically storing multiple time-sensitive versions of data objects. Additionally, language facilities are provided to retrieve data by time-oriented queries (in research, these facilities are usually extensions to SQL).

Because temporal databases can store huge volumes of data and quickly overwhelm any mass storage environment, these systems must be used wisely when they become widely available. That is, even though it is "interesting" to retain multiple versions of most data objects online (or near-line), the business needs of the organization must dictate the extent to which such technology is used. Coupled with data warehouses

- A given employee's salary and rank at some point in the past.
- A list of all price changes that occurred when a particular person was the manager of a particular store.

With these requirements in mind, and using today's commonly available relational database technology, your design process will yield the following tables with their corresponding rows:

```
CREATE TABLE movies (
    movie_title          char (30) not null,
    movie_type           char (20),
    our_cost             decimal (5,2),
    current_rental_price decimal (5,2),
    ...
)
```

MOVIE_TITLE	MOVIE_TYPE	OUR_COST	CURRENT_RENTAL_PRICE
Last Action Hero	Adventure	15.99	2.99
Jurassic Park	Adventure	13.99	2.99
Addams Family	Comedy	14.99	1.99
Star Trek XXIII	Adventure	18.99	2.99

. . . .

(see Chapter 4), in which time-oriented *summarized snapshots* are used to provide an historical perspective of the organization's data, temporal databases will shortly provide a richer set of capabilities for time-sensitive information gathering than is available with today's technology.

What This Technology Can Do for You

An understanding of both the capabilities and limitations of temporal data environments is essential to making intelligent decisions about whether or not they are applicable to your organization, and if so, to what extent. The guiding factor should be the dictates of business needs rather than "it would be *interesting* if we could see multiple versions of . . ." Such requests are better met in data warehouse environments (as described in Chapter 4) than by maintaining temporary data in an organization's operational databases.

```
CREATE TABLE employees (
    emp_last_name        char (30) not null,
    emp_first_name       char (30) not null,
    emp_address          char (20),
    emp_city             char (20),
    ...
    current_salary       decimal (5,2),
    current_rank         char (10),
    ...
)
```

EMP_LAST_NAME	EMP_FIRST_NAME	...	CURRENT_SALARY	CURRENT_RANK
Jones	Charlie		15,000	Manager
Twindell	Clifford		14,000	Asst_Mgr
Smith	Mary		12,000	Clerk
Kirk	Dianne		15,000	Manager
Picard	Max		11,000	Stock_Mgr
Sulu	Betty		12,000	Clerk
Scott	Daryl		16,000	Manager

```
CREATE TABLE movie_rental_price_changes (
    movie_title         char (30) not null,
    price               decimal (5,2),
    date_in_effect      date,
    who_changed         char (30) )
```

MOVIE_TITLE	PRICE	DATE_IN_EFFECT	WHO_CHANGED
Last Action Hero	2.99	12/15/1994	Smith
Last Action Hero	2.50	11/26/1994	Smith
Last Action Hero	1.99	10/10/1994	Jones
Last Action Hero	2.99	3/17/1994	Twindell
Jurassic Park	2.99	12/15/1994	Smith
Jurassic Park	1.99	10/10/1994	Jones
Star Trek XXIII	2.99	3/24/1994	Kirk
Star Trek XXIII	1.99	1/15/1994	Picard
Star Trek XXIII	2.99	4/30/1993	Scott
	.99	3/30/1993	Sulu

```
CREATE TABLE emp_salary_history (
    emp_last_name       char (30) not null,
    emp_first_name      char (30) not null,
    salary              decimal (5,2),
    effective_date      date,
    manager_was         char (30) )
```

EMP_LAST_NAME	EMP_FIRST_NAME	SALARY	EFFECTIVE_DATE ...
Jones	Charlie	15,000	10/1/1994
Jones	Charlie	14,000	10/1/1993
Jones	Charlie	12,000	4/1/1993
Twindell	Clifford	14,000	10/1/1994
Twindell	Clifford	12,500	10/1/1993
Smith	Mary	12,000	10/1/1994
Smith	Mary	10,000	10/1/1993
Kirk	Dianne	15,000	9/1/1994

. . .

```
CREATE TABLE emp_rank_history (
    emp_last_name       char (30) not null,
    emp_first_name      char (30) not null,
    rank                char (10),
    effective_date      date,
    manager_was         char (30) )
```

With those table structures and their respective data, you can then issue time-oriented queries that will, for example, provide you with the complete price change history for the specified movie:

```
SELECT movie_title, price, date_in_effect
  FROM movie_rental_price_changes
  WHERE movie_title = "Gone With The Wind"
```

Suppose, though, that you are asked by the users to design your database to support queries such as "What was the average rental price on a given date?" Now, you groan, you could conceivably reconstruct that information, using data from both the MOVIES table (with current pricing information) and the MOVIE_RENTAL_PRICE_CHANGES history, using some horrendous combination of JOIN operations and subqueries. Because some prices may never have changed from their original entry into the system (you had decided to create a table of price *changes*, not necessarily initial value assignments), you need to utilize tables. It's difficult to do, but being a clever database programmer you figure out a way and add capabilities for those queries to your applications.

Now, however, you are asked to provide a nearly identical capability, not the average rental price but the average *sales* price of the videotapes. You had never anticipated a need for this information, so to satisfy this query you need to start going through archive backup tapes or old files, *if* that information exists. (A complete archival history back to the start of the system probably doesn't exist, because in most systems, tapes and other archival media tend to be reused after a certain point.)

Of course, it doesn't stop there. You are then beset by requirements to support the following queries:

- What is the most number of copies of "Sgt. Pepper's Lonely Hearts Club Band" that have ever been in inventory, and when did that occur?
- When Mike, the store manager at the Main Street store, was a sales person at the mall store, what was his highest salary?
- Consider the day after Christmas for the past ten years; how many movie tapes were in stock at noon on each of those respective days, at each store?

By now you get the idea that time is a dimension not easily handled in traditional databases. Effective management of the temporal dimension through traditional databases requires much foreknowledge, as the very structure of the database must be created to support the aspect of time. Since temporal operations are mostly of an ad hoc querying nature, envisioning all the *meaningful* temporal queries during design of the database structures and creation of the data capture mechanisms is nearly impossible.

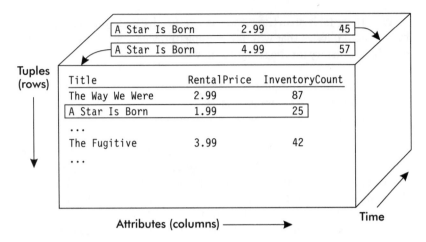

Figure 15-1 The Three-Dimensional Temporal Relation[1]

The solution to this problem can be found in *temporal databases,* which have an aspect of time orientation *built into the database structure itself.* That is, you don't need to create historical information tables based on anticipated queries. Instead, appropriate portions of your databases automatically have a dimension of time.

Additionally, temporal databases feature language constructs (such as extensions to SQL) to issue temporal queries and, indeed, even the rare update operation, as we'll discuss.

In this chapter, we'll look at the many aspects of temporal databases, focusing on the emerging technology and where it will go in the next few years. We'll discuss the principles of temporal databases, the architectural foundations, language extensions (including proposed standardization efforts), metadata management, and other topics.

15.2 Principles of Temporal Databases

The principle of temporal databases can be simply (perhaps over-simply) summed up in a *Twilight Zone* manner: "You're traveling through another dimension, through time."

Most of the temporal database research to date has focused on extensions to the relational model. Relations are two-dimensional objects comprised of tuples (rows) and attributes (columns). By adding a third dimension, time, a *temporal relation* can be created (Figure 15-1).

Contrast the three-dimensional relation in Figure 15-1 with the additional tables required in a traditional relational database to represent time, as we saw in the previous section. In a temporal database, no additional relations are needed to model time; the temporal dimension is built into the relation itself.

Concepts	Original terms	Current terms
When a fact becomes effective in reality	Effective time	Valid time
When a value is actually posted into a database	Registration time	Transaction time

Figure 15-2 Time for Temporal Databases

However, viewing temporal databases as consisting merely of three-dimensional relations is an oversimplification. Indeed, many other principles apply to temporal databases, including multiple definitions of time.

When initial work on temporal databases was done in the late 1970s and early 1980s, one of the first tasks was to define exactly what was meant by "time." Jacov Ben-Zvi introduced two different concepts here: effective time and registration time.[2] *Effective time* was defined as the time "when a fact becomes effective in reality" (this is now known as *valid time*); *registration time* (now called *transaction time*) is the time when a new value is posted into a database.[3] The terms and their definitions are presented in Figure 15-2. A third type of time is applicable to temporal databases. Known as *user-defined time*, it is an "uninterpreted time domain" managed by users. User-defined times are easy to support but contain less semantics than the other two types (only input, output, and comparison operations are supported) and aren't representable as a time cube.[4]

As one might expect, temporal database experts disagree on the necessity of having multiple definitions of time. Some argue that transaction times do little more than complicate the temporal dimension of a database and add little meaning with respect to time.[5] In some temporal models, only valid time has meaning, although clearly transaction time does not always equate to valid time (e.g., something becomes a reality at a given time, but the state change isn't made in the database until some time afterwards). *Bitemporal databases*[6] can support both valid time and transaction time. When evaluating temporal technology as it emerges (that is, what does *your* application need to model in the area of time?), you'll have to consider bitemporal versus temporal databases.

You could view a traditional database (whether relational, object-oriented, home-grown, or following some other model) as a snapshot database; that is, only the current states of the database objects are known. Looking back at archived versions of the database only enables you to view earlier snapshots.

Valid-time databases, though, contain the history of the system the database supports, to the extent that the history is known. Transaction-time databases, on the other hand, are the perfect vehicle for effortless rollback to previous database states through their support of transaction time.

Let's take a look at candidate architectures for temporal databases and the directions in which they are heading.

15.3 Models of Temporal Databases

As with most of the areas we discuss throughout this book, temporal database research follows many different directions with respect to architectural support of the time dimension. From the earliest days, temporal database research has focused on extensions to a relational foundation in much the same way that object-oriented extensions to a relational basis have developed and are still evolving (as discussed in Chapter 9). One temporal database approach involves *lifespan* with database objects of varying granularities, from an entire database down to individual rows or tuples.[7] Lifespans might be used to denote portions of time when a particular state of some object is relevant; therefore they can also be used as a parameter to retrieve information. Lifespans at the database level have little relevance, because each relation (table) and every tuple within each relation will not likely have the same lifespan, though, of course, associating a lifespan at a very coarse level of granularity is easier to implement than relation-level or tuple-level lifespans, much as database-level locking is easier to implement than row-level or column-level locking (Figure 15-3). However, the standard relationship of ease of implementation being inversely proportional to usefulness applies in both of these areas. Because of this limited usefulness, very little research has been done into database-level lifespans.[8]

The lifespan concept could even be drawn to the *attribute* (column within a row) level, as shown in Figure 15-4. Again, an analogy can be drawn between tuple- and attribute-level lifespans as compared with element-level locking and row-level options locking for database concurrency control.

Just as the basic relational data model supports the unary operations of *select* and *project*, the extended relational model used within the HRDM example features an additional unary operation: *time-slice*.[9] Under a temporal data model such as HRDM, the time-slice operations may be applied against some relation as a limiting search criteria for *when*, in much the same way that select performs similar limitations for *where* (Figure 15-5).

Another architectural approach to temporal databases, one also within the extended relational model, is the Temporal Relational Model (TRM).[10] A temporal database under TRM is defined as "the union of two sets of relations R_s and R_t, where R_s is the set of all static relations and R_t is the set of all *time-varying relations*."[11] *Time intervals*, conceptually similar to HRDM lifespans, include two mandatory timestamp attributes, representing starting and ending times (e.g., lower and upper bounds of a time interval, respectively).

Under TRM, every tuple of the time-varying relation (also known as a TVR) has a precise start-time value. In some cases, the ending time may be known, even if that time has not yet occurred (e.g., a contract employee is hired for a specific project and for a period of time; the starting and ending times of the relevance of tuples relating to that employee are both determin-

Relation-level lifespans

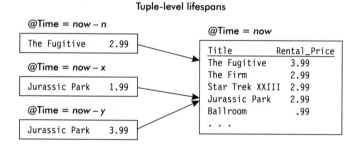

Tuple-level lifespans

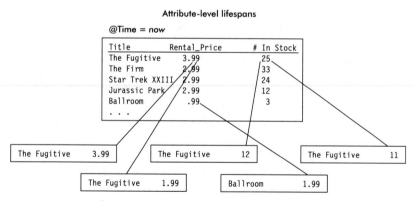

Figure 15-3 Lifespans at the Relation and Tuple Levels

Attribute-level lifespans

@Time = now

Title	Rental_Price	# In Stock
The Fugitive	3.99	25
The Firm	2.99	33
Star Trek XXIII	2.99	24
Jurassic Park	2.99	12
Ballroom	.99	3
. . .		

The Fugitive	3.99

The Fugitive	12

The Fugitive	11

The Fugitive	1.99

Ballroom	1.99

Figure 15-4 Attribute-Level Lifespans: A Finer Level of Granularity

able at that time). In other cases, the end time is not known. However, the end time in those cases may be either infinite (e.g., a specific videotape goes into stock and may very well stay there forever) or may *not* be infinite (but still isn't known, as when a contract employee is hired for a specific job of a finite but uncertain duration). Recalling our discussion in section 15.2 about the different types of times in temporal databases, TRM utilizes valid time, though

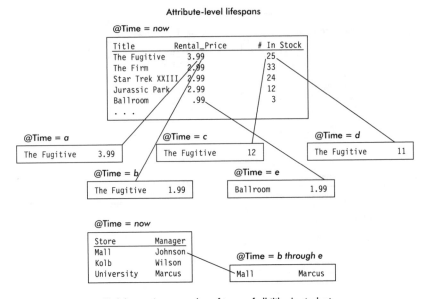

Find the maximum number of tapes of all titles in stock at
the mall store *when* Susan Marcus was the manager there.

Figure 15-5 Time-Slices as a "When" Operator

transaction and user-defined times can be included if necessary.[12] Figure 15-6
summarizes TRM concepts.

Given the relational foundations of temporal data models such as TRM, it
seems only natural that normalization will play some role in extended models.
The TRM model includes a concept of *time normal form* (TNF), defined as
follows: "A relation is in TNF if and only if it is in BCNF (Boyce-Codd Normal
Form) and there exist no temporal dependencies among its nonkey attributes."[13]

We could apply the TRM model to our example relations in section 15.1.
If we start off with a "base relation" that isn't in time normal form, we might
have the following:

EMP_LAST_NAME	EMP_FIRST_NAME	SALARY	T_S	T_E	Rank	T_S	T_E
Jones	Charlie	15,000	10/1/1994	Now	Manager	9/1/90	Now
Jones	Charlie	14,000	10/1/1993	9/30/1994			
Jones	Charlie	12,000	4/1/1993	9/30/1993			
Twindell	Clifford	14,000	10/1/1994	Now	Manager	9/1/97	—
Twindell	Clifford	12,500	10/1/1993	9/30/1994	AsstMgr	1/2/94	8/30/96
Twindell	Clifford				Clerk	10/1/93	1/1/94
Smith	Mary	12,000	10/1/1994	Now			
Smith	Mary	10,000	10/1/1993	9/30/1994			

R_s

Store	Manager
Mall	Johnson
Kolb	Wilson
University	Marcus
...	

R_t

Store	Manager	Ts	To
Mall	Marcus	1/5/93	2/4/94
Mall	Adams	4/5/92	1/4/93
Mall	Babson	3/3/89	4/4/92
Mall	Young	5/5/95	–
...			

Now = 2/1/1995; Young is scheduled to become manager at the mall store on 5/5/1995, with an undetermined ending date for that position. This is stored in the time-varying relation.

Figure 15-6 Temporal Relational Model (TRM)

Note that even though the above relation is a TVR and includes the attributes of start time and end time, individual tuples "have problems" with data representation. Because there is no correlation between the start-time and end-time attributes applicable to salary and rank, that particular table has problems very similar to those of a relation violating 2NF or 3NF. Therefore, TNF would require that the relations be decomposed into multiple ones.

However, this model is more closely defined with the traditional relational model's time representation structure than one in which the multiple time values for individual attributes are handled "behind the scenes" rather than at the structural level. In effect, we have what might be considered a light rather than a deep extension to a relational foundation (a deep extension requires attribute-level metadata to maintain the multiple time versions of attributes).

Another aspect in which the temporal dimension might be useful is management of future time, such as in HDBMS.[14] HDBMS supports the following rules for temporal operations:

- The separation of historical, current, and future data into different segments, with that separation transparent to the user.
- Supporting all types of transactions on future states and entities.
- Placing no unnecessary restrictions on the time-ordering of future transactions (e.g., basic transaction synchronization principles.

Management of future data can, for many applications, be just as important as the capability to query historical data. Just as the bulk of historical access is query-oriented (though some models support retrospective updates, in which errors may be corrected or other retrospective actions taken),[15] transactions against future data tend to be update-oriented (e.g., change employee X's salary on July 15, 1996; increase all videotape rental prices by

5 percent on December 15, 1997; and so on). Queries could, of course, be processed against future time (e.g., What will our average videotape sales price be in September, 1995?).

We have different alternatives for handling transactions against future time. Conceivably, a transaction such as future changes to salaries or prices might be registered within the database (this is a case where active databases, discussed in Chapter 16, would be valuable), and at that point some action is triggered to execute the transaction. Such a model could be accomplished without any temporal extensions to the database itself, though future-oriented *data* are not present in the database. With a temporal dimension to the underlying data model, whether HDBMS, TRM, or any other model, data of the future *are* present in the database. Using the start time and end time (T_S and T_E) of the TRM model as we discussed earlier, a time-varying relation may be created and managed *which is separate from the basic system data*. This is called *static relation*.

In short, management of the future within a temporal database can be just as important as query capabilities of the past. As temporal databases evolve, such capabilities will likely be included in commercial products.

15.4 Temporal Extensions to Database Languages

If temporal databases are typically extensions of conventional data models, then the temporal aspects should be accessible through extensions to traditional database languages. Interestingly, though, neither the SQL-92 standard nor the work on SQL3 to date includes any temporal extensions to SQL. A situation very similar to object-oriented extensions to SQL is then likely to occur: Object-oriented extensions will first appear in SQL3, which won't be an official standard until the mid-1990s, but OODBMSs based on extensions to the relational model have already introduced their own versions of object-oriented SQL, which are mostly incompatible with one another.

The same situation will likely occur with temporal databases. Research in the 1980s and early 1990s on the architecture of temporal databases has often been accompanied by language extensions with temporal properties. And, because most of the research revolves around temporal extension to relational databases, the logical choice as a foundation for such extensions was SQL.

What might temporal SQL look like? Let's take a quick look at some of the SQL extensions utilized to date.

15.4.1 TempSQL

One version, known as TempSQL, includes *temporal expressions,* which return temporal elements (in addition to the traditional relational operations, which return relations).[16] TempSQL uses a WHILE clause similar to the SQL WHERE clause for temporal expressions. The format of TempSQL SELECT statements is as follows:[17]

```
SELECT { select list }
  WHILE { temporal expression }
  FROM { list of relations }
  WHERE { where-clause }
```

TempSQL allows subqueries to be included in WHILE clauses.

15.4.2 TSQL

Another variation is known as TSQL, used as an interface to the Temporal Relational Model (TRM, discussed in section 15.3 with respect to time normalization and time normal form).[18] TSQL uses a WHEN clause (instead of the TempSQL WHILE clause), and also includes the following:[19]

- Retrieval of timestamps
- Retrieval of temporally ordered information
- Using the TIME-SLICE clause to specify a time domain
- Using the GROUP BY clause for modified aggregate functions

Within the WHEN clauses, a number of *temporal comparison operators* may be used, including[20]

- BEFORE
- AFTER
- DURING
- EQUIVALENT
- ADJACENT
- OVERLAP
- FOLLOWS
- PRECEDES

The syntax of the SELECT ... WHEN statement is

```
SELECT { select list }
  FROM { list of relations }
  WHERE { where-clause }
  WHEN { temporal clause }
```

15.4.3 HSQL

Another example of extended SQL is HSQL, used to model the Historical Data Model (the model that designates transaction time as a complicating factor to avoid, as we discussed in section 15.2).

An interesting aspect of HSQL is that the data definition language (DDL) includes temporal extensions, via the WITH TIME GRANULARITY clause. For example[21]

```
CREATE STATE TABLE prices (
    movie_title      CHAR (30) NOT NULL,
    price            DECIMAL (5,2),
    )
WITH TIME GRANULARITY DATE.
```

The clause is used to designate that DATE is a sufficient level of granularity for rows within this table. That is, two movies with price changes that occur on the same day will be treated as if those changes occurred simultaneously, even if they really occurred at different times during that same day. When finer levels of granularity are necessary, you might specify a granularity of DATE:HOUR or DATE:HOUR:MIN:SEC.[22]

The above example is for a state relation (table); relations may also be events. *Events* are special cases in which the states prevail over a single time instant, in contrast to states that prevail over an interval of time.[23] Event tables are created by a CREATE EVENT TABLE statement.[24]

The historical database represented by the above syntax will add two columns to the table's rows, used for temporal operations:

CURRENT-PRICE	MOVIE_TITLE	PRICE	FROM	TO
HISTORY-PRICE	MOVIE_TITLE	PRICE	FROM	TO

FROM and TO are used to define a non-null interval of time. For the CURRENT-PRICE, the TO attribute will always be represented by the keyword NOW. For the other rows, a FROM and TO date or time (whichever granularity has been specified; in our above example, DATE) will be maintained. These two relations are also union-compatible.[25]

HSQL also includes built-in functions such as[26]

- CURRENT ()—Provides the current tuples of a relation.
- HISTORY ()—Provides only historical tuples of a relation.
- ELAPSEDYEARS ()—Provides the elapsed number of years between two arguments.
- ELAPSEDMONTHS ()—Results in the elapsed months between two arguments.

- PRED ()—Gives the instant that precedes some time argument, in the granularity of that argument.
- SUCC ()—The same as PRED () above, except for the instant that succeeds some argument.
- UPTO*x* ()—Used to convert granularities for comparisons (e.g., UPTO-MONTHS (1973:09:28) will result in 1973:09, in effect dropping the day component of the date).

HSQL also provides built-in conversion to change granularities into comparable values. Further, it allows two arguments to be compared even if they are of different granularities, if that comparison makes sense (e.g., January, 1990 is < February 1, 1992; 1996 is > October 10, 1946).

HSQL uses a variety of clauses to support temporal operations, including[27]

- IN INTERVAL within the WHERE clause, used to limit searches to a specific time interval.
- FROMTIME . . . TOTIME, *prefacing* a query with a time interval.
- CONTAINS, used for limiting INTERVALS to a specific point in time.

HSQL also includes a capability for *retrospective updates*, which in effect are used to update historical data. While not a commonly used operation within most applications, the ability to make corrective changes is valuable. HSQL designates two types of retrospective updates: delayed maintenance, where INSERT, UPDATE, and DELETE operations act as normal operations, but a user-supplied time is employed to override transaction time; and error correction, in which changes may be applied to the time attributes as well as user-defined attributes (the data columns).[28]

Error corrections are prefaced by FOR CORRECTION, as in

```
FOR CORRECTION
FROMTIME < some time value> TOTIME < some time value >
  DELETE...
    WHERE...
```

Finally, more recent HSQL work includes capabilities for handling future time, as in triggering actions at some future time (e.g., price changes, employee salary increases). In effect, a third type of relation, FUTURE, is added to HISTORY and CURRENT.[29]

15.4.4 Other SQL Extensions

Other temporal extensions to SQL have surfaced over the years. Jacov Ben-Zvi's work included the following SQL extensions:[30]

- SELECT statements may be prefaced with a TIME-VIEW clause.
- A CHANGES clause may be included within a SELECT statement, and it is used to query changes to a database:

```
SELECT ...
    CHANGES FROM {some date} TO {some date}
        FROM ...
        WHERE ...
```

15.4.5 Standardized Temporal SQL

As you can see from the previous sections, extensions to SQL to support temporal databases have varied widely. In 1992, an effort began among database researchers with interests in temporal databases to develop a consensus Temporal SQL.[31] As we mentioned earlier, no current provisions exist for incorporating into SQL3 a consensus Temporal SQL (or, for that matter, any of the other SQL extensions we looked at in the previous sections). Even with the absence of temporal aspects from SQL3, though, efforts toward achieving a consensus with SQL extensions will likely help with compatibility and portability in the temporal database world.

15.5 Metadata and Temporal Databases

Several aspects of metadata are important in supporting temporal databases. The first is fairly obvious: temporal attributes and other characteristics of the temporal database model being implemented must be handled within the DBMS catalog. Using the SQL-92 and SQL3 Information Schema (discussed in Chapter 12), a temporal DBMS based on the TRM discussed in section 15.3 might have INFORMATION_SCHEMA views (and corresponding DEFINITION_SCHEMA base tables) such as

```
create view static_table (
    catalog            char (40),
    schema             char (40),
    table_name         char (40),
    ...,
)

create view time_varying_table (
    catalog            char (40),
    schema             char (40),
    table_name         char (40),
    ...,
```

```
start_time          date,
end_time            date,
...,
)
```

With the above table definitions, a DBMS could manage both the static tables and those representing time-varying relations. A DBMS that supports both valid time and transaction time would need to account for both within any temporal aspects of the metadata objects.

Consider the following situation, though. Our examples so far, particularly those from the previous section on SQL extensions, have all been under the following assumption, one that is bound to be faulty: the schema itself does *not* vary over time. Real-world databases have tables added and deleted; column definitions added, modified, and deleted; domains created, modified, and deleted; and so on. Temporal queries, regardless of what version of extended SQL or any other language is used, must be processed against the *appropriate schemata in effect during the time of interest.*

This situation forces a temporal aspect on the metadata, not just the user data, of a temporal database. In the case of a temporal SQL-based DBMS, we may have time-varying INFORMATION_SCHEMA tables, with associated lifespans at the tuple or attribute level used to represent schemata changes and applicable times of relevance.

Why is a temporal aspect important to metadata? Simply because a temporal query against a TVR (or whatever term is used for an instantiated temporal model) may be occurring against a database structure long in the past. In our video and music store example, at one time in the 1970s we likely had database objects representing 45 rpm records (singles) and 8-track tapes. As time—and the music industry—marched on, we stopped handling such merchandise, replacing them with CD singles, digital audio tapes (DATs), and other newer products. Similarly, in the early 1970s we didn't carry videotapes at all, and when we began in the late 1970s we had Beta format tapes; they also went the way of 8-tracks. At some point, we removed the representation of that obsolete inventory from our database, in effect causing metadata changes to the database (e.g., we did an ALTER MOVIES . . . DROP COLUMN BETA_TAPES . . . operation and similar operations for the other obsolete products).

If, however, we wish to issue a temporal query such as "produce an entire average monthly inventory for *Abbey Road* and all singles with songs from the album, regardless of the type of medium (LPs, regular cassettes, DATs, 8-tracks, singles, CDs, CD singles, and so on)," the temporal query, regardless of what form it takes, must know that there are old table structures of interest to us for this particular query but that no longer exist. If the temporal database supports the maintenance of all historical user data about *Abbey Road* and all of its songs, then appropriate metadata must also exist to access that historical user data. This way, a temporal query such as in our example would know to look at a given set of columns in a given table during an interval, some other columns in other tables during some other interval, and so on. In effect, the query engine must make use of the temporal nature of the metadata in order to create the appropriate query graph. If, for example, a model such as TRM is used, then query components must be processed against the static tables (e.g., the current data) as well as against all time-varying tables, regardless of any form changes ("shape-shifting") they have undergone during the interval of interest.

A formal model to manage the schema evolution, such as SQL/SE,[32] is therefore necessary to fully support a temporal database environment. That model proposes SQL language extensions, similar to those we discussed in the previous section on other temporal models. The language extensions of SQL/SE are oriented toward the schema evolution itself, such as the inclusion of a SCHEMA-AS-AT clause (SCHEMA-AS-AT *some time reference*).[33] In this sense, the temporal queries may be directed at a particular point in time, using the schema in force at that time. These types of operations, though, are applicable to historical snapshots rather than intervals of time, because any given interval may span multiple schemata formats and structures.

SQL/SE provides facilities via transaction time inclusion for supporting schemata rollback, but such support may be "too costly to implement in many cases."[34] Regardless of whether or not language extensions are eventually used for schema evolution management within temporal databases, though, the fact remains that metadata must be temporally managed if user data are to be temporally managed.

15.6 Object-Oriented Temporal Databases

Earlier in this chapter, we stated that the majority of temporal database research has focused on extensions to a relational foundation. As object-oriented databases have come to fruition and are considered a key component of future information management, some temporal research has shifted to the object orientation.

Note that a relational engine extended with object-oriented capabilities (abstract data types, inheritance, and so on, as discussed in Chapter 9) could conceivably be extended with temporal capabilities in much the same way that a "basic" relational DBMS could. That is, a tuple could have historical data maintained (as well as future data, if applicable) even if that data is of some abstract type representing perhaps voice, image, or video. Conceivably, a TRM time-valued relation could represent annual photographs of video store employees in the same way that salary histories and rank histories could be maintained.

As discussed in Part III, however, the OODB/OODBMS world is following two different paths with respect to underlying models. In addition to extensions to the relational model, many OODBMS vendors have created their own engines and storage managers without the foundations of the relational model. Research into temporal extensions to such models has started in recent years, and it now represents another branch from which commercial temporal databases may emerge.

An example of OODBMS roots in the temporal world is found in extensions to the OODAPLEX model, which in turn is an extension to the DAPLEX functional model first formulated in the early 1980s.[35]

In a temporally extended OODB model, each object has a function lifespan that is issued to return the time interval of the object's existence. Based on the values returned from that function, temporal operations may be processed against objects in the database.[36] Note that the real-world representation of OODBs usually means that objects play specific roles within the world being modeled, roles that can vary over time. A specific object may represent an employee of a video store, but that employee may play different roles at different times (e.g., a clerk during one interval, an assistant manager during another, and a store manager during yet another interval). Therefore, the lifespan of an object as an instance of one type will likely be different than the lifespan of the same object as an instance of another type.

Temporal queries similar to those of the various SQL extensions we saw may also be expressed through object-oriented languages. Considering the future importance of the ODMG-93 languages, including the object query language (OQL), temporal object-oriented DBMSs will likely include extensions to ODMG-93 languages (OQL, OML, ODL) as those languages find their way into commercial products.

15.7 Indexes for Temporal Database Support

Let's briefly mention *indexing techniques*, which are an implementation-specific aspect of temporal databases. Because of the historical nature of temporal data, queries based on time-oriented specifications (e.g., specified against one or more intervals of time) should have some type of index structure for efficient processing of those operations. Indexing techniques such as segment, mixed-media, and lopsided indexes are being researched for temporal database support.[37]

Of particular note are mixed-media indexes, which can span both magnetic and optical media. Organizational historical data is increasingly stored on optical disks, both write-once read-many (WORM) or rewritable write-many read-many (WMRM). Time-oriented operations inevitably will span multiple media, as high-performance temporal DBMSs come to market, regardless of the underlying engine (relational or object-oriented). Mixed-media indexes will therefore likely play an important role in the temporal database world.

15.8 Conclusion

The utility of temporal databases is inarguable. The informational (as opposed to the operational or transactional) needs of databases and information management systems will inevitably lead to the desire for an increased level of time orientation to queries and database information requests.

The major unknown factor is the direction from which robust, highly capable temporal database capabilities will emerge. Although the majority of research in the discipline has been based on relational extensions, the following observation can be made: relational DBMS vendors are busy working on extensions to their products, but those extensions are in the area of object-oriented capabilities. Temporal capabilities are secondary.

This observation is supported by the direction of SQL3. The extensions to both the underlying model and the language are predominantly in the area of adding object-oriented capabilities. As we mentioned, while SQL3 currently contains no temporal language extensions, it does have many object-oriented extensions to the underlying relational base. Given the major efforts vendors will undertake to add object-oriented capabilities to their products, temporal extensions are likely to wind up in the "maybe someday" category.

Temporal extensions will likely emerge from the OODBMS world. The concept of multiple versions of objects, critical for CAD, CASE, and many other OODB-based applications, is closely related to temporal properties of database contents. Since research work in temporal extensions to OODBMSs has increased in recent years, this area will probably provide the foundation for production-quality temporal databases.

Because this discipline is not well known to those outside of database research and students of information systems, we have not seen much demand for temporal capabilities from information management system users. This is likely to change in the near future, but not necessarily to the same degree as client/server connectivity standards or object-oriented capabilities, which have generated far more interest. Nevertheless, temporal databases are certainly an area worth watching.

Outlook

Short-term

- Temporal properties will appear in commercial DBMS products
- Applications that are required to maintain historical information will begin to be developed on top of or moved to temporal database systems

Long-term

- More robust temporal DBMS products will appear, with extensions to the DBMS engine
- Data warehouse environments (Chapter 4) will incorporate temporal databases as an underlying storage manager to maintain historical summarized information

Additional Reading

- C. S. Jensen, J. Clifford, S. Gadia, A. Segev, and R. T. Snodgrass, "A Glossary of Temporal Database Concepts," *SIGMOD Record* (September 1992).
- J. F. Roddick, "SQL/SE—A Query Language Extension for Databases Supporting Schema Evolution," *SIGMOD Record* (September 1992).
- A. Tansel et al., *Temporal Databases: Theory, Design, and Implementation* (Redwood City, CA: The Benjamin/Cummings Publishing Company, 1993).

Endnotes

1. Adapted from a figure in A. Tansel et al., *Temporal Databases: Theory, Design, and Implementation* (Redwood City, CA: The Benjamin/Cummings Publishing Company, 1993), 2.

2. S. Gadia, "Ben-Zvi's Pioneering Work in Relational Temporal Databases," in Tansel et al., *Temporal Databases*, 202.

3. Tansel et al., *Temporal Databases*, xviii.

4. Tansel et al., *Temporal Databases*.

5. N. L. Sarda, "HSQL: A Historical Query Language," in Tansel et al., *Temporal Databases*, 113.

6. Tansel et al., *Temporal Databases*, xviii.

7. J. Clifford and A. Crocker, "The Historical Relational Data Model (HRDM) Revisited," in Tansel et al., *Temporal Databases*, 7–9.

8. Clifford and Crocker, "(HRDM) Revisited," 8.

9. Clifford and Crocker, "(HRDM) Revisited," 22.

10. S. B. Navathe and R. Ahmed, "Temporal Extensions to the Relational Model and SQL," in Tansel et al., *Temporal Databases*, 93.

11. Navathe and Ahmed, "Temporal Extensions."

12. Navathe and Ahmed, "Temporal Extensions."

13. Navathe and Ahmed, "Temporal Extensions," 96.

14. Sarda, "HSQL," 137–138.

15. Sarda, "HSQL," 132.

16. S. K. Gadia and S. S. Nair, "Temporal Databases: A Prelude to Parametric Data," in Tansel et al., *Temporal Databases*, 37.

17. Gadia and Nair, "Parametric Data," 38.

18. Navathe and Ahmed, "Temporal Extensions," 99.

19. Navathe and Ahmed, "Temporal Extensions."

20. Navathe and Ahmed, "Temporal Extensions," 100.

21. Adapted from sample DDL in Sarda, "HSQL," 114.

22. Sarda, "HSQL," 117.

23. Sarda, "HSQL," 111.

24. Syntax for table definitions shown in Sarda, "HSQL," 123.

25. Sarda, "HSQL," 114.

26. Sarda, "HSQL," 118.

27. Sarda, "HSQL," 129–131.

28. Sarda, "HSQL," 132.

29. Sarda, "HSQL," 138.

30. Gadia, "Ben-Zvi's Pioneering Work," 206.

31. C. S. Jensen et al., "A Glossary of Temporal Database Concepts," *SIGMOD Record* (September 1992), 35.

32. J. F. Roddick, "SQL/SE—A Query Language Extension for Databases Supporting Schema Evolution," *SIGMOD Record* (September 1992), 10.

33. Roddick, "SQL/SE," 13. The author states that such a facility, while supported in the SQL/SE model, "may not merit the cost of implementation . . ."

34. Roddick, "SQL/SE," 14.

35. G. T. J. Wuu and U. Dayal, "A Uniform Model for Temporal and Versioned Object-oriented Databases," in Tansel et al., *Temporal Databases*, 231.

36. Wuu and Dayal, "Uniform Model," 238.

37. C. Kolovson, "Indexing Techniques for Historical Databases," in Tansel et al., *Temporal Databases*, 418–432.

CHAPTER
16

Database Intelligence: The Active Database Approach

A Note to the CIO

Many of the topics in this book—data warehouses, repositories, and others—as well as general applications architecture can benefit from active database properties. *Active database* properties mean that procedural aspects of your overall environment are embedded in your database systems and are managed declaratively. Active databases have been identified as one of the major trends that will revolutionize applications development. The philosophy behind this movement—storing data operations and procedures with the data—is pervasive in

16.1 Introduction

Traditionally, databases have been passive entities. Data objects are put into databases, typically by a user or application. Objects are retrieved, again by an external source. Information is exchanged among database storage locations (e.g., from one table to another), similarly driven by an outside source.

Business rules applied against database contents (e.g., the rules for updating a particular item, successive actions against other items as a result of that update) are again typically managed from an outside source. In short, databases have not been active players in information systems but, instead, have had a storage-oriented, organizational role.

other areas such as object-oriented databases, so even if OODBs don't figure prominently in your three- to five-year plans, you can still obtain that particular benefit of OODBMSs by incorporating active database constructs into your environments.

Executive Summary

While much has been written and discussed since the early 1950s about the convergence of artificial intelligence (AI) and database technologies, commercial implementations of thinking, self-learning databases are as elusive as ever. In the meantime, much intelligence can be pushed into the data management component of information systems through active database technology.

Though the terms are not widely known in the commercial world, the underlying technologies of active databases have been increasingly used since the late 1980s. These include

- Database triggers, which are "fired" at the occurrence of a pre-specified event (or combination of events).

This role has been changing in recent years, and the concept of *active databases* will grow in importance over the rest of the decade. In fact, some would argue that active database technology is the gateway toward the knowledge bases envisioned by artificial intelligence (AI); indeed, at the end of this chapter, we'll briefly discuss some visions of the convergence of artificial intelligence and databases.

Before that, though, we'll discuss the principles, technologies, and directions of active database systems, from basic trigger/stored procedure models to more complex technology.

16.2 Principles of Active Database Systems

As we mentioned, database systems have traditionally been passive. In the video store example in Figure 16-1, applications, users, operating system software, or some other external source must tell the DBMS how to store, retrieve, or reorganize information. Even outside the realm of ad hoc user operations, we still have the bulk of the processing logic of database contents contained within entities such as applications programs.[1]

- Stored procedures, which embed procedural logic in the database environment rather than in the application subsystem.

- DBMS-based monitoring facilities, which act as controllers for the active nature of these pseudo-intelligent databases and direct trigger and stored procedure actions.

The primary difference between active databases and traditional, passive databases is that in the latter, all of the procedural logic, including retrieval and modification of DBMS-managed data, is coordinated from outside the data management realm; if the result of a particular data update operation (an event) is supposed to cause some other sequence of actions, the execution of those other actions must be initiated by logic from the application or some other external agent. In contrast, an active database environment supports the initiation and control of those other actions from within the database environment according to preset rules, without the need to obtain further guidance from the applications or from other outside sources.

In addition to the basic principles of active databases, issues such as transaction processing models, state transition models, and handling

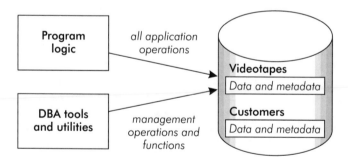

Figure 16-1 Passive Database System

Active database systems, on the other hand, provide facilities so that[2]

- A degree of processing logic is contained within the database itself and is managed by the DBMS rather than applications software.

- A form of monitoring events and conditions that affect data and can initiate the database-maintained processing is provided.

- A means by which those events and conditions can trigger the logic within the database is also included.

more than one trigger per event will help expand the capabilities of today's active database technology into the realm of intelligent databases.

What This Technology Can Do for You

As active database technology becomes more widely available, a number of advantages may be gained by users. These advantages fall in three different areas: business rule specification and maintenance, application development, and operational performance.

Business Rules

One of the most heavily hyped areas of computing today is the representation and management of business rules, or the specifications of the ways in which information flows from one information system entity (e.g., users, systems) to another and the conditions under which those flows occur. Active databases provide one platform for business rules to be represented, maintained, and efficiently executed within a single information system environment.

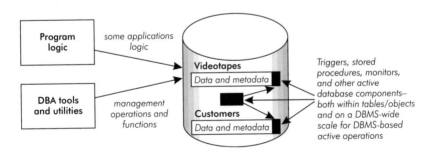

Figure 16-2 Active Database System

As shown in Figure 16-2, these three features—the logic, triggers for the logic, and monitoring facilities to activate the triggers—are pushed from the application programs into the database itself, providing a closer coupling of system data and data operations than in traditional, passive database-driven systems.

Several basic database constructs aid in creating active environments: constraints, assertions, stored procedures, and triggers. Let's discuss each of these.

Application Development

Specification of business rule components (specifically, triggers and the sequence of actions following the firing of those triggers) is *declarative* in active databases, rather than *procedural* as in traditional DBMSs. That is, SQL statements such as CREATE TRIGGER and CREATE ASSERTION specify components of the business rules, and stored procedures may be attached to the objects upon which they operate.

Declarative specification of business rules is a more productive process than the procedural specification required in passive systems, primarily because the controlling logic (the monitors, recovery mechanisms) is already present within the DBMS environment and doesn't need to be custom-developed within the applications.

Operational Performance

Consider client/server database environments (discussed in Chapter 3). With traditional, passive databases, complex business rule processing, in which the result of some action causes the execution of one or the other alternatives, requires the following steps:

16.2.1 Constraints and Assertions

Constraints are relatively simple constructs, ranging from primary and foreign key relationships used for referential integrity to SQL-like CHECK constraints (used for range and lists of values checking).[3] Constraints might be viewed as the first means of embedding business rules within a database instead of within application logic.

Constraints of this kind are usually attached to a specific database object such as a table or certain columns within a table. A more generalized type of constraint, supported in the SQL-92 standard, is the *assertion*, a stand-alone constraint in a schema, which is used to specify a restriction that may affect more than one table.[4] That is, instead of a constraint structure that might look like

```
CREATE TABLE table_name (
  row-1...,
  row-2...,
  ...
  row-n,
  CONSTRAINT constraint_name
  constraint-definition...
  )
```

1. The client application issues a database operation request (e.g., an SQL UPDATE statement to modify a data item value) to the server.

2. The database server executes the requested operation and returns a SUCCESS status to the client application.

3. Based on the new value set by the UPDATE operation, one of two possible database operations will follow. In the first case, another UPDATE operation request will be sent from the client to the server. In the second case, a series of SELECT statement requests will be issued from the client to the server, with possible subsequent actions based on the values retrieved by the SELECT statements.

In this scenario, each step requires communication across whatever network medium is being used (LAN, WAN, or others) to connect the client to the server.

Alternatively, the active database paradigm could support the execution of the steps in #3 inside the server *without* having to return across the network to the client to obtain further processing instructions. The

an assertion has a structure like this:

```
CREATE ASSERTION assertion_name
   assertion_definition
```

Assertions have a primary advantage over basic constraints. Assertions are stand-alone entities that need not be contained within a table definition, so business rules affecting two or more tables can be naturally represented within the body of an assertion, as in the following:[5]

```
CREATE ASSERTION maximum_inventory
   CHECK ( ( SELECT SUM (our_cost)
                FROM movies )
          + ( SELECT SUM (our_cost)
                FROM music_titles )
          < 500000 )
```

This assertion will ensure that the maximum value of inventory, including both videotapes and music titles (CDs, tapes, and so on) will be less than $500,000. Since this business rule spans more than one table, representing it in a stand-alone fashion is more natural.

combination of the active DBMS and the business rule logic helps push the processing intelligence into the database environment itself.

Taken together, business rule specification, application development productivity, and operational performance improvement are substantial reasons not only to investigate today's active database technology but also to carefully track present trends and future directions in this area.

Through widespread usage of constraints and assertions, a great percentage of the business rules applicable to an information system can be specified within the confines of the database.

16.2.2 Stored Procedures

In many cases, the basic constructs of constraints and assertions are inadequate for expressing complex business rules. DBMSs that support *stored procedures*, or database-contained programming logic, have further capabilities of expressing more complex business rules.

A stored procedure is similar to an application program module, except that it "belongs" to the database rather than to an external programming system using the database. Stored procedures can be defined against one or more databases just as constraints and assertions are.

16.2.3 Triggers

There must be some means to evaluate business rules expressed through database constructs, and to cause specified actions to occur.

In Chapter 12, we discussed SQL3 and the inclusion of triggers, noting that triggering capabilities have already found their way into most commer-

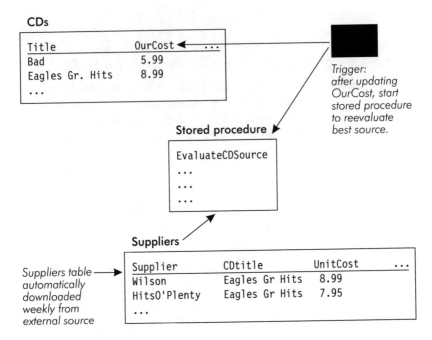

Figure 16-3 Database Triggers

cial relational DBMS products. Triggers are a key component in turning a database into an active environment. After insertion, update, and/or deletion operations, triggers attached to certain objects can be "fired," resulting in evaluation of certain business rules or execution of specific actions (Figure 16-3).

The DBMS must be capable of monitoring its environment, detecting conditions that will cause triggers to fire and the procedural logic contained within stored procedures to be executed.

16.3 Extensions to the Active Database Model

In the previous section, our discussion focused on active database implementations based on existing and emerging technology. In this section, we'll expand to a more general view of active databases.

Active databases can be characterized as following Event-Condition-Action rules.[6] The key to future active database systems is to have the capability to express these rules in an advanced, declarative manner that permits extensions into artificial intelligence constructs such as inferencing via forward chaining (e.g., following a set of rule-based actions and inferring some type of result from the chained actions).[7] For example, IBM's Starburst system supports the concept of *state transitions*—an S → S' transition—and the capability to model system execution as a sequence of such transitions.[8]

Starburst includes other capabilities, such as database transactions that not only execute predefined rules but also create new rules based on some transaction logic; deactivate one or more rules; or alter the priority of one or more rules.[9] Basically, an active database environment should allow rule-based operations not only against objects such as tables and columns but also against rules themselves.

Another system, POSTGRES, provides other rule-based active capabilities, such as a *do instead* rule that says if a certain event or state occurs during a database operation, do a certain other operation instead; and a *do refuse* rule that refuses to do an operation unless a particular constraint is satisfied (for example, don't allow a videotape price to be updated unless the user is either a store manager or assistant manager).[10] Again, note that the procedural characteristics of such operations are hardly new, having been coded in probably millions of applications over the past 40 years. However, the declarative nature of such rules, and the role of the DBMS as the primary maintainer and enforcer of them, are emerging technology.

16.4 Transaction Models and Active Databases

In section 20.3 of Chapter 20, we'll discuss different models of transaction processing, including nested transactions (transactions contained within other transactions). This model is particularly appropriate for active databases, because the hierarchical structure of the nested transaction model easily accommodates the relation between the triggering transaction and the execution of the rules. Since child transactions can run in parallel with one another, multiple rule processing functions can occur simultaneously.[11]

Figure 16-4 illustrates active database usage of a nested transaction model. The user transaction runs as the root (top-level) transaction, with various rule classes running in the nested transactions. These rule classes include[12]

- *Immediate*, in which a triggering transaction T_1 is suspended, and a rule R is fired and executed as a child transaction of T.
- *Deferred*, in which the rule R is created just before T commits and is performed as a child of T.
- *Decoupled*, in which a new top-level transaction is started.
- *Causality*, where a triggered top transaction T_2 is serialized after a transaction T_1; if T_1 is aborted, then T_2 is aborted.

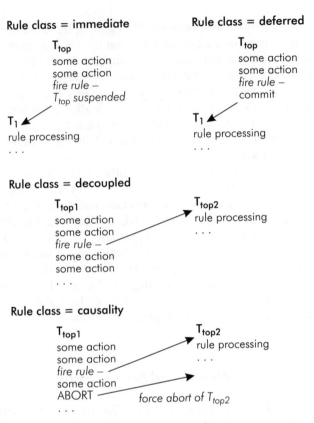

Figure 16-4 Nested Transactions and Active Databases

See section 20.3.4 for further discussion on the general commit and rollback policies of nested transactions. It should be noted here, though, that transaction specification languages (see section 20.7) could, for active database environments, be extended with a rich model of constraint, procedure language, and triggering mechanisms in addition to specifications of chaining and nesting models for the transactions themselves.

16.5 Limitations of Active Database Models

With today's technology, there are some limitations to active database models that require research.[13] First, the events, conditions, and actions are limited to database operations (e.g., queries, update statements, and transaction management); even the most robust active database environment can't stand alone but must interoperate with other systems services (e.g., communications, user interface, systems services).

Second, only one trigger per event is typically supportable. That is, for any given relational table, usually only one trigger is described per statement type (delete, update, insert, and so on). Any multiple-trigger (multiple-rule) processing models must be processed sequentially rather than in parallel. A richer rule specification model must be able to support the definition of parallel trigger execution paths.

Finally, implementation techniques are rather limited. As we mentioned, the DBMSs themselves must be capable of supporting active operations rather than just locking, retrieving, or updating objects, and related functions. Monitoring and similar capabilities must be available.

16.6 Production Rules and Database Environments

In section 16.1, we mentioned that active database environments represent a basic combination of artificial intelligence and data management. Throughout this chapter, we've discussed various ways of expressing business rules within the context of database systems, a key component of making databases active.

Another way of looking at such rules is in the artificial intelligence sense of *production rules*, which take the form of *pattern -> action*.[14] This model is known as *pattern-based* rules, meaning that the rule is triggered when some pattern is matched by data in the working memory, and that the specified action will modify working memory. Alternatively, the pattern may be considered a *condition* or *predicate*.[15]

AI rule languages (pattern-based languages) assume that rules are triggered only when new data are in the working memory that match the pattern, while database rule languages are, as we've seen in this chapter, based on rules triggered by database events (e.g., insertions and updates).[16] In many ways, though, the rule languages of AI and databases are conceptually similar, leading to the vision that at some point in the future, the two areas will be more tightly integrated.

16.7 Artificial Intelligence and Database Technology

And just how would the two disciplines of AI and database technology be more closely related? For many years, we've been hearing about *knowledge bases* and *knowledge-base management systems* (KBMSs), which include intelligence and not just data within a DBMS environment. Interestingly, though, those in the AI and database disciplines have rarely interacted with one another. Michael Brodie noted that two separate workshops were held in 1988 on AI-database integration, one by AI researchers and the other by database researchers; he was the only person to attend both workshops.[17]

Part of the problem might be that even though a high degree of interest in AI-database integration dates back to Alan Turing's Turing Test in 1951, in which a machine was envisioned that might imitate human intelligence, creating such a machine would require some sort of data management capabilities in which the "intelligence" would be maintained.[18]

Some AI areas in which a tighter integration with database technology would be valuable include[19]

- *Knowledge sharing*, or a common knowledge base shareable among multiple applications and users.
- *Knowledge representation independence*, or limiting the negative effects of system changes.
- *Knowledge distribution*, in which the knowledge representation is partitioned and replicated much the same as data in a distributed database environment.

Whether or not the particulars of "true" AI-database integration in these areas eventually evolve, active database technology as discussed in this chapter will go a long way toward meeting these goals. For example, active database capabilities (triggers, assertions, and others) built on top of a distributed DBMS environment would lead to a model of knowledge distribution. Similarly, a semantically rich conceptual data model (with a robust rule expression capability), on which applications can be developed, could arguably be the realization of knowledge representation independence.

In short, then, it's uncertain when commercially successful knowledge-base management systems or AI databases will ever be widely deployable, or if they will remain entrenched in experimental, research-oriented domains. Pushing rule specification and processing into the database itself, though, certainly goes a long way toward improving information management.

16.8 Conclusion

Active database technology covers a wide spectrum, from basic triggering capabilities common in today's commercial products to robust rule specification and execution models under the control of nested transactions, which will likely become common in the near future. Further, active databases provide what might be considered a gateway to the elusive future of intelligent databases with rich levels of artificial intelligence technology. Regardless of where the AI-database integration model heads, active databases *will* provide a key application development tool through DBMS management of business rules.

Outlook

Short-term

- Triggers and stored procedures will be widely used, providing active database properties to many information management environments
- Further research into "database intelligence" will provide more robust means of business rules representation than are available today

Long-term

- Active databases will be extended with robust business rule representation mechanisms in the commercial world
- Active database capabilities will become a dominant property of most commercial DBMS products
- The big question in artificial intelligence and databases will be: Will the marriage of the two disciplines be any further along (in terms of deployable technology) by the year 2000 than had been envisioned in the early 1950s?

Additional Reading

- U. Dayal and J. Widom, "Active Database Systems," *Tutorial for the 1992 ACM SIGMOD International Conference on Management of Data.*
- J. Mylopoulos and M. L. Brodie, eds., *Readings in Artificial Intelligence and Databases* (San Francisco: Morgan Kaufmann Publishers, 1989).
- J. Widom and S. Ceri, *Active Database Systems: Triggers and Rules for Advanced Database Processing* (San Francisco: Morgan Kaufmann Publishers, 1995).

Endnotes

1. U. Dayal and J. Widom, "Active Database Systems," *Tutorial for the 1992 ACM SIGMOD International Conference on Management of Data*, 2. Slides provided courtesy of Jennifer Widom, IBM Almaden Research Center, San Jose, CA.

2. Dayal and Widom, "Active Database Systems," 3.

3. D. McComb and T. Griffin, "Leveraging Your Database Smarts," *Database Programming & Design* (August 1992), 30.

4. J. Melton and A. Simon, *Understanding the New SQL: A Complete Guide* (San Francisco: Morgan Kaufmann Publishers, 1992), 211.

5. Melton and Simon, *New SQL*, 213.

6. Dayal and Widom, "Active Database Systems," 5.

7. Dayal and Widom, "Active Database Systems," 6.

8. Dayal and Widom, "Active Database Systems," 15.

9. Dayal and Widom, "Active Database Systems," 26.

10. Dayal and Widom, "Active Database Systems," 33.

11. Dayal and Widom, "Active Database Systems," 50.

12. Dayal and Widom, "Active Database Systems."

13. Dayal and Widom, "Active Database Systems," 69.

14. E. N. Hanson and J. Widom, *Research Report: An Overview of Production Rules in Database Systems* (San Jose, CA: RJ 9023 (80483), IBM Research Division, October 12, 1992), 4. Provided courtesy of Jennifer Widom.

15. Hanson and Widom, *Production Rules*.

16. Hanson and Widom, *Production Rules*.

17. M. Brodie, "Future Intelligent Information Systems: AI and Database Technologies Working Together," in J. Mylopoulos and M. L. Brodie, *Readings in Artificial Intelligence and Databases* (San Francisco: Morgan Kaufmann Publishers, 1989), 624.

18. Brodie, "Intelligent Information Systems," 627.

19. Brodie, "Intelligent Information Systems," 631–632.

CHAPTER

17

Space, Shapes, and Words: Spatial Databases, Multimedia and Image Information Management, and Text Management Systems

A Note to the CIO

We mentioned at the beginning of Chapter 15 that the concept of temporal databases probably only applies to a portion of your applications environment. The same is true of the subjects in this chapter: spatial, image, multimedia, and text data. Many of your most basic applications have little or no need for multimedia data or special extensions in the form of spatial databases. They do, however, apply to special classes of applications within your organization, and an understanding of the principles and future directions of each is important as you decide whether or not investments in these technologies should be made.

There is little doubt, though, that the other subjects covered in this chapter—multimedia data and management systems for text and documents—are of intense interest to both your short- and long-term planning. Both areas are extremely "hot" today, and will continue to be so for the rest of the decade.

Executive Summary

Database planners and practitioners are used to thinking of data in a "flat" sense. Even in the context of object-oriented systems, corporate-level implementations usually focus on information about customers and employees, inventory, and other data that fit nicely into one database paradigm or another (i.e., relational, network, object-oriented).

17.1 Introduction

In Part II, we discussed the future directions of object-oriented information management, noting that object-oriented capabilities such as abstract data types, methods, and encapsulation were a part of the trend of more closely modeling the real world. If abstract data types are incorporated, either as part of a "pure" OODBMS product or through a relational DBMS extended with object-oriented features, the increased power over simple binary large objects (BLOBs) provides application developers and end users with a high degree of semantic equivalence between real-world concepts and underlying information systems implementations.

In many situations, though, the basic object-oriented model capabilities are themselves insufficient to capture the semantics of specific types of application needs. Earlier we discussed the need for temporal databases (see Chapter 15), and noted that the temporal attributes are most powerfully implemented through extensions to the underlying DBMS model; the same holds true for other areas, including

- Spatial, or space-oriented, data
- Image data
- Multimedia data and delivery systems
- Text data and document management

Today and tomorrow's complex applications require a means to represent and manage data in ways that don't mesh quite so easily with either traditional database models or, at the simplest base levels, object-oriented databases. Some examples include

- *Spatial databases:* These deal with geometric points, commonly used in *geographic information systems* (GISs). Applications such as route planning and reconfiguration require spatial databases.

- *Image information systems:* Instead of using flat files to store image data, intelligence is applied to the components of the image being supported with database logic questions like "Show the left lung" (in a radiology application), rather than forcing the application to do all of the processing.

In this chapter, we'll look at the future directions of these information management areas, focusing on usages and model extensions.

17.2 Principles of Spatial Data

In the simplest sense, spatial data are space-related matters. Spatial information management deals with points, lines between points, and other geometrical attributes. Among the properties of the geometric relationships that must be preserved within the spatial database are[1]

- Connectivity (from one road to another)
- Adjacency (what neighborhoods are divided by a given road)
- Order (linear sequencing of landmarks along a road)
- Metric relations (approximate distances such as "near," "far," and "overnight trip")

In reality, there is little conceptual difference between spatial and temporal data (the latter being our subject in Chapter 15), at least in terms of their relationship with an underlying "normal" data model. In one sense, the concept of *parametric data* applies to both spatial and temporal data;[2] that is, a set of parameters that define either space or time concepts resides on top of base relations or objects. Temporal and spatial data are simply special cases of the more general concept of parametric data. They overlap in many other

- *Multimedia data:* One of the hottest areas today (witness the popularity of CD-ROMs and multimedia PCs, an area that boomed in 1993) and no doubt tomorrow. The conglomeration of different types of data—audio, video, still image, text, and traditional relational-like data—into single applications and delivery systems will be one of the dominant trends throughout the 1990s.

- *Text retrieval and document management:* As with multimedia systems, the unification of different types of documents—e.g., spreadsheets, word processing documents, textual portions of graphics and presentations—into a consolidated retrieval system will be a major objective of most organizations as they struggle to control billions of bytes of text dispersed physically and across different application types.

areas as well: a recent ACM SIGMOD bibliography[3] noted that of approximately 350 papers dealing with temporal databases and over 800 papers on spatial data structures, approximately 100 papers overlapped both topics.

Part of the reason for the overlap, in addition to the fact that both are extensions to basic underlying database models, is that spatial databases must have a temporal dimension. For example, street name changes, exit number changes, temporary characteristics (e.g., the left two lanes of I-70 between Denver and Idaho Springs are closed between May 15 and July 18), and other time-oriented properties should seem familiar from our discussion in Chapter 15. Spatial databases with temporal qualities are highly desirable, and information management systems designed to support spatial requirements will likely provide a certain number of temporal qualities as well.

Spatial data very often relates to geographic usages through geographic information systems (GISs). That is, the basic geometric principles of points and lines may be extended to geographic representations: streets and roads, air corridors, highways, and so on.

To better understand the properties—and challenges—of spatial data, let's look at a typical implementation of spatial data in the form of navigational systems.

17.2.1 Navigational Systems: A Case of Spatial Data Management

One of the classic examples of the need to manage, manipulate, and display spatial data is the use of navigational systems. Whether in the air, on the sea,

What This Technology Can Do for You

As we discussed in Chapter 1, information management in today and tomorrow's organizations involves more than databases and DBMSs. Further, underlying base DBMS technology is often not sufficient to support complex applications involving geographic and multimedia data. Instead of manipulating complex data types exclusively in such applications, the trend of pushing intelligence into the database (discussed in Chapter 16) can help support efficient development and maintenance of those types of systems.

Additionally, technology to help gain control over gigabytes of dispersed text data is always welcome. Just as the philosophy of logical centralization is one of the guiding principles of database technology (i.e., all applications ideally operate against a logically centralized

or on land, many applications require navigation along throughways and around detours. Facilitating such applications requires the ability to represent objects such as roads and streets, aggregations of simple objects (e.g., neighborhoods, city blocks), and the properties of each of these objects and aggregations.[4]

For example, the following simple and complex objects might have these properties:

Object	Property	Example Value
Road	Name	Coleridge Street Interstate-195 Route 122
	Exit_Number	22N 22S
	Old_Exit_Number	68A 68B n/a
	Restrictions	One-Way:EastBound One-Way:SouthBound NoHAZMAT NoTrucks TruckMax:10000 GVW BridgeClear:8'6"

database rather than numerous program-specific data files, a paradigm that holds true even in distributed database systems), that approach can help with the searching, retrieval, and manipulation of text documents that aren't, or can't be, stored in the corporate database environment. Documents with text data are certainly as important to an organization as data within the databases, and application of data management principles can help improve productivity by dispensing with long, exhaustive manual searches for documents based on contents, being forced to recreate such documents if the desired ones aren't found, and so on.

Object	Property	Example Value
	Speed_Limit	55 45Night
	Tolls	none .60_flat .10_per_mile .05*GVW*per_mile
	Traffic_Load	Heavy BumperToBumper AccidentBlocked
Neighborhood	Name	Stanton Heights
	Bounds	{list of roads on boundary}
Exit	Type	Normal CloverLeaf
	Number	22N
	Direction	N5°
Intersection	Participants (*multivalued*)	Coleridge Street Woodbine Street

Object	Property	Example Value
	Intersection_ID	1
	Num_Times_Intersect	2 (in many instances, the same 2 roads might intersect more than once)
Building	Building_Name	USX Building
	Address	555 Grant Street
	Num_Floors	65

Using the geographic objects stored in some type of database environment (more on that in a moment), the following are representative of the types of queries and operations you might issue through a GIS:[5]

- Find the shortest path between Philadelphia and Manhattan.
- Find the cheapest path between Philadelphia and Manhattan.
- Are there any roads currently undergoing construction between Philadelphia and Pittsburgh?
- I'm carrying hazardous materials; are there any tunnels between Albany and Syracuse that I can't travel?
- I want to go from Stanton Heights to downtown; what is the best route at 10:00 A.M.?
- Same question as above, but for 5:00 P.M. rush hour.

In response to these queries and requests for information, one of the challenges of geographical information systems—and, more specifically, navigational systems—is determining the form in which an answer might be returned. For example, the "best route" from one location to another within a metropolitan area might have the results returned 1) before a trip commences or 2) in real time during a trip. In the first case, a route might be preplanned based on known information in the geographical database (e.g., what roads are particularly heavy during a particular time, and so on), but this is of questionable value when changes in conditions occur after the route has been chosen (e.g., an accident occurs).

In the second case, a real-time link to some type of information feeder must be maintained in order to provide up-to-the-second accuracy, and a real-time database update capability must be part of the system (Figure 17-1).

Another real-time requirement has to do with making instructions and feedback reported to users of the database application as useful as possible. For

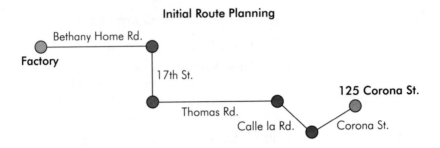

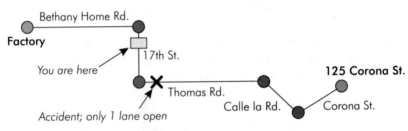

Figure 17-1 Navigational Planning and Real-Time Updates

example, accident reporting and rerouting as illustrated in Figure 17-1 could take one of several different forms:

1) "Turn left on Indian School": For system users (e.g., drivers) familiar with the area, this information might be sufficient.

2) "Turn left, 1.85 miles, road = Indian School": For system users less familiar with the area, who need clearer directions.

3) "Turn left, 1.85 miles": If, perhaps, the turn puts you onto an unmarked road (e.g., desert roads or trails on the city outskirts).

Additionally, users should be able to select from one of several types of output, including the following:

- A map with routes highlighted (similar to Figure 17-1).
- A list of instructions, minus the map.
- Some other combination of output (e.g., audio output of list-based instructions, with voice requests for a heads-up display of a highlighted map).

Although our subject of interest in this book isn't directly related to input and output, the point we will make in Chapter 18 about hypertext and hypermedia as future-oriented front ends to databases and repositories can also be made about spatial data. Consultant Joe Celko notes that geographic information systems, or "geobases," might be viewed as a combination of databases, CAD systems, and hypertext with specialized geographic data.[6]

In addition to the obvious need to handle complex data types and relationships, other requirements must be met in spatial databases intended for use in applications such as navigation, including[7]

- *Data volumes:* Requirements range from land vehicle (car, truck) navigational systems, with "very large" storage requirements (perhaps 600 megabytes, using the U.S. Census Department's TIGER files as a reference), to terabyte databases used in remote sensing applications. Paradoxically, an individual object's storage requirements might be rather small, perhaps just an x and y coordinate pair, but with many thousands of relationships with other points. Part of the reason for this large number of relationships is the bill-of-materials nature of navigational data types: a point on a map is part of a road, which is part of a neighborhood, which in turn is part of a city, which is part of a county, and so on.
- *Real-time access:* Certain classes of queries must be answered in a real-time manner; data properties such as data density, granularity of the information, travel speed, and many other mobile computing issues (see section 22.2 of Chapter 22 for a discussion on mobile and nomadic database requirements) must be factored into the retrieval side of the data management environment.
- *Query processing:* Obviously, standard relational queries are insufficient for retrieving spatial data; it's hard to imagine anyone, whether a truck driver or a computer programmer, formulating JOIN and PROJECT operations on the fly during a traffic jam. Different classes of spatial data operations require different classes of queries. For example, basic spatial data is queried most naturally in a navigational form, moving from object to object through space, while route planning requires information about connectivity among objects, which are then built into a route. Map presentations, however, require boundaries to be presented and the appropriate level of granularity retrieved and presented within the bounds of the map. A great deal of work needs to be done in this area, including

extended queries such as predicting (inferring) the type of information a driver or other user might need along a given route (e.g., the system reports a speed trap but the driver isn't speeding, so this information need not be reported).

- *Granularity:* Different levels of detail are often stored within a spatial database for the same object; depending on the query type, user profile, and other requirements, approximations or more precise information might be returned. Reporting that the distance from one neighborhood to another is approximately six miles might be sufficient in general, but public utility planning, for example, would likely need to know precise distances, often down to the foot or inch.

In the next section, we'll turn our attention to a related topic: image information systems.

17.3 Image Information Systems

In many ways, image information systems are very much like other types of spatial environments such as navigational systems. If you consider image-intensive applications such as medical CAT scans and MRIs, some spatial capability is useful to set the boundaries of the image that must be retrieved and managed.[8] In fact, characteristics such as a navigation plan (going from one image to another according to a user request or even inferred rules) are pertinent to image information systems.

Figure 17-2 shows the conceptual architecture of an image information system. Note that the components and their relationship to one another are similar to nearly any other type of information system one might imagine.

For our purposes, the image database system is of the greatest interest. This component must perform three functions:[9]

1) *Image analysis and pattern recognition:* A binary large object (BLOB) data type is completely different from an abstract data type (ADT). Semantics are attached with the abstract but not with the BLOB data type. An image database system must similarly be capable of analyzing a raw image and *recognizing* what that image as well as its components are. The database system, rather than a higher-level application, must have the capability to analyze bit streams and determine the contents and characteristics of some image (say, an X-ray, a map, a photograph). In short, the conceptual query "show the left lung" should retrieve the image of someone's left lung from an X-ray. Much of this processing is done via *pattern recognition*, using encoding of image objects within the "knowledge base" to understand the query.

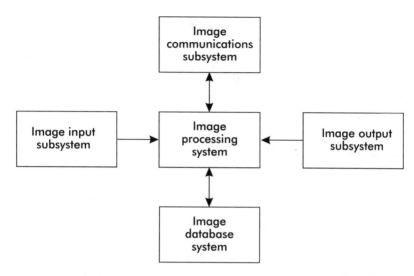

Figure 17-2 Conceptual Architecture of an Image Information System[10]

2) *Image structuring and understanding:* Some applications merely require that an object be retrieved and displayed, with no further structuring necessary. Other applications require some degree of structuring for spatial reasoning (see the third item here); in order to perform spatial reasoning, icons on an image (e.g., a lane on a road) must be defined.

3) *Spatial reasoning and image information retrieval:* "Find all roads from an aerial photograph that have four or more lanes" is an example of spatial reasoning from an image. Another example is to retrieve all X-rays in which a patient has a liver enlarged by some specified percentage.

Interestingly, the traditional ANSI SPARC 3-schema approach—external, conceptual, and internal—might be used within an image database. As illustrated in Figure 17-3, the external view, accessible by users and applications, might represent objects such as X-rays, lungs, roads, and so on. Underneath, a conceptual model controls the relationships among objects, including appropriate aggregations (e.g., a body is composed of lungs, a heart, and other organs; a heart contains ventricles; and so on). Finally, the internal model, used by the image database, uses whatever representation is most appropriate and efficient for its environment, with appropriate mappings to the conceptual model.

Since image databases and spatial data in general can grow extremely large (especially when motion is added to form video, as we'll discuss in section 17.4 on multimedia), a tiered approach is advised for information management. One method[11] provides a set of preview images and associated text in the form of a catalog from which desired images might be selected. The large image base is then stored in another location, perhaps in near-line

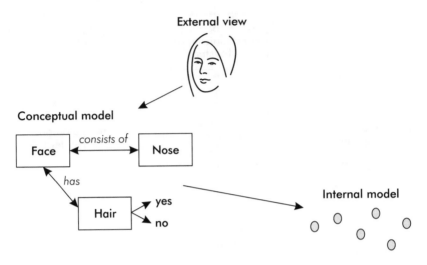

Figure 17-3 The Three-Schema Approach and Image Databases

media, for retrieval. With this approach, keyword searches may be performed on the text. While not quite the image-based query capability envisioned for the future (e.g., "Find all faces with blue eyes" actually retrieves information based on eye color in the image base, not keyword-based information), a tiered approach is an adequate stopgap measure until full image-driven functionality comes about.

While still images are quite useful in many applications, they might be considered a subset of multimedia information systems, which we'll discuss next.

17.4 Multimedia Information Systems

In the next generation of computer-based applications, few are more exciting than multimedia. Adding audio, video, text, and image to traditional application types is yet another step in the march toward more closely aligning computer systems with the real-world concepts they are intended to represent. The tremendous growth in sales of CD-ROM-equipped personal computers, particularly during the 1993 holiday buying season, signals the desire of individuals and business organizations to bring multimedia computing into their homes and companies.

Even the general class of *informational* applications can greatly benefit from multimedia systems. One example is a system that began operating in 1993 at the U.S. Holocaust Memorial Museum in Washington, D.C.[12] Through 25 workstations, users can retrieve articles, play recordings, watch newsreels and other video, and scan maps. When initially fielded, the system was

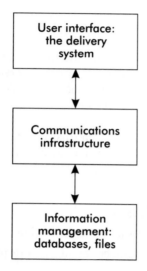

Figure 17-4 Conceptual Architecture of Multimedia Information Systems

self-contained within the museum; remote database access from the Library of Congress has been discussed, using fiber-optic cable as the communications medium.

This particular multimedia system is interesting in that the hardware and overall system design were relatively easy to create; the most difficult step was "organizing the material,"[13] that is, creating a conceptual model of the multimedia data. As we discussed in section 17.3 with respect to image databases, conceptual modeling through a semantically rich technique is extremely important; concepts such as classification, aggregation, and generalization must be thoroughly investigated among the objects of a multimedia system.[14]

17.4.1 Architecture

At the simplest level, a multimedia information system is conceptually similar to any other information system; the environment is compartmentalized into a delivery system (the user interface), some form of underlying information management capability, and a communications infrastructure. In the case of multimedia systems, all three levels have different properties from more traditional computer environments, including the way applications are developed (Figure 17-4).

Consider the delivery system, through which the user makes requests and receives information back from the system. Hypermedia interfaces will be the primary delivery system for the next generation of multimedia applications. These interfaces allow a user to browse through an information base consisting of many different types of data in ad hoc, unpredictable ways, which is essential to getting the most out of the information base. (We'll discuss hypertext and hypermedia in Chapter 18.)

The information base itself—the multimedia information system—could be considered a conglomeration of the many different types of data discussed in this chapter and throughout the book. The following are included in the typical multimedia information system:

- "Normal" types of database data (that could be found in a relational or network database or in application-owned flat files)
- Still image data, as in photographs
- Other types of graphics
- Moving image data (video)
- Audio (e.g., voice, musical sounds, animal noises)
- Text data, such as might be found in word processing documents or spreadsheet files

We've discussed the delivery system and the information base. Now we will consider the communications infrastructure. A general rule of thumb with respect to support requirements for multimedia information systems is as follows: the more "lifelike" the data, the greater the bandwidth that is required. By "lifelike" we mean data such as video or high-quality (e.g., stereo) audio. Not only do these data types take up tremendous amounts of storage space if data compression isn't used (one minute of untreated video to be delivered at 15 frames per second, which is only half of television speed, requires 117 megabytes of storage),[15] but high-throughput networking is required to support the data type. This is true not only for local area systems, but also across wide area environments. Emerging wide area networking (WAN) technologies such as Asynchronous Transfer Mode (ATM) or Switched Multimegabit Data Service (SMDS) are necessary to adequately support large-scale transfer of the complete range of multimedia data types.[16]

One simple way to understand the space requirements for full-fledged multimedia computing on the desktop is through "the 4 G's": a gigabyte of main memory, a minimum of a gigabyte of secondary storage, giga operations per second, and gigabit-per-second data transfer rates.[17] Given the rapid pace of advancements in hardware technology to which we've become accustomed, such base technology will undoubtedly emerge.

For multimedia information management, the principles of temporal and spatial data are often very important in composing a multimedia document. For example, creation of an electronic video requires that frames be sequenced properly; to do so, especially when source data for the video is being consolidated from a number of different origins, implies a temporal property to that information. Likewise, composition on a multimedia document—an electronic magazine, for example—means that a spatial relationship among data must be supported, not only as a document is composed from different media types (e.g., the video goes to the left of the text and above the audio), but within a given media type as well. (For example, for a map composed of spatial data from multiple sources, what is the proximity of New York State to Pennsylvania? Which one should be displayed where?)[18]

17.4.2 Standards

In addition to the standards on data management we've discussed throughout this book, other standards apply to the multimedia systems world. Microsoft's Multimedia PC (MPC) specification has emerged as the de facto standard for multimedia desktop machines. Other standards include[19]

- Joint Photographics Expert Group (JPEG) for still-image compression.
- Moving Picture Coding Expert Group (MPEG) for moving-image compression.
- Multimedia and Hypermedia Information Coding Expert Group (MHEG) for hypermedia information compression.

More standards will undoubtfully emerge to promote interchangeability and interoperability among multimedia systems.

17.4.3 Application Development Methodology

Traditional application development methodologies don't translate well to multimedia systems. "Programming" doesn't really apply to multimedia applications; "authoring" is a more appropriate term. Rather than programming languages and compilers, the dominant development paradigm emerging in multimedia is scripting systems (e.g., Microsoft Viewer). Because so many hypermedia applications are being developed, scripting facilities must be available to create application logic that enables users to function in a hypermedia environment (e.g., moving randomly among topics).[20]

More and more multimedia development systems will appear on the marketplace, enabling high productivity as applications become commonplace.

17.5 Text Retrieval and Document Management Systems

Though many data administrators are forced to focus on the database area of data management, it comes as no surprise that a great deal of an organization's data are not under the control of any database but rather are stored within many different types of documents, including "plain old text documents" from word processors and editors. The advent of desktop computing through low-cost personal computers has, of course, greatly increased user productivity since the days of centralized, mainframe-based computing. However, as with personal computer databases and the dispersal of DBMS-managed data, the scattering of documents to desktops across the corporation has greatly complicated the management of text data.

Consider the following scenario. You need to *quickly* locate all documents that relate to the Ricardo Band Instruments, Inc. (also known as "RBI" in informal documents) contract for a meeting that will commence in one hour. You know that many different staff members have worked on many documents concerning that project. Some of those documents were prepared in Microsoft Word for Windows, others in the Macintosh version of Microsoft Word. Some were also done on an MS-DOS system in an old version of WordPerfect by a temporary agency worker who only knew that package.

The documents also include some spreadsheets, also prepared on different systems using a variety of spreadsheet packages. There may be some graphics, too; you think someone did a presentation last month on the Ricardo account.

You get the idea. The process of assembling many different types of documents, even simply *finding* what computers they're on and the correct file names, is hardly trivial. A document management system is needed that operates similarly (at least conceptually) to the distributed database architectures we discussed in Part II.

Traditionally, document management systems have been limited to text documents (e.g., ASCII or EBCDIC files, word processing documents) and have been in one of two different areas:[21]

1) *Text retrieval systems*, which use file indexes to locate documents containing certain keywords or text strings (more on that in a moment).

2) "*Textbases*," also known as *component document managers*, which compartmentalize documents into user-specifiable units (e.g., chapters, sections, or even as granular as paragraphs) and enable those units to be managed as objects (e.g., checked out, modified, checked back in).

These two types of systems are, however, coming together in document management systems, which (along with underlying tools) are capable of performing all of these functions and much more. Figure 17-5 illustrates the architecture of such systems and their relationship with other aspects of distributed information management.

Along with hypermedia interfaces (discussed in Chapter 18) capable of providing unpredictable, ad hoc access to the underlying base of information, and middleware (discussed in Chapter 3) to provide standards-based connectivity and interoperability, document management systems provide interfaces

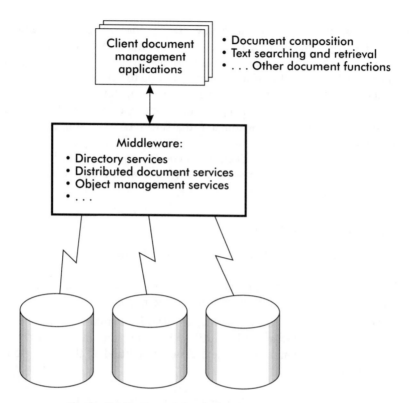

Figure 17-5 Architecture for Emerging Distributed Document Management Systems

to and coordination of a variety of document managers including word processors, editors, spreadsheet programs, graphics and presentation systems, and others.

The media that support the overall document management system include the following:

- CD-ROMs particularly for PC-managed multimedia data.

- Optical disks for both multimedia and very large documents, typically attached to LAN servers or mid-range systems.

- Magnetic disks, for "normal" files (e.g., text, spreadsheet).

Returning to our earlier example, the user, via the hypermedia interface, would issue the query "Find all documents that reference Ricardo Band

Instruments, Inc." Once such a request reaches the distributed document management system (DDMS), a global index is searched, which yields 1) the location(s), 2) the file name(s), and 3) the particular data manager(s) (e.g., a list of products) that will yield documents referring to the request text string. Through the component document management capabilities of such a system, a finer granularity than simply a file name may be provided (e.g., a particular chapter or section within a textual document, or a single page of a multipage graphics file).

Questions arise: How are documents checked into the global management system? How is the index structured? Who or what decides what should go into the index?

17.5.1 Document Check-in

Two methods are available to check documents into the system:

1) Optical character recognition (OCR) scanning of documents (which usually requires editing services to verify correctness).

2) "Online loading" of documents that are already maintained in machine-readable form. This might be a utility that scans the universe of documents on all systems within the organization, building the index from that base.

17.5.2 Index Structure

Textbase systems typically use an *inverted list* data structure, in which a complete list of all words or phrases of interest is maintained with pointers to the appropriate document. For example, requests to find the following text combinations would be satisfied by cross-referencing the pointers and coming up with the correct list of documents:

- "Ricardo Band Instruments" and "1994": The index structure would yield the data, which would tell the retrieval system that a group of documents contains *both* of these text strings; this data would be determined by the *intersection* of the pointers (e.g., which documents were common to both text strings).

- "Ricardo Band Instruments" or "RBI": All pointers from the index entries of both of these text strings would be returned (the *union*).

- ("Ricardo Band Instruments" or "RBI") and ("1992" or "1993"): Two different union operations are performed, then the intersection of those is taken,[22] resulting in a list of all documents that deal with the client and events in either 1992 or 1993.

17.5.3 Index Loading

The traditional method used in text retrieval systems involves a person with the function of "text data administrator" (though he or she would rarely be called that) who would determine what keywords constitute the search criteria managed through the index. One problem with this approach is that if a specific keyword isn't provided, then it isn't available for use. Further, textbases are not static (created at one time, with all necessary keywords in place initially); as new documents are checked into the textbase over time, new keywords must be added to the index. Requiring human intervention may cause a tremendous time lag between when a document is checked in and when it becomes "usable" (i.e., subject to being found in a search).

Alternatively, an automatic index loading scheme may be used at the time of document loading, effectively making an entry for every word into the index. If a word already exists, a new pointer is added; if not, a new index entry is made along with the pointer. The disadvantage to this model is the vast amount of storage required for the index structure. Though human-specified keyword indexes run the risk of excluding something that might be of interest, the automatic loading model usually requires the loading and maintenance of much that will *never* be of interest. Models that incorporate both aspects (automatic loading with an *exception list* of words that should never be loaded) show promise, but the text search algorithms must account for the absence of words such as "the" and "an," if so selected for exclusion.

17.5.4 Component Document Management

Consider the model of *full-text retrieval*, in which the index described in the previous section would lead a user directly to one or more documents, in their entirety, that are likely to be of interest. The primary disadvantage of this type of environment is that documents have traditionally been treated as monolithic units, with no lower levels of decomposition for management. To combat this problem, text management systems have begun (and will continue) to add context areas to their storage environments.[23] A *context area* is used to confine a document search to one or more components of interest to a user, a component being a chapter, section, paragraph, or some other significant unit level. Allowing the user to structure documents according to the user's most meaningful context levels should be a goal of document management systems.[24]

In terms of standards-based document storage, the Standard Generalized Markup Language (SGML) has somewhat surprisingly played a part in component management.[25] SGML was originally conceived in the early 1980s as a standard means to interchange documents from one system to another, and it is based on tags. *Tags* are used to specify the components of a document, as in

```
<chapter>Chapter 17: Space, Shapes, and Words: Spatial
Databases, Multimedia and Image Information Management, and Text
Management Systems</chapter>

<abstract>discussion of non-traditional data types</abstract>

<para> . . . some text . . . </para>
<para> . . . some more text . . . </para>
```

SGML and similar tag-based systems weren't widely used for a long time because PCs and workstations favored WYSIWYG (what you see is what you get) word processors. Having to actually compile your document once finished to see if you had all the tag placements correct made writing a document in SGML extremely inconvenient.

What has brought SGML to the forefront of document management is its ability to specify components via paragraph, section, chapter, and other tags, which can then feed into a text database system capable of managing those components and providing full-text search capabilities. Because SGML is by definition a standard, most word processing packages are moving toward providing SGML output as an option that allows documents, once created, to be inserted into the text DBMS environment for management.

17.5.5 Future Directions and Issues

If the above scenario and examples sound familiar, recall the transparent global schema approach to distributed databases, discussed in Chapter 6. Though that approach has long been pursued in research and, to some extent, has been successfully implemented in commercial products, the technology currently does not scale well to corporation-wide distributed databases, and numerous problems still exist that must be resolved.

The same is true of widely distributed document management systems, which have the following issues:

- *Document loading:* This task cannot be handled simply by using a combination of OCR and online loading of documents (section 17.5.1). Document loading into the textbase and associated indexes is a *major* job; documents are likely already distributed across the corporation among numerous PCs, and inevitably multiple versions of the same document exist (on different users' PCs). This is a time-intensive process, and one that requires translators to numerous underlying text managers (e.g., word processor formats, spreadsheet, and graphics packages) that will have text checked into the system. Export/import facilities may have to be written for products or systems that don't currently have interfaces to the document system.

- *The user interface:* In section 17.4.1, we noted that a hypermedia interface would provide multimedia ad hoc access. While hypermedia is rapidly evolving, the underlying workflow management of such requests is still developing. For example, what sequence of events must occur if a user makes a request of the textbase that requires a wide-area search, possibly of systems not currently online? Should all of a user's result be presented at one time, or can documents "trickle in" as they become available? These workflow paradigms must be specified and managed.

- *Access rules:* At the user interface level, a system should include a way to prevent a user from issuing a request such as "retrieve all documents in which the word 'and' appears"; such a request would adversely affect the overall system and could quite possibly bring the entire infrastructure of the corporation to a grinding halt.

- *Multiple text source:* We noted that textbases and document management systems will be multimedia in nature, meaning that text occurrences in graphics, spreadsheets, and other packages must be indexed. Though many newer versions of PC packages have added textual capabilities to spreadsheets and graphics packages (e.g., "find" functions and spell checkers in a presentation graphics program), older packages may not have such facilities. These documents must have their text contents analyzed for incorporation into the textbase, possibly requiring utility programs to pick through proprietary data structures.

- *Concurrency control:* Remember that a textbase is not a database, and transaction semantics such as concurrency control are not found here. The document management system most likely will need to support long transaction paradigms of the type common to object-oriented databases, enabling documents to be checked out, modified, and checked back in (and the appropriate index or indexes updated).

- *Index server architecture:* In a widely distributed environment, should the index be 1) centralized, 2) distributed among a small number of "index servers," or 3) widely distributed among servers across the corporation? This is the same problem that applies to directory servers for globally transparent distributed databases.

- *Ownership and security:* Bringing documents into a corporation-wide document management system raises the question of who *owns* a document, with respect to permissible operations. Can a user indiscriminately delete a spreadsheet file on his or her PC? Suppose someone else needs that file; what ownership rules apply?

These are some of the major areas that must be addressed as organizations struggle to provide a level of control to distributed document management through the rest of the decade.

17.6 Conclusion

We've taken a look at types of nontraditional data and how the information management world is evolving to account for them. Most of what we've discussed in this chapter could conceivably be database extensions in a general sense. For example, to handle spatial data (like temporal data, as we discussed in Chapter 15) some extensibility to a basic database is desirable.

Different data classes have not only different input and output requirements (e.g., audio, still image, video) but also different information management requirements. Spatial data must have a very large number of properties and relationships captured for what might be a relatively simple set of data items, perhaps a long series of X-Y map coordinates. Document management for full-text retrieval introduces the concept of component management.

Each of the subjects we've discussed in this chapter is in its infancy at the present time, with some degree of functionality in commercial systems; of course, a tremendous amount of research is under way. One could argue that the future of spatial, image, and multimedia data is heavily influenced by developments in object orientation. That is, as ODMG (see Chapters 10 and 13) and extended relational systems with SQL3 (see Chapters 9 and 12) evolve, they will provide the basic capabilities for spatial properties, multimedia data, and other advanced information management needs.

Outlook

Short-term

- Layers on top of OODBMSs will provide image, spatial, and multimedia capabilities
- Libraries of complex data types for image, spatial, and multimedia data will be available for reuse by many organizations
- Interest in multimedia systems will continue to increase as multimedia desktop computers become commonplace
- Various text management product types (retrieval, text databases, authoring) will have their capabilities merged into single document management systems that can be layered on top of widely dispersed corporate resources for consolidated management of textual data
- Standards for querying text will be approved; compliant products will become commonplace

Long-term

- Image, spatial, and multimedia capabilities will be incorporated into DBMS product engines

- Standards for text queries will evolve and include more features; products will keep pace
- Management of the types of data discussed in this chapter will be commonplace in most organizations

Additional Reading

- K. Al-Taha, R. T. Snodgrass, and M. D. Soo, "Bibliography on Spatiotemporal Databases," *SIGMOD Record* (March 1993).
- C. Bidmead, "Finding the Right Words," *Which Computer?* (February 1993).
- M. Blattner and R. B. Dannenberg, *Multimedia Interface Design* (New York: ACM Press, 1992.)
- M. J. Egenhofer, "What's Special about Spatial? Database Requirements for Vehicle Navigation in Geographic Space," *Proceedings of SIGMOD 1993.*
- S. Khoshafian and B. Baker, *Imaging and Multimedia Databases* (San Francisco: Morgan Kaufmann Publishers, in press).
- P. Marshall and P. Watt, "Text Retrieval," *InfoWorld* (May 1993).
- "Multimedia Information Systems," *IEEE Computer* (October 1991). Various articles on the subject.
- "Multimedia in the Workplace," *Communications of the ACM* (January 1993). Various articles on the subject.

Endnotes

1. M. J. Egenhofer, "What's Special about Spatial? Database Requirements for Vehicle Navigation in Geographic Space," *Proceedings of SIGMOD 1993*, 400.

2. S. Gadia, "Parametric Databases: Seamless Integration of Spatial, Temporal, Belief, and Ordinary Data," *SIGMOD Record* (March 1993), 15.

3. K. K. Al-Taha, R. T. Snodgrass, and M. D. Soo, "Bibliography on Spatiotemporal Databases," *SIGMOD Record* (March 1993), 59.

4. Egenhofer, "What's Special about Spatial?," 399.

5. Adapted from the examples in Egenhofer, "What's Special about Spatial?," 399.

6. J. Celko, "DBMS Report," *Systems Integration* (November 1991), 39. Celko actually noted that *relational* databases were part of the geobase equation, but the article was written in 1991, before the accelerated growth in OODBMSs in the past two or three years. We've elected to generalize the component to databases of all types.

7. Egenhofer, "What's Special about Spatial?," 400–401.

8. S. K. Chang and A. Hsu, "Image Information Systems: Where Do We Go from Here?," *IEEE Transactions on Knowledge and Data Engineering* (October 1992), 432.

9. Chang and Hsu, "Image Information Systems," 431–432.

10. Chang and Hsu, "Image Information Systems," 431.

11. A. Abernathy, "New Image Databases Adept at Handling Many Large Files," *MacWEEK* (January 18, 1993), 36–38.

12. J. Burgess, "Making Multimedia Work," *Washington Business* (June 14, 1993), 19.

13. Burgess, "Multimedia," 26.

14. C. Meghini, F. Rabitti, and C. Thanos, "Conceptual Modeling of Multimedia Documents," *IEEE Computer* (October 1991), 24.

15. D. C. Churbuck, "Lights! Camera! Manual!" *Forbes* (January 17, 1994), 93.

16. ATM and SMDS are discussed in A. Simon, *Implementing the Enterprise* (New York: Bantam Books/Intertext, 1993), Chap. 3.

17. A. Desai Narasimhalu and S. Christodoulakis, "Multimedia Information Systems: The Unfolding of a Reality," *IEEE Computer* (October 1991), 6.

18. T. D. C. Little and A. Ghafoor, "Spatio-temporal Composition of Distributed Multimedia Objects for Value-Added Networks," *IEEE Computer* (October 1991), 42–46.

19. Little and Ghafoor, "Distributed Multimedia Objects," 7.

20. Churbuck, "Lights! Camera! Manual!," 93.

21. P. Marshall and P. Watt, "Text Retrieval," *InfoWorld* (May 24, 1993), 123.

22. In practice, a different sequence of events might occur as part of the text query optimization scheme, but the logical outcome is the same.

23. Meghini, Rabitti, and Thanos, "Conceptual Modeling," 24.

24. Meghini, Rabitti, and Thanos, "Conceptual Modeling."

25. K. G. Barkes, "Documents on Demand," *DEC Professional* (August 1993), 18.

CHAPTER

18

Hypertext and Hypermedia

A Note to the CIO

Hypertext and hypermedia have, perhaps unfairly, been considered something of a "toy" by information systems; their purpose in the PC world is small-scale applications, the party line goes. With the expansion of technology in this area, coupled with growth in client/server utilization in which PCs and corporate mainframes, mid-ranges, and other servers are integrated with one another, hypermedia systems will inevitably be desirable as easy-to-use interfaces not only for general applications but also for database operations (e.g., queries and updates). Therefore, an understanding of the foundations of hypertext and hypermedia (normally outside the realm of corporate information systems) as well as the future directions of the technology is important to help determine its applicability to your environment.

18.1 Introduction

The history of hypertext goes back to 1945, when Vannevar Bush proposed a MEMory Extender (Memex) system, which bears a striking resemblance to the commercial hypertext environments that began appearing in the mid-1980s.[1] Bush's theories, which were actually developed between 1932 and 1933 and described in a paper in 1939, were never implemented, and his grand vision of a sort of windowing environment with access to multimedia forms of data is still some years away from widespread implementation. Bush's vision for Memex was predicated on the explosion of scientific information at the time,

Executive Summary

Hypertext and hypermedia reached prominence in the mid-1980s with Apple Macintosh implementations of HyperCard. Having faded somewhat from the scene after an initial flurry of applications, hypermedia is gaining new life as the front end for CD-ROM-based multimedia data.

As with most other areas discussed here, the concept of layering pervades the hypermedia world, with mix-and-match architectures featuring hypermedia GUIs on top of middleware and underlying databases.

and he recognized the need for maintaining traversable associations among many different sources of information, regardless of format.[2]

Prototypes based on Memex concepts appeared from the mid-1960s through the mid-1980s, but it wasn't until the Apple Macintosh came to market in 1984 and, more specifically, the introduction of Apple's HyperCard in 1987, that hypertext gained widespread popularity and became a serious subject for research in the area of information management. Part of this sudden popularity was the inclusion of HyperCard in every Macintosh sold after 1987, giving Mac users the ability to produce HyperCard-based applications, known as *stackware*.[3]

In this chapter, we'll discuss hypertext and hypermedia—two closely related subjects—and their future in information management. We'll take a close look at the basics of hypertext and hypermedia, as well as their role in information management. Finally, we'll discuss the directions in which hyper-information technologies are headed.

18.2 Definitions of Hypertext and Hypermedia

First, it's important to put hypertext and hypermedia in the context of our discussions in this book on the future directions of information management (we'll refer to both of them collectively as hypermedia, except when we define them or when a given concept is particular to one or the other). Hypermedia is a user interface paradigm to underlying information, revolutionary (its nearly 50-year history notwithstanding) when considered next to traditional

What This Technology Can Do For You

Many types of applications are suitable for hypermedia interfaces. Almost any desktop application with complex flows of execution can be fitted with graphical user interface (GUI) layers on top of hypermedia, which in turn may be layered on top of local or remote (or both) databases. Executive information system (EIS) applications, as discussed in Chapter 4 in the context of data warehouses, are representative of such applications. So too are PC applications that use CD-ROM multimedia data.

An understanding of the directions of hypermedia, particularly in the area of complex layered systems construction, is important to creating the next generation of desktop applications geared to decision making or personal productivity.

human-computer interfaces such as character cell terminals and block mode terminals. In comparison to graphical user interfaces (GUIs), hypermedia can be viewed as an interface layer on top of basic GUI primitive operations (e.g., menu bars, windows, icons); hypermedia can exist in environments other than GUI, but GUI technology makes hypermedia that much "prettier."

So, just what are hypertext and hypermedia? *Hypertext* is a nonsequential manner of looking at text-based information. That is, even though a manual, book, report, or some other document may be stored within a computer system in a sequential manner, hypertext provides an interface so that any number of nonsequential links may be followed by the user, allowing the user to easily access an item of interest even if it is not the next sequentially stored item.[4]

Perhaps more importantly, hypertext includes the capability to return to the point from which a given traversed path began. Random access to a sequential document by itself is nothing special; you could use any text editor or word processor and, while scanning an online document, do a FIND or SEARCH operation for a text string and go to another section, or call up a related document in another GUI window. Hypertext, though, maintains an infrastructure of information nodes and links, with pointers used to facilitate browsing and navigation among objects rather than user-induced search operations.[5]

Hypermedia extends the hypertext paradigm into multimedia (see Chapter 17). Instead of navigation among text objects, hypermedia offers links among text, video, images, voice—pretty much the whole spectrum of multimedia information.

Figure 18-1 illustrates an example of a hypertext system, and Figure 18-2 extends that model to a hypermedia environment.

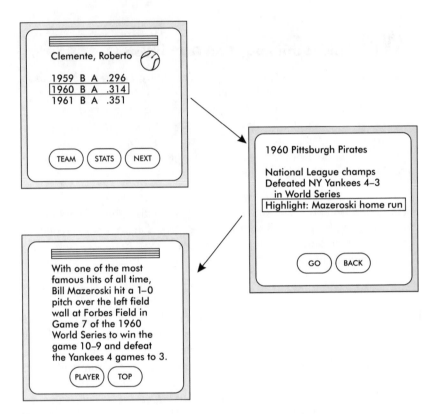

Figure 18-1 Hypertext Example

18.3 Architecture of Hypermedia Systems

Hypermedia systems typically have a three-level architecture:[6]

1) *Presentation, or user interface level*, which includes the constructs and presentation forms of how commands are presented to users (e.g., what buttons are presented with a particular screen, noting what paths may be followed), display parameters for the information within the window, and so on.

2) *Hypertext (or hypermedia) abstract machine (HAM)*, which includes an abstract definition of the nodes within the application environment as well as the links among those nodes. Basically, this level might be viewed as a conceptual implementation-independent layer that represents the data model against which the presentation level is written, much as applications may be developed against a conceptual data model with mappings to the underlying physical data structures.

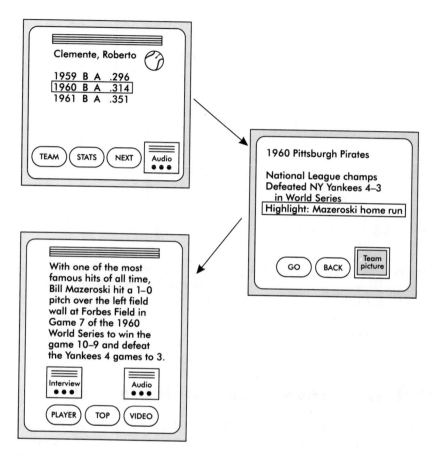

Figure 18-2 Hypermedia Example

3) *Database level*, which is the underlying physical data representation of the information presented and managed through the hypermedia system. In early commercial hypermedia systems and even basic hypertext environments, without multimedia support, the "database" level was far from a database as we understand the concept; it lacked multi-user concurrency control, security, and other database properties.

At the database level, integration with existing database technology must occur on a larger scale than it does today, to provide a more robust data management environment. Application developers using hypermedia models to create information systems have clamored for underlying DBMS capabilities on top of which hypermedia may be layered. Object-oriented database capabilities in particular are greatly desired[7] (Figure 18-3).

Indeed, the paradigm of object orientation ideally should extend not just to the underlying database model, but to the hypermedia development envi-

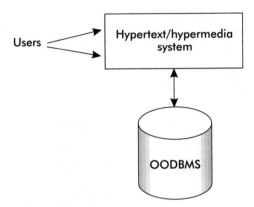

Figure 18-3 The Integration of Database Technology with Hypermedia

ronment as a whole: the abstract machine level (e.g., an object-oriented conceptual model for the underlying data) and the programming environment itself (e.g., the capability to create windows and contained objects through inheritance; firing methods to automatically traverse a particular link to another screen; and so on).

18.4 Hypermedia and Information Management

Hypermedia may be a user interface for many types of information management. Let's look at how hypermedia can interface with some of the other subjects we discuss in this book.

Let's look at data warehouses (see Chapter 4) first. You'll recall that the primary purpose of data warehousing is to provide decision support system (DSS) and executive information system (EIS) capabilities against an informational database, offloading such processing from operational databases. Because a great deal of EIS and DSS processing is of the what-if variety, traversing different paths based on what is important to different people, hypermedia is a natural interface paradigm for such environments (Figure 18-4). With a hypermedia abstract machine (HAM) built on top of the underlying data warehouse structure, the EIS/DSS applications could then be written against the HAM to permit browsing and drill-down analysis against multiple levels of warehouse granularity (see section 4.4 of Chapter 4). By using a hypermedia application capable of managing multimedia data, your EIS/DSS application can have access to voice, video, and image data as well as text or tabular information.

Although the purpose of data warehousing is to offload informational processing from operational databases, there are no rules actually forbidding

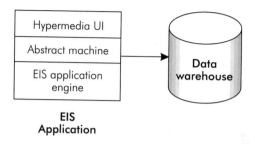

Figure 18-4 Data Warehouses and Hypermedia

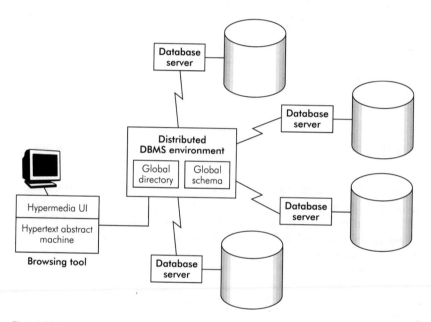

Figure 18-5 Hypermedia Access to Heterogeneous Distributed Databases

such informational actions even against distributed data managers. In Chapter 7, we noted the argument in favor of client/server interfaces to distribute data over global transparent access. Figure 18-5 illustrates an architecture in which a hypermedia user interface is used for browsing capabilities against a heterogeneous distributed database environment. The HAM level operates as client applications, calling remote database servers for access to the applicable underlying data represented by a particular hypermedia node.

Another area of information management where hypermedia will be valuable is repository tools, discussed in section 19.6 of Chapter 19. Briefly, tools to browse and manage repository objects are a very important part of a full-functioned repository environment, as we'll discuss in Chapter 19. With

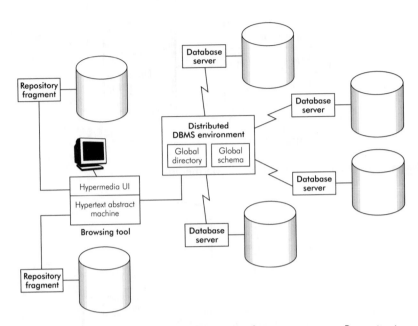

Figure 18-6 Distributed Hypermedia on Top of Heterogeneous Repositories

an architecture similar to the one shown in Figure 18-5, heterogeneous information repositories may be integrated through a distributed hypermedia system.[8] A distributed hypertext, with multiple workstation- or PC-based clients run against a single server that maintains the links and nodes (the HAM), can then be mapped against the underlying distributed repository facilities (Figure 18-6).

18.5 Future Directions in Hypermedia

We've already discussed a closer relationship between hypermedia interfaces and underlying information management technology. What else does the future hold for hypermedia systems? Jakob Nielsen identified short-, intermediate-, and long-term advances and directions for the technology in 1990.[9]

Nielsen stated that in the short term (1993 to 1995) the technology itself wouldn't undergo any radical shifts, though a mass market would emerge for hypermedia as well as a closer integration of hypermedia with other computing facilities (discussed in the previous section).

In the intermediate term (1995 to 2000), Nielsen suggested, we would see widespread publishing of hypermedia-based material, particularly in document management. Hypermedia-based documents would become a viable form of information dissemination, with interchange formats among hypermedia systems (perhaps through standardization of the hypermedia abstract machine and mapping algorithms to underlying information sources), permitting multiple platforms to work with the same hypermedia systems. (This author would add that multimedia interchange algorithms, such as those used in Adobe Systems' Acrobat system, should have direct applicability to hypermedia environments.)

For the long-term future of hypermedia (from the year 2000 on), Nielsen took the same cautious tone as we have done in this book with other subjects, concluding that the future "is for the science fiction authors to tell."[10] He did note, though, that many of the concepts we read about, such as electronic, personally composed magazine subscriptions (articles customized to an individual's preferences), will likely play a role in the hypermedia systems of the future.

Regardless of where hypermedia technology is headed, though, we can assume that, through a layered approach based on a hypermedia abstract machine (or similar mapping layer), wherever the various disciplines of information management go, they will be provided with hypermedia interfaces along with APIs for developers and other types of interfaces.

18.6 Conclusion

To date, hypertext and hypermedia environments have mostly been complete systems, from user interfaces to underlying proprietary data managers. As information management technology evolves in the many ways we've discussed in this book, the decoupling of the various layers in hypermedia systems will continue, and formal database managers (most likely with object-oriented capabilities, regardless of how they are actually implemented) will replace the proprietary lower levels of hypermedia systems. Through abstract machines in the middle, various user interface implementations of hypermedia can be mapped against underlying database systems, centralized or distributed, in much the same way that other user interface paradigms are placed against DBMSs. Information management technologies, from distributed DBMSs to data warehouses to repositories, can benefit from the natural ad hoc browsing capabilities inherent in hypermedia.

Hypermedia might arguably be the most valuable ad hoc user interface for tomorrow's information management environments.

Outlook

Short-term

- A closer coupling of hypertext and hypermedia technology with underlying information managers, particularly object-oriented databases, will occur

- Hypermedia may become the dominant ad hoc user interface for certain classes of applications on the desktop

- Commercial products will incorporate a layered architecture with interchange and interface mechanisms at the middle (hypermedia abstract machine) level

Long-term

- Hypermedia will be widely used in personalized electronic publishing environments

Additional Reading

- J. Nielsen, *HyperText and HyperMedia* (San Diego: Academic Press, 1990).

- J. Noll and W. Scacchi, "Integrating Diverse Information Repositories: A Distributed Hypertext Approach," *IEEE Computer* (December 1991).

Endnotes

1. J. Nielsen, *HyperText and HyperMedia* (San Diego: Academic Press, 1990), 29.

2. Nielsen, *HyperText*, 29–30.

3. Nielsen, *HyperText*, 30–40.

4. Nielsen, *HyperText*, 1–2.

5. Nielsen, *HyperText*, 2.

6. Nielsen, *HyperText*, 101. This model is known as the Campbell and Goodman model, and it isn't unanimously accepted; other models exist, but this three-level is suitable for our discussions in this chapter.

7. D. Crabb, "What's in the Cards for HyperCard's Future?," *MacWEEK* (May 11, 1992), 37.

8. J. Noll and W. Scacchi, "Integrating Diverse Information Repositories: A Distributed Hypertext Approach," *IEEE Computer* (December 1991), 38–44.

9. Nielsen, *HyperText*, 181–192.

10. Nielsen, *HyperText*, 187.

PART VI

Supporting Functions

CHAPTER

Repositories and Metadata Management

A Note to the CIO

Corporate metadata management in the form of repository control is a growing area, but has lagged behind the operational databases realm in general technology and standardization. As corporation-wide integration becomes more and more important, repository technology is seen as one of the keys to a robust system. This chapter discusses different models of distributed repositories, important for developing an overall long-range information management strategy.

19.1 Introduction

A repository is just a database with metadata instead of user data, right?

At the simplest level, we can give that summation a qualified yes. However, as we'll see in this chapter, repositories actually are more complex, and they arguably represent one of the keys to corporation-wide information management. Also, as we'll discuss, a repository itself is only part of the metadata management picture; user and application tools are absolutely critical to the effectiveness of any repository implementation.

In this chapter, we'll discuss the basics of repositories, with an emphasis on present trends and future directions.

Executive Summary

A *repository* may simply be viewed as a database for systems-related data rather than for user-oriented data. Much of the leading-edge database technology discussed in this chapter is directly applicable to present trends and future directions of repositories.

Repository technology dates back to data dictionaries used by software systems. As functionality and advanced capabilities have been incorporated into the data dictionary, the scope has been extended to encompass, ideally, corporation-wide metadata management.

Unlike databases, though, the repository field has a problem with standards. While several efforts have been underway for a number of

19.2 Principles of Repositories

First, let's give more substance to our "a repository is just a database" definition. Philip Bernstein defines a *repository* as "a shared database of information about engineered artifacts requiring control functions in addition to those provided by database systems."[1]

In the world of repositories, the *shared* property requires that the entities sharing the repository—tools and run-time systems—agree on the format of the metadata objects stored within that repository as well as on interobject relationships. *Engineered artifacts* include CASE, project management, and system configuration: components of information systems that are themselves *about* information systems.

Finally, the *control functions* required by a repository include the following:

- Check-in/check-out paradigm and formal procedures for objects under the management of the repository (regardless of where the objects themselves reside, and in what form).
- Ability to maintain multiple versions of objects, as well as configuration control procedures over those objects.
- Ability to notify tools and run-time systems about events of interest, such as changes to the format or semantics of repository-controlled objects.
- Context management, or different ways of looking at repository objects (such as database views).
- Ability to define and manage the work-flow of repository-based objects, such as tracking object status and executing predefined work-flow actions (e.g., notifying a set of users or some other tool about the progress to date).

years (particularly the IRDS effort at both the national and international levels), they are far behind database standards such as SQL in terms of maturity and commercial product implementations.

One of the growing areas will be repository tools, helping system developers and users browse through voluminous amounts of data. Another growing area will be the use of powerful repository capabilities in integrated CASE (I-CASE) environments, supporting systems development at different life-cycle stages by maintaining and reporting relationships among metadata objects from different phases (e.g., how a particular requirement is implemented in the operational database environment, or, conversely, helping to trace the requirements from which a relational table or column is derived).

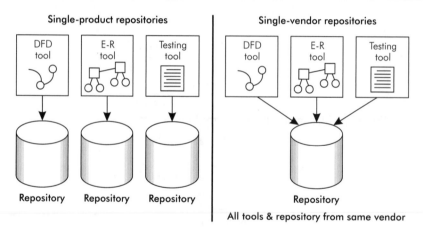

Figure 19-1 Single-Product and Single-Vendor Repository Environments

In addition to Bernstein's definition, two other characteristics are very important to the future directions of repositories: vendor independence and extensibility.[2]

To date, repository implementations have been primarily vendor-specific, even product-specific, with a very limited role to play. In the product-specific sense, a repository functions simply as a storage manager for metadata of use to that tool, DBMS, application, or whatever that product's role was to be. Expanding from an individual product to multiple products from a vendor, the repository's role changes from a simple storage manager to one encompassing interproduct communication of metadata. Even at this level, though, we're still dealing with proprietary object formats, communications protocols and notification mechanisms, versioning schemes, and other repository functions (Figure 19-1).

What This Technology Can Do For You

Having a good understanding of today's and tomorrow's repository technology is important, and you shouldn't get caught up in the hype surrounding "corporation-wide metadata management through a single repository." In reality, we're looking at a number of years, perhaps as late as 2000, until such repository capabilities are available across an entire worldwide information systems environment. In the meantime, department-class and other subcorporation systems can be equipped with repository facilities, to set the stage for eventual integration as technology catches up with ambition.

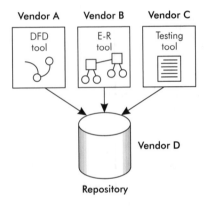

Figure 19-2 Vendor-Independent Repository Environment

Repositories supporting *vendor independence*, however, are capable of accepting plug-in interfaces from many different tools, run-time systems, and other users of the repository (Figure 19-2). The key to repository vendor independence is the same as with information management in general, and in fact the entire information systems marketplace: standards. We'll discuss repository standards in section 19.3.

The other characteristic mentioned, *extensibility*, means that repositories must be capable of extending the predefined schema supplied with the product. Extensions include adding new objects, modifying objects and properties, and otherwise customizing the repository environment for a particular organization (Figure 19-3).

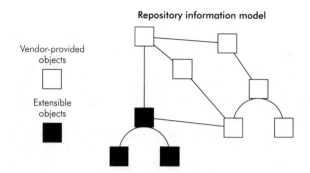

Figure 19-3 An Extensible Repository

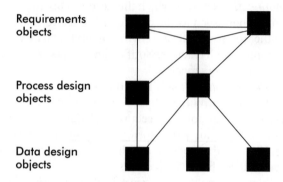

Figure 19-4 Intertool Object Relationships in a Repository

So what does a repository do? Exactly what is its role other than to "manage system metadata?" Let's look at a scenario illustrating the functions a repository is envisioned to do.[3]

Suppose your organization implements a wide range of computer-aided software engineering (CASE) tools at various life-cycle stages, from requirements collection to data modeling to process modeling to testing, as well as numerous other functions. During the development cycle, you will need to capture the interrelationships among objects from the many CASE tools you use: a particular requirement A is related to data modeling object B as well as database DDL definition C; a test X relates back to a code module Y, which in turn is traceable to both requirements A and Z (this scheme is shown in Figure 19-4).

Consider the trends in the CASE marketplace—specifically, the growing role of CASE environments such as Hewlett-Packard's SoftBench, with the ability to accept interfaces from many different tools, according to data and control integration standards.[4] From this we can infer that no single vendor will provide tools to serve each and every life-cycle stage; rather, many different tools from many different vendors, as well as multiple run-time environments (e.g., compilers, DBMSs, 4GL systems), will comprise the typical organization's development environment. To support the types of interrelationships shown in Figure 19-4, a repository must be capable of interfacing with that many tools and run-time systems.

However, in addition to the repository objects, the tools themselves need some means of communicating among themselves. For example, a change to that data modeling object B should be automatically conveyed to the manager of DDL object C (likely some DBMS product), as well as the programs, test plans, and other system entities affected by that change and all of its propagations. Figure 19-5 shows two ways such notification may occur. Outside of the repository, a *notification server* to which the various tools interface can accept notifications of changes such as the one described above, and can broadcast those facts to other tools and software environments that have registered their interest in learning of such changes. Notification servers are typically outside the scope of the repository services.

Repository-based notification allows the methods or operations of the objects themselves to control the intertool notification. Active database concepts, such as triggers and stored procedures (relational) or methods (object-oriented), can be used for repositories built on top of such database environments. In short, the repository itself contains the knowledge of which tools should be notified about which events.

Basically, then, we can describe a key role of the repository as supporting the necessary control and data integration for information systems development and management, even when many different vendors' products are involved (as well as home-grown tools and systems). And, as we'll discuss next, standards are key to attaining that integration.

19.3 Repository Standards

Standards and repositories are an odd couple. At least five major standards efforts are under way for repositories,[5] none of which could arguably be termed "mature" (as of 1993), in the way that SQL is mature in the relational DBMS world.

The repository standards range from those supporting a very limited set of functionalities—the CASE Data Interchange Format (CDIF) standard, for example—to one intended as a general repository facility for nearly any information system, the Information Resource Dictionary System (IRDS).[6]

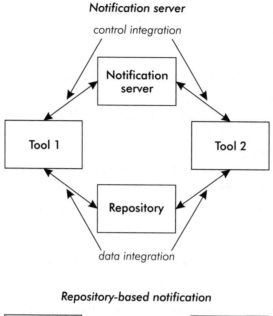

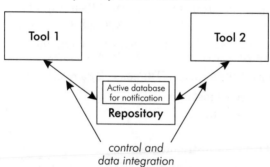

Figure 19-5 Alternative Forms of Intertool Communications

The other efforts are the Portable Common Tool Environment (PCTE), also for CASE environments; A Tools Integration Standard (ATIS); and IBM's revised AD/Cycle CASE platform, unofficially known as AD/Platform.[7]

Let's focus on IRDS, because of its general nature as opposed to the CASE-specific nature of three of the others (ATIS is being considered for integration into the next version of the IRDS standard).

IRDS was first published by the American National Standards Institute (ANSI) in 1988; its roots are in the ANSI X3H4 subcommittee. Because it was never based on a hardware- or software-dependent proposal, IRDS is considered to be vendor-independent.[8]

At the time of this writing, many different proposals are under review by X3H4 to extend the IRDS standard beyond the original seven modules, which are[9]

1) The core standard, which addresses minimum requirements for claiming IRDS compliance.
2) The basic functional IRDS schema, which addresses the implementation of extensions to the core metamodel.
3) IRDS security.
4) Extensible life-cycle phase facility, which addresses the life-cycle management of IRDS contents.
5) A procedure facility, for the definition and execution of IRDS command procedures.
6) An API.
7) Entity lists, used to name groups of entities and how to manipulate those groups.

Among the proposals that will likely find their way into the next version of IRDS (and will affect the standards of repositories in general) are[10]

1) An ATIS-based service interface, for the API
2) Export/import file formats (CDIF may play a role)
3) An object-oriented metamodel
4) Distribution capabilities

With that last item, distributed IRDS capabilities, let's now shift our focus to the distribution characteristics of the repositories of the future.

19.4 Distributed Repository Capabilities

As with databases, varying degrees of distribution exist among repositories. At the simplest level, we have client/server interfaces to server-based repositories, with architectures roughly equivalent to client/server databases. Indeed, since most repositories are now (and will continue to be) built on top of a DBMS, a client/server interface based on ODBC, IDAPI, or a similar client/server standard (see Chapter 3) will likely play a role in client/server repository environments (Figure 19-6).

On the other end of the spectrum, we have distributed repositories similar in concept to distributed database environments. *Distributed repositories* (Figure 19-7) are subject to the same rules of distributed databases; that is,

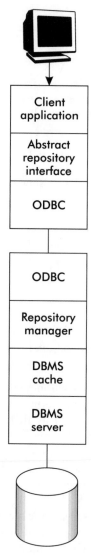

Figure 19-6 Client/Server Repository Interface[11]

updates that cross repository instances must be under two-phase commit (2PC) or a similar distributed concurrency control algorithm to maintain the atomicity of repository transactions (atomicity meaning that an all-or-nothing principle must apply to transactions, whether centralized or distributed; see section 20.2 of Chapter 20 for discussion). Partitioning and replication (see section 2.4.2 of Chapter 2) apply to repository objects just as they do to database information.

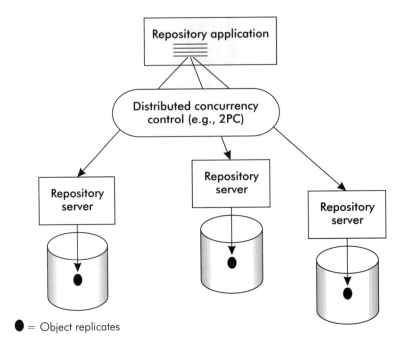

Figure 19-7 Repositories, Replication, and Distribution

As with distributed database environments, distributed repositories of the future will likely involve heterogeneous products that must be integrated with one another. While standards such as IRDS will arguably help with the heterogeneity problem, one needs only look at relational DBMS products based on "standard SQL" to see that issues such as vendor extensions and variations from standards will lead to integration problems. Likewise, attempts to integrate, say, an IRDS repository with an existing proprietary one (e.g., a metadata legacy system) will lead to the types of problems we discussed regarding distributed databases: semantic inconsistency, representation mismatches, and so on. Additionally, problems will occur if one or more repository servers are unavailable when a multiple-server update is attempted. Bernstein notes that all solutions to this issue are expensive, and that none is in widespread use, because each represents a beyond-the-state-of-the-art model of repository concurrency control.[12]

Repositories involve variations on the replication theme. Recall that in section 19.2, we mentioned that repositories should support a check-in/check-out model of work. Figure 19-8 shows an attractive setup in which one or more objects from one or more repository servers may be checked out by a user (or a group of users, who would then apply groupware cooperative working paradigms to the checked-out material). While those objects reside within the domain of a local PC or workstation—or perhaps on some type of LAN server—they can be considered to be replicated; that is, versions exist in

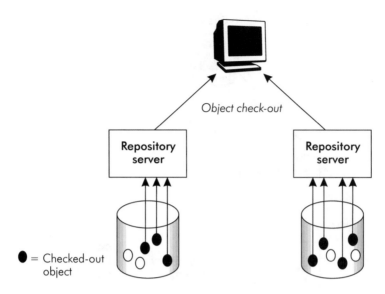

Figure 19-8 Check-out Model of Replication

multiple places, even if across-server replication isn't used in that particular environment. Therefore, check-in/check-out configuration control and the ability to maintain multiple versions of objects are imperative capabilities of repositories.

Bernstein also notes that replication may be avoided by using *surrogates*, or live links from one repository to another (Figure 19-9). Under a surrogate-based repository model, a single instance of each repository object exists somewhere in the environment, though multiple repository servers are accessible by client applications and tools. Surrogates of the objects are dispersed among the collective whole of the repository servers according to whatever type of distribution policy is deemed appropriate for that particular environment (e.g., a complete set of surrogates at every site; partitioning of surrogates among logically grouped servers). If a client attempts to access or check out a particular object that really doesn't reside at that server (that is, a surrogate of that object is there), the live link would locate the real object wherever it resides, and a remote check-out of that object is then executed.[13]

At first glance, the value of surrogates may not be apparent, since any check-out of or access to the real object still involves a remote repository operation. By storing basic properties of the object such as identifying characteristics and other critical information with the surrogates, the "pre-access" functions (e.g., "Is this really the object I want?") may be performed against that surrogate with lower overall system costs (network, processing) than if all functions were performed against remotely managed repository servers. Only when that object is indeed desired would the remote repository operation be executed.

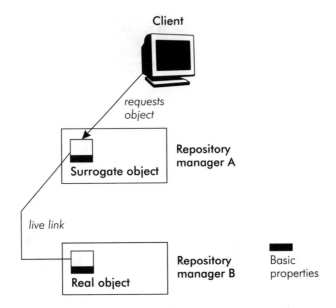

Figure 19-9 Using Surrogates in Distributed Repository Environments

As with intertool notification mechanisms (see section 19.2), active database facilities will likely be very valuable in surrogate-based architectures in future repository environments. "Where is the real object and how do we get it?" rules may be stored with the surrogates themselves; when a tool or user signifies that the real object should be obtained, the appropriate triggers may fire, invoking the object access procedures (Figure 19-10).

19.5 Granularity Issues

When considering the future direction of repositories, one issue is absolutely essential to support the type of functionality we've discussed in this chapter. Repositories need to maintain the finest levels of granularity, regardless of a distributed implementation or the types of distribution.

Traditionally, repository environments other than single-product systems have maintained objects at a rather coarse level of granularity. That is, objects representing DESIGNS and MODELS would be maintained within the repository, with links back to local tool-specific metadata managers (e.g., an SQL DBMS INFORMATION_SCHEMA implementation), where finer levels of granularity were supported (e.g., metadata for every table, column, domain, and other database objects would be stored there). This scheme is shown in Figure 19-11.

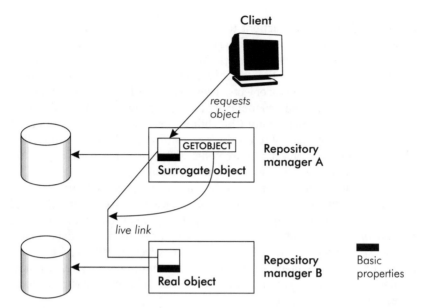

Figure 19-10 Active Database Technology for Surrogate Management in Distributed Repositories

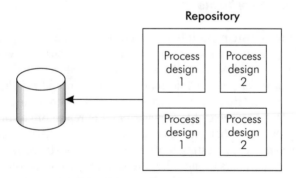

Figure 19-11 Repositories and Coarse Granularity

This implementation may have been sufficient for basic repository services, but not for the type of interobject relationships illustrated in Figure 19-4. Performing corporation-wide functions such as *impact analysis* (determining the impact across the entire information systems if an object x were to be modified) and *requirements traceability* (ensuring that all requirements are handled throughout every subsequent life cycle stage) requires a much finer level of granularity. Typically this means to the level of storing not only every object at the lowest level (e.g., data flows, entities, database column definitions) but also higher-level abstractions (e.g., designs and models, and components of each)—as well as all applicable interrelationships among objects of any level.

There are two challenges to repository services' support of this level of granularity. First, we have the issue of complexity: every tool must be capable of defining multiple levels of objects, down to the finest granularity, applicable to its own needs, with no two tool types having exactly the same needs. As we mentioned earlier, extensibility (the ability to create new repository object classes) is a requirement of tomorrow's repositories, and the tools must first identify all of their object requirements and extend the basic repository models to add new objects and interobject relationships.

The second issue is the massive amounts of space needed to store finely granular information across a corporation. Basically, we have a terabyte-sized database problem (e.g., voluminous data storage requirements for perhaps billions of objects) that exists in metadata rather than user data. Likely solutions applicable to the DBMS include massively parallel architectures managing partitions of metadata, distributed multirepository (e.g., multi-database) solutions based on client/server access through predefined procedures, and so on.

19.6 Repository Tools

Perhaps Philip Bernstein put it best: Nobody wants repositories; people want tools that benefit from repository technology, and a repository without tools is basically useless.[14] Just as databases are of little value without application programs capable of putting information into them and *intelligently and efficiently* retrieving that information, so too are repositories useless without an adequate toolset capable of taking advantage of repository technology.

Throughout this chapter, we've discussed how tools use repositories, including data modeling, testing tools, and run-time systems. We can extend the toolset requirements beyond those tools that *use* the repository to tools that help *manage* it. For example, the ability to browse the contents of a distributed repository—indeed, even the ability to obtain information about the repository structure itself (e.g., how many repository servers exist, what information objects are stored at what servers, to what degree objects are replicated—is extremely useful, and tools are needed for that as well.

Since repository contents and the instances of objects controlled through the repository (e.g., database programs, database contents including multimedia data and tool drawings) are likely to be of radically different forms (e.g., text-based, image, voice), such tools must be capable of supporting those different forms of data. One solution is to use a hypertext-based tool to manage repository contents (see Chapter 18 for a discussion of hypertext). This is particularly true when heterogeneous repositories are to be integrated, and the data formats of those repositories vary widely from one another.[15]

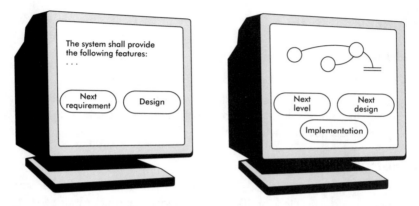

Figure 19-12 Hypertext-Based Repository Management Tools

For example, suppose you wish to browse objects within the repository, following hypertext links among objects as you learn about the contents of the system. Figure 19-12 illustrates a simple example of hypertext-based traversal of repository contents.

19.7 Conclusion

Even though repositories and databases share a number of common characteristics, we can now draw distinctions between the two areas, primarily based on how the two are used. Both manage data of some type (metadata for repositories, user data for databases), but the usage paradigms of their respective contents vary somewhat from one another.

Today, most underlying storage managers for repository implementations are either relational DBMSs or home-grown structures; a significant level of mapping from repository schema models (typically based on either entity-relationship or object-oriented formats) to the underlying storage managers is required. This often 1) significantly slows performance and 2) makes it hard to manage large volumes of repository contents. As object-oriented databases (either "pure" OODBs or hybrid relational and object-oriented models) continue to grow in prominence, we will inevitably see today's underlying storage managers being replaced by OODBMS or extended relational implementations. As this occurs, a more robust set of repository tools and interaction mechanisms will likely evolve.

Repository implementations will likely head in the same direction as DBMSs and database environments: widespread use of clients linked to distributed repository servers, heterogeneous distribution among those repository servers, and managed replication of repository contents should all become commonplace.

Outlook

Short-term

- The IRDS standard will be approved
- Commercial products that are IRDS-compliant will appear in the marketplace; these products will be capable of managing metadata for heterogeneous distributed environments

Long-term

- As integrated CASE (I-CASE) environments and frameworks become more robust near the year 2000, high-capacity repositories will serve as the focal point for entire information system environments, from development tools to run-time systems

Additional Reading

- J. Noll and W. Scacchi, "Integrating Diverse Information Repositories: A Distributed Hypertext Approach," *IEEE Computer* (December 1991).
- A. Simon, *The Integrated CASE Tools Handbook* (Van Nostrand Reinhold/Intertext, 1993).
- A. Tannenbaum, *Implementing a Corporate Repository: The Models Meet Reality* (New York: John Wiley & Sons, 1993).

Endnotes

1. P. Bernstein, "Repositories and Client/Server: Do They Fit?," *Proceedings of the DCI Database World*, Vol. I (June 1993), D9-3.

2. A. Tannenbaum, "U.S. Market Seeing Repository Rebirth," *Software Magazine* (June 1993), 47.

3. Adapted from various portions of A. Simon, *The Integrated CASE Tools Handbook* (New York: Van Nostrand Reinhold/Intertext, 1993).

4. See Simon, *CASE Tools*, Chapters 1, 12, and 14 for a discussion of CASE integration principles and Hewlett-Packard's SoftBench.

5. Tannenbaum, "Repository Rebirth," 54.

6. Tannenbaum, "Repository Rebirth."

7. Tannenbaum, "Repository Rebirth."

8. Tannenbaum, "Repository Rebirth."

9. Tannenbaum, "Repository Rebirth."

10. Tannenbaum, "Repository Rebirth."

11. Based on Bernstein, "Repositories," D9-9.

12. Bernstein, "Repositories," D9-13.

13. Bernstein, "Repositories," D9-14.

14. Bernstein, "Repositories," D9-6.

15. J. Noll and W. Scacchi, "Integrating Diverse Information Repositories: A Distributed Hypertext Approach," *IEEE Computer* (December 1991), 38–44.

CHAPTER

Transaction Processing

A Note to the CIO

Many of the early 1980s' visions of transaction processing, particularly more robust models than basic "flat" transactions, are just now coming into the commercial world. The architecture of your applications currently under development, as well as those created in the future, will be influenced by the supporting transactional models. Chained and nested transactions, for example, allow you to design distributed applications in a much different, and hopefully more efficient, manner than if only rudimentary transaction models were available. The material in this chapter (which, by the way, crosses the bounds of information management into general applications structures) is a must.

20.1 Introduction

Throughout this book, we've discussed transaction processing (TP) concepts and directions. We've looked at transaction processing and its role in distributed database and information management, as well as TP requirements for object-oriented databases.

In this chapter, we'll take a closer look at the trends and future of transaction processing as that discipline applies to information management systems in general. Specifically, we'll look at the following topics:

Executive Summary

Transaction processing capabilities are essential to maintaining the integrity of the corporation's information. Though many research advances have been made in the areas of complex transaction models (i.e., paradigms more suitable to distributed computing than those used for years in centralized, mainframe environments), these models are just now finding their way into real-world products and applications.

Key to complex transaction models is the ability to partition transaction units into multiple subcomponents (subtransactions). Those subtransactions can, subject to the particular transaction model, 1) be restarted upon system failure without having to redo the entire transaction, 2) be processed either synchronously or asynchronously with other subtransactions, and 3) be rolled up under a "master transaction" that can abnormally terminate underlying subtransactions even if they have successfully completed their own units of work.

- The background and principles of information systems transaction processing
- Recent developments in the world of commercial transaction processing systems
- Transaction processing languages
- Alternative transaction models
- Emerging standards
- Likely directions for the next generation of transaction processing systems

20.2 Background in Transaction Processing Fundamentals

Transaction processing may be generalized to include paradigms ranging from batch processing to simple terminal-based interactive processing (in fact, computer-based transaction processing has its roots back in Sumerian clay tablet recordings of royal transactions, several millenia before computers were even imagined).[1] More specifically, the TP discipline has grown to include functions that provide essential support for communications-based and other computer applications. In a global sense, a transaction processing system includes everything pertinent to the computer system, including databases and repositories as well as the networks and operating systems.[2]

A major trend in distributed transaction processing is the emergence of standards, in two areas: the formats and protocols (i.e., message sets and models of how certain messages are answered by recipients), and the application programming interfaces (APIs), which will help promote the portability of transaction processing applications among heterogeneous platforms.

What This Technology Can Do for You

Long-held notions of transaction processing models that served the centralized mainframe need to be revisited with respect to widely distributed environments. Models with a single level of control do not function well in organizations where multiple processors are involved in transaction processing, yet there are many different ways in which subtransaction models may be grouped together to support complex environments.

For our purposes, we'll focus on the core services of transaction processing systems along a generational line, in the same evolutionary manner as programming languages (e.g., 3GLs, 4GLs, 5GLs) and databases (e.g., the "Third-Generation Database Manifesto," which we discussed in Chapter 1, and fourth-generation database systems, which we'll discuss in Chapter 23). In transaction processing, we have the following classifications (Figure 20-1):[3]

- *First generation:* Single monolithic systems, based on dumb terminal models of user interaction.

- *Second generation:* Multiple vendor support, intelligent client systems, multiple database systems support typically through two-phase commit protocols (the second generation represents the state of the art today).

- *Third generation:* The emerging generation, with a closer relationship to the modeling of business activities than is possible today (we'll discuss third-generation characteristics in more detail in section 20.8).

Even though the concept of transaction processing applies to nearly all computerized environments, particularly in the business world, formal usage of transaction processing monitoring facilities has traditionally been limited to large-scale mainframe-based data processing centers, in application environments such as airline reservations or international banking.[4] In recent years, partially due to increasing distribution and heterogeneity in corporate-class information systems, many other vertical applications (e.g., health care, insurance, sales) are equipped with transaction processing monitoring capabilities,

Also important is the ability to match the appropriate complex transaction model with the *business needs* of a particular organization. For example, nested transactions offer a great deal of flexibility to complex subtransaction processing and control, yet they are extremely complex to implement and may be unnecessary for an organization. In such a case, a chained transaction model may be more appropriate, particularly when asynchronous processing of subtransactions is appropriate to support the business functions.

An understanding of emerging standards, and which areas are covered by various standards, is important for every reader.

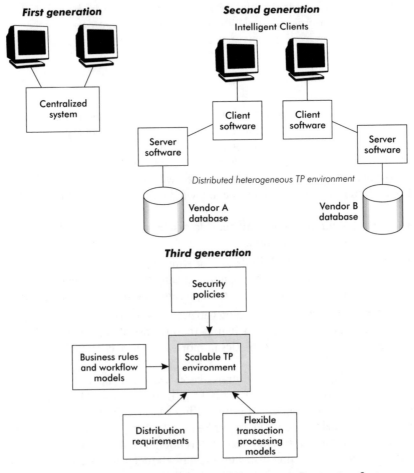

Figure 20-1 Generational Classification of Transaction Processing Systems

and it is estimated by the Gartner Group that 1995 will see 50 percent of newly developed relational DBMS-based applications employing TP monitoring capabilities.[5]

Let's next look at the fundamental properties and basic models of transactions, which guide the use of TP facilities in database and other information systems environments.

20.3 Transaction Principles and Models

A set of properties known as the ACID properties are applicable to all transactions. ACID stands for the following components:[6]

- *Atomicity:* The transaction consists of a collection of actions. The system provides the all-or-nothing illusion that either all or none of these operations are performed—the transaction either commits or aborts.

- *Consistency:* Transactions are assumed to perform correct transformations of the abstract system state. The transaction concept allows the programmer to declare such consistency points and allows the system to validate them by application-supplied checks.

- *Isolation:* While a transaction is updating shared data, that data may be temporarily inconsistent. Such inconsistent data must not be exposed to other transactions until the updates commit (this means until all modifications are "officially completed"). The system must give each transaction the illusion that it is running in isolation, that is, that all other transactions appear to have run either previous to the start of this transaction or subsequent to its commit.

- *Durability:* Once a transaction commits, its updates must be durable. The new state of all objects updated will be preserved, even in case of hardware or software failures.

Many different transaction models exist that embody these principles; they range from flat transactions (discussed next) to more complex models such as nested and chained transactions. Let's take a brief look at these models, especially since the more complex models are directing transaction processing in commercial information systems.

20.3.1 Flat Transactions

Flat transactions have a single control layer for an arbitrary number of simple actions. In most of today's information systems, it is the only transaction model supported at the application level, though other components of the system, such as SQL itself, may exhibit more flexible transaction models; they just aren't available at the application programming level. We'll discuss the pseudo-nesting of SQL in section 20.3.4.[7]

Flat transactions are the basic building blocks for implementing the atomicity principle; in other words, designating any set of actions as components of a flat transaction enforces the all-or-nothing mandate.

In many application environments, particularly those with centralized processing and resource management (e.g., databases and files), flat transactions have over the years provided sufficient capabilities for the creation and execution of applications; simple state transformations are appropriate for inclusion within an atomic unit of work.[8]

With the advent of widespread distribution of processing and data resources, though, the all-or-nothing nature of flat transactions will inevitably become a hindrance. Consider the example in Figure 20-2. With flat transactions, the processing rules would state that each and every component of that global transaction must succeed, or none can. So, for example, if the only failure within a transaction is the update of a remote database under the control of a particular resource manager, then all other components of that transaction must roll back to their previous states before the transaction occurred. Taking into account the amount of information within large-scale organizations or even medium-sized environments with perhaps many PC-based LAN servers or mobile computing databases (see section 22.2 of Chapter 22 for a discussion on database and transaction processing in mobile computing), the probability of at least one site failing within a highly distributed transaction increases dramatically. Using a flat transaction model, all portions of that transaction would be repeated, heavily increasing demands on the overall processing and throughput loads of a system.

Clearly, some sort of decomposition to flat transactions is desirable, particularly in this age of widely distributed computing. A modification of the flat transaction model, preserving atomicity while providing some relief from what could conceivably be unnecessary repetitive actions ("do-overs"), is the use of savepoints, which we'll discuss next.

20.3.2 Savepoints

Savepoints are used within an application program to establish points where the execution flow could be restarted if problems occur. Ideally, savepoints should be at partially consistent states (e.g., after building the second temporary table in a program, which will then be used for processing against some other table).

When a particular savepoint within a transaction is reached, the completion of the actions up to that point creates a new atomic action, which then carries on with the processing. Only the final atomic action within a sequence can initiate a COMMIT WORK of the transaction; that COMMIT WORK is then passed back to all of the previous atomic actions until the transaction is committed.[9] Unlike chained transactions (our next topic), each savepoint does

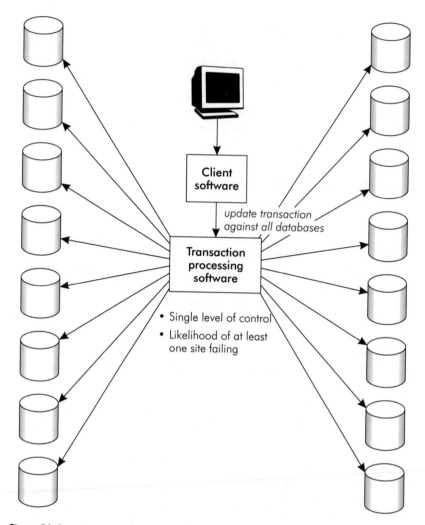

Inside figure:

Client software

update transaction
against all databases

Transaction processing software

- Single level of control
- Likelihood of at least one site failing

Figure 20-2 Flat Transactions in Large-Scale Enterprises

not initiate an irrevocable COMMIT WORK of the work done up to that point within the transaction.

Rollbacks may be initiated from any atomic action and not just the last one, though at any given point in time only the most recently created one can initiate a rollback (once a savepoint has been reached for an atomic action, that action can't subsequently decide to roll back the work). The rollback action may be to any previous savepoint, so a transaction manager supporting savepoints must have the capability to accept some type of parameter that indicates which savepoint is being targeted (and, ideally, the application must contain processing logic that will determine which savepoint is appropriate as the target of the rollback).[10]

The concept of *persistent savepoints*, which make their way to a disk-based form or to some other type of persistent storage for use after total system crashes, has been investigated, but Gray and Reuter point out that "no commonly accepted conclusion seems to be within reach."[11] This isn't too much of a problem, though, because two other emerging advanced transaction models, chained transactions and nested transactions, provide similar capabilities, but through more formally understood and agreed-upon paradigms. Let's look first at chained transactions.

20.3.3 Chained Transactions

Conceptually similar to savepoints, *chained transactions* (Figure 20-3) involve the application programming *committing* the work done up to some point, not just marking that point as a potential place of reexecution; all rights to roll back that work are waived.[12]

However, the application *remains within a transaction*; chained transactions do not start one transaction, finish it, start another, then finish that one, and so on. Rather, chained transactions retain all contexts that are still needed (e.g., database cursors, open files) though resources no longer needed may be released.[13]

Chained transactions involve a CHAIN WORK request—a combination of COMMIT WORK and BEGIN WORK within the same request—which is *not* the same as handling COMMIT and BEGIN as separate requests. With separate statements, the context is lost, thereby allowing for the possibility of some other transaction, say, modifying the database that is needed by the next chain before the next part of the chain could acquire that context again.[14] As we said earlier, chained transactions are conceptually similar to savepoints, except that with chaining, rollbacks can only occur to the immediately prior action instead of to any earlier savepoint.[15]

Both savepoints and chained transactions permit applications to create sequences of actions, with the rollback and persistence distinctions we noted in this section and the previous one. The final model we'll discuss is nested transactions, in which hierarchies rather than sequences of transactions may be created.

20.3.4 Nested Transactions

Nested transactions involve a top-level transaction that controls the activities of the entire hierarchy. Within the hierarchy, lower-level transactions, which may be nested even further (Figure 20-4), may also be present. The leaf levels on the transaction hierarchy are flat transactions. Note that individual branches of the hierarchy may have different distances from the top-level transaction (the tree root) to its leaf transactions.[16]

Rules and models for nested transactions were first developed by Elliot Moss in 1981. Moss's model permitted actual work to be done only by leaf

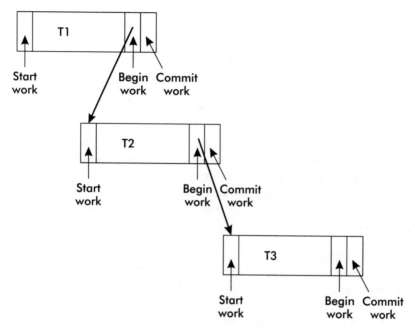

Figure 20-3 A Conceptual View of Chained Transactions

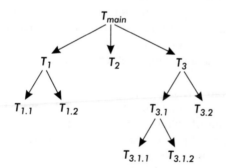

Figure 20-4 Structure of Nested Transactions

nodes, but Gray and Reuter note that this restriction limits the functionality of transaction nesting, and that an increased level of parallelism on shared objects within an environment can be attained against a layered abstraction of objects.[17]

Moss proposed three rules to govern the behavior of nested transactions:[18]

- *Commit Rule:* The COMMIT WORK of a subtransaction makes the results of that subtransaction visible only to the parent transaction. The "real" committal of the work of a subtransaction only occurs when its parents and all of its ancestors back to the top-level root transaction have committed.

- *Rollback Rule:* If a subtransaction at any level of nesting (including the top-level root transaction) is rolled back, all of its subtransactions must do likewise, regardless of any local commital status. Therefore, the rollback by root transactions causes the entire transaction to roll back its work.

- *Visibility Rule:* All changes done by a given subtransaction are visible to its parent transaction at the time that subtransaction commits. Further, all objects held by a given transaction can be made accessible to its subtransactions. Sibling transactions (those at the same level and with the same parent) do not have such visibility, given the possibility of parallel concurrent execution.

Of the ACID properties, atomicity, consistency, and isolation do apply to subtransactions, but because a subtransaction COMMIT isn't really a COMMIT until the entire overall transaction commits, durability is not present and therefore a subtransaction is not equivalent to a flat transaction.[19]

As with other transaction models, nested transactions have variations, including *multilevel* transactions, in which a subtransaction ST1 "precommits" its work. In this model, though, a *compensating transaction* exists which can reverse the work of ST1 back to its original state in case the overall transaction rolls back. Compensating transactions are used for near–real time reversal of results, thereby avoiding a "time traveling" recovery scenario in which precious online resources are used to recover a consistent database state (e.g., using logs and piecing together a puzzle of what the consistent database state should be).[20]

Although one can envision application and system models in which chained or nested transactions would be very useful, it wasn't until the early 1990s that the flat transaction model was superseded in the commercial world (we'll discuss Transarc's Encina in section 20.4). Interestingly, though, an examination of basic SQL transactions indicates some "pseudo-nesting" with respect to how statements are handled (this is currently not available to application developers; however, at present SQL3 includes savepoints and will likely include chained transaction statements).

Figure 20-5 shows the execution of an SQL transaction. Each statement within the transaction, say a sequence of UPDATE and DELETE statements, may succeed or fail. Even if one or more statements were to fail, the transaction as a whole would still proceed, unless the logic programmed into it were to force an ABORT, and rollback would commence. Any successfully completed statements before the one that determines the rollback (which are sort of the subtransactions in this model) would then have their work undone via the rollback.

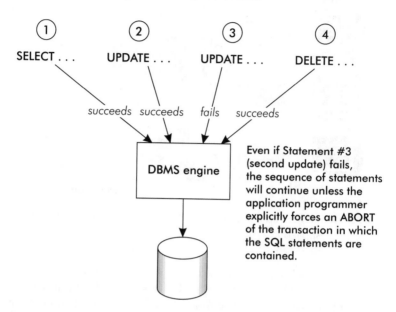

**Transaction-based
sequence of SQL statements**

(1)   (2)   (3)   (4)

SELECT . . .   UPDATE . . .   UPDATE . . .   DELETE . . .

succeeds   succeeds   fails   succeeds

DBMS engine

**Even if Statement #3
(second update) fails,
the sequence of statements
will continue unless the
application programmer
explicitly forces an ABORT
of the transaction in which
the SQL statements are
contained.**

Figure 20-5 SQL as a Pseudo-Nested Transaction Model

Application developers have had to work around the fact that pseudo-nesting hasn't been available in SQL, creating tricks to achieve a transaction architecture more applicable to their work than simple flat transactions. When SQL3 comes to market in the mid-1990s, and compliant products begin to appear (recall our discussion from Chapter 12 in which we note that features often appear in commercial products before they are incorporated into standards), SQL-based database developers will be able to take advantage of these facilities directly.

While we're on the subject of commercializing transaction models more complex than classic flat transactions, let's examine the Encina TP monitor.

20.4 Encina and DCE

The Encina transaction processing monitor from Transarc Corporation can be considered a second-generation commercial product[21]—albeit an advanced one, representing the state of the art. Encina incorporates a nested transaction structure and builds on the Distributed Computing Environment (DCE) of the Open Software Foundation (OSF).

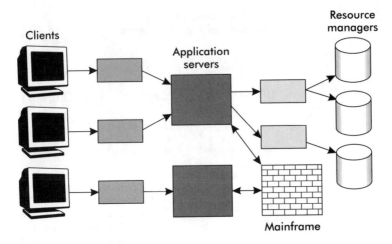

Figure 20-6 Representative Open Distributed Transaction Processing Application Architecture[22]

The roots of Encina are in the Camelot prototype transaction processing system, developed at Carnegie-Mellon University in Pittsburgh. The technology behind Camelot and the accompanying Avalon persistent programming language are documented in *Camelot and Avalon: A Distributed Transaction Processing Facility*.[23] Camelot is generally considered to be the "first proven implementation of nested transactions in a general facility"[24] (as contrasted with the pseudo-nesting we discussed in the previous section or with system-internal nesting not available to applications developers).

The architecture in Figure 20-6 illustrates the degree of distribution common in newly developed information systems, as well as those on the drawing board. The use of application servers follows the philosophy (introduced in Chapter 2) of externalizing procedures to manage data rather than externalizing the data themselves. Though direct browsing of remote databases could be accomplished by authorized users, the general goal is to give data management control to the application servers.[25]

Figure 20-7 illustrates a typical layered approach to distributed transaction processing, as used within DCE. Encina, from its DCE roots, uses abstract layers for the management of resource and communications managers, and it provides direct connection to non-DCE resource and communication managers. This modularity and layering, so common in emerging open systems and corporate computing architectures,[26] is finally finding its way into transaction processing. It stands to reason that tomorrow's commercial products and research efforts will continue this incorporation of open systems concepts into transaction processing.

One of the challenges faced by Encina is to support the ACID properties in a client/server database environment, given that clients and servers have distinct records of what a transaction state might be.[27] Under Encina, code

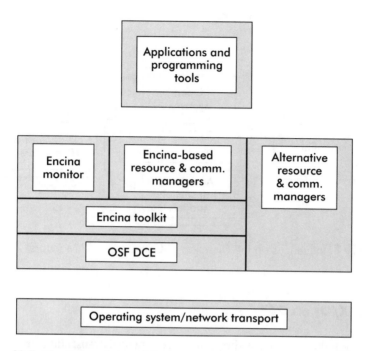

Figure 20-7 The Encina Layered Transaction Processing Architecture[28]

used to maintain ACID properties is retained within the resource managers (see Figure 20-7); the commit and rollback requests are then issued by applications or other higher-level software in concert with the resource managers, which are then directed against the appropriate lower-level resources.[29]

Within Encina is a Transactional C application development facility, with a collection of macros and libraries used for creating and managing transactions. The keyword TRANSACTION is used to designate top-level transactions as well as those nested within other transactions. Functions ONABORT and ONCOMMIT specify actions to take when an any-level transaction commits or must roll back. A program may call ENCINA_ABORT_ALL to force a rollback of the entire transaction.[30]

Future developments, not only in the Encina product but in the entire area of "open transaction processing," will be interesting to observe. The trends of distribution and heterogeneity we discussed in Chapter 1, which help to drive database and information management technology, demand that some degree of openness make its way into each component of an information system (operating system services, security management, databases and repositories, and transaction processing monitors). While long-existing proprietary products will continue to exist as long as the hardware and operating system platforms they support, the trends shown in Figure 20-8 will inevitably influence the direction of transaction processing systems.

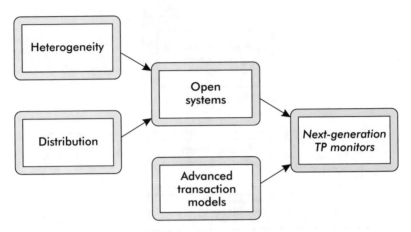

Figure 20-8 Influences on the Direction of Commercial TP Monitors

20.5 X/Open DTP

Another influence on the direction of commercial transaction processing products will come from the standards community. The International Standards Organization (ISO) has defined a two-part protocol designed to support interoperability of transaction processing systems. These two parts are[31]

- *OSI-TP:* For transaction processing services, 1992
- *OSI-CCR:* For commit, control, and recovery operations, 1990

Together, the OSI standards define formats and protocols, but *not* application programming interfaces, for a standard two-phase commit (2PC) protocol designed to sit on top of the OSI communications protocol stack.

The API issue is being addressed by X/Open, in the form of the *X/Open Distributed Transaction Processing (DTP) API*. The goal of the X/Open DTP is to permit a transaction manager to use a combination of proprietary and OSI-TP protocols for internal and interoperating environments, respectively. X/Open DTP is an emerging standard and one with its share of controversy. Specifically, there is disagreement as to 1) definitions of TP monitor environments for the purposes of standardization, and 2) the relative merits over transactional remote procedure calls (TRPC) and peer-to-peer communications models (both approaches are currently in the model, at least for the time being).[32]

X/Open DTP supports not only flat transactions, but also chained and nested transactions (in the latter, a transaction will abort if any branch aborts, unlike the more robust model we discussed in section 20.3.4).[33]

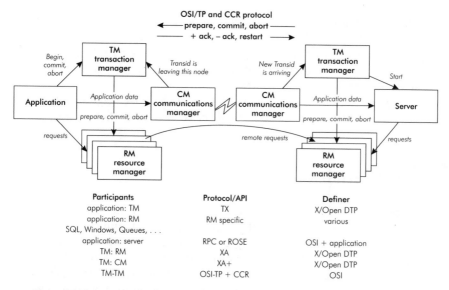

OSI/TP and CCR protocol
prepare, commit, abort
+ ack, – ack, restart

Participants	Protocol/API	Definer
application: TM	TX	X/Open DTP
application: RM	RM specific	various
SQL, Windows, Queues, . . .		
application: server	RPC or ROSE	OSI + application
TM: RM	XA	X/Open DTP
TM: CM	XA+	X/Open DTP
TM-TM	OSI-TP + CCR	OSI

Figure 20-9 Standards-Based Transaction Processing Environment[34]

In a standards-based distributed TP environment, a combination of protocols is used to define intercomponent interfaces. Some of these protocols, such as the OSI Remote Operations Service (ROSE), are general to the OSI protocol stack; others are specific to X/Open DTP or OSI-TP. Figure 20-9 illustrates the interfaces in a standards-based distributed TP environment and the appropriate protocols and APIs.

20.6 Transaction Processing System Classification

As next-generation, standards-based transaction processing systems emerge, classifying them in terms of their functionality becomes useful. Such a classification is proposed by Avraham Leff and Calton Pu of Columbia University, using five dimensions:[35]

- M—A set of machines
- P—A set of processes
- H—The degree of heterogeneity among the set of machines and system software
- D—A set of logical data
- S—A set of sites

The model represents each transaction processing system, ranging from "base systems" (P_1,M_1,H_1,D_1,S_1) to more complex multiple-site, multiple–data set, heterogeneous environments (P_n,M_n,H_n,D_n,S_n). In their 1991 paper, the authors presented a set of three-dimensional models against which various research and commercial systems were measured.[36]

This classification, or one similar to it, would be extremely valuable in assessing the functionality and extensibility of TP systems as they emerge.

20.7 Transaction Languages

In section 20.4, we discussed Transarc's Encina, which includes a set of libraries and macros that comprise the Transactional C environment. Another way to express transaction processing directives and requests is through a separate language facility. An example from researchers is the InterBase Parallel Language (IPL), part of the InterBase heterogeneous distributed database environment we discussed in Chapter 6. IPL is designed to support a high degree of parallelism and provide synchronization and inter-subtransaction communication within some global transaction.[37] IPL was intended to support transactions of varying types (e.g., mixed transactions) as well as to provide for a system-independent *declarative* language to achieve transaction management transparency.

Following is the general structure of an IPL subtransaction:[38]

```
subtrans NAME_OF_TRANSACTION (ARGUMENTS): OUTPUT_TYPE at NODE
    use RESOURCE_MANAGER between STARTING_TIME
    and ENDING_TIME lasts MAXIMUM_EXECUTION_TIME
  guard SOME_FORCED_TRANSACTION_TERMINATION_BECAUSE_OF_
                   SOME_CONDITION
  beginexec
    operations
  endexec
  beginconfirm
    operations to confirm the subtransaction
  endconfirm
  beginundo
    operations to cancel the subtransaction
  endundo
  endsubtrans;
```

An entire IPL program would include record declarations, along with appropriate subtransactions, within the bounds of a *program–endprogram* block. Since IPL is being continuously researched, and a GUI interface and an object-oriented version are still being investigated, the reader is directed to the InterBase project at Purdue University for more up-to-date information.

A variation on transaction specification is to focus the transaction language not against some global schema or a product-specific implementation but rather against a neutral semantic data model.[39] With the increasing importance of data modeling, applying the transaction architecture against the semantic model itself is valuable.

Part of the value of this capability is in helping to integrate the process and data sides of conceptual modeling. Classic 1970s-era model integration focuses on the mapping of, say, data flow diagram (DFD) data flows against entity-relationship diagram (ERD) entities and attributes.[40] Object-oriented modeling promotes a closer definition of objects and their operations, but both of these lack the capability to express transaction semantics. By providing transaction language capabilities against some form of data model, and eventually shifting those transactional semantics into a graphical representation from which nesting, chaining, and other advanced transaction models might be specified, a much greater degree of productivity and reliability in the creation of transaction processing systems will be possible in the future.

20.8 Third-Generation TP Monitors Revisited

Before we leave this chapter, let's revisit third-generation transaction processing monitors, which we briefly mentioned in section 20.2. The characteristics of the next generation of transaction processing facilities include[41]

- *The capability to model and manage the execution of business activities:*
  In the previous section, we investigated research directions in transaction languages. The current transaction processing philosophy, even with OSI-TP and X/Open DTP environments, calls for embedding the transaction specification and management logic within the applications themselves. Highly desirable is an independent, declarative facility through which those transaction semantics could be specified against (or, more appropriately, *modeled in conjunction with*) the business operations they are intended to support.

- *Work flow integration:* Regarding the independent modeling and specification noted in the previous item, a closer tie to the emerging area of work flow computing (briefly mentioned in Chapter 1 as part of the trend toward a closer mapping between computer systems and the real-world systems they are designed to represent). A high-level work flow language or graphical system can be used to specify interuser, interprocess, and interapplication flows of information. The transaction semantics could then be applied against the work flow specification in much the same way they could be applied against some semantic data model. The development environment, preferably one rich in system generation tools, could then generate transaction management facilities (compliant with X/Open DTP, most likely), along with the procedural and data representations needed to implement the combined work flow/transaction/data model.

- *Extended transactions:* In Chapter 11, we discussed the need for long-duration transactions for object-oriented databases. While this necessity is understood, new abstractions are required to capture and implement the properties of those transactions. A third-generation transaction processing monitor must be capable of supporting long-duration transactions in addition to, or preferably in conjunction with, traditional short-duration transactions.

- *Extensibility:* A third-generation TP monitor should be capable of being dynamically extended with new transaction models (e.g., generalizing nested transaction support to include compensating transactions, or modifying the nested transaction rules currently in place).

- *Security:* In Chapter 21, we'll discuss the many aspects of database and information management security. Security encompasses efforts from all resources across an environment (e.g., network, operating system, DBMS). Security properties, particularly support for multiple levels of security within a given environment, must find their way into next-generation TP monitors.

- *Scalability:* A transaction processing architecture optimized for 100 resource managers does not necessarily scale to one suitable for 1,000 or 10,000 resource managers. Next-generation TP monitors must be capable (perhaps through the extensibility requirement mentioned above) of scaling among varying amounts of resources.

20.9 Conclusion

Transaction processing is evolving much like other areas of information and computer systems. Even though concepts such as nested transactions were identified in the early 1980s or even before, not until very recently have models other than those supporting flat transactions as single atomic units made it from the research laboratories into commercial products.

Transaction processing will inevitably be influenced by factors such as distributed computing resources and the need for interoperability. For that reason, standards-based efforts, such as DCE-based TP products (e.g., Encina), OSI-TP, and X/Open DTP, will become increasingly important as organizations struggle to get a handle on managing their information.

Outlook

Short-term

- More commercial products with advanced transaction processing models (e.g., chained and/or nested transactions) will appear
- The X/Open DTP will be formalized and development of compliant products will begin

Long-term

- Third-generation TP monitors that feature work flow integration, long transaction handling, and other capabilities will become commercially viable

Additional Reading

- U. Dayal et al., "Third Generation TP Monitors: A Database Challenge," *Proceedings of the 1993 ACM SIGMOD.*
- J. L. Epinger, L. B. Mummert, A. Z. Spector, eds., *Camelot and Avalon: A Distributed Transaction Processing Facility* (San Francisco: Morgan Kaufmann Publishers, 1991).
- J. Gray and A. Reuter, *Transaction Processing: Concepts and Techniques* (San Francisco: Morgan Kaufmann Publishers, 1993).
- A. D. Wolfe, Jr., "Transarc Encina, *Distributed Computing Monitor,* Patricia Seybold Group (November 1992).

Endnotes

1. J. Gray and A. Reuter, *Transaction Processing: Concepts and Techniques* (San Francisco: Morgan Kaufmann Publishers, 1993), 3.

2. Gray and Reuter, *Transaction Processing*, 5.

3. U. Dayal et al., "Third Generation TP Monitors: A Database Challenge," *Proceedings of the 1993 ACM SIGMOD*, 394.

4. S. Dietzen, "Distributed Transaction Processing with Encina and the OSF DCE," Draft, Transarc Corporation, September 1992, 2. Provided courtesy of Transarc Corporation, Pittsburgh, PA.

5. Dietzen, "Distributed Transaction Processing."

6. J. Gray, "A Transaction Model," RJ2895 (San Jose, CA: IBM Research Division, August 1980). The ACID principles were also discussed in the context of SQL and databases in J. Melton and A. Simon, *Understanding the New SQL: A Complete Guide* (San Francisco: Morgan Kaufmann Publishers, 1992), 39–40.

7. Gray and Reuter, *Transaction Processing*, 167.

8. Gray and Reuter, *Transaction Processing*, 171.

9. Gray and Reuter, *Transaction Processing*, 189.

10. Gray and Reuter describe rules for savepoint-based rollbacks, and variations on the theme with respect to the rules in Gray and Reuter, *Transaction Processing*, 189–190.

11. Gray and Reuter, *Transaction Processing*, 190.

12. Gray and Reuter, *Transaction Processing*, 192.

13. Gray and Reuter, *Transaction Processing*.

14. Gray and Reuter, *Transaction Processing*.

15. Gray and Reuter, *Transaction Processing*, 193.

16. Gray and Reuter, *Transaction Processing*, 195.

17. J. E. B. Moss, "Nested Transactions: An Approach to Reliable Computing," LCS-TR-260, Massachusetts Institute of Technology, Cambridge, MA, 1981, cited in Gray and Reuter, *Transaction Processing*, 195.

18. Moss, "Nested Transactions," 196–197.

19. Moss, "Nested Transactions," 197.

20. Gray and Reuter discuss multilevel transactions, nested transactions, and other variations in detail that are beyond our scope in this book. The reader is referred to Gray and Reuter, *Transaction Processing*, 203–210.

21. U. Dayal et al., "Third Generation TP Monitors," 394.

22. Dietzen, "Distributed Transaction Processing," 7.

23. J. L. Epinger, L. B. Mummert, and A. Z. Spector, eds., *Camelot and Avalon: A Distributed Transaction Processing Facility* (San Francisco: Morgan Kaufmann Publishers, 1991).

24. Gray and Reuter, *Transaction Processing*, 223.

25. Dietzen, "Distributed Transaction Processing," 7–8.

26. See A. Simon, *Enterprise Computing* (New York: Bantam Books/Intertext, 1992), and A. Simon, *Implementing the Enterprise*, (New York: Bantam Books/Intertext, 1992), for numerous examples of layered and modular approaches in these areas.

27. A. D. Wolfe, Jr., "Transarc Encina," *Distributed Computing Monitor*, Patricia Seybold Group (November 1992), 5.

28. From "Encina: Enterprise Computing in a New Age," Product Overview, 8.

29. Wolfe, "Transarc Encina."

30. From Transactional C code sample in Wolfe, "Transarc Encina," 9.

31. Gray and Reuter, *Transaction Processing*, 260.

32. Gray and Reuter, *Transaction Processing*, 961.

33. Gray and Reuter, *Transaction Processing*.

34. Gray and Reuter, *Transaction Processing*, 84.

35. A. Leff and C. Pu, "A Classification of Transaction Processing Systems," *IEEE Computer* (June 1991), 63–65.

36. Leff and Pu, "Transaction Processing Systems," 73.

37. J. Chen, A. Elmagarmid, and O. Bukhres, "The Interbase Parallel Language: Supporting Distributed Transaction Applications," SERC-TR-119-P, Purdue University, West Lafayette, IN, July 1992.

38. Chen, Elmagarmid, and Bukhres, "Interbase Parallel Langauge," 5.

39. S. B. Navathe and A. Balaraman, "A Transaction Architecture for a General Purpose Semantic Data Model," in *Proceedings of the Tenth International Conference on Entity-Relationship Approach: Bridging the Gap*, ed. T. J. Teorey (Ann Arbor, MI: University of Michigan, 1991).

40. See A. Simon, *The Integrated CASE Tools Handbook* (Van Nostrand Reinhold/Intertext, 1993), Chap. 6, for more details.

41. Based on Dayal et al., "Third Generation TP Monitors," 394–396, with additional comments from this author.

CHAPTER 21

Database Security

A Note to the CIO

Protection of corporate information system assets is no small task, and this is particularly true of data. Database security technology has typically lagged behind areas such as networks and communications. Many of the models first proposed in the mid- and late 1980s (in particular, databases with data from multiple security levels stored in the same database) are just coming into commercial use. Even though government—specifically, defense—considerations have long driven all aspects of database security, commercial considerations are now coming more into play. Much of the research to date will likely apply to commercial information security, though it remains to be seen how important certain areas (e.g., the need for multilevel security) really are. Nevertheless, it's important to recognize that commercial products now undergoing National Computer Security Center (NCSC) validation have derived their security requirements from the defense sector, and tremendous investments have been made in certain technologies and

21.1 Introduction

You can make two definitive statements about database security: it doesn't come easy, and it's not cheap.

Despite concerted efforts since the early 1980s, not until the early 1990s did advanced security policies find their way into commercial DBMS products. And even the accomplishments to date have been far behind what is envisioned for the secure database environments of the future.

models. Because of this, any commercial-specific database security that evolves will likely be similar to defense-driven models, so even if your organization has nothing to do with defense computer systems, the security models presented in this chapter may come to play an important role in your database security program.

Executive Summary

Database security has long fallen into the rather simplistic realms of the SQL GRANT/REVOKE model, where owners of data grant permission for various read/write operations to other system users. In reality, these simple models do little or nothing to protect data, not only from those determined to compromise the organization's security but also from accidental security violations.

The U.S. government has long been interested in database and information security models, and a number of efforts in the early and

Technical difficulties (which we'll discuss in detail in this chapter) are not the only challenges. There are other issues, such as the following:[1]

- Security in general, and database security specifically, is costly and inconvenient. Nearly every security measure one might apply compromises advances in other areas, such as connectivity, interoperability, ease of use, and performance.

- In these days of corporate and organizational cutbacks, taking a long-term view with respect to investment is often difficult and is often from the standpoint of perceived payback periods and returns on investment. Hence we have the focus on downsizing, standardization, and other popular trends of the 1990s. Security expenditures typically don't offer an immediate return on their investment and might be viewed in the same light as insurance: the payoff doesn't come until something bad happens, and the odds of that occurring aren't great.

- In light of the previous statement, it's interesting that the mover in security has traditionally been the U.S. government, specifically the Department of Defense. Commercial security concerns, important in certain industries such as banking, and in certain areas such as virus prevention, have lagged behind government efforts. Ironically, as Sushil Jajodia of George Mason University points out, "It would be extremely rare that a major security breach would cause a nation to topple, regardless of how serious that breach is; it is quite conceivable, though, that a

mid-1980s focused attention on this area (along with other information system security areas, such as networks and communications). A great deal of research has been done in these areas over the past decade, and commercial products are appearing that incorporate new security technologies.

The commercial world has lagged behind the government in both interest and implementations, but the high-profile network security breaches of the late 1980s and early 1990s (e.g., viruses, worms) have brought new attention to commercial security. What is unclear, though, is which commercial database security models will emerge, since government models aren't necessarily applicable to commercial needs.

What This Technology Can Do for You

Protection of corporate information is absolutely necessary! Whether the threat comes from competitors or foreign intelligence services who

security break of similar magnitude would cause a company or business concern to go under."[2]

Because information is such a highly valuable asset for corporations and governments in the U.S. and around the world, information security is certainly a critical need. Increasingly, organizations are starting to realize this need and are instituting, or at least investigating, security programs that span the computer disciplines of communications, operating systems, and information management.

Part of the challenge is that different organizations have widely varying requirements to protect their information. In some commercial organizations, accidental leakage of information would be a relatively minor problem (other than possible Privacy Act complications). Such companies are more concerned about system availability, preventing application corruption caused by viruses, Trojan horses, and worms, and perhaps most importantly preventing unauthorized changes to their data (particularly financial data such as bank and account balances).

However, in other organizations—military services, for example—accidental release of highly classified data could cause serious damage. Divulgence of names of spies, battle plans, and similar entities could seriously impair the ability of military organizations to successfully operate.

Database security has long been in the background to areas such as communications and network security (this has been particularly true of

no longer target military enemies, attempts to steal information and compromise operations of business organizations will doubtless increase in number and affect most large corporations, and many mid-size businesses as well.

While current government thinking is probably out of synch with corporate needs, it is at least a start, and can be used to begin applying long-neglected security practices to corporate data. It is important to understand two points: first, what passes for security in today's commercial DBMS products is woefully inadequate to provide real protection; and second, security is an end-to-end mission, involving not only DBMSs and information managers but also the network, operating system, and other facilities of each system.

commercial organizations), but high-profile events such as the Michelangelo virus and the Internet worm have brought the protection of databases and information assets to the attention of corporate planners. With that in mind, advances in database security may come more quickly than they might otherwise have.

Computer and communications security has been a major issue for a number of years, since the U.S. Department of Defense (DOD) issued its *Trusted Computer System Evaluation Criteria* in 1985. This document, known as the Orange Book (because of the color of its cover), outlines a standardized approach to computer systems security, based on a hierarchical division and class structure. Four divisions, ranging from D (the lowest level of protection) to A (the highest level), were designated, with multiple classes within the C and B divisions (C1, C2, B1, B2, and B3, from lowest to highest levels).

Detailed coverage of the various divisions and classes is beyond the scope of this book (the Orange Book will likely be replaced by new government security standards anyway). What is important about the Orange Book is its role as the basis for the National Computer Security Center's *Trusted Database Management System Interpretation of the Trusted Computer System Evaluation Criteria*, a document commonly known as the TDI, released in April 1991. The role of the TDI is to put a database "spin" on the Orange Book, providing guidelines, or interpretations, for the building and evaluation of trusted DBMSs. The TDI influences many of the recent advances and future directions of database and information security that we'll discuss.

In this chapter, then, we'll look at principles behind database security, and recent developments (since the late 1980s) that will affect the trends in database security over the next several years. We'll cover subjects such as multilevel secure databases, polyinstantiation implementations (in which multiple tuples exist to represent different views of reality to different classes of users), covert channels and database security, and the current research in database security.

21.2 A Basic Database Security Model

At a very basic level, database and information management security is rather simple. Two fundamental principles must be supported: authorization and authentication. *Authorization* means that a specific user or information system process has a set of authorized actions that can be performed against certain objects. *Authentication* is the determination beyond any doubt that a user or process attempting to perform authorized actions is indeed who he, she, or it claims to be. Let's take a look at each of these.

21.2.1 Authorization

Figure 21-1 illustrates the basic authorization model. You could conceivably build a security matrix, matching all users and processes in the system against all objects within the enterprise. Every intersection point on the matrix would contain from 0 to n operations that the user or process is allowed to perform against that object. An all-powerful, incorruptible security management system that could control that matrix *and enforce its use* by every action within the environment could conceivably provide a high degree of information security (though, as we'll discuss, the real-world issues are much more complex than that).

Figure 21-2 shows how a basic authorization model is *not* sufficient by itself for any degree of database security. If, say, Process 2 successfully masquerades as Process 1, it can perform actions and operations permissible only to Process 1 and not Process 2. Additional measures are required, which we discuss next.

21.2.2 Authentication

Because of the problem just described, a model of authentication must be present within the security environment, in which claimed identities are unfailingly verified. Authentication has become even more important than before with the advent of widespread distributed computing. With the high degree of connectivity available today, the pipelines into computer systems must be controlled.

	Sales.Total	Sales.Per_Store	Sales.Total_Units	Payroll.Total	Payroll.Salary	Payroll. Bonus	
Jones	R,U	R,U,C,D		R,U,C,D	R,U,C,D		
Smith	R,C,U		R,U,C,D		R,C,U		
Wilson	R,U,C,D		R,C,U				
Evans	R,U,C,D						
Michaels		R,U,C,D			R,C,U		
Walters	R,U,C,D	R,U,C,D	R,U,C,D				
Peters							
Sanders		R,C,U		R,U,C,D			
Trumble	R,C,U		R,C,U		R,U,C,D		
...							

R = Read
C = Create
U = Update
D = Delete

Figure 21-1 A Simple Authorization Model

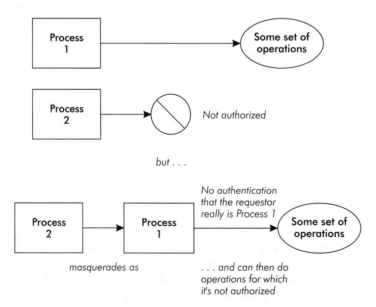

Figure 21-2 The Need for Authentication in Addition to Authorization

Authentication typically falls within the realm of communications and network security, so we won't discuss it further except to note the following. In end-to-end computer system security, where operating systems, networks, databases, and other services cooperate to provide a comprehensive security program, authentication is certainly applicable to database security. We'll discuss other areas in this chapter that are typically dependent on sufficient authentication.

Note that the security model of basic authorization and authentication provides no relief for problems such as stolen user IDs and passwords or malicious intentions on the part of authorized users—for example, a programmer working on an accounting system with full access to the accounting database who is determined to place a Trojan horse in the code for theft or similar purposes. It's beyond the scope of our discussion of trends and future directions of database security, but you should be aware that an information systems security program encompasses not only interrelated technical areas (e.g., network, database, operating system) but also physical security, personnel security (e.g., background checks), audits, and a host of manual or partially automated procedures. Even if every concept we discuss in this chapter could be easily implemented, the potential for problems still exists if the program isn't complete.

21.3 Multilevel Secure Databases

The combination of authorization and authentication is a potent weapon in the fight for database and information security. If all users on a system, whether interactive or ones running applications, are sufficiently trusted to the highest level of information managed within that environment, then the security policies may very well be adequate. For example, a computer system with information ranging from unclassified to top secret (we'll discuss security classifications in a moment) whose users all have permission to access top secret information, could conceivably function with powerful authorization and authentication enforcement. This model is known as "running at system high."

This model falls apart, though, when organizations attempt to implement multilevel secure computing environments. *Multilevel security* means that 1) information at various classifications is contained within a computer system, and 2) some users are *not* cleared to the highest classification of that information.[3] An example specific to information management is a military computer system where a single logical database (whether centralized or distributed) may contain information ranging from unclassified to top secret, and the clearances of the users could also range from unclassified to top secret. That is, an unclassified user must be capable of performing his or her job on a computer system that contains top secret data in the database, but must never be permitted access to those data.

Multilevel secure databases are typically based on the Bell-LaPadula model, which manages *subjects*, active processes that may request some access to information, and *objects*, the files, views, records, fields, or whatever else is applicable to that particular information model.[4]

Objects receive *classifications*, and subjects receive *clearances*. Collectively, classes and clearances are known as either *access classes* or *levels*.[5]

An access class has two components. The first is a hierarchical component. The second is a set of nonhierarchical categories, which may be applied against a level of the hierarchy. For example, the U.S. military uses the following hierarchy (highest to lowest):

- Top secret
- Secret
- Confidential
- Unclassified

The second component might be composed of the following:

- Nuclear weapon clearance
- No foreign government release
- No contractors

As another example, a private company might impose the following hierarchy (highest to lowest):

- Secret
- Restricted distribution
- Confidential
- Sensitive
- Unlimited distribution

This same company's second component might include these categories:

- No subcontractors
- Corporate financial data
- Salary data

You could conceivably create a matrix of nonhierarchical versus hierarchical components. For example, one object might be classified as top secret, but it has no nonhierarchical component and therefore could be released to foreign governments, while a secret data object might have a "no foreign government" classification and therefore must not be released. But the Bell-

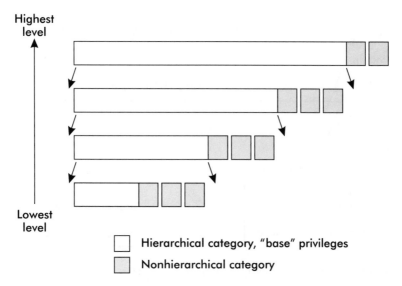

Highest
level

Lowest
level

☐ Hierarchical category, "base" privileges

☐ Nonhierarchical category

Figure 21-3 The Bell-LaPadula Access Class Lattice

LaPadula model creates a lattice in which the nonhierarchical component of any level in the hierarchy is automatically included in the next higher hierarchical level (a reverse inheritance, if you will). This is shown in Figure 21-3.

So far, our discussion has been relatively straightforward. It follows that a subject with a given clearance CL1 is permitted read access to objects with a classification CL2 that is equal to or less than CL1. For example, a top secret user can access data that are top secret, secret, confidential, or unclassified; secret users can access secret, confidential, and unclassified; and so on. In the Bell-LaPadula model, this is known as the *simple security property*.[6]

Not quite as obvious, though, is a companion known as the **-property,*[7] which permits subjects to have write access to objects only if the clearance of the subject is identical to or *lower than* that of the object being written. That is, information is never permitted to be written from a given level into some "thing" that has a lower level than the source; this could potentially lead to inadvertent downgrading of the classification of information.

Taking into account the two Bell-LaPadula access restrictions (simple security property and *-property), we could envision a multilevel secure database model like the one in Figure 21-4. Note that Subject 1, a user or process with a top secret clearance, is permitted read access to all three tuples (rows) within the relation, but under the *-property is only permitted to write to the tuple with a top secret classification (subjects can write "up the hierarchy," but not "down the hierarchy"). Subject 2, with a clearance of secret, can't read the top secret row but can read the other two. Subject 2 can, though, write into either the row classified secret (the same level) or the top secret row ("writing up").[8]

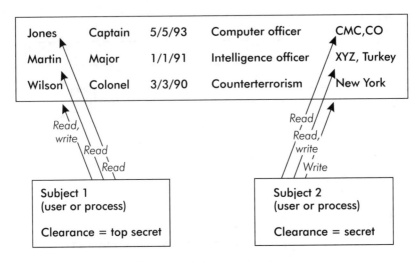

Figure 21-4 Examples of Bell-LaPadula Access Rules

As with most areas of computing and information management, and particularly in the security of both, the above simplistic model is of little real-world value, like the basic authorization/authentication model we discussed in section 21.2. While the principles of Bell-LaPadula are sound, the requirement to support multiple levels of security within a single table (or, for that matter, a single database) causes serious complications.

Consider the following situations:

- Individuals in a military unit with personnel records stored in a multi-level secure database might have a "real" mission, say, counterterrorism or intelligence, and a "cover story" position, like Air Force marching band member. The real information as well as the cover story need to be represented in the database.

- A sergeant turns out to be a counterintelligence major; or a disgraced, dishonorably discharged veteran is in reality the country's most closely guarded secret weapon and an active duty Army colonel to boot (most of us have seen this in movies or read books about it).

- The name of the government's top counterterrorism expert is classified top secret; the cover story position is that of a retired postal worker.

We could expand the model in Figure 21-4 to add a security property, in addition to the tuple/row level, at the element level (that is, each column within each row will have a classification). This expansion, however, introduces serious problems, namely that any given column within a row could have multiple values, depending on the classification one is viewing (Figure 21-5). At the fundamental level, this violates first normal form (the multiple

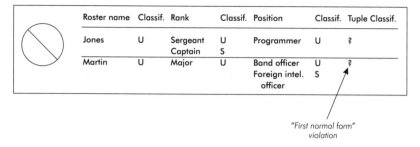

Roster name	Classif.	Rank	Classif.	Position	Classif.	Tuple Classif.
Jones	U	Sergeant	U	Programmer	U	?
		Captain	S			
Martin	U	Major	U	Band officer	U	?
				Foreign intel.	S	
				officer		

"First normal form"
violation

Figure 21-5 Element-Level Classifications and Associated Problems

Roster name	Classif.	Rank	Classif.	Position	Classif.	Tuple Classif.
Jones	U	Sergeant	U	Programmer	U	U
Jones	U	Captain	S	Programmer	U	S
Martin	U	Major	U	Band officer	U	U
Martin	U	Major	U	Foreign intel. officer	S	S

Figure 21-6 Polyinstantiation

values acting as a sort of repeating group), one of the guiding principles of relational databases. Therefore, a solution to this problem must be determined. We'll discuss that solution, polyinstantiation, next.

21.4 Polyinstantiation

One solution to the element-level classification problem described in the previous section is *polyinstantiation,* in which multiple tuples that have the same primary key exist within a relation.[9]

Figure 21-6 illustrates an example of polyinstantiation, in which military members show their true mission and ranks as well as their cover stories. Figure 21-7 shows the two Bell-LaPadula access rules against a polyinstantiated database.

Polyinstantiation was first introduced in the SeaView (Secure Data Views) secure database model in 1988.[10] Over the succeeding years, a great deal of research and writing, much of it by Sushil Jajodia and Ravi Sandhu of George Mason University, have been conducted on variations of polyinstantiation.

One research area is *polyinstantiation integrity,* introduced with the polyinstantiation concept in SeaView. Without going into excessive detail, the SeaView polyinstantiation integrity rules include a functional and a multi-valued component, which limit the set of all possible polyinstantiated instances to *only* those instances that satisfy the polyinstantiation integrity

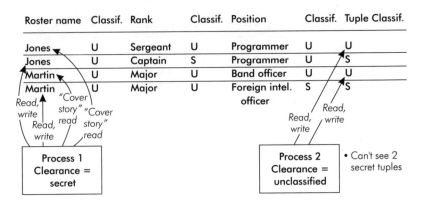

Figure 21-7 Polyinstantiation and Bell-LaPadula Properties

constraints. Because this area has been viewed by some as being too restrictive under the rules of SeaView, a paper entitled "Polyinstantiation Integrity in Multilevel Relations"[11] has proposed ways in which relaxation of the polyinstantiation integrity rules may occur. The paper describes various polyinstantiated instances and scenarios in which a database should maintain each and every instance, and the paper also proposes the multivalued dependency portion of polyinstantiation integrity as a candidate for elimination.[12]

So what is the bottom line on polyinstantiation? Even without the need for cover stories, as we discussed above, polyinstantiation has become an accepted part of multilevel secure databases. To illustrate why, and to lead us to our next subject (covert channels), consider the following situation.

If we disregard polyinstantiation, the multilevel secure relation in Figure 21-8(a) might be handled as follows: the multilevel secure DBMS could conceivably mask elements that are inaccessible to a user or process because of security reasons, and this masking might typically be accomplished through null values (Figure 21-8(b)).

Recall that there is only a single instance of each tuple; therefore an unclassified process might attempt to write unclassified data into what are believed to be null-valued (empty) columns within a tuple (Figure 21-9). This presents a problem for the multilevel secure DBMS, since these columns are in fact not empty and their values are not to be overwritten. This attempted update should be rejected on security grounds, correct?

Rejecting the update operation, though, opens what is known as a covert channel, or an indirect means by which the classification of information might be downgraded (deliberately or inadvertently, as we'll discuss later).[13] Rejecting what should be a perfectly acceptable database transaction in a multilevel database against null fields is a giveaway that those elements aren't

(a) "Real" tuples in the database

Roster name	Classif.	Rank	Classif.	Position	Classif.	Tuple Classif.
Jones	U	Captain	S	Programmer	U	S
Martin	U	Major	U	Foreign intel. officer	S	S

(b) What processes of different clearances see

Roster name	Classif.	Rank	Classif.	Position	Classif.	Tuple Classif.
Jones	U	null	?	Programmer	U	?
Jones	U	Captain	S	Programmer	U	S
Martin	U	Major	U	null	?	?
Martin	U	Major	U	Foreign intel. officer	S	S

Process 1 Clearance = secret

Process 2 Clearance = unclassified	• Sees null values instead of secret elements

Figure 21-8 Masked Views of Data for Security Reasons

Roster name	Classif.	Rank	Classif.	Position	Classif.	Tuple Classif.
Jones	U	null	?	Programmer	U	?
Jones	U	Captain	S	Programmer	U	S
Martin	U	Major	U	null	?	?
Martin	U	Major	U	Foreign intel. officer	S	S

Attempted operation:
```
UPDATE ROSTER
    SET POSITION = "Band Officer"
    WHERE NAME = "Martin" ;
```

Process 2 Clearance = unclassified

• Process 2 *thinks* that ROSTER.POSITION has a null value for Major Martin.

• If the UPDATE is rejected because SECRET data exists in that element, Process 2, which is UNCLASSIFIED, now knows that SECRET data exists there.

Figure 21-9 Attempted Update of Masked Objects

really empty, that in fact classified data reside there. Simply acknowledging the presence of higher classified information in a given location to an unauthorized user or process will open a covert channel.

Conceivably, the multilevel secure DBMS could simulate the acceptance of those updates, avoiding the rejection that would trigger the opening of the covert storage channel. What happens, though, if the user who already made the virtual update attempts to run a query or application that touches that tuple, and that data doesn't exist? We have another avenue for opening a covert channel.

What if the multilevel secure DBMS were to keep a type of log in which such changes are maintained for subsequent retrieval attempts? If that sounds familiar, it should; we've just described polyinstantiation. Even if we envision a specific solution to polyinstantiation—for example, maintaining duplicate versions of the tuples affected—that solution is implementation-specific. Polyinstantiation is a phenomenon of multilevel data;[14] how it's implemented doesn't affect the need of multiple views for users at various levels, though implementation models are a continuing area of research.

When thinking about the implementation of polyinstantiation, note the conceptual similarities between polyinstantiated tuples in a multilevel secure database and multiple valued tuples in temporal relational database architectures (as we discussed in Chapter 15). You will recall that in most temporally extended relational architectures, multiple instances of a single tuple with the same primary key need to exist, representing the current state as well as historical information. A relational model extended with multilevel security properties basically involves the same kind of representation, with the distinction that the determining properties for the multiple tuples are *time* in temporal databases and *access classes* in secure databases. Even though the two areas share little else besides implementation issues, and temporal database access isn't governed by anything so formal as the Bell-LaPadula properties, the commercialization of temporal and secure databases may utilize similar algorithms for multiple tuple representation and access.

Summarizing, then, polyinstantiation has grown from its roots in the SeaView project to a widely accepted model for multilevel secure databases, particularly in relational DBMSs. Indeed, polyinstantiation has entered as well into object-oriented database security research (an area much further behind the relational, as we'll discuss later, but that will be increasingly important as OODBMSs attempt to take their place in commercial and government environments).

We won't discuss here the many other nuances of polyinstantiation; the reader is directed to the references at the end of this chapter. Suffice it to say that the future directions of database security will be tied to multilevel secure models, and because of the issue of covert channels, polyinstantiation will play an important role.

21.5 Covert Channels

At the higher levels of Orange Book computer systems and database security (B2, B3, and A1), the issue of covert channels becomes important. A *covert channel* is a means through which subjects operating at a high clearance provide information to other subjects with a lower clearance.[15] Given that enforcement of the Bell-LaPadula *-property prohibits direct writing to a lower level, covert channels are often opened through *indirect* passing of information.

The Orange Book identifies two types of covert channels:[16]

1) Covert storage channels
2) Covert timing channels

Though covert storage channels are the more relevant of the two to databases,[17] covert timing channels are important as well; we'll look at examples of both.

A *covert storage channel* opens when a specific storage location such as a database object is directly or indirectly used as the vehicle for unauthorized downgrading of classified material. In the previous section, we discussed several examples in which a covert storage channel might be opened. Without enforcement of the Bell-LaPadula *-property, classified data might be easily downgraded, perhaps via a Trojan horse explicitly writing top secret data to a secret or unclassified location for pickup by an uncleared user or process.

Even with *-property enforcement, information could be downgraded in an indirect manner, again by a Trojan horse process. The earlier example in Figure 21-8 showed the non-polyinstantiated example in which masking via null values is used to hide information from a lower-level process. We discussed how rejecting a low-level process update of those null values would open a covert storage channel by indicating that classified information was hiding behind those masking null values—though this wouldn't release the information itself. Using that same model, however, a Trojan horse could, via cooperation with a lower-level process, send the actual classified data through a type of signaling mechanism. The Trojan horse could open a transaction, create a bogus table according to a prearranged structure, and populate the table with both fake classified data and selected null-valued masks. The lower-level process could then, at a prearranged time, attempt a sequence of updates against that table and interpret the success and failures against selected rows or attributes according to a code. The code could be as simple as the bit patterns of downgraded ASCII data. For example, every eight rows within the table would be assigned a 1 value for a successful update by the lower-level process or a 0 for a rejected update; the eight 0 or 1 values would then be interpreted as an octet character representation. Or a more complex code could be invented. Following the usage of the covert channel, the high-level process could then DROP the table.

Even though this type of covert channel is susceptible to detection (e.g., the database logs should capture the sporadic creation and deletion of tables, though this could be difficult to detect in an active database environment), other means are available to use existing tables to pass information. The database security policy therefore must take these factors into account.

As we mentioned above, *covert timing channels* do have some degree of applicability to multilevel secure databases. An unclassified or low-level network analysis tool might monitor traffic patterns and response times for all system operations. Noting how long it takes a low-level process to transfer data (e.g., a personnel roster) and comparing that time to a known data transfer of highly classified information, data set sizes could be estimated. Even without having unclassified instances for comparison, or even the record structures of classified data, the knowledge of bandwidth, protocols (for overhead determination), and other network characteristics could be used against a secure transmission to determine data volumes. By comparing these volumes to one another over time, inferences might be made. For example, if a top secret personnel or equipment roster is known to be sent periodically to a remote field site in a foreign country, and over time the transmission takes longer and longer until the transfer time is regularly twice as long as when the monitoring began, one could infer that twice as many people or equipment items are considered important enough to have data transferred for their support, indicating that a buildup of some degree has occurred.

Covert timing channels are typically overcome by communications solutions, such as *traffic padding*, in which communications throughputs are masked to hide their true volumes. Again, covert timing channels are primarily a communications issue, though as databases become more distributed in the future and security becomes more important, they must be considered along with covert storage channels for trusted database environments.

Here is another example of a covert channel.[18] Since high-level processes are permitted to read data from objects with lower-level classifications, the following situation might occur. Suppose the high-level process sends an SQL query against some remote low-level DBMS, with the query reading

```
SELECT name, rank, date_of_birth
  FROM roster
  WHERE duty_building = 445
```

While this could simply be an innocent query attempting to access personnel information from anyone working in Building #445, it could also conceivably be a Trojan horse–generated query in which the information leakage is encoded in the query itself. Perhaps 445 tanks or armored personnel carriers are being sent to some location for a top secret mission, or the

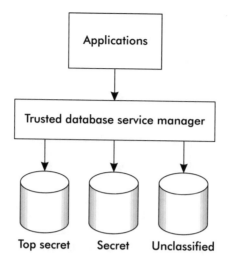

Figure 21-10 Separate Back-End Architecture for Secure Distributed DBMSs

number 445 might have some other hidden meaning (perhaps readable through deciphering of the bit pattern). This problem is particularly important and it leads us into our discussion of secure *distributed* database environments. So far, the issues and directions we've discussed are applicable to database environments in general. Adding distribution to databases introduces new security concerns and issues. The state of the art in secure distributed DBMSs is considerably behind centralized databases, as we'll discuss, though a significant amount of research is being directed at associated issues and problems.

21.6 Secure Distributed Database Environments

While multilevel secure databases have had greater agreement on basic concepts (such as the need to handle the polyinstantiation phenomenon) if not the actual implementations, the state of distributed DBMSs is somewhat less mature.

The roots of secure DDBs are traceable back to the 1982 U.S. Air Force Woods Hole study, in which two candidate distributed DBMS architectures were defined.[19] A common feature to each was a single trusted front-end component that would be connected to two physically separated DBMSs. In one architecture (shown in Figure 21-10), one DBMS would store the high data and the other would contain low data; the front end would receive all database operations (including queries) and route them appropriately. Queries for high data access from appropriately cleared processes and users would be

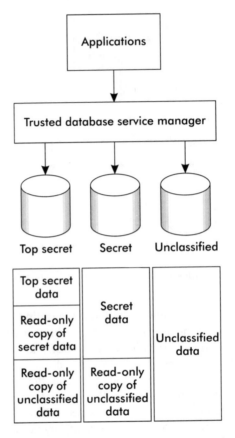

Figure 21-11 Pseudo-Multilevel Back End for Secure Distributed DBMS Architecture

routed to the high DBMS, while multilevel queries would be decomposed and routed accordingly.

This basic architecture, though, doesn't address the multilevel secure databases and the advances made in that area. Though distributed applications could be processed through the trusted front end and could conceivably see a single integrated global schema (as we discussed in Chapter 2), the distributed DBMS principle of locally autonomous applications running against a local database (also discussed in Chapter 2) would be lost, at least for multilevel applications (e.g., no single back-end multilevel secure DBMS for non-distributed multilevel processing).

The alternative architecture, shown in Figure 21-11, is more complex and includes multiple levels within a single DBMS, though it isn't truly multilevel. Low operations are processed as with the other architecture, but high and multilevel operations are processed against a DBMS that contains the high-level data plus copies of the low-level data. Note that this architecture introduces replication issues not unlike those we discussed in Chapter 2, which would then mandate a replication manager and appropriate data integrity policies.

In the mid-1980s, work commenced under the sponsorship of the Rome Air Development Center (RADC) of the U.S. Air Force with the charter to expand on the 1982 recommendations and develop specifications for a multilevel secure DDBMS.[20] This program, known as SD-DBMS, was *not* designed to be a distributed DBMS in the classical sense (that is, to allow horizontal and vertical partitioning of tuples according to network cost algorithms or organizational reasons), but rather to use data distribution as the means to enforce mandatory access control (MAC).[21] SD-DBMS was designed to be LAN-based, in fact running on a multilevel secure LAN.

SD-DBMS follows the basic Bell-LaPadula model (e.g., hierarchical and nonhierarchical components of access classes, subjects and objects, as discussed in section 21.3). The system enforces discretionary access control (DAC) through *access views*, or a virtual relation derived from base relations not unlike traditional SQL views. Subjects (users and processes) are *not* permitted to access base relations, but rather must go through the DAC-controlled views.[22]

As an aside, note the similarities between this mandatory view-based access and that introduced for metadata management in the SQL-92 standard via the INFORMATION_SCHEMA (see section 12.3.2), in which all metadata access must be through views rather than base tables.

DAC is managed via an attached access control list (ACL) with users (individuals or groups) specifically noted as to permissible operations. MAC is enforced by associating access classes with individual base relation tuples. The *derived relation*, or the result of a relational operation against an access view, yields a set of derived tuples, which then are subject to MAC labeling.[23] The labeling procedures are areas of continuing research. As the derived tuples are created, varying algorithms might be used to manage them.[24]

The SD-DBMS architecture was still based on physically separate back ends, one per access class (Figure 21-12). When a user created a multilevel relation, that relation would then be horizontally partitioned into single-level fragments, which would be stored within the appropriate back end according to security classification.[25]

Policies and candidate architectures were developed for SD-DBMS to overcome obstacles such as the high-level user query in which data might be encoded within the query itself (the last of the covert channel examples we discussed in the previous section).[26]

Secure distributed database work continues in areas such as developing an architecture capable of supporting both local and global multilevel processing. Another research area is security in heterogeneous multidatabase

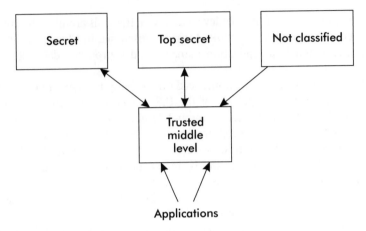

Figure 21-12 SD-DBMS architecture[27]

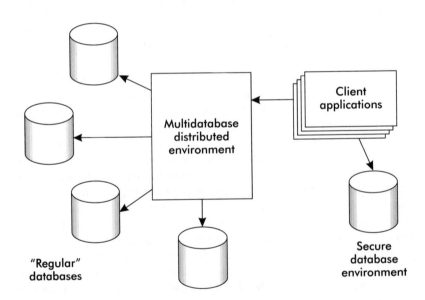

Figure 21-13 A Possible Architecture to Support the Coexistence of
Multidatabase and Multilevel Secure Database Environments

systems. The extent to which powerful multilevel security will ever be successfully applied to corporation-wide multidatabase environments is uncertain,
given the many complexities in that area (see Chapters 6 and 7).

What may occur is that a particular corporation will have islands for
secure processing, including secure databases and information managers,
divorced from any grandiose plans for overall connectivity (Figure 21-13). A
multilevel secure user may have access to a highly secure environment, perhaps

one encompassing a secure DDBMS, which is *not* part of any corporate-wide data integration strategy regardless of the implementation, the level of transparency, and other multidatabase issues.

21.7 Languages for Secure Databases

In Chapter 15, we discussed SQL language extensions to support temporal databases, but noted that neither the SQL-92 standard nor the current state of SQL3 supports such facilities. The same is true of language extensions for multilevel secure databases.

It's important to note that even though security-oriented statements exist within SQL (the GRANT and REVOKE statements, for example), these do *not* constitute multilevel (nor for that matter any type of MAC-based) security. The capability to GRANT certain access and update privileges against selected objects, to pass some or all of your privileges to other users (through the WITH GRANT OPTION clause), and to revoke privileges (either directly or by following a trail through WITH GRANT OPTION–granted privileges), simply constitute components of discretionary access control (DAC). Even though the SQL-92 security model is far more robust than any previous versions of the standard (though many SQL-based commercial relational DBMSs have had product-supplied security extensions for some time, above earlier editions of the standard), those facilities are hardly sufficient for tomorrow's database security or indeed even today's.

As multilevel DBMSs come to market, they will likely provide multilevel extensions to their languages. A research example of such extensions is MSQL (Multilevel SQL), the language of SeaView.[28] MSQL includes capabilities for DDL-based classification specification, such as[29]

```
create relation roster (
    name                char (30) [U:S] primary-key,
    rank                char (10) [U:S],
    job_code            char (10) [U:TS],
    duty_location       char (20) [U:TS],
    ...
)
```

MSQL allows primary keys to be made from a group as well, as in

```
create relation roster (
   group (last_name char (20), first_name char (10),
     middle_initial char (1) ) [U:TS] primary-key,
   ...
)
```

As in the above examples, an attribute might be assigned an enumerated set of classifications rather than a range:

```
create relation missions (
  ...
  task              char (30) [S; TS NUCLEAR; TS INTEL]
  ...
)
```

In the previous example, the TASK column can have values of either Secret, Top Secret/Nuclear, or Top Secret/Intelligence.

MSQL allows classification constraints to be specified that are conceptually similar to SQL integrity constraints:

```
create class-constraint JOBCodeRules
  on roster as
  name.class = SECRET,
  rank.class = SECRET,
  mission.class =
    (if roster.mission = "COUNTERINTELLIGENCE' then
        TOP SECRET else SECRET)
```

Note that a metadata property *class* is defined for each attribute, to process statements.

MSQL includes functions such as HIGHEST-CLASS to deal with polyinstantiated classification information (e.g., SELECT operations where information will be returned at the highest classification for which the user or process is cleared).

Although SQL3 currently has no MLS commands and these capabilities will likely reside within extensions provided by vendors, we can make some predictions about MLS language extensions:

- SQL will provide the basis for security language extension in relational databases, though untraditional statements like those of MSQL (e.g., CREATE RELATION rather than CREATE TABLE) will likely shift toward standard SQL syntax.

- As polyinstantiation implementations hit commercial DBMSs to support multilevel security, language extensions—not just DDL, but functions such as MSQL's HIGHEST-CLASS—will be included. Examples might be HIGHEST-COVER-STORY and LOWEST-COVER-STORY, which would return the cover stories with the highest and lowest classifications, respectively.

- As secure DBMSs evolve in OODBMSs, vendor extensions to the ODMG languages discussed in Chapter 13 (OQL, OML, and ODL) may receive multilevel extensions similar to those of extended SQL (though, of course, the vendors need to first implement the ODMG languages themselves into their products, which may take several years). OODBMS users interested in multilevel security may have an opportunity to influence vendor and standards directions regarding secure OODBMS language.

21.8 Secure OODBMSs

Let's shift our focus a bit from the relational-oriented security approach to one in which object-oriented databases are the focus. As OODBMS products mature and begin to be used in other than small, compartmentalized applications, and, concurrently, as database and information management security continues to grow in importance, secure OODBMSs and OODBs will become increasingly significant. In this section, we'll discuss the directions of secure OODBs.

You could make two generalizations about secure OODBs:

1) Development is behind that of secure relational DBs, but primarily because of the relative ages of relational and object-oriented technology.
2) Multilevel security principles developed in relational databases, such as an understanding of polyinstantiation and the reliance on the Bell-LaPadula model, have made their way into secure OODBs.

The object-oriented counterpart to SeaView is SODA, or the Secure Object-Oriented Database. SODA uses the Bell-LaPadula security policies and a labeling strategy to denote object classifications.[30] SODA supports two different types of labels:

1) *Instance-variable labeling:* Each instance variable may be labeled independently according to the specified classification range; this is similar to relational element-level classification, where each column in a row might have its own permissible classification range and its own actual classification, independent of other elements.
2) *Object labeling:* Similar to tuple-level classification (e.g., one classification for the entire tuple or object).

Different issues exist within OODBMSs with respect to the classification of composite and noncomposite objects. Briefly, a set of properties (defined by B. Thuraisingham) can be used to govern security levels of instances, objects, and the relationship among instances and objects for both types of objects.[31]

Since OODBs, unlike relational databases, currently lack standardization for terminology and models (though the ODMG-93 standard will help correct that situation), OODB security research has typically been conducted against somewhat varying models. Because, as we noted earlier, most of the relational security principles are finding their way into OODBs, the convergence of OODB models toward an ODMG standard will likely present a common framework for commercialization of secure OODBMSs.

21.9 Conclusion

So where is database security headed? Though a tremendous amount has been accomplished in recent years, particularly in multilevel security (e.g., identifying the phenomenon of polyinstantiation, developing policies to deal with the issue, and refining those policies based on further research), the fact remains that commercial implementation is significantly lagging behind research. As Sushil Jajodia claims, "It's relatively easy to be 99% secure; it's that last 1% which not only is very costly, but it may not be practical to try to achieve it."[32]

A handful of DBMS products are being certified today at the B1 level, which means that issues such as covert channels aren't being sufficiently addressed in the vendor-supplied solutions of today. Mandatory access control (MAC) policies are just beginning to find their way into commercial ventures.

We have, however, much further to go. Teresa Lunt identifies the following areas, which will give you a good idea of where the next generation of database security advances will likely occur:[33]

- *Defining operational semantics for multilevel database operations:* Meaning, for example, that we must determine exactly what a multilevel UPDATE or DELETE operation does to all affected objects. The semantics are required to advance the ways polyinstantiation is handled, from the current state to a state implementable by commercial DBMSs. This author would add that standardization is important in this area, because a multilevel DELETE in one DBMS must work identically to the same operation in another DBMS.

- *Extending multilevel security to other models and distributed databases:* We discussed this topic with respect to OODBs and distributed databases in this chapter. Research is also focused on entity-relationship models and deductive databases, though these arguably have less long-term commercial potential.

- *Preventing undesired inferences:* The inference problem occurs when two or more pieces of information at a security classification C1 could, when considered together, infer complete or partial information at a higher level C2. For example, consider the following individual information units and their respective classifications:

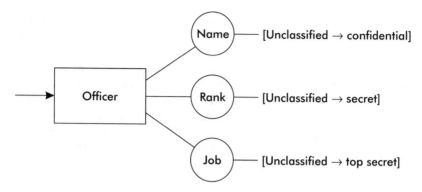

Figure 21-14 CASE-Based Security-Extended Entity-Relationship Model

"Captain Smith is a spy"—SECRET

"Captain Smith is scheduled to go to {name of country} tomorrow"—CONFIDENTIAL

"Captain Smith leaves on a flight at 1:45 A.M."—CONFIDENTIAL

"Captain Smith's leave (vacation) ended earlier than it was scheduled to end"—UNCLASSIFIED

Taking all of this information together, you could determine that Captain Smith, the spy, ended his scheduled vacation early to leave on a 1:45 A.M. flight to go to {country unknown}, most likely to do some spy-type stuff. This inferred information might be classified at a very high level, perhaps TOP SECRET, a level higher than any of its individual components. As Lunt notes, of all the work done in this area of *multilevel inference,* no formal or quantitative definitions of the problem, let alone any solutions, have been found.

• *Tools for designing and developing multilevel secure databases:* Consider the entity-relationship diagram in Figure 21-14. Because elements and tuples in a secret relational database, or attributes and object instances in an OODB, may exist at multiple levels of classification, it stands to reason that a modeling tool to create multilevel database structures should support the definition of those classifications. A security-extended entity-relationship model (or any other conceptual model, for that matter) could then be mapped into a security-extended DDL, similar to SeaView's MSQL, which we investigated in section 21.7.

Another area where security will begin to make inroads is high-performance databases, including parallel databases (discussed in Chapter 3) and multilevel deductive databases.[34]

In conclusion, we predict that database security will continue to forge ahead, simply because it must. We live in a dangerous world, not only in a geopolitical sense but also in terms of commercial concerns. Industrial espionage is on the rise, and the protection of corporate information is becoming an increasing necessity.

Where the uncertainty lies, though, is the extent to which complete database security will be realized. That "last one percent" to which Sushil Jajodia refers may indeed turn out to be the biggest obstacle to one hundred percent assured security. However, the advances in the near future, and their incorporation into commercial products, will likely provide greater levels of security than we have today, perhaps enough to protect against all but the most skilled person determined to compromise security.

Outlook

Short-term

- More B1-compliant commercial DBMS products will appear
- Will commercial products go past B1? This is unclear, since commercial database security concerns are different than government and defense; given the downplaying of defense systems, vendors may opt to shift security emphasis to emerging commercial concerns
- New standards in the government to replace the Orange Book
- Research into commercial database security requirements will gain momentum, possibly surpassing defense-related issues in importance

Long-term

- Commercial database security models will be better understood than they are today, and products that support those models will be available
- Database security concerns for aggregation will be resolved, and aggregation management tools will be available

Additional Reading

- S. Jajodia and R. Sandhu, "Polyinstantiation Integrity in Multilevel Relations," *Proceedings of the 1990 IEEE Computer Society Symposium on Research in Security and Privacy.*
- S. Jajodia and R. Sandhu, "Toward a Multilevel Secure Relational Data Model," *Proceedings of ACM SIGMOD 1991.*
- T. F. Lunt, ed., *Research Directions in Database Security* (New York: Springer-Verlag, 1992).
- National Research Council, *Computer at Risk: Safe Computing in the Information Age* (Washington, D.C.: National Academy Press, 1991).

Endnotes

1. S. Jajodia, private communication, May 1993.

2. Jajodia, private communication.

3. T. F. Lunt, "Security in Database Systems: A Research Perspective," *Computers and Security* (March 1992), 41.

4. S. Jajodia and R. Sandhu, "Toward a Multilevel Secure Relational Data Model," *Proceedings of ACM SIGMOD 1991*, 51.

5. Jajodia and Sandhu, "Secure Relational Data Model."

6. Jajodia and Sandhu, "Secure Relational Data Model."

7. Jajodia and Sandhu, "Secure Relational Data Model."

8. It may not be obvious why a secret user is able to write information into a top secret object; keep in mind that this does not equate to a secret user writing top secret data, but rather writing into an area capable of holding top secret data. Once those data are stored, however, they become classified as top secret. Logically, a secret user or process would not have access to any top secret information to put into that area, but rather would be putting secret, confidential, or unclassified information there which some top secret user or process might need to use.

9. Jajodia and Sandhu, "Secure Relational Data Model," 52.

10. T. F. Lunt, "Security in Database Systems," 44, and T. F. Lunt, "SeaView," in T. F. Lunt, ed., *Research Directions in Database Security* (New York: Springer-Verlag, 1992).

11. S. Jajodia and R. Sandhu, "Polyinstantiation Integrity in Multilevel Relations," *Proceedings of the 1990 IEEE Computer Society Symposium on Research in Security and Privacy*, 104.

12. Jajodia and Sandhu, "Polyinstantiation Integrity."

13. Jajodia and Sandhu, "Secure Relational Data Model," 52.

14. Lunt, "Security in Database Systems," 43.

15. Jajodia and Sandhu, "Secure Relational Data Model," 51–52.

16. U.S. Department of Defense, *Department of Defense Trusted Computer Systems Criteria*, December 1985, 81.

17. G. W. Smith, "Session Report: The Semantics of Data Classification," in Lunt, ed., *Research Directions in Database Security*, 139.

18. Adapted from an example in J. P. O'Connor et al., "An Investigation of Secure Distributed DBMS Architectures," in Lunt, ed., *Research Directions in Database Security*, 53.

19. O'Connor et al., "Investigation," 41.

20. O'Connor et al., "Investigation," 41.

21. O'Connor et al., "Investigation," 43.

22. O'Connor et al., "Investigation," 45.

23. O'Connor et al., "Investigation," 45–46.

24. See O'Connor et al., "Investigation," 46, for a detailed discussion.

25. O'Connor et al., "Investigation," 47.

26. O'Connor et al., "Investigation," 59–61.

27. O'Connor et al., "Investigation," 48.

28. Lunt, "SeaView," 21.

29. Code examples based on those in Lunt, "SeaView," 25.

30. T. F. Keefe and W. T. Tsai, "Security Model Consulting in Secure Object-Oriented Systems," *Proceedings of the 5th Computer Security Applications Conference*, 1989, 290–291.

31. B. Thuraisingham, "Multilevel Secure Object-Oriented Data Model—Issues on Noncomposite Objects, Composite Objects, and Versioning," *Journal of Object-Oriented Programming*, Focus on OODBMS, Special Issue, 1992, 121–130.

32. S. Jajodia, private communication, May 1993.

33. Lunt, "Security in Database Systems," 54–55.

34. B. Thuraisingham, "Current Status of R&D in Trusted Database Management Systems," *ACM SIGMOD Record* (September 1992), 46.

PART VII

The Finishing Touches

CHAPTER

Other Database and Information Management Topics

A Note to the CIO

While some of the topics in this chapter (for instance, benchmarking) may be more appropriate to your technical staff members, others such as mobile computing databases are likely to be of concern to you as you struggle to incorporate personal digital assistants and other mobile devices into your overall computing environment. Areas such as mobile computing can be truly classified as emerging technology, and they merit careful watching over the next few years.

22.1 Introduction

Even a book as comprehensive as this one is can't cover the trends and future directions of every single topic related to databases and information management. When you consider that most of these subjects have entire books written about them, our task has been to boil down the most critical subjects in information management to a chapter or two (or six, in the case of distributed technology).

To round out our technical discussions, this chapter will include a number of miscellaneous subjects, from benchmarking to mobile computing information management to main memory databases. Grouping these subjects into a single chapter by no means implies that they are insignificant. In the case of mobile computing databases, for example, we have an area of technology just emerging and about which very little is known, other than an

Likewise, the responsibility of managing voluminous amounts of data may require you to incorporate near-line and offline devices into your overall database picture, not just in order to archive but as an active part of your database storage environment. Tertiary storage may, then, be important to you, and the discussion in this chapter will likewise be of value.

Executive Summary

In this chapter, we present several other topics that deal with present trends and future directions in information management. Some of these, like mobile computing databases, are in their infancy. Others, like benchmarking standards, have been around for a while but are evolving to meet changes in information management.

The subjects discussed in this chapter are

- *Mobile computing databases:* Query processing and transaction models, user interfaces, and other aspects of this area are different

identification of the challenges ahead. Another subject, compression, will no doubt grow as multimedia and image data become more important for applications in the future. One could spend a great deal of time on compression algorithms; however, we prefer to present the issues and other future-related material in a concise manner.

And with that, let's look at our first subject: mobile computing information management.

22.2 Databases and Information Management for Mobile Computing Environments

Laptops, palmtop computers, personal digital assistants, and special inventory management tracking and ordering devices are all examples of the emerging area of *mobile computing* (sometimes called nomadic computing, for the "wandering around" method of working). In mobile computing, the desktop PC is unleashed from its stationary office or home environment by the laptop. The applications software running on those laptops is basically the same as on a stationary PC. In stand-alone mode, this presents no problem; however, when sporadic communications are required from those laptops back to a host or server system (that communication typically occurs via a modem/

from traditional environments, and the problems are just starting to be understood.

- *Benchmarking:* New standards are evolving to meet new information management paradigms, including decision support systems and corporation-wide computing.

- *Data compression:* Multimedia data, particularly video and audio, demand new data compression algorithms to enable today's storage devices to accommodate applications featuring such data.

- *Main memory databases:* As main memory grows dramatically in capacity, some applications can have entire databases stored in data. Because of the volatility of today's memory technology, some degree of persistence must be provided by supporting utilities and DBMS components.

- *Tertiary storage:* On the other end of the spectrum from main memory, very large database (VLB) environments will continue to make use of mass storage devices other than magnetic disk. Instead of simply archiving data on tapes and optical devices, such

telephone line interface, though cellular communications usage is increasing), commonly used models of information management tend to be insufficient. Further, this problem will only worsen as palmtops, personal digital assistants, and other devices become more commonplace.[1]

As laptop systems gain far more capacity in terms of secondary storage than was possible when they were introduced, and as processing power increases with the 486, Pentium, and other extremely fast CPUs, we have mobile devices capable of supporting complex database operations that only a year or two earlier would have been chained to the desktop. (Still a few years earlier, these feats would have required mid-range or mainframe computing support.) And, with wireless network technology (e.g., cellular communications) on the rise, it is entirely conceivable and desirable that mobile computing devices become an active part of distributed information systems.[2] This means that database consistency between those on mobile devices and home systems, as well as transaction processing, repository access, security, and many other areas *must* play a role in mobile computing.

It is quite likely, though, that mobile computing "changes fundamentally some of the assumptions underlying existing protocols, models and algorithms for database systems."[3] Specifically, here are some areas that will require extensive research if mobile computing is to be brought into the mainstream of information management:[4]

storage media ideally will be included as part of the run-time database environment. New models of handling multiple storage media are evolving to enable this approach.

- *Design models and CASE tools:* New data modeling techniques and supporting CASE tools will continue to evolve to support corporation-wide data design.

- *Network operating system (NOS) databases:* Network operating systems have, in recent years, incorporated a great deal of data-base functionality into the operating systems; one example is a NetWare Loadable Module (NLM) version of a DBMS product.

What This Technology Can Do for You

The many different subjects in this chapter round out discussion in this book. As a decision maker and strategic planner for information systems, you need to have a good understanding of various technical areas. In information management, the subjects discussed in this

- *Distributed query processing:* In Chapter 7, we discussed the issue of query processing and the challenges for distributed information management (e.g., optimization and reoptimization issues). Consider the mobile device with a roving database that must periodically connect via a network interface to a centralized site for database query operations and information download. That connection will, by definition, vary from instance to instance. For example, it could vary from a different place within a city or a different city, state, or country; by different network connections (wireless sometimes, modem or telephone at other times); and so on. This means there is an issue of query costs varying widely from one connection instance to another.

Another area of research in query processing is the nature of the queries themselves. Queries may be parameterized by the current location where that query originates; for example, "How many XYZs can you ship me within the next two hours?" or "Where is the closest source of 35 ABCs?" posed to a central site will have a different answer if those queries come from a city close to a warehouse as opposed to overseas. Other parameters may include direction and speed in which the computer itself is moving.

- *Transaction processing:* Mobile queries arguably may be of the "docking/download" model; that is, instead of frequent short-term communications common in traditional environments, we will have fewer but

chapter are likely to be considered for part or all of your organization's information system environment.

Some topics, such as mobile computing databases, bear watching if your business needs dictate such computing paradigms. Other subjects, such as benchmarking, are more passive (i.e., they play a supporting role in evaluation and are not a base technology), but they are important to your decision-making process. In the case of benchmarking, you should understand that benchmarks oriented for high-throughput transaction processing are ill-suited for decision support systems or widely distributed corporate computing, and you should ignore vendor hype.

morboo

longer-term connections with large amounts of information transferred from one direction to another. This means that the transaction models will be different from stationary computing. Long-running transaction models may need to be implemented for mobile computing even for database environments that would likely require more traditional short-term transactions if the databases and systems involved were stationary.

- *Failure and recovery:* Mobile computers may often be unavailable due to circumstances such as system failure or merely the need to recharge batteries. A means must be available by which the mobile computer can register its unavailability in advance, when possible, so that information management models can compensate for this (e.g., download information in advance of the unavailability, hold information transfer and associated actions until a "ready to receive" signal is returned, and so on).

- *Security*—The security issues discussed in Chapter 21, including some such as authentication that are arguably within the scope of network services, are more serious in mobile environments than in their stationary counterparts. Impersonation becomes problematic and is compounded by physical issues such as stolen mobile computing devices.

- *Human-computer interfaces:* Screen space is shrinking; even though today's laptops mirror desktop PC screen layouts, palmtops and other smaller mobile devices won't have screens with 24 rows and 80 columns.

Therefore, new ways of phrasing queries (perhaps pushbutton-intensive) and receiving large amounts of output from a remote site must be investigated.

Even areas such as *energy efficient data management*[5] (efficiently managing the mobile device's use of energy for database operations) need a great deal of investigation. For example, data transmission consumes an order of magnitude power more than the act of receiving data,[6] which means that database operations must be carefully planned in accordance with power requirements and refresh capabilities—functions certainly not included in traditional stationary computing environments.

Applications in which mobile computing, and therefore mobile information management, are likely to play an important role include

- *Delivery services*, where such devices are already in use today.
- *Directory information services,* such as local "yellow pages," which provide significantly more information than currently provided in telephone book form.[7]
- *Mail-enabled applications,* in which electronic mail forms the messaging backbone of interapplications communications.[8]

In summary, mobile, or nomadic, computing is a growing area of technology in which traditional means of database and information management must be rethought to account for the characteristics of mobile environments.

22.3 Benchmarking

Benchmarks have much more value than simply providing advertising fodder for DBMS vendors, who are prone to choose the benchmark most favorable to their particular product and base their "we are the fastest" campaigns on those results. Benchmarks *do* provide some means of consistent comparison from one product to another, and taking a look at the future directions of the benchmarking business is useful.

The benchmarking business is controlled by the Transaction Processing Council (TPC), which formulates a series of transaction-based test suites to measure database/TP environments in a (more or less) even playing field. In mid-1993, TPC approved a new benchmark designed for decision support system measurement, known as TPC-D.[9] TPC-D, like its companions TPC-A, TPC-B, and TPC-C (all three designed to measure various transaction processing modes of operations), is a printed specification and is accompanied by ANSI C source code, which populates a database with data according to a preset standardized structure. In the case of TPC-D, the database structure is designed for large aggregations, full-table scans, and four- and five-way join operations—basically, decision support and executive information system application functions.[10]

As of this writing, TPC-D is only a draft benchmark, so vendors are prohibited from using results for competitive purposes. Upon formal publication, the TPC-D specifications will be used in the way that its companion specifications are.[11]

TPC is also working on the TPC-E benchmark, which is designed for corporate computing environments. TPC-E is expected to be generally available in 1995.[12]

Another development in benchmarking is the recent release of benchmark specifications for object-oriented databases. In March 1993, the University of Wisconsin released the 007 benchmark, developed by Michael Carey, David DeWitt, and Jeffrey Naughton; this benchmark is designed to be more comprehensive than the 001 de facto standard benchmark.[13]

007 is designed to simulate a CAD/CAM environment and tests system performance in the area of object-to-object navigation over cached data, disk-resident data, and both sparse and dense traversals. It also tests indexed and unindexed updates of object fields, repeated updates, and the creation and deletion of objects. A variety of query types are included, such as exact-match lookup, ranges, and ad hoc joins.[14]

Summarizing, we can make the following observation: as new models of database and information management appear and become widely used, the means to competitively measure vendors' performance on products designed to support those new models will inevitably follow. For example, mobile computing systems (discussed in the previous section) will likely have some type of benchmark developed once a significant number of mobile data management solutions are in place.

22.4 Data Compression

Data compression? Didn't that go away when PCs started adding gigabyte-sized disks replacing all of those old 10- and 20-megabyte disks?

Not really. Recall that several times throughout this book (e.g., in the discussion of parallel database systems in Chapters 5 and 7), we've mentioned that terabyte-sized databases would be commonplace and indeed already are underway in most organizations. You can throw all the high-capacity disk devices you want at the storage problem, but the fact remains that organizations will store more and more data as time goes on. Multimegabyte images, billion-row relational tables, and so on will continue to require some degree of compression.

It's important to note that data compression algorithms must be reversible, and all of the original precompression information must be restorable in its entirety. This precludes data compaction (e.g., nonreversible data compression) actions, such as removing leading and trailing blanks or leading zeroes.[15]

In addition to the obvious storage space advantages of compressing data, other advantages will become increasingly important in the next few years. These include[16]

- *Communications data transfer:* The transmission of compressed data from one site to another will take less time, and therefore yield a higher transfer rate, than uncompressed data.

- *Backup and recovery:* Backing up very large databases is a problem under investigation. Even at the highest transfer rates, terabyte-sized database backup would take days using today's technology. With data compression, this problem is alleviated somewhat, for the same reasons as communications data transfer (e.g., higher transfer rates and overall throughput). Additionally, fewer backup devices are needed to store compressed than uncompressed data.

- *Performance:* Index structures may be able to pack more keys into a given index block when compression is used. Key values used for searching are first compressed and then compared against an index with compressed keys comprising its tree structure or hash tables. Therefore, having more keys stored in a given index block will result in fewer I/O operations until the index block necessary to access the data is found.

For all the wonders of compression, though, it also has disadvantages, the most obvious being the processing overhead necessary to encode and decode compressed data. One of the research areas for this problem involves using VLSI technology to implement compression through hardware rather than software, which would then reduce the processing overhead.[17]

Specific to the actual process of compression, a great deal of work still must be done to identify the best compression techniques and algorithms for a given environment; 40 years of data compression technology has produced numerous algorithms, and as with nearly every other subject we've discussed in this book, no single algorithm is most effective in every type of environment.[18]

Finally, recall that in section 19.5 we discussed repositories and granularity issues, noting that the ultimate repository environment would support the finest levels of granularity for all system objects—but would result in a nightmarish storage requirement problem. The area of metadata compression, which uses standard compression techniques of one form or another, still needs to be researched for a greater understanding of the effects of such compression on overall system performance.[19]

22.5 Main Memory Databases

Until recently, memory-resident databases were used only in special applications where the need for performance outweighed all else, including retention of data in the event of system failure. Applications tended not to be of the traditional transaction processing or decision support variety, but rather were message-driven, processing- and algorithmic-intensive applications that needed very fast access to a relatively nonvolatile set of data. Data structures were typically home-grown, based on direct pointers to memory addresses.

With chip densities and available semiconductor memory on the rise in recent years, storing conventional-type databases in main memory is far more feasible than it has been in recent years.[20] These *main-memory databases* (MMDBs) differ significantly from the more traditional disk-based varieties, in several ways:[21]

- Main memory access time is orders of magnitude less than that of disk storage, resulting in extremely fast database performance.

- Main memory is volatile, while disk storage is stable (though nonvolatile main memory is technologically feasible but expensive).

- Main memory is not block-oriented as disks are, since disks must overcome a relatively high fixed cost per access that doesn't apply to main memory.

- Data layout, so important for performance in disk environments, is of less importance in memory.

- Disks are not normally directly accessible by processors, while main memory is; the performance improvement for memory databases, though, is counteracted by main memory being more susceptible to software errors.

Even with much higher memory capacities than in the recent past, very large databases (again, our terabyte-class databases) do not and likely will never fit completely into main memory. Even in such environments, though, a distinction may be made between *hot data*, information that is accessed frequently, and *cold data*, which are rarely accessed. Hot data will usually be of significantly lower volume than cold data, so a database could be partitioned between main memory and disk storage according to access frequency.[22]

The problems of memory databases, outside of storage capacity, can basically be boiled down to the question "What happens when the system fails?" Adding battery backups and uninterruptible power supplies to systems can help reduce the probability of externally induced failures (e.g., power failures or spikes), but there is always the possibility that failure could occur anyway; as with disks, you can attempt to increase the mean time between failures (MTBF) but failures will occur at some point. Unlike disks, though,

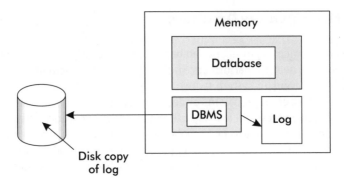

Figure 22-1 Main Memory Databases and Recovery Mechanisms

the volatility of memory could conceivably wipe out an entire database in the event of some type of media failure. This could, of course, happen with disk-based databases as well, such as during a head crash, which is why backup to some other type of media is important for MMDBs as well as disk databases (Figure 22-1).

MMDBs typically are checkpointed to a disk-based version, possibly during periods of lower activity. Along with logs (discussed next), those checkpoint versions may be used to reconstruct the MMDB contents in the event of failure.

With respect to the logs, transaction processing in MMDBs follows a paradigm similar to traditional databases, which we discussed in Chapter 20. That is, commit processing within the context of transaction control and ACID principles applies to MMDBs; it is entirely conceivable that an application may determine that it must roll back operations within a transaction, thus recovering the consistent state of the database before the transaction began. With MMDBs, storage of the recovery log on disk would present a bottleneck that could significantly slow performance—the primary reason for implementing an MMDB environment in the first place. One alternative is to keep the primary log in a small amount of nonvolatile stable main memory, which is then posted periodically to disk, possibly by a special processor.[23] This will help alleviate log-based bottlenecks while still providing recovery and rollback mechanisms.

Other MMDB issues dictate differences in processing from disk-based environments. Because the processing speed is orders of magnitude faster than disk environments, even the most complex traditional transactions (*not* long-running transactions, as in OODBMS environments) will complete much more quickly in an MMDB than in a disk-based system. Therefore, locking requirements could conceivably be at the database level rather than at the finer levels of granularity typically needed when trying to improve traditional database multitransaction performance (e.g., table-, row-, or element-level locking). Basically, this will force transactions into a serialized mode of execution (that is, one transaction *really* executing after another, rather than having to ensure that serializability is emulated by the transaction processing model).[24]

Many other issues are pertinent to MMDBs: index structures, data representation, recovery algorithms, and so on. The interested reader is directed to a special issue of *IEEE Transactions on Knowledge and Data Engineering*[25] in which these subjects and example implementations are discussed at length over several papers.

22.6 Tertiary Storage

On the flip side of main memory databases we have databases stored on *tertiary storage*: tapes, optical disks, and other devices that follow offline or near-line access models. Given the ever-popular need to store terabytes of data for some environments, storing nonvolatile, sporadically used data on devices other than magnetic disks is often more cost-effective (as is main memory, for that matter, based on our discussion in the previous section). Archival data into tapes or optical devices is hardly new. What *is* new is the desire to put that information under the control of a database management system rather than a general file system.[26] Instead of having to bulk-load or selectively load desired data into a disk-based database and then perform database operations on that information, direct DBMS access to and control of such data objects is the desired goal.

To date, we have little DBMS technology to report in this area other than simple metadata management (e.g., recordings about where data objects are located and on what type of devices).[27] A great deal more research must be done.

In the previous section, we stated that MMDBs could in effect be considered as functional equivalents to disk-based DBMS environments (although transaction models and backup/recovery utilities would have to be adapted to them). This is not true for tertiary storage data, however; those devices cannot be treated as if they were just another disk system, chiefly because in most cases the devices themselves (tapes, optical disks) are not always on line.[28] Even when tape cartridge silos and optical disk jukeboxes are used for near-line storage, we still have fundamental differences in data availability when compared to disk systems. Further, as we know, tapes are not random access devices. Therefore, query processing and optimization techniques and algorithms must be adjusted to take into account the medium from which data is to be accessed, not just the format, organization, relationships, and all of the other individually complicated factors that go into query processing in databases.

Figure 22-2 illustrates the typical view of different levels of data storage, which is usually organized in a pyramid.[29] Unlike file system–based data movements among levels of the hierarchy, though, tertiary storage (the level

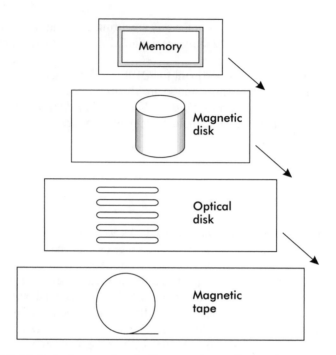

Figure 22-2 Multiple Storage Levels Organized as a Pyramid

below magnetic disk storage, regardless of whether tape, optical disk, or some other device type is used) does not have its data necessarily moved into disk before it is placed into memory, nor can data not found at a particular level be automatically searched for at the next lowest level (e.g., if it's not in memory, try the disk; if not there, try the tape).[30] Basically, the policies of the database environment itself will control the data media search patterns, as well as data migration.

Note that within tertiary storage, different devices may exist (e.g., tape and optical disk, as we've mentioned), as well as different classes within each device type (e.g., reel tape and cartridge tape). The storage architecture defines how data migrates from one level to another (e.g., permanent movement due to an event, such as for the next six months a particular data set will be frequently used in query processing), as well as caching policies (temporary copies of data at some other level).[31] Further, the data handling policies (how traditional DBMS functions are performed) must also be described within the overall multiple-storage-level framework.[32]

One possible specification calls for DDL extensions, conceptually similar to those we discussed for multiple-level security in database environments (see Chapter 21) and temporal databases (see Chapter 15), using those extensions to denote home storage devices, either explicitly or on a range-based partitioning model similar to distributed databases. Michael Stonebraker first proposed such extensions,[33] and the POSTGRES next-generation DBMS includes such capabilities.[34]

Key to understanding the problems and possible solutions of DBMS environments encompassing tertiary storage is to first analyze what types of applications are likely to require such multiple-level architectures. Michael Carey and Laura Haas of the University of Wisconsin and Miron Livay of IBM Almaden Research Center[35] are currently researching this area.

22.7 Design Models and CASE Tools

Another topic is the trends and future directions in database design and modeling techniques, as well as the CASE tools used to implement them.

Data modeling today shows a lack of agreement on which modeling techniques (extended entity-relationship [EER], binary-relationship, IDEF1x, object-oriented, and others) are most useful. This situation will continue, which is probably as it should be. Some people prefer EER, others favor object-oriented modeling, and users should be able to select whichever technique they feel comfortable with.

An increase in the use of object-oriented data modeling is likely, simply because of the expected growth in object-oriented database or object-extended relational database implementations. It makes sense to include the definition of methods and operations, inheritance, and other object-oriented capabilities in the model itself.

In the area of CASE support, the primary achievement throughout the rest of the 1990s will be the closer integration of data modeling tools with other design tools (e.g., data flow diagramming tools, object-oriented modelers, and so on) through enhanced repository capabilities (see Chapter 19) as well as CASE integration frameworks and environments. The stand-alone nature of modeling tools—indeed, tools at any of the life-cycle stages—will eventually fade away as more robust integration models and implementations come to market.[36]

22.8 Network Operating System Databases

Many PC-LAN environments are built around network operating systems (NOSs) such as Novell's NetWare. Prior to NetWare Version 3.11, complex, unwieldy client/server architectures were needed to run most DBMS products in Novell LAN environments; the DBMS server software could not run on the NetWare server due to operating system mismatches, and client requests to the DBMS server had to be routed through the NetWare server to the physical processor where the database server functions would occur. Further complicating the architecture were protocol mismatches between NetWare's IPX LAN protocol and the TCP/IP that would be necessary to communicate with the DBMS server.[37]

With an NLM architecture, the DBMS runs on NetWare as an extension of the network operating system itself, removing the need for protocol conversions and separate database server hardware. The upside to this configuration is that transaction throughput in the LAN environment is greatly improved over the kludge-like architecture discussed above. The downside includes the lack of a protected mode of operation (which makes crash analysis nearly impossible), preemptive job schedulers, and robust memory management.[38]

Despite these shortcomings, which are being overcome by the DBMS vendors, the NLM database market has grown dramatically, from an estimated 10,300 units in the 1991 installed base to an estimated 35,675 by 1992, a threefold increase.[39]

With the dramatic increase in recent years in the use of PC-LAN environments in corporate settings (as contrasted with small businesses), the trend toward network operating system DBMS servers is worth watching, not only for NLM systems but for other NOSs as well.

22.9 Conclusion

In this chapter, we've put the finishing touches on our discussion of the database and information management technology of tomorrow. From memory-resident databases to those encompassing tapes and optical devices, from nomadic, mobile data management requirements to new ways of benchmarking emerging information management models, the future of information management not only involves refinement of existing technologies but the emergence of new ones as well.

In our next and final chapter, we'll shift our focus on technology a bit, to discuss management and business issues relative to incorporating that technology into your organization.

Outlook

Short-term

- Research into mobile computing database requirements will provide guidance for commercial implementation
- Similarly, research into both main memory databases and tertiary storage requirements will continue

- More network operating system (NOS) versions of commercial DBMS products; note also that most of the same DBMS vendors are also introducing parallel database systems (see Chapter 5), indicating a tremendous amount of investment in research within those companies
- New benchmarks (e.g., TPC-D, TPC-E, 007, others) will be widely used for their respective areas

Long-term

- Commercially viable mobile computing database products, with hooks into corporate database environments, will be available
- Further research into the topics discussed in this chapter, as well as new information management subjects, will occur, and commercial products will appear in these areas

Additional Reading

- R. Alonso and H. Korth, "Database System Issues in Nomadic Computing," *Proceedings of the 1993 ACM SIGMOD.*
- M. J. Carey, L. M. Haas, and M. Livay, "Tapes Hold Data, Too: Challenges of Tuples on Tertiary Storage," *Proceedings of the 1993 ACM SIGMOD.*
- T. Imielinski and B. R. Badrinath, "Data Management for Mobile Computing," *ACM SIGMOD Record* (March 1993).
- M. A. Roth and S. J. Van Horn, "The Advantages of Data Compression," *Database Programming & Design* (July 1993).
- A. Simon, *The Integrated CASE Tools Handbook* (New York: Van Nostrand Reinhold/Intertext, 1993).
- M. Stonebraker, "Managing Persistent Objects in a Multi-Level Store," *Proceedings of the 1991 ACM SIGMOD.*

Endnotes

1. R. Alonso and H. Korth, "Database System Issues in Nomadic Computing," *Proceedings of the 1993 ACM SIGMOD,* 388.

2. Alonso and Korth, "Nomadic Computing."

3. Alonso and Korth, "Nomadic Computing."

4. Alonso and Korth, "Nomadic Computing," 389–392.

5. T. Imielinski and B. R. Badrinath, "Data Management for Mobile Computing," *ACM SIGMOD Record* (March 1993), 37.

6. Imielinski and Badrinath, "Data Management."

7. Imielinski and Badrinath, "Data Management," 38.

8. Imielinski and Badrinath, "Data Management." Mail-enabled applications are discussed in A. Simon, *Enterprise Computing* (New York: Bantam Books/Intertext, 1992), Chap. 3.

9. D. Richman, "Undeterred, TPC Approves Another Benchmark," *Open Systems Today* (July 5, 1993), 62.

10. Richman, "Another Benchmark."

11. Richman, "Another Benchmark."

12. Richman, "Another Benchmark."

13. D. Richman, "New OODBMS Test Suite Gets Nod," *Open Systems Today* (March 29, 1993), 3.

14. Richman, "New OODBMS Test Suite."

15. M. A. Roth and S. J. Van Horn, "The Advantages of Data Compression," *Database Programming & Design* (July 1993), 54.

16. Roth and Van Horn, "Data Compression," 58–59.

17. Roth and Van Horn, "Data Compression," 59.

18. Roth and Van Horn, "Data Compression," 60.

19. Roth and Van Horn, "Data Compression."

20. H. Garcia-Molina and K. Salem, "Main Memory Database Systems: An Overview," *IEEE Transactions on Knowledge and Data Engineering* (December 1992), 509.

21. Garcia-Molina and Salem, "Main Memory."

22. Garcia-Molina and Salem, "Main Memory."

23. Garcia-Molina and Salem, "Main Memory," 511.

24. Garcia-Molina and Salem, "Main Memory."

25. *IEEE Transactions on Knowledge and Data Engineering,* December 1992, 509–565.

26. M. J. Carey, L. M. Haas, and M. Livay, "Tapes Hold Data Too: Challenges of Tuples on Tertiary Storage," *Proceedings of the 1993 ACM SIGMOD,* 413.

27. Carey, Haas, and Livay, "Tapes Hold Data Too."

28. Carey, Haas, and Livay, "Tapes Hold Data Too."

29. Carey, Haas, and Livay, "Tapes Hold Data Too," 414.

30. Carey, Haas, and Livay, "Tapes Hold Data Too."

31. Carey, Haas, and Livay, "Tapes Hold Data Too."

32. Carey, Haas, and Livay, "Tapes Hold Data Too."

33. M. Stonebraker, "Managing Persistent Objects in a Multi-Level Store," *Proceedings of the 1991 ACM SIGMOD,* 2–11, cited in Carey, Haas, and Livay, "Tapes Hold Data Too," 415.

34. POSTGRES is described in M. Stonebraker and G. Kemnitz, "The POSTGRES Next-Generation Database Management System," *Communications of the ACM* (October 1991), 64–77. This particular issue of *Communications of the ACM* includes a special section on Next-Generation Database Systems, including the article describing the 1990 NSF Future Database Technology Workshop we discussed in section 1.6.3 of Chapter 1.

35. Carey, Haas, and Livay, "Tapes Hold Data Too," 417.

36. Integrated CASE environments are discussed in A. Simon, *The Integrated CASE Tools Handbook* (New York: Van Nostrand Reinhold/Intertext, 1993).

37. P. Korzeniowski, "NetWare Loadable Module DBMSs Sparking Debate," *Software Magazine Client/Server Computing Special Edition* (March 1993), 37.

38. Korzeniowski, "NetWare," 37–38.

39. Korzeniowski, "NetWare," 38. Cited from Forrester Research, Inc. study.

CHAPTER

Managerial and Business Issues

A Note to the CIO

Since you work in information systems, you know that technology does not stand by itself. In this final chapter, our discussion will take a turn toward the business side of the database and information management future, exploring in particular product and technology evaluation and migration/transition strategies.

Executive Summary

Discussions of future technology in databases and information management must be considered in the context of business needs. Business

23.1 Introduction

In this final chapter, we'll take a step back from our technology-focused discussions of the previous chapters and look at some business and managerial issues. These issues will be important as you attempt to make use of emerging database and information technology that is just becoming available, as well as in the future.

We'll first address the interrelationship of many of the disciplines we've discussed throughout the book, and then we'll help you determine which areas are most applicable to your particular environment. Finally, we'll take a brief look at strategies you can use to begin implementing new information management technology, despite the pressures you face in the continued maintenance of your legacy environments.

requirements determine what technologies are initially explored and eventually implemented on either small-scale or corporation-wide systems. Also, the process of incorporating those technologies into existing operational environments is extremely difficult.

Finally, claims of technical and business benefit, whether from researchers or from product vendors, should be *carefully* evaluated for accuracy.

23.2 Interrelationships of Information Management Disciplines

From the previous chapters it is clear that many—in fact most—of the information management technologies we've discussed are interrelated. The directions of the Xbase language and PC databases are intertwined with the use of middleware, such as ODBC and IDAPI, to decouple interfaces from the database engines. Triggers, an important addition to the SQL3 standard now under development (though, as we discussed in Chapter 12, triggers are already implemented in many commercial products), are critical for active databases and may be very useful in data warehouse environments. Advances in transaction processing are crucial for distributed multidatabase and other systems. Further, the overall trends we discussed in the first chapter, such as heterogeneity and distribution of resources, affect most areas of information management. In short, none of the subjects we discussed exists in a vacuum, whether we're looking at today's state of the art or where each subject is headed.

One view, which puts this interrelationship into context, is described by Jim Gray as "the great convergence."[1] His belief is that many of the areas we've discussed are converging into what might be termed a fourth-generation DBMS (4GDBMS). Interestingly, Jim Gray was one of the authors of the "Third-Generation Database Manifesto" which we discussed in section 1.6.1 of Chapter 1. As shown in Figure 23-1, advances in the following areas will lead to a 4GDBMS:

- Transaction processing
- Client/server computing
- Object-oriented computing
- Active databases
- SQL
- Distributed database technology

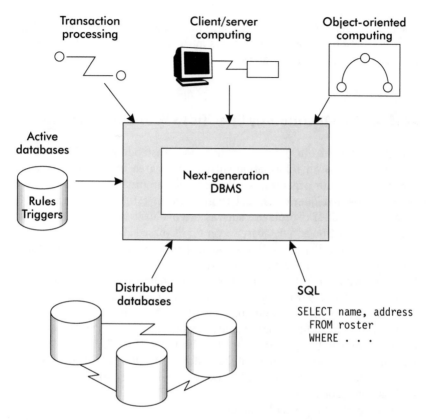

Figure 23-1 Jim Gray's "Great Convergence" of Information Management Technologies

We've already discussed the directions of each of these areas in earlier chapters. As a brief example of the interrelationships and interdependencies of the emerging technologies, consider the following:

- SQL3 will add triggers and abstract data types (ADTs), reinforcing the incorporation of relational databases with object-oriented capabilities.
- The triggers will play a key role in active databases.
- The ADTs will allow multimedia and geographical/spatial data to be stored within SQL databases.
- Services utilizing middleware standards based on SQL/CLI, such as IDAPI or ODBC, can be used by Xbase or Windows-based PC database applications to access remote or distributed multimedia and spatial data; other applications may use ODMG-93–specified languages such as OQL to access that same data.

The point to remember is that except in rare cases, future-oriented database and information management planners must track trends, standards efforts, and directions in numerous areas.

23.3 Utilize Technology Specific to Your Environment

Our discussion in the previous section notwithstanding, specific areas or directions within an information management area may be of particular importance to your organization. For example, an organization with a need for time-oriented queries should thoroughly investigate temporal DBMS products, regardless of problems such as lack of object-oriented extensions or inability to function as a database server for PC-based clients.

Or, sometime in the late 1990s, your organization may have a tremendous investment in C++ applications software with embedded SQL2 DML, and you feel that it's now time to add object-oriented database characteristics to your applications. Faced with a choice between using OML and OQL from ODMG-93, or SQL3 MOOSE syntax (discussed in Chapters 14 and 12, respectively) to achieve those capabilities, logic would probably dictate migrating those applications from SQL-92 support to the SQL MOOSE syntax. That would likely be a cleaner transition path than totally switching to ODMG-93 OML, particularly if your relational tables will be extended with object-oriented columns such as images or voice.

However, your particular application environment might have a clean demarcation between the relational data and the object-oriented information that will be incorporated, and an ODMG-93–type hierarchy is more appropriate than relational-oriented ADTs for your system. In that case, you may develop new subroutines with their own bindings to OODBMS servers compliant with ODMG-93, use OML for access to the object-oriented data, and present that to users separate from the relational-based data. Clearly, every information systems environment is different, and the path to incorporate new technologies will vary for each environment.

Some situations may be so critical to your particular environment that advances in that area override every other information management consideration. A crucial need for multilevel security, perhaps at the A1 level (see Chapter 21), that could be satisfied by some centralized DBMS product may override any desires for distribution, heterogeneity, and other properties that may be present in less secure database products. Therefore, focusing on the requirements of your information management environment and not just a wish list with standard entries of "distributed databases, object-oriented databases, and, oh yes, throw in some next-generation transaction processing, too" should form the basis on which advanced information management technology can be introduced to your environment.

23.4 Assessing Next-Generation Vendor Products and Research Advances

Let's briefly discuss the issue of assessing vendor and research claims in terms of capabilities and standards conformity, technology "breakthroughs," and similar statements you will likely encounter.

In Chapter 12, we discussed the three levels of SQL-92 compliance: Entry, Intermediate, and Full. Therefore, as you will soon investigate DBMS products to bring SQL-92 capabilities into your organization, vendor claims of "SQL-92 compliance" should be met with at least one question: What level of SQL-92? Similar questions should be asked of vendor claims of compliance with the X3J19 Xbase standard, OODBMSs based on the ODMG-93 standard, and so on.

Vendor claims of supporting "heterogeneous distributed database management" should be greeted with a barrage of questions about transaction management alternatives, what type of global model is supported, the degree of local autonomy, the underlying local data models, what middleware standards are supported, and so on.

Ideally, the process of discussing product features for new or greatly enhanced technology with vendors should be done in conjunction with your own thorough investigation of the principles and fundamentals of that technology (e.g., what characteristics should a multilevel secure DBMS have?) along with a comprehensive analysis of your information management needs. Appropriate investigation of vendors' products and their future directions can help determine the suitability of various products to your particular environment and its development.

Similar considerations apply to emerging technology from research communities, whether from the research labs of vendors or from the universities. One caveat (which is *not* meant to take anything away from the research accomplished at many fine institutions and labs): many research products don't have all of the real-world features needed for immediate implementation of prototypes or basic technology.

One way you can gauge research efforts is by reading the sections in papers that discuss future directions. Typically, authors of academic papers on prototype development or similar research will indicate areas needing further work, as well as corollary topics in which little or no research has been done. For example, you may be interested in some exciting research into hypertext, but your environment requires multilevel secure (MLS) information management. University researchers working on next-generation hypertext interfaces would not likely include MLS capabilities into a prototype (though, of course, it's always possible). This might be an opportunity for your organization to sponsor research into a hypertext/MLS combination, or you could utilize any available prototypes within your organization's own research arm, investigating the security properties important to specific applications you may have pending.

Whether you're assessing vendor or research products and developments, one thing is crucial: you must be as up-to-date as possible with all related aspects of information management, not just a narrow area in which you're interested. This principle extends outside of information management, of course: user interfaces, communications, and other service areas of information systems should be considered along with their interdependencies.

23.5 Getting from Here to There: Transitioning to New Information Management Technology

Throughout this book, we've discussed the emerging technology and future direction of information management and databases. "That's fine," you might be thinking, "But how can I concern myself with object-oriented databases, temporal databases, and future hypertext systems when my organization has 700 COBOL and network DBMS programs that are costing us $10 million a year just to maintain? It's hard enough just keeping these systems running and supporting users, let alone considering future-oriented technology. Maybe next year when the budget is better . . ."

These problems are difficult but not insurmountable. As information technology has evolved, possible solutions to the database transition problem have appeared in several forms.

One solution involves migration and conversion tools. Converting procedural code such as COBOL programs is not a trivial task, but it can be relatively simple, depending on the amount of redesign one wants to introduce into the transition process. Indeed, automated conversion tools began to appear in the 1980s that assisted users with conversion of procedural code.

This period also saw the emergence of tools that aided in the transition of the database component of applications. Some of these tools were straightforward, like the conversion of the table definitions and underlying data from one relational DBMS product to another. Others could assist with intermodel structural transformations, for example, to convert network DBMS structures to those of a relational product.

Another class of tools appeared, interoperability tools to aid the transition process at run-time (as compared with those discussed above, which operated on databases in a static environment). Recall our earlier discussion on the division of a centralized database environment among the data center and one or more departmental systems, which would often lead to data redundancy and the potential for inconsistent data. Interoperability tools are used to allow heterogeneous database environments to interact with one another. Initially, interoperability tools tended to be "extraction-oriented" in nature. That is, a department application with underlying DBMS A could extract information from a remote data center application that featured DBMS B. The extracted information could be downloaded into local structures and used during the course of application processing (Figure 23-2).

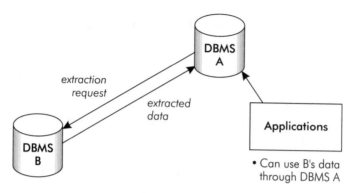

Figure 23-2 Database Extraction Scenario

Subsequent interoperability tools permitted update of remote database structures in addition to the extraction model. Through client/server middleware, as we discussed in Chapter 3, these capabilities can be extended to include some degree of standardization. The legacy systems (the existing databases), which add middleware server capabilities, may have their data accessible in a much easier manner than in the recent past.

So where do the capabilities of these tools lead us? It's one thing to say that tools can greatly aid the transition process. However, without a firm methodology and vision of the technical and managerial issues involved in the transition process, tools are relatively useless.

In general, you are likely to encounter three major classes of information management transitions. These classes are, from simplest to most complex:

- Same product
- Same database model, different product
- Different database models

23.5.1 Same-Product Transitioning

The simplest type of information management transition is accomplished within the boundaries of the same product in the source and target environments. By "same product," we typically mean the database or information management product is by the same vendor in your source and target environments but is typically a different release or version in each. For example, the following are examples of same product transitioning:

- ORACLE Version 6 to ORACLE7
- Rdb/VMS Version 4.x to Rdb/VMS Version 5.0

This might just sound like upgrades and not a true transition process, but the principles and guidelines discussed in this chapter do indeed apply to even these seemingly simple transitions. The following three actions and decisions apply to same-product transitions:

1. *New features:* New versions of an existing product often add features, such as
   - New data types
   - New data definition statements (such as new constraints)
   - New data manipulation statements
   - New functions
   - New (or modified) interfaces to other software subsystems such as transaction processing monitors or repositories
   - New tools and utilities

   The mere addition of SQL-92 capabilities to a new product version, or of standards-based Xbase to a new version of a PC DBMS, can be considered a major upgrade, worthy of implementing some sort of formal transition methodology.

2. *Deprecated features:* As new features are introduced, seldom-used features are sometimes deprecated, or "marked for elimination in a future version." Your applications may, however, make extensive use of such to-be-eliminated features, and you need to prepare for this change now while the feature is still supported.

3. *Advanced technology support:* A new version of a product may offer you first glimpses at support for advanced information management technology, such as ODBC or IDAPI interfaces. You may choose to implement these technologies as you transition from the old version to the new one.

23.5.2 Same Model, Different Product

Let's add a degree of complexity to our transition model. Assume that you currently operate a centralized environment featuring a relational DBMS, say product R. As part of your overall information system evolution strategy, you wish to implement some of your DBMS on another platform, one in which relational DBMS product X is supported but product R is not.

An interproduct transition introduces further complexity:

1. *Language incompatibilities:* As we discussed in Chapter 12, vendors typically provide extensions to "standard" languages such as SQL to differentiate their product from competitors. These extensions may be available in your source environment (DBMS product R) but not on product X in your target environment. Additionally, not all applications are developed using a host 3GL and SQL; some are built around forms managers or other visually oriented user interfaces, which may be DBMS-product-specific. Even if both products support SQL, you must consider other compatibility issues for your applications:

- *Binding style:* Whether the target product supports the same binding style (typically embedded SQL or module SQL) as the source product.
- *SQL support level:* As we mentioned in Chapter 12 and earlier, multiple levels of SQL may be supported by vendors (Entry, Intermediate, and Full).

Note that these language incompatibilities may be present in both the data definition language (DDL), which may force redefinition of data tables and columns, and the data manipulation language (DML), which could result in application redesign.

2. *User data conversion:* Products R and X are not likely to have the same underlying file and storage structures to maintain user data (and, for that matter, metadata). Therefore, some degree of conversion is usually necessary for data. In some cases, a direct product-to-product conversion utility may be available. In other cases, a load/unload mechanism through some other file structure may be necessary.

23.5.3 Intermodel Transition

Finally, let's look at one of the more perplexing problems in information management transition today, a problem that will only increase in the future.

Both same-model and intermodel transitions assume that the same information management model will be used in the target environment as in the source, whether the same vendor's products are used or not. In reality, many database transitions involve not only a movement to a new product, but a conversion from one information management model to another.

For example, as relational databases and their DBMS products grew to prominence in the 1980s, not all of the relational applications and the underlying databases that were developed were for "new" applications. Many applications took data structures and user data from a mainframe-based application that utilized a hierarchical or network DBMS and converted the metadata and data into a relational form. In these situations, all of the issues we discussed earlier (new, different, or absent features; language incompatibilities; user data conversion; and so on) were accompanied by a mandated redesign of the database structure itself. The physical linkages of hierarchical and network databases, together with such concepts as CODASYL sets, had to be fitted into a table-and-column structure.

Fortunately, the state of the art of intermodel schema conversion is much more advanced than it was in the mid-1980s, due to the growth in middleware products such as Information Builders, Inc.'s Enterprise Data Access/SQL (EDA/SQL), and widespread work in global schema representations as part of multidatabase environments. These intermodel mapping algorithms may be applied in a migration/transition manner, not just as part of a layered global schema approach.

Much more can be written about database transition, but it's beyond our scope here. One last item, though, is very important: datacentric transition does not exist in a vacuum; rather, it should be part of an overall transition program involving the appropriate networks, systems software, user interfaces, and other information system services. A transition program will most likely involve many or even all of these individual service areas, and no one service can be done in isolation. You can refer to several reference sources that describe in detail methodologies for pursuing transition programs.[2]

23.6 Conclusion

To close this book, let's look at a presentation by Michael Stonebraker at the June 1993 DCI Database World conference.[3] Stonebraker's presentation, entitled "Headache Replacement," was based on the premise that most of today's database and information systems problems will soon become irrelevant—only to be replaced by an entirely new set of problems.

These new problems include many of the topics we've discussed throughout this book: transitioning to new information systems environments (discussed in the previous section), decision support performance (discussed in the context of data warehouses in Chapter 4), database integration and impedence mismatches (discussed in Chapter 7), and the incorporation of OODBMSs into corporate data processing environments.

Particularly interesting, though, was Stonebraker's "non-problem," the fanatical pursuit of performance improvement for transaction processing environments. Stonebraker noted the tremendous amount of tuning, physical data placement, transaction processing monitor tuning, and other efforts that have traditionally constituted the solution for performance improvement. Because of two relatively recent developments, Joy's Law and RAID (both discussed next), Stonebraker contended that the solution to transaction processing performance no longer lies in the traditional methodology, but in fact has now become almost a given within the next two to three years.

23.6.1 Joy's Law

Joy's Law itself isn't exactly new; it was defined in 1984 by Bill Joy, and basically predicated that single-chip CPU performance would double every year. Over the next six years, this performance doubling wasn't quite achieved, despite the commercialization of RISC and advances in that area. However, the 1991 level of improvement over 1990 was more than double (30 MIPS maximum in 1990 on the MIPSCO RS3000 to 71 MIPS on Hewlett-Packard hardware), and a tremendous leap again occurred by 1992, reaching 175 MIPS on Digital Equipment's Alpha processor. In short, real-world performance is finally converging on the target numbers of Joy's Law; processors are getting faster, and will continue to do so.

23.6.2 RAID

The other half of the unanticipated solution, RAID, handles the storage side. Redundant Arrays of Independent Disks (RAID) use a large amount of inexpensive disks ($3\frac{1}{2}$-inch or $2\frac{1}{4}$-inch disks, with 1-inch disks on the horizon) as an alternative to traditional large-capacity disk drives.

The downside of these configurations is that system reliability decreases dramatically (e.g., with perhaps 75 $3\frac{1}{4}$-inch disks in a RAID, the first component failure will occur much sooner than with larger disks). However, the increase in the number of disk arms means that much more data may be accessed much more quickly.

To compensate for imminent failure, RAID configurations use a parity-like setup, with a bit used for "cross-disk parity." If a disk fails, the failed drive may be reconstructed from the "parity" bits plus the other data drives. Alternative parity handling methods are also available, such as striping the parity over all the drives.

Stonebraker claimed that because of the reconstruction capabilities of RAID configurations, the technology would evolve to a mean time between failures (MTBF) for a disk array of 500 years (at which time, he noted dryly, we should all be retired).

So we conclude that the combination of rapidly increasing processing power, coupled with much faster disk I/O as a result of including RAID configurations within an organization, will actually lead to an environment where throwing hardware at a transaction processing performance problem is the acceptable and desirable solution.

23.6.3 Future Challenges

While the specific technology Stonebraker addressed is interesting in itself, the process leading to the solution is more pertinent to the discussion of trends and future directions in information management. This particular example is indicative of a scattershot approach to database and information management; in fact, the solutions to problems often come from unexpected places. The answer to problems in corporate-wide decision support and executive information systems will likely be not from globally accessible schemas on top of operational databases but rather from periodically updated informational data warehouses. Externalizing procedures for distributed data management may turn out to be a superior solution for some organizations to transparently distributed databases. You can never tell what might come along that can make your computing and database management life easier.

Even within information management, solutions often come from unforeseen sources. In Chapter 21, we noted that multilevel security in databases causes the phenomenon of polyinstantiation, and that polyinstantiation is conceptually similar to multiple instances of tuples in temporal databases (although secure databases involve security classifications versus the time dimension in temporal models). Conceivably, the implementors of polyinstantiation could look to temporal databases for solutions in handling multiple instances of the same tuple, or vice versa. Probably many other areas exist where you can find a cross-discipline relationship within a future-oriented solution.

In conclusion, keep your eyes and ears open, not only for advances in areas that are of the greatest interest to you at the moment, but in corollary areas as well.

Outlook

Short-term and long-term

- "The Great Convergence" described in this chapter will drive the direction of many commercial products
- Today's problems will be solved, but new ones will arise; those will be solved, and yet more will surface
- Migration and transition methodologies will be well understood, allowing for fewer problems with transitions from source to target environments

Endnotes

1. J. Gray, "The Great Convergence," *Proceedings of DB Expo/93*, May 4, 1993, 175–190.

2. Sources for migration-oriented information include:

    A. Simon, *Systems Migration: A Complete Reference* (New York: Van Nostrand Reinhold/Intertext, 1992). A general methodology and migration/transition checklist.

    A. Simon and S. Shaffer, *Transitioning to Open Systems* (San Francisco: Morgan Kaufmann Publishers, forthcoming). Open systems-specific transitioning.

    M. Stonebraker and M. Brodie, *Migrating Legacy Systems: Gateways, Interfaces, and the Incremental Approach* (San Francisco: Morgan Kaufmann Publishers, in press). Methodologies and case studies dealing with legacy systems migration, focusing on the database realm.

3. M. Stonebraker, "Headache Replacement," *Proceedings of the DCI Database World Conference*, June 1993, E2-1–E2-47.

Index

A

abstract data types (ADTs)
in image information systems, 302
in object-oriented databases, 176–177
in SQL3, 419
abstraction, mediator support for, 117
access classes in Bell-LaPadula security
model, 376, 382
access control lists (ACLs) in
SD-DBMS, 387
access rules in text retrieval systems, 313
access views in SD-DBMS, 387
ACID properties in transaction
processing, 351
ACLs (access control lists) in SD-DBMS, 387
active databases, 279–280
and artificial intelligence, 280, 289–290
benefits of, 282–285
constraints and assertions in, 283–285
in data warehouses, 85–86
extensions for, 286–287
limitations of, 288–289
principles of, 280–286
production rules in, 289
in replication, 100–101
stored procedures in, 281–282, 285
transaction models for, 287–288
triggers in, 281–282, 285–286, 289
activity management in multidatabase
systems, 114
Ada language
for object-oriented databases, 153
SQL bindings for, 207
adjacency in spatial data, 295
AD/Platform, 335
ADTs (abstract data types)
in image information systems, 302
in object-oriented databases, 176–177
in SQL3, 419
AFTER INSERT trigger option (SQL), 213
AI (artificial intelligence)
and active databases, 280, 289–290

mediators as, 118
AIX operating system, 251–252
ALTER statement (SQL), 211
ALTER TABLE statement (SQL), 205
ANSI standards
for repositories, 335
for SQL, 200
for Xbase, 242–245
applications in MPP systems, 98
artificial intelligence (AI)
and active databases, 280, 289–290
mediators as, 118
assertions in active databases, 283–285
ASSIST mode (dBASE), 247
Asynchronous Transfer Mode (ATM), 306
ATIS (A Tools Integration Standard), 335
ATM machines, global schema for, 129–132
atomicity
in distributed repositories, 337
in transaction processing, 184, 186–187,
351–352
A Tools Integration Standard (ATIS), 335
attributes
conflicts in, 116
in multidatabase systems, 116
in navigational systems, 297–299
in object-oriented databases, 19, 149,
175–176
in ODMG-93 standard, 228
in repositories, 330
in temporal databases, 264–265
AUDITOR, SQL-92 standard for, 210
authentication in security, 373–375
authoring systems, 307
authorization in security, 373–374
automated conversion tools, 422
automatic index loading, 311
autonomy
in client/server computing, 60, 126–127
in distributed databases, 40
in multidatabase systems, 120

B

Bachman, Charles, 14, 28
backups, data compression for, 406
bandwidth for multimedia systems, 306
batch queries in MPP systems, 98
battery backups for main-memory
   databases, 407
BEFORE INSERT trigger option (SQL), 213
BEFORE UPDATE trigger option (SQL), 213
behavior of object-oriented database
   objects, 149
Bell-LaPadula security model, 376–383, 391
benchmark, 007, 405
benchmarking, 404–405
Ben-Zvi, Jacov, 263, 271
Bernstein, Philip, 330, 338–339, 342
best route solutions in navigational
   systems, 299
binary large objects (BLOBs), 162,
   249–250, 302
bindings
   in object-oriented databases, 172
   in ODMG-93 standard, 233–234
   in product transitions, 425
   in SQL-92 standard, 207
bitemporal databases, 263
BLOBs (binary large objects), 162,
   249–250, 302
Borland Object Component Architecture
   (BOCA), 63
bottom-up distributed database systems,
   47–52, 135
Brodie, Michael, 289
browsing distributed databases, 134
Bush, Vannevar, 317–318
business issues, 417–418
   interrelationships, 418–420
   product assessment, 421–422
   technology transitions, 422–426
   technology use, 420
business rules for active databases, 283

C

C language, SQL bindings for, 207
C++ language
   for object-oriented databases, 151, 153,
      164, 192
   in ODMG-93 standard, 226, 231–233

CAD (computer-aided design)
   object-oriented databases for, 144, 184
   relational databases for, 18
Call-Level Interface (CLI) standards, 63–65
CALL statement (SQL), 214
Camelot prototype transaction processing
   system, 358
Carey, Michael, 405, 411
CASE (computer-aided software
   engineering)
   object-oriented databases for, 144, 184
   relational databases for, 18
   repositories for, 333–334
   tools for, 411
CASE Data Interchange Format (CDIF)
   standard, 334
CASE...END CASE structure (SQL), 214
catalogs in IDAPI draft, 64
causality rule class in active databases,
   287–288
CDIF (CASE Data Interchange Format)
   standard, 334
CD-ROMs
   in document managers, 309
   in multimedia information systems, 304
Celko, Joe, 301
cellular communications, computing
   environments for, 401
centralized data warehouses, 80–81
chained transactions, 354–355
CHAIN WORK statement, 354–356
Chamberlin, Donald D., 198
CHANGES clause (SQL), 272
changing history in data warehouses, 82–83
CHECK clause (SQL), 215
check-in/check-out paradigm for
   repositories, 330, 338–339
checkpoints in transaction groups, 187
classes
   in object-oriented databases,
      150–151, 177
   in ODMG-93 standard, 226
   with SQL, 165
classifications
   in Bell-LaPadula security model, 376–377
   in MSQL, 389–390
   in object-oriented databases, 391
   of transaction processing systems,
      361–362

clearances in Bell-LaPadula security
    model, 376–377, 383
CLI (Call-Level Interface) standards, 63–65
client/server databases, 55–59
    autonomy in, 60, 126–127
    benefits of, 59
    in data warehouses, 83–84
    for distributed repositories, 336–337
    Encina support for, 358–359
    future of, 136–137
    guidelines for, 60–61
    standards for, 56, 58–59, 61–65
clustering in ODMG-93 standard, 233
COBOL language
    converting programs from, 422
    importance of, 246
    for object-oriented databases, 153–154
CODASYL (Conference on Data Systems
    Languages), 14, 20–21
Codd, E. F., 15–16, 18, 28
code reuse in object-oriented databases, 148
cold data in main-memory databases, 407
commit rule for nested transactions,
    355–356
COMMIT statement (SQL), 206
COMMIT WORK statement, 352–353
Common Object Request Broker
    Architecture (CORBA), 188–191
communications
    data compression for, 406
    in multimedia systems, 305–306
comparison operators in TSQL, 269
compatibility
    .DBF format for, 250
    in product transitions, 424
compensating transactions, 356
complexity issues in repository tools, 342
component document managers, 308,
    311–312
compression, data, 405–406
computational completeness in
    object-oriented databases, 172
computer-aided design (CAD)
    object-oriented databases for, 144, 184
    relational databases for, 18
computer-aided software engineering (CASE)
    object-oriented databases for, 144, 184
    relational databases for, 18
    repositories for, 333–334

tools for, 411
conceptual database design, 17
conceptual modeling, semantic data
    models for, 363
concurrency control
    in distributed repositories, 337
    in multidatabase systems, 120
    for replication, 100
    in text retrieval systems, 313
conditions in active databases, 289
Conference on Data Systems Languages
    (CODASYL), 14, 20–21
conflict resolution
    mediators for, 117–118
    in multidatabase systems, 115–117
    in transaction groups, 187
connectivity
    in client/server computing, 60
    demand for, 8
    vs. security, 388–389
    in spatial data, 295
consistency
    in object-oriented databases, 148
    in transaction processing, 351
constraints in active databases, 283–285
CONTAINS clause (HSQL), 271
context areas in text retrieval systems, 311
context management for repositories, 330
continuous operations in distributed
    databases, 40
control functions in repositories, 330
control statements, SQL3 standard for,
    214–215
cooperative transaction model, 184–188
CORBA (Common Object Request Broker
    Architecture), 188–191
core language in SQL3 standard, 218
cost reductions in object-oriented
    databases, 148
costs of security, 370
covert channels
    in SeaView database model, 380–382
    in security, 382–385
CREATE statement (SQL), 211
CREATE TABLE definitions, 208
cross-database integrity in multidatabase
    systems, 118–119
cross-disk parity with RAIDs, 427
CURRENT function (HSQL), 270

D

DAC (discretionary access control), 387, 389
database design in MPP systems, 98
database languages, 21. *See also* SQL
    language; Xbase language
  in client/server computing, 60
  compatibility of, 424
  for object-oriented databases, 151–154,
      164–166, 177–178, 192, 223–234,
      248–250
  and product transitions, 424
  for security, 389–391
  for temporal databases, 268–272
  for transaction processing, 362–363
database level in hypermedia, 321
database machines, 29
database management systems (DBMSs),
    4–8
database models, distribution and
    extended, 18
Data Base Task Group (DBTG), 14–15
data compression, 405–406
data conflicts in multidatabase systems,
    115–117
data conversions in product transitions, 425
data definition in IDAPI draft, 64
data definition language (DDL)
  in DBTG model, 14–15
  in MSQL, 389
  in product transitions, 425
data independence in multidatabase
    systems, 113
Data Language/I (DL/I), 13
data manipulation language (DML)
  in DBTG model, 14–15
  in IDAPI draft, 64
  in object-oriented databases, 150
  in product transitions, 425
data mining in next-generation
    databases, 26
data modeling, 17
data reorganization in MPP systems, 98
data types
  in object-oriented databases, 147, 150,
      173–174, 176
  in SQL3 standard, 217
  in SQL-92 standard, 206

in Third-Generation Data Base System
    Manifesto, 23
  in Xbase standard, 244
data volumes in navigational systems, 301
data warehouses, 71–72
  active databases in, 85–86
  benefits of, 75
  changing data in, 82–83
  client/server databases in, 83–84
  in digital libraries, 87
  distributed, 79–82
  hypermedia in, 322–323
  hypertext in, 86
  multiple media for, 77–78
  principles of, 72–77
  summarization in, 78–79
  vs. temporal databases, 259
  temporal databases in, 86–87
Date, C. J., 39
DATE data type, SQL-92 standard for, 206
Date's Rules for Distributed Databases,
    39–42
DB2 databases, 251–252
dBASE databases, 17
  ASSIST mode in, 247
  history of, 21, 199–200
  IDAPI support for, 63–64
  and Xbase, 238–240
.DBF file format, 250
DBMSs (database management systems),
    4–8
DBTG (Data Base Task Group), 14–15
DCE (Distributed Computing
    Environment), 357–360
DDBMSs (distributed database
    management systems), 39
DDBs. *See* distributed databases (DDBs)
DDL (data definition language)
  in DBTG model, 14–15
  in MSQL, 389
  in product transitions, 425
DDM (Distributed Data Management)
    Architecture, 62
decentralization, 6–8
decision support systems (DSSs), data
    warehouses for. *See* data warehouses
decoupled rule class in active databases,
    287–288

deferred rule class in active databases,
287–288
DEFINITION_SCHEMA
SQL3 standard for, 214
SQL-92 standard for, 208–210
delivery services and systems
in mobile computing environments, 404
in multimedia information systems,
305–306
Department of Defense security, 191,
370, 372
dependencies in multidatabase systems,
118–119
deprecated features in same-product
transitions, 424
derived relations in SD-DBMS, 387
designing distributed databases, 135
design models, 411
design transactions in object-oriented
databases, 173
DESTROY operator (OML), 233
DeWitt, David, 405
diagnostics in IDAPI draft, 65
digital libraries, data warehouses in, 87
directory information services in mobile
computing environments, 404
discretionary access control (DAC), 387, 389
disk-based processing model, 12–13
disks
in document management, 309
optical, 309, 409–410
in parallel systems, 93
Distributed Computing Environment
(DCE), 357–360
distributed database management systems
(DDBMSs), 39
distributed databases (DDBs), 37–39
browsing, 134
client/server, 55–65
data warehouses in. *See* data warehouses
definition and characteristics of, 39–42
designing, 135
four-phase approach toward, 42
future of, 123–137
gateways in, 66–67
global transparency in, 125–132
heterogeneous, 27, 46–47, 105, 134
homogeneous, 46–47

middleware in, 65
models of, 18, 45–52, 125–132
MPP systems in, 132–133
multidatabase systems, 107–119
partitioning in, 47–51, 89–99
promising areas for, 136–137
query processing in, 40, 135–136
replication in, 40, 51, 99–101
requirements for, 44–45
scalability of, 134–135
security in, 134, 385–389
semantic inconsistency in, 133–134
taxonomy of, 106–111
top-down vs. bottom-up, 47–52
transaction processing in, 41, 135
uses for, 43–45
Distributed Data Management (DDM)
Architecture, 62
distributed data warehouses, 79–82
distributed query processing in mobile
computing environments, 402
Distributed Relational Database
Architecture (DRDA), 61–62,
79–80, 84, 251
distributed repositories, 336–340
distribution
of information management systems, 6–8
in knowledge-base management
systems, 290
in object-oriented databases, 173
DL/I (Data Language/I), 13
DML (data manipulation language)
in DBTG model, 14–15
in IDAPI draft, 64
in object-oriented databases, 150
in product transitions, 425
document check-in in text retrieval
systems, 310
document loading in text retrieval
systems, 312
document management systems, 307–310
component document management in,
311–312
document check-in in, 310
future of, 312–313
hypermedia in, 325
indexes for, 308, 310–311
index loading in, 311

domains, SQL-92 standard for, 205–206
downsizing of information management
    systems, 6–7
DRDA (Distributed Relational Database
    Architecture), 61–62, 79–80, 84, 251
drill-down analyses for data warehouses,
    74, 78–79
DROP statement (SQL), 211
DROP TABLE statement (SQL), 205
duplication of data
    in file-oriented processing model, 12–13
    in hierarchical databases, 14
durability in transaction processing, 351

E

effective time in temporal databases, 263
ELAPSEDMONTHS function (HSQL), 270
ELAPSEDYEARS function (HSQL), 270
encapsulation
    in multidatabase systems, 114
    in object-oriented databases, 147–148
    in Third-Generation Data Base System
        Manifesto, 24
Encina transaction processing monitor,
    357–360
end-user tools in client/server computing, 60
energy management in mobile computing
    environments, 404
engineered artifacts in repositories, 330
entry SQL level, 203
Event-Condition-Action rules for active
    databases, 286–287
events
    in active databases, 289
    in data warehouses, 85–86
    in HSQL, 270
exception lists in text retrieval systems, 311
EXCEPTION statement (SQL), 214
execution skew in partitioning, 96
executive management systems (EISs),
    data warehouses for. *See* data
    warehouses
expressions
    in ODMG-93 queries, 230–231
    in TempSQL, 268–269
extended database models, 18
extended relations forms of object-oriented
    databases, 159–165

extended transactions in transaction
    processing, 364
extensibility
    in object-oriented databases, 172
    of repositories, 331–332, 342
    in transaction processing, 364
extension flaggers in SQL standards, 219
extents in object-oriented databases, 176

F

failure handling
    in main-memory databases, 407–408
    in mobile computing environments, 403
FAP (formats and protocol) specifica-
    tions, 61
FD:OCA architecture, 62
federated databases, 110–111
file formats, 250
file-oriented processing model, 11
file systems, 4
filtering in multidatabase systems, 114
first generation databases, 23
first generation transaction processing
    systems, 349–350
flat files, 4
flat transactions, 351–352
FOR...END FOR structure (SQL), 215
formats, file, 250
formats and protocol (FAP) specifica-
    tions, 61
FORTRAN language, 153–154
fragmentation independence in distributed
    databases, 40
FROMTIME...TOTIME clause (HSQL), 271
full SQL level, 204
full-text retrieval models, 311–312
functions
    in HSQL, 270–271
    in SQL-92 standard, 207–208
    in Third-Generation Data Base System
        Manifesto, 24

G

gateways in distributed databases, 66–67
generalization, mediator support for, 117
geobases, 301
geographic information systems (GISs), 296
geometrical information. *See* spatial data

global queries in multidatabase systems, 120
global schema
    in distributed database systems, 49–50
    in multidatabases, 109–112
global scoping in Xbase standard, 245
global transparency, pros and cons of,
        125–132
GRANT statement (SQL), 210, 389
granularity
    in navigational systems, 302
    in repositories, 340–342
graphical user interfaces (GUIs)
    future of, 248–249
    history of, 246–247
    with hypermedia, 319
    for real-world modeling, 9
Gray, Jim, 125, 354–355, 418–419
great convergence, 418–419

H

Haas, Laura, 411
HAM (hypertext abstract machine) level,
        320, 322–323
hardware independence in distributed
        databases, 41
hashing partitioning in MPP systems, 95–97
HBX (hybrid index) structures in MPP
        systems, 97
HDBMS, 267–268
heterogeneity in information management
        systems, 7–8
heterogeneous distributed database
        systems, 46–47, 105
    National Science Foundation Workshop
        on, 27
    standards in, 119
hierarchies
    in Bell-LaPadula security model, 376–377
    in databases, 13–15
    in object-oriented database classes,
        150–151
HIGHEST-CLASS function (MSQL), 390
Historical Data Model, 270
history changing in data warehouses, 82–83
HISTORY function (HSQL), 270
homogeneous database systems, 46–47, 111
horizontal partitioning
    in distributed database systems, 48–49

standards for, 209
host languages in client/server computing, 60
hot data in main-memory databases, 407
HSQL language, 270–271
hybrid forms of object-oriented databases,
        158–164
hybrid index (HBX) structures in MPP
        systems, 97
HyperCard, 20–21, 318
hypermedia, 20–21, 317–318
    architecture of, 320–322
    benefits of, 319
    definition of, 318–319
    future of, 324–325
    in information management systems,
        322–324
    in multimedia systems, 305–306
hypertext, 4, 20–21, 317–318
    in data warehouses, 86
    definition of, 318–319
hypertext abstract machine (HAM) level,
        320, 322–323

I

IDAPI (Integrated Database Application
        Programming Interface), 63–65, 67, 84
identifiers
    for security, 375
    in Third-Generation Data Base System
        Manifesto, 24
identity of object-oriented database objects,
        149, 177
IDS (Integrated Data Store) DBMS, 14
IF...END IF structure (SQL), 214
image information systems, 302–304
immediate rule class in active databases,
        287–288
impact analyses, repositories for, 341
implementation issues
    in active databases, 289
    in object-oriented databases, 176
    in SQL-92 standard, 204–205
    in Third-Generation Data Base System
        Manifesto, 25
IMS (Information Management System), 13
IMSs. See information management
        systems (IMSs)
inconsistency, semantic, 133–134

incorrect-entry data conflicts in
multidatabase systems, 116
independence
in client/server computing, 60
in distributed databases, 40–41
in knowledge-base management
systems, 290
in multidatabase systems, 113
in repositories, 331–332, 335
indexes
for MPP systems, 97
for temporal databases, 275
for text retrieval systems, 308,
310–311, 313
inferences
in object-oriented databases, 173
in security, 392–393
in Xbase standard, 244
informational applications, 304–305
information filtering in multidatabase
systems, 114
information highways, data warehouses
in, 87
Information Management System (IMS), 13
information management systems (IMSs),
4–6
client/server computing in, 56–57
database languages in, 21
distribution and decentralization of, 6–8,
18, 38
extended database models, 18
heterogeneity in, 7–8
hierarchical and network databases,
13–15
hypertext and hypermedia, 20–21, 322–324
interrelationships in, 418–420
and multimedia systems, 305–306
object-oriented databases, 18–20
pre-DBMS, 11–13
real-world modeling in, 9
relational model in, 15–17
service areas in, 9–10
standards in, 8
Information Resource Dictionary System
(IRDS), 334
Information Schema
SQL3 standard for, 214
SQL-92 standard for, 208–210

Information Warehouse architecture, 62, 79
inheritance
in object-oriented databases, 19, 144,
150, 172–173
in ODMG-93 queries, 230
in Third-Generation Data Base System
Manifesto, 24
IN INTERVAL clause (HSQL), 271
instance-variable labels in SODA, 391
Integrated Database Application
Programming Interface (IDAPI),
63–65, 67, 84
Integrated Data Store (IDS) DBMS, 14
integration
in data warehouses, 75–76
mediator support for, 117
integrity in multidatabase systems, 118–119
intelligent databases. See active databases
interactive commands in Xbase standard, 244
InterBase Parallel Language (IPL), 362–363
interchangeability in client/server
computing, 57–59
interdependence
in multidatabase systems, 118–119
in next-generation databases, 26
interfaces
for document managers, 308–309
in hypermedia, 320
hypermedia as, 319
in mobile computing environments,
403–404
in multimedia information systems,
305–306
in object-oriented databases, 176
in ODMG-93 standard, 226, 228–229
for repositories, 334
in text retrieval systems, 313
interim results, mediator support for, 117
intermediate SQL level, 204
intermodel transitions, 425–426
International Standards Organization
(ISO) standards
for RDA, 61
for SQL, 200
for transaction processing, 360–361
interoperability
demand for, 8
gateways for, 66–67

in information management systems, 10
middleware for, 65
in multidatabase systems, 111, 113–114
tools for, 422–423
intersection of pointers in text retrieval
   systems, 310
inverted list data structures in text
   retrieval systems, 310
IPL (InterBase Parallel Language), 362–363
IRDS (Information Resource Dictionary
   System), 334
ISO (International Standards
   Organization) standards
   for RDA, 61
   for SQL, 200
   for transaction processing, 360–361
isolation in transaction processing, 351

J

Jajodia, Sushil, 370, 379, 394
Joint Photographics Expert Group (JPEG)
   standard, 307
Joy, Bill, 426
Joy's Law, 426–427

K

KBMSs (knowledge-base management
   systems), 289–290
keywords in text retrieval systems, 311
Kim, W., on multidatabase conflicts, 116
knowledge bases, 289

L

labels in SODA, 391
languages. *See* database languages; SQL
   language; Xbase language
laptop computing environments, 400–404
late binding in object-oriented databases, 172
layered approach in transaction processing,
   358–359
LEAVE statement (SQL), 215
Leff, A., 361
legacy systems, 4–5
levels
   in Bell-LaPadula security model,
   376–377
   in SQL3 standard, 217

in SQL-92 standard, 203–204
in Xbase standard, 243
lifetimes of object-oriented database
   objects, 177
lifespans in temporal databases, 264–265
links
   for distributed repositories, 339–341
   in hypermedia, 319
Livay, Miron, 411
live data access in client/server
   computing, 60
local prototyping in client/server
   computing, 60
local scoping in Xbase standard, 245
location autonomy
   in client/server computing, 126–127
   in distributed databases, 40
location independence in distributed
   databases, 40
location mapping, mediator support
   for, 118
locking requirements in main-memory
   databases, 408
logs for main-memory databases, 408
LOOP...END LOOP structure (SQL), 215
LTRIM function (ORACLE7), 207
Lunt, Teresa, 392

M

Macintosh systems, databases for, 241–242
magnetic tapes, 11, 409–410
mail-enabled applications in mobile
   computing environments, 404
main-memory databases (MMDBs), 407–409
Major Object-Oriented SQL Extensions
   (MOOSE), 164
   ODMG-93 mappings to, 226
   in SQL3 standard, 216–217
managerial issues, 417–418
   interrelationships, 418–420
   product assessment, 421–422
   technology transitions, 422–426
   technology use, 420
mandatory characteristics of
   object-oriented databases, 171–172
mapping, mediator support for, 118
maps and navigational systems, 296–302
MARKMODIFIED operator (OML), 233

massively parallel processing (MPP)
architectures, 89
benefits of, 91–92
concepts in, 90–94
future of, 98–99, 132–133, 136–137
in object-oriented databases, 188
partitioning in, 50–51, 90–99
relational operators and index structures
in, 97
security for, 393
mass load model for data warehouses, 76
master files
in disk-based processing model, 12–13
in file-oriented processing model, 11–12
McGoveran, David, 124
media for data warehouses, 77–78
mediators in multidatabase systems,
117–118
MEMory Extender (Memex) system,
317–318
memory in parallel systems, 92–93
metadata, 5
data compression for, 406
for data warehouses, 81
managing. *See* repositories
SQL-92 standard for, 208–210
in temporal databases, 272–274
tertiary storage for, 409
metamiddleware, 67
methods
with object-oriented database objects,
149–150, 177
with object request brokers, 190
with SQL, 165
metric relations in spatial data, 295
MHEG (Multimedia and Hypermedia
Information Coding Expert Group)
standard, 307
middleware, 57, 65, 67
in document management, 308–309
for intermodel transitions, 425
for interrelationships, 419
migration tools, 422
minicomputers, relational databases on,
16–17
mismatch resolution in multidatabase
systems, 115–117
MMDBs (main-memory databases),
407–409

mobile computing environments, 400–404
modeling, real-world, 9
modularity in Xbase standard, 244–245
monitoring facilities
in active databases, 281–282
for transaction processing, 363–364
MONTHS function (HSQL), 271
MOOSE (Major Object-Oriented SQL
Extensions), 164
ODMG-93 mappings to, 226
in SQL3 standard, 216–217
Moss, Elliot, 354–356
Moving Picture Coding Expert Group
(MPEG) standard, 307
MPC (Multimedia PC) standard, 307
MPP. *See* massively parallel processing
(MPP) architectures
MSQL (Multilevel SQL) language, 389–390
multidatabase systems, 107–111
conceptual architecture of, 111–113
conflict resolution in, 115–117
cross-database integrity in, 118–119
database services in, 113–114
mediators in, 117–118
problems and issues in, 119–120
multilevel security, 375–379, 386–389,
391–393
inferences in, 393
Multilevel SQL (MSQL) language, 389–390
multilevel transactions, 356
multimedia, 304–305. *See also* hypermedia
architecture of, 305–307
in next-generation databases, 26
scripting systems for, 307
standards for, 307
Multimedia and Hypermedia Information
Coding Expert Group (MHEG)
standard, 307
Multimedia PC (MPC) standard, 307
multiple inheritance, 172–173
multiple sources in text retrieval
systems, 313
MUMPS language, SQL bindings for, 207

N

NATIONAL CHARACTER strings, 206
National Science Foundation Workshop,
25–27

Naughton, Jeffrey, 405
NAV/CLI component, 64
navigational systems, 296–302
navigation in Third-Generation Data Base
    System Manifesto, 25
nested transactions, 354–360
network databases, 13–15
network independence in distributed
    databases, 41
network operating system (NOS)
    databases, 411–412
new features in same-product transitions,
    424
NEW statement (SQL), 214
next-generation databases, workshop on,
    26–27
Nielsen, Jakob, 324
nomadic computing environments, 400–404
nonvolatility of data warehouses, 73, 76
normalization in database design, 17
NOS (network operating system)
    databases, 411–412
notification servers for repositories, 334

O

Object Database API (ODAPI), 63
Object Database Management Group
    (ODMG), 170, 174–175.
    See also ODMG-93 standard
object definition language (ODL)
    for object-oriented databases, 178
    in ODMG-93 standard, 225–229, 231–232
object IDs (OIDs) in object-oriented
    databases, 149, 177
object labels in SODA, 391
object manipulation language (OML)
    for object-oriented databases, 177
    in ODMG-93 standard, 232–233
object-oriented database management
    systems (OODBMSs), 19, 141–142,
    150–153
object-oriented databases (OODBs), 18–20,
    28, 141–142
    attributes in, 19, 149, 175–176
    benefits of, 143–146
    characteristics of, 142–148, 171–174
    classes in, 150–151, 177
    development methodology in, 152–153

engines and models for, 169–178
future of, 192–193
hybrid and extended relational forms of,
    157–166
inheritance in, 19, 144, 150, 172–173
languages for, 151–154, 164–166,
    177–178, 192, 223–234, 248–250
methods in, 149–150, 177
object identity in, 149, 177
object request brokers in, 188–191
persistence in, 150–152
for real-world modeling, 9
security in, 191, 390–392
standards for, 169–170, 174–178,
    224–225
temporal, 274–275
transactions in, 173, 184–188
Object-Oriented Database System
    Manifesto, 25, 170–174
object query language (OQL)
    for object-oriented databases, 178
    in ODMG-93 standard, 229–232
object request brokers (ORBs), 66–67, 114,
    188–191
objects
    in Bell-LaPadula security model, 376
    in navigational systems, 297–299
obsolete data in multidatabase systems, 116
OCR (optical character recognition), 310
ODAPI (Object Database API), 63
ODBC (Open Database Connectivity),
    63–65, 67, 83–84
ODL (object definition language)
    for object-oriented databases, 178
    in ODMG-93 standard, 225–229, 231–232
ODMG (Object Database Management
    Group), 170, 174–175
ODMG-93 standard
    benefits of, 225
    C++ with, 231–233
    object definition language in, 225–229,
    231–232
    object manipulation language in,
    232–233
    object query language in, 229–232
    principles in, 224–225
    Smalltalk with, 234
OLTP queries in MPP systems, 98

OML (object manipulation language)
for object-oriented databases, 177
in ODMG-93 standard, 232–233
online loading in document management
systems, 310
online utilities in MPP systems, 98
OODBMSs (object-oriented database
management systems), 19, 141–142,
150–153
OODBs. *See* object-oriented databases
(OODBs)
Open Database Connectivity (ODBC),
63–65, 67, 83–84
open features of object-oriented databases,
173–174
open-host languages in client/server
computing, 60
Open Systems Environment Application
Portability Profile (OSE/1 APP)
reference model, 10
open systems in Third-Generation Data
Base System Manifesto, 24–25
open transaction processing, 359
operating system independence in
distributed databases, 41
operational semantics in security, 392
operations
in distributed databases, 40
for object-oriented database objects, 147,
149–150
in ODMG-93 standard, 228
optical character recognition (OCR), 310
optical disks, 309, 409–410
optimized queries
in distributed databases, 136
in MPP systems, 98
optional characteristics of object-oriented
databases, 172–173
OQL (object query language)
for object-oriented databases, 178
in ODMG-93 standard, 229–232
ORACLE database manager, 198
Orange Book, 372
ORBs (object request brokers), 66–67, 114,
188–191
order in spatial data, 295
OS/2 operating system, 251–252
OSI-CCR standard, 360

OSI-TP standard, 360
Öszu, M. Tamer, 125, 135
overriding features in object-oriented
databases, 172
ownership in text retrieval systems, 313

P

packages in SQL3 standard, 218
palmtop computing environments,
400–404
Paradox database manager, 240–241
parallel database systems, 89
benefits of, 91–92
concepts in, 90–94
future of, 98–99, 132–133, 136–137
in object-oriented databases, 188
partitioning in, 50–51, 90–99
relational operators and index structures
in, 97
security for, 393
parallelism
models of, 92
in next-generation databases, 27
in object-oriented databases, 188
parallel queries in MPP systems, 98
parametric data and spatial data, 295
parity with RAIDs, 427
partitioned parallelism, 92
partitioning, 89–90
in distributed database systems, 47–51
in distributed repositories, 337
models for, 94–97
in MPP systems, 90–94, 97–99
standard for, 209
passwords in security, 375
patterns
in active databases, 289
in image information systems, 302
in transaction groups, 187
PCTE (Portable Common Tool
Environment), 335
performance with data compression, 406
persistence in object-oriented databases,
150–152
persistent savepoints in transaction
processing, 354
personal computers, relational databases
on, 16–17

personal digital assistants, computing environments for, 400–404
physical pointers in hierarchical databases, 14–15
pipelined parallelism, 92
plug and play model, 57
pointers
  in hierarchical databases, 14–15
  in text retrieval systems, 310
points. *See* spatial data
polyinstantiation in security, 379–382, 391
polytransactions in multidatabase systems, 118–119
portability
  in client/server computing, 57–59
  in object-oriented databases, 175
Portable Common Tool Environment (PCTE), 335
POSTGRES system, 287
PRED function (HSQL), 271
predicates in active databases, 289
presentation level in hypermedia, 320
primary keys in MSQL, 389–390
private scoping in Xbase standard, 245
privileges, SQL-92 standard for, 210–211
procedures
  for object-oriented database objects, 149–150
  in replication, 100
  SQL3 standard for, 214–215
production rules in active databases, 289
products
  assessing, 421–422
  changes in, 422–425
programming. *See also* database languages
  in multimedia information systems, 307
  in object-oriented databases, 173
properties. *See* attributes
protection. *See* security
prototyping in client/server computing, 60
pseudo-nested transactions, 356–357
Pu, Calton, 361
public scoping in Xbase standard, 245
PUBLIC statement (SQL), 211

Q

QUEL language, 21, 200
queries
  in distributed databases, 40, 135–136
  in mobile computing environments, 402
  in MPP systems, 98
  in multidatabase systems, 114, 120
  in navigational systems, 301–302
  in ODMG-93 standard, 229–231
  temporal. *See* temporal databases

R

RAIDs (Redundant Arrays of Independent Disks), 427
range partitioning in MPP systems, 95–96
RDA (Remote Database Access) specification, 61
Rdb/VMS language, 200
real-time requirements in navigational systems, 299–301
real-world modeling, 9
records in relational databases, 16
recovery
  data compression for, 406
  in main-memory databases, 408
  in mobile computing environments, 403
RECURSIVE UNION statement (SQL), 214
Redundant Arrays of Independent Disks (RAIDs), 427
reference models in information management systems, 10
referential integrity in multidatabase systems, 118–119
registration time in temporal databases, 263
relational calculus, 21
relational model, 15–17
relational operators in MPP systems, 97
relations
  in ODMG-93 standard, 228, 233
  in relational databases, 16
  in spatial data, 295
  temporal. *See* temporal databases
reliability with RAIDs, 427
Remote Database Access (RDA) specification, 61
Remote Operations Service (ROSE) protocol, 361
remote requests in distributed databases, 42
remote units of work in distributed databases, 42

repetition of data
  in file-oriented processing model, 12–13
  in hierarchical databases, 14
replication, 90
  in distributed database systems, 40, 51,
    99–101
  in distributed repositories, 337–338
repositories, 329–330
  benefits of, 332
  distributed, 336–340
  granularity issues for, 340–342
  hypermedia in, 323–324
  principles of, 330–334
  standards for, 334–336
  tools for, 323–324, 333–334, 342–343
representation independence in
    knowledge-base management
    systems, 290
representation systems in object-oriented
    databases, 173, 177
requests in distributed databases, 42
requirements traceability, repositories
    for, 341
research assessment, 421–422
RESIGNAL statement (SQL), 215
resources
  in IDAPI draft, 64
  sharing, in parallel systems, 92–94
retrospective updates in HSQL, 271
RETURN statement (SQL), 214
reusing code in object-oriented
    databases, 148
Reuter, A., 354–355
REVOKE statement (SQL), 210–211, 389
rollback rule for nested transactions, 356
rollbacks. See transactions and transaction
    processing (TP)
ROLLBACK statement (SQL), 206
ROSE (Remote Operations Service)
    protocol, 361
round-robin partitioning in MPP systems,
    95–97
RTRIM function (ORACLE7), 207
rules
  for active databases, 283, 286–289
  for nested transactions, 355–356
  in next-generation databases, 27
  in text retrieval systems, 313

  in Third-Generation Data Base System
    Manifesto, 24
running at system high model, 375

S

SAA (Systems Applications Architecture), 62
SAG (SQL Access Group), 61–65
same-product transitions, 423–424
Sandhu, Ravi, 379
savepoints in transaction processing, 216,
    352–354, 356
scalability
  of distributed databases, 134–135
  of global transparency, 128–129
  of MPP systems, 90
  in next-generation databases, 27
  of transaction processing, 364
schemas
  in distributed database systems, 107
  in IDAPI draft, 64
schematic conflicts in multidatabase
    systems, 115–116
scoping in Xbase standard, 245
scripting systems, 307
SD-DBMS program, 387
search criteria in text retrieval systems, 311
SeaView database model, 379–382
second generation databases, 23
second generation transaction processing
    systems, 349–350
Secure Object-Oriented Database
    (SODA), 391
security, 369–373
  benefits of, 371–372
  covert channels in, 382–385
  in distributed databases, 134, 385–389
  future of, 392–394
  languages for, 389–391
  in mobile computing environments, 403
  model of, 373–375
  in multidatabase systems, 120
  multilevel, 375–379, 386–389, 391–393
  in object-oriented databases, 191,
    390–392
  polyinstantiation in, 379–382, 391
  SQL-92 standard for, 210–212
  in text retrieval systems, 313
  in transaction processing, 364

segments in hierarchical databases, 14
SELECT statement (SQL), temporal
    extensions for, 272
self-learning databases. *See* active databases
semantic loss and inconsistency
    in distributed databases, 133–134
    in object-oriented databases, 145–147
    in traditional databases, 142–145
    in transaction groups, 187
semantic modeling, 18, 363
semantics for security, 392
Seo, J., 116
SEQUEL language, 198
servers. *See also* client/server databases
    autonomy of, 60
    IDAPI support for, 63–64
    independence of, 60
service areas, 9–10
SET statement (SQL), 214
SFQL (Structured Full-Text Query
    Language), 218
SGML (Standard Generalized Markup
    Language), 311–312
shared properties in repositories, 330
shared resources
    in knowledge-base management
        systems, 290
    in parallel systems, 92–94
SIGNAL statement (SQL), 215
simple security property in Bell-LaPadula
    model, 377
site autonomy in multidatabase
    systems, 120
skewing in partitioning, 96
Smalltalk language
    for object-oriented databases, 151, 153,
        164, 192
    in ODMG-93 standard, 226, 234
SMDS (Switched Multimegabit Data
    Service), 306
SODA (Secure Object-Oriented
    Database), 391
spatial data, 293–295
    in multimedia information systems, 306
    navigational systems, 296–302
    principles of, 295–302
spatial reasoning in image information
    systems, 303

SQL2 standard, 201
SQL3 standard, 201, 212–213
    issues in, 217–218
    MOOSE in, 216–217
    ODMG-93 mappings to, 226
    relation-like database concepts in,
        213–216
    savepoints in, 356
    triggers and ADTs in, 419
SQL-92 standard, 202–203
    implementation issues in, 204–205
    language features in, 205–212
    leveling in, 203–204
SQL Access Group (SAG), 61–65
SQL/DS product, 198
SQL language, 21, 197
    benefits of, 200–201
    history of, 198–203
    with object-oriented database
        languages, 165
    in product transitions, 425
    pseudo-nested transactions in, 356–357
    SQL3 standard for, 212–219
    SQL-92 standard for, 203–212
    in Third-Generation Data Base System
        Manifesto, 24–25
SQL MM standard, 218
SQL/SE model, 274
SQLSTATE status code, 206
stackware, 318
Standard Generalized Markup Language
    (SGML), 311–312
standards
    for client/server databases, 56, 58–59,
        61–65
    for heterogeneous distributed
        databases, 119
    for information management systems, 8
    for middleware, 65
    for multimedia information systems, 307
    for object-oriented databases, 169–170,
        174–178, 224–225
    for repositories, 334–336
    for SQL, 198–219
    for Temporal SQL, 272
    for transaction processing, 135, 360–361
    for Xbase, 240–246
Starburst system, 287

statements in IDAPI draft, 64
states of object-oriented database objects, 149
state transitions in active databases, 287
static optimization of distributed database
  queries, 136
status parameters, SQL-92 standard for, 206
Stonebraker, Michael
  on database debate, 28
  on future problems, 426–427
  on parallel systems, 92–93
  on SQL and object-oriented databases, 216
  on tertiary storage, 410
  on uncertainty, 29
storage
  for multimedia information systems, 306
  in next-generation databases, 26
  for repositories, 342
  tertiary, 27, 409–411
stored procedures
  in active databases, 281–282, 285
  in replication, 100
  in repositories, 334
striping parity with RAIDs, 427
Structured Full-Text Query Language
  (SFQL), 218
subject orientation of data warehouses,
  73, 75
subjects in Bell-LaPadula security model,
  376–377
subroutines in Xbase standard, 244–245
subtasks in transaction groups, 186
SUCC function (HSQL), 271
summarization in data warehouses, 78–79
supertypes in object-oriented databases, 176
support issues in same-product
  transitions, 424
surrogates in distributed repositories,
  339–341
Switched Multimegabit Data Service
  (SMDS), 306
synchronization of replications, 51
System R database, 198
Systems Applications Architecture
  (SAA), 62

T

table conflicts in multidatabase systems,
  115–116

tables
  in relational databases, 16
  SQL-92 standard for, 205, 208–209, 212
tags in text retrieval systems, 311–312
tasks in transaction groups, 186
TDI (Trusted Database Interpretation),
  191, 372
technology transitions, 422–423
  different product, 424–425
  intermodel, 425–426
  same-product, 423–424
templates in object-oriented databases, 176
temporal databases, 257–262
  benefits of, 259
  in data warehouses, 86–87
  indexes for, 275
  language extensions for, 268–272
  metadata in, 272–274
  models of, 264–268
  in multimedia information systems, 306
  object-oriented, 274–275
  principles of, 262–263
  and spatial data, 295–296
temporal expressions in TempSQL, 268–269
Temporal Relational Model (TRM), 264–268
Temporal SQL standards, 272
temporary tables, SQL-92 standard for, 212
TempSQL language, 268–269
tertiary storage, 27, 409–411
textbases, 308
text retrieval systems, 307–310
  component document management in,
    311–312
  document check-in in, 310
  future of, 312–313
  indexes for, 308, 310–311
  index loading in, 311
Third-Generation Data Base System
    Manifesto, 22–25
third-generation transaction processing
    systems, 349–350
time normal form (TNF), 266
time-oriented queries. *See* temporal
    databases
time-slices in temporal databases, 264
time-variance in data warehouses, 76–77
time-varying relations in temporal
    databases, 264

TIME-VIEW clause (SQL), 272
timing channels in security, 383–384
TNF (time normal form), 266
tools
    for CASE, 411
    in client/server computing, 60
    for interoperability, 422–423
    for migration, 422
    for repositories, 323–324, 333–334,
        342–343
    for security, 393
Tools Integration Standard (ATIS), 335
top-down distributed database systems,
    47–52, 135
TP. See transactions and transaction
    processing (TP)
TPC (Transaction Processing Council), 404
traffic padding in covert timing
    channels, 384
Transactional C language, 359, 362
transaction files
    in disk-based processing model, 12–13
    in file-oriented processing model, 11–12
transaction groups, 186–188
TRANSACTION keyword (Transactional C),
    359
Transaction Processing Council (TPC), 404
transactions and transaction processing
    (TP), 5, 347–348
    ACID properties in, 351
    in active databases, 287–288
    chained, 354–355
    classifications of, 361–362
    in distributed databases, 41, 135
    Encina monitor for, 357–360
    flat, 351–352
    fundamentals of, 348–351
    in IDAPI draft, 64
    languages for, 362–363
    in main-memory databases, 408–409
    in mobile computing environments,
        402–403
    monitors for, 363–364
    in multidatabase systems, 113, 118–119
    nested, 354–360
    in next-generation databases, 27
    in object-oriented databases, 173,
        184–188

    savepoints in, 216, 352–354, 356
    in SQL3 standard, 216
    in SQL-92 standard, 206
    standards for, 135, 360–361
transaction time in temporal databases, 263
transitions in active databases, 287
transitions in technology, 422–423
    different product, 424–425
    intermodel, 425–426
    same-product, 423–424
transparency, pros and cons of, 125–132
tree structures
    in databases, 13–15
    in MPP systems, 97
triggers
    in active databases, 281–282, 285–286,
        289
    for data warehouses, 85–86
    in replication, 100–101
    for repositories, 334
    in SQL standards, 202–203, 213–215, 419
    in Third-Generation Data Base System
        Manifesto, 24
TRIM function (SQL), 207
TRM (Temporal Relational Model), 264–268
Trojan horses, 371, 375, 383–384
Trusted Database Interpretation (TDI),
    191, 372
TSQL language, 269
Turing, Alan, 290
Turing Test, 290
two-phase commit (2PC) models, 91–92,
    99–100, 337
types, data
    in object-oriented databases, 147, 150,
        173–174, 176
    in SQL3 standard, 217
    in SQL-92 standard, 206
    in Third-Generation Data Base System
        Manifesto, 23
    in Xbase standard, 244

U

unified approach to object-oriented
    databases, 158, 161
unified schema in distributed database
    systems, 107
uniformity in object-oriented databases, 174

uninterruptible power supplies, 407
union of pointers in text retrieval
    systems, 310
unique identifiers (UIDs) in
    Third-Generation Data Base System
    Manifesto, 24
units of work in distributed databases, 42
UNIX operating system, 251–252
updates in HSQL, 271
UPTO function (HSQL), 271
user data conversions in product
    transitions, 425
user-defined data types
    in object-oriented databases, 147
    in SQL3 standard, 217
user-defined time in temporal
    databases, 263
user IDs for security, 375
user interfaces. *See* interfaces
utilities in MPP systems, 98

V

Valduriez, Patrick, 125, 135
valid time in temporal databases, 263
variables in Xbase standard, 245
vendor claims, assessing, 421–422
vendor independence for repositories,
    331–332, 335
versions
    in next-generation databases, 27
    in object-oriented databases, 173
    in repositories, 330, 338–339
vertical partitioning, 49
viruses, 371–372
visibility rule for nested transactions, 356

VLSI technology for data compression, 406

W

what-if analyses, data warehouses for,
    82–83
wide area networks (WANs) for multimedia
    systems, 306
Winter, Richard, 132
wireless network computing
    environments, 401
WMRM (write-many read-many) optical
    disks, 275
Woods Hole study, 385–386
work areas in Xbase standard, 245
work-flow management
    in real-world modeling, 9
    for repositories, 330
    in transaction processing, 363–364
WORM (write-once read-many) optical
    disks, 275
worms, 371–372
write-many read-many (WMRM) optical
    disks, 275
write-once read-many (WORM) optical
    disks, 275
write operations in transaction groups, 187

X, Y, Z

Xbase language, 21, 237–238
    with data warehouses, 83–84
    history of, 238–240
    standards for, 240–246
X/Open Distributed Transaction Processing
    (DTP) API, 360–361